Penguin Education

Price Theory

Edited by Harry Townsend

Penguin Modern Economics Readings

General Editor
B. J. McCormick

Price Theory

Selected Readings

Edited by Harry Townsend

Penguin Education

Penguin Education
A Division of Penguin Books Ltd,
Harmondsworth, Middlesex, England
Penguin Books Inc., 7110 Ambassador Road,
Baltimore, Md 21207, U.S.A.
Penguin Books Australia Ltd,
Ringwood, Victoria, Australia

First published 1971
Reprinted 1973
This selection copyright © Harry Townsend, 1971
Introduction and notes copyright © Harry Townsend, 1971

Made and printed in Great Britain by
Cox & Wyman Ltd, London, Reading and Fakenham
Set in Monotype Times

Contents

Introduction

An economist's involvement with price theory runs the course of true love – delight, disillusion, dependence. At first price theory is a revelation. The bourgeois gentleman's discovery that he had been talking prose for forty years without knowing it is as nothing to the student's discovery that he and everyone else around him has been living economically without knowing it. New mysteries of everyday life are continually revealed and resolved.

Alas, this heady state does not last, problems begin to look too simplified and solutions too glib. The assumptions of arguments seem chosen for the convenience of the theorist and not for relationship to anything real. Analysis looks tendentious, better suited to justifying the *status quo* than explaining it. Mountains of argument are moved to reveal a conclusion the size of a mouse. Worse still, whilst a good many parts of theory still satisfy, it becomes more and more difficult to see how they fit together to explain the working of the economic system as a whole.

Such a catalogue of tribulation may make it difficult to understand how anyone perseveres with the subject; but lots of us do. Light dawns, arguments fall into place and as we proceed to apply economic theory it is found that what we are applying in nine cases out of ten is price theory. The tenth application is that of national income theory to some grand concern of Treasury, Chancellery or Bureau of the Budget. Most of the time we are dependent on price theory.

These Readings have been assembled for students making the transition from disillusionment to dependence. In terms of the literature, they have been working on W. J. Baumol's *Economic Theory and Operations Analysis*, K. E. Boulding's *Economic Analysis, vol. 1*, K. Lancaster's *Introduction to Modern Microeconomics*, R. H. Leftwich's *The Price System and Resource Allocation*, W. J. L. Ryan's *Price Theory*, G. J. Stigler's *The Theory of Price*, or one or other of the many competitive books which carry one beyond the introductory texts. The very number of such books suggests that there are some peculiar difficulties to overcome. It is hoped that these Readings will help by supplementing rather than replacing the efforts of the textbook authors.

Texts expound price theory at three levels of abstraction, the economy as a whole, individual markets within the economy and individual firms within markets. G. C. Archibald edits a companion volume of Readings in the Penguin Modern Economics series on the *Theory of the Firm*, so this present volume concentrates on the two upper levels of economy and markets. Some overlap is unavoidable, however, if each selection is to meet the needs of students. It could be argued that the theory of costs and of all but perfectly competitive markets belongs properly to the theory of the firm; but a book on price theory that omitted all reference to costs and imperfect competition would be odd, if not downright deception. We have, therefore, covered these fields, but not so thoroughly that Archibald's volume is no longer worth consulting. Readings in the *Theory of the Firm* complement Readings in *Price Theory* and vice versa.

We begin with two articles that demonstrate the ways in which prices link together the scattered and heterogeneous resources of nature, hand and mind with the equally widespread and diverse tastes and needs of householders, to form an integrated system. The fact that the price system is indeed a system and not simply a means of solving separate problems such as the supply and allocation of peanuts is easily grasped to begin with. Textbooks describe how, for example, wheat, meat, butter, fodder, fruit, tea, tobacco and timber are brought from the other end of the earth, and aircraft, motor cars, electrical equipment, chemicals, textiles and machinery are sold in return, all without the intervention of a central directorate. Goods move in response to the opportunities for profit signalled by prices. As one becomes immersed in indifference curves and isoquants the vision is apt to fade. The mechanics of a social system is what price theory is all about, and so we begin with F. A. von Hayek and Oskar Lange.

Von Hayek emphasizes the importance of the price system as

a means of organizing 'the knowledge of the particular circumstances of time and place' which is spread throughout the community and which is needed for efficient deployment of resources. A common criticism of price theory is that it assumes greater knowledge on the part of suppliers and demanders than they in fact possess. This criticism sometimes has cogency, but it shrinks to small proportions when it is recognized that the price system is a means for coping with ignorance, for organizing the bits of knowledge spread through the population.

The work of von Hayek and Lange became intertwined in the economics of Socialism. It will be seen that the article by von Hayek published here was in part written in reaction to Lange's exposition of the economic theory of Socialism. Lange's solution of the problem of allocating publicly owned resources by means of market mechanisms predated by a quarter of a century the efforts of Communist countries to reform their economic systems along these lines. His article is included here, however, not so much for its application of conventional theory to the allocation of resources and products in a Socialist State, as for its explanation of the working of the Capitalist system which precedes the analysis of collectivism.

Part Two is devoted to the two main traditions in price theory. In English-speaking countries the dominating influence has been that of Alfred Marshall, founder of the oral tradition at Cambridge, and last in the line of classical authors who could attempt to encompass the whole of economics in a volume of *Principles*. Students are no longer led to the great book with the admonition that 'it is all in Marshall'; but a surprising number of the innovations of recent years can be traced to the *Principles*. The monumental scholarship of C. W. Guillebaud's variorum edition (1961), together with the appearance of the 8th edition in paperback ensure that the influence of the *Principles* will continue at first as well as second hand.

Ragnar Frisch, from the vantage point of Scandinavia, provides a fresh and sympathetic insight into the main features of Marshall's theory of value, with emphasis on the Marshallian period analysis. The distinction between the long and short period has suffered from Keynes's quip that in the long run we are all dead, which is true enough but, with a life expectancy of sixty-nine for men and seventy-five for women, the end of the run is on average thirty-four and a half to thirty-seven and a half years away, depending on sex. Separate analysis of the short period provides the means for explaining why firms continue in operation despite failure to cover their full 'costs': witness cyclical behaviour in almost any industry and more lasting behaviour in declining industries such as textiles. The long-period theory demonstrates that changes in costs or demand eventuate in adjustments in output rather than permanently enhanced or diminished profits, and explains why businessmen are usually defenders of whatever is the present state of affairs, the situation to which they are becoming adjusted.

Following Marshall we take problems of manageable magnitude and analyse them one at a time by examining partial equilibria. This contrasts sharply with the approach of Léon Walras who brought all economic activities together within one great mathematical schematization. Walras has exerted his greatest influence on continental economists. To quote Schumpeter (1954):

So far as pure theory is concerned, Walras is in my opinion the greatest of all economists. His system of economic equilibrium, uniting, as it does, the quality of 'revolutionary' creativeness with the quality of classic synthesis, is the only work by an economist that will stand comparison with the achievements of theoretical physics. Compared with it, most of the theoretical writings of that period – and beyond – however valuable in themselves and however original subjectively, look like boats beside a liner, like inadequate attempts to catch some aspect of Walrasian truth. It is the outstanding land-mark on the road that economics travels towards the status of rigorous or exact science.

Walrasian modes of thought lie behind the analysis in Lange's article. It was difficult to decide what Reading to add in order to present a more formal exposition of general equilibrium theory. The theory is essentially mathematical and most contributions in this area assume more than passing acquaintance with mathematics. This is an assumption which is well on the way to be satisfied by economics students; but it would be a pity to rob literary-types of a view of the grand architecture of the Walrasian system. Hence the choice of Gustav Cassel's popularization of Walras's ideas. The Walrasian equilibrium has been generalized beyond the stage explained in this Reading. Cassel achieves simplicity by assuming fixed supplies of fully-employed factors and fixed technical coefficients of production; but he brings out the flavour of general equilibrium analysis.

We return to recent extensions of general equilibrium theory in Part Six. In between are contributions which stem from the Marshallian tradition.

Part Three is devoted to the theory of demand. Armen Alchian's paper makes light work of the concept of utility measurable up to a linear transformation, demonstrates its application to choices involving risk, and explains why men choose both to gamble and take out insurance. Consumption theory seemed at one stage more of a cult or conspiracy of examiners than a specially exciting field of inquiry. A theory of consumer behaviour was required to explain the interdependence of demand curves, and consumer well-being needed to be ranked for welfare economics; but the interest was strictly theoretical. This has changed dramatically and we now find the economic theory of choice being applied far beyond the bounds of economics. One indication of this spread is the Penguin Modern Psychology Readings in *Decision Making* edited by W. Edwards and A. Tversky (1967). These Readings might have been included with equal propriety in the economics as in the psychology series.

Reading 6 by Richard Stone introduces the element of time into demand theory. Stone's model allows for consumers learning about, holding and replacing goods instead of simply purchasing them at a constant rate per period of time. His model applies to the measurement of demand. Measurement is also the subject of E. J. Working's classic paper on what statistical 'demand curves' do and do not show.

Discussion of demand is placed before that of costs so as to follow the usual order of treatment; but the conventional order is of doubtful merit. The same apparatus of thought is employed in consumption theory and production theory; but whereas the mapping of consumer preferences and assumption that consumers seek to maximize satisfaction may cause anomic, deviant, frustrated, impulsive, sentimental or sanctimonious students to balk, the mapping of possible factor combinations and assumption that firms strive to minimize costs for particular outputs seems acceptable as objective circumstance from the start. This appearance is not deceptive. L. Cookenboo, Jr, identifies a production function with only two main variables, pipe diameter and horse-power, and so provides an analysis of the determination of actual costs of production following closely the theorist's categories.

Om P. Tangri shows in Reading 9 that even the most familiar analytical tools deserve careful attention. He helps to clear up difficulties met as one sorts out the relationships between input and output summed up in the law of variable proportions. The symmetry between region I of the typical total product curve, where there is too little variable factor working with the fixed factor, and region III, where there is too much variable factor (i.e. too little fixed factor working with the variable factor), had been acknowledged but seldom fully worked out before Tangri's neat exercise.

Alchian's second paper on costs and outputs also clears up a good deal of confusion, in this case the confusion surrounding the idea of economies of scale. The introduction of calendar time into the discussion of costs parallels Stone's discussion of the variation of demand over time, and it enables the crucial distinction to be made between costs at different rates of output and at different cumulative totals of output.

Costs and demands influence the working of the economy through markets, the areas of discourse of Marshall's partial equilibrium analysis. Among the main developments in price theory in recent years have been the adding of precision to the definition of the structure of markets and the multiplication of models for investigating conduct and performance within these structures. J. S. Bain has himself played a notable part in these developments, and he took the opportunity of the Chamberlin *Festschrift* (1967) to provide the survey of recent contributions to price theory which is reprinted as Reading 11. Bain pays special attention to work on defining markets and analysing oligopoly situations. He also politely places in proper perspective Chamberlin's model of large-group monopolistic competition. Ease of textbook exposition and examination marking have often given this construction a prominence which has overshadowed the areas where the most productive theorizing was taking place.

The models of markets which are of greatest current importance and some of the more sophisticated tools for analysing them are discussed by W. J. Baumol. Baumol wrote his paper for marketing managers. The ambition shown in attempting to explain so much contemporary price theory in so few words to a lay audience is only equalled by the triumphant success with which he brings it off. It is a paper which clearly deserves a larger audience.

Parts Three and Four include articles which incorporate time as an explicit variable in demand, and cost analysis. Calendar time has not usually been included so successfully in theories of the working of markets as a whole. This may change, however, as computers offer the ability to trace complex patterns of price and quantity adjustments. It sometimes seems that computers are simply correlation machines for Ph.D. students; but K. J. Cohen and R. M. Cyert show that computers have great potentiality for theory construction as well as for calculation.

In Part Six we return to the Walrasian tradition in price theory. General equilibrium theory has probably made its greatest impact on the pure theory of international trade, where adjustments analysed are typically too large to allow the *ceteris paribus* assumption of partial equilibrium analysis to hold. The Penguin Modern Economics Readings on *International Trade* edited by J. Bhagwati (1969) are therefore well worth consulting for their interest in terms of price theory. There has also been important work on general equilibrium theory performed within confines of closed economies. Some of the most subtle theorizing is to be found in this area, which has involved economists in their highest flights into abstraction. J. S. Chipman shows what is involved when we face some of the most basic questions: Why does exchange take place? Is there harmony of interests in exchange? How does the large number of participants in perfect competition lead to a determinate price? What are the sources of instability? How does the process of adjustment work from a disequilibrium situation?

F. M. Bator follows up some of the same ideas as Chipman. He spells out, for example, Chipman's comment that 'it is amazing how many economic laws stand or fall with this principle' of convexity. In Bator's case they are the laws of general equilibrium and the conditions of welfare maximization, first in a $2 \times 2 \times 2$ economy (two factors, two products, two consumers) and then in an economy of many factors, products and consumers. The elegance of analytical geometry is well illustrated in Bator's paper, for example, in his Figure 2 (see page 374) which illustrates optimum production combinations, optimum consumption combinations, and the necessary equality of marginal rates of substitution in production and consumption for the combined optimum of production and consumption.

General equilibrium analysis has always had appeal from virtuoso performances by the most high-flying theorists, but admiration had to be tempered by recognition that argument was being conducted a good distance above solid ground. W. Leontief has shown the way in which general equilibrium may be brought down to earth, and in developing input–output analysis has provided the main operational theory of economic planning. Reading 16 is a straightforward account of input–output theory.

Part Seven concludes the Readings.

References

KUENNE, R. E. (ed.) (1967), *Monopolistic Competition Theory: Studies in Impact, Essays in Honor of Edward H. Chamberlin*, Wiley.
MARSHALL, A. (1890), *Principles of Economics*, 9th (variorum) edn by C. W. Guillebaud, 2 vols., Macmillan, 1961.
SCHUMPETER, J. A. (1954), *History of Economic Analysis*, Allen & Unwin.

Part One The Price System

In the early innocent days of television there was a quiz
game 'What's my Line?' in which a panel had to discover the
occupations of challengers from a mime and a series of 'yes'
or 'no' answers. The game turned up some weird and
wonderful occupations, a saggar-maker's bottom knocker,
and so on; yet no one saw cause to question how anyone
could possibly get into such lines. We take the allocation of
people to different tasks and their organization into cooperative production for granted. Guidance to particular
places of work, and incentives to produce particular products,
are two of the main functions of the price system.

F. A. von Hayek emphasizes that these processes of allocation
depend upon the interconnection of bits of knowledge spread
throughout the community. The price system is, in a sense, a
vast communications network. Oskar Lange shows that this
network is politically neutral in that it may be used to guide
people and resources to work, and products to people in any
political set-up. Socialist countries do not usually use the
price system for the main tasks of deciding what, how and
for whom to produce because they are mostly centralized
dictatorships. There is no reason in economic theory why they
should be this way.

1 F. A. von Hayek

The Use of Knowledge in Society

F. A. von Hayek, 'The use of knowledge in society', in *Individualism and Economic Order*, Routledge & Kegan Paul, 1949, pp. 77–91. (First published in *American Economic Review*, vol. 35, 1945, pp. 519–30.)

What is the problem we wish to solve when we try to construct a rational economic order? On certain familiar assumptions the answer is simple enough. *If* we possess all the relevant information, *if* we can start out from a given system of preferences and *if* we command complete knowledge of available means, the problem which remains is purely one of logic. That, is, the answer to the questions of what is the best use of the available means is implicit in our assumptions. The conditions which the solution of this optimum problem must satisfy have been fully worked out and can be stated best in mathematical form: put at their briefest, they are that the marginal rates of substitution between any two commodities or factors must be the same in all their different uses.

This, however, is emphatically *not* the economic problem which society faces. And the economic calculus which we have developed to solve this logical problem, though an important step toward the solution of the economic problem of society, does not yet provide an answer to it. The reason for this is that the 'data' from which the economic calculus starts are never for the whole society 'given' to a single mind which could work out the implications and can never be so given.

The peculiar character of the problem of a rational economic order is determined precisely by the fact that the knowledge of the circumstances of which we must make use never exists in concentrated or integrated form but solely as the dispersed bits of incomplete and frequently contradictory knowledge which all the separate individuals possess. The economic problem of society is thus not merely a problem of how to allocate 'given' resources – if 'given' is taken to mean given to a single mind which deliberately solves the problem set by these 'data'. It is rather a problem of how to secure the best use of resources known to any of the members of society, for ends whose relative importance only these individuals know. Or, to put it briefly, it is a problem of the utilization of knowledge which is not given to anyone in its totality.

This character of the fundamental problem has, I am afraid been obscured rather than illuminated by many of the recent refinements of economic theory, particularly by many of the uses made of mathematics. Though the problem with which I want primarily to deal in this paper is the problem of a rational economic organization, I shall in its course be led again and again to point to its close connections with certain methodological questions. Many of the points I wish to make are indeed conclusions towards which diverse paths of reasoning have unexpectedly converged. But, as I now see these problems, this is no accident. It seems to me that many of the current disputes with regard to both economic theory and economic policy have their common origin in a misconception about the nature of the economic problem of society. This misconception in turn is due to an erroneous transfer to social phenomena of the habits of thought we have developed in dealing with the phenomena of nature.

In ordinary language we describe by the word 'planning' the complex of inter-related decisions about the allocation of our available resources. All economic activity is in this sense planning; and in any society in which many people collaborate, this planning, whoever does it, will in some measure have to be based on knowledge which, in the first instance, is not given to the planner but to somebody else, which somehow will have to be conveyed to the planner. The various ways in which the knowledge on which people base their plans is communicated to them is the crucial problem for any theory explaining the economic process, and the problem of what is the best way of utilizing knowledge initially dispersed among all the people is at least one of the main problems of economic policy – or of designing an efficient economic system.

The answer to this question is closely connected with that

other question which arises here, that of *who* is to do the planning. It is about this question that all the dispute about 'economic planning' centres. This is not a dispute about whether planning is to be done or not. It is a dispute as to whether planning is to be done centrally, by one authority for the whole economic system, or is to be divided among many individuals. Planning in the specific sense in which the term is used in contemporary controversy necessarily means central planning – direction of the whole economic system according to one unified plan. Competition, on the other hand, means decentralized planning by many separate persons. The halfway house between the two, about which many people talk but which few like when they see it, is the delegation of planning to organized industries, or, in other words, monopolies.

Which of these systems is likely to be more efficient depends mainly on the question under which of them we can expect that fuller use will be made of the existing knowledge. This, in turn, depends on whether we are more likely to succeed in putting at the disposal of a single central authority all the knowledge which ought to be used but which is initially dispersed among many different individuals, or in conveying to the individuals such additional knowledge as they need in order to enable them to dovetail their plans with those of others.

It will at once be evident that on this point the position will be different with respect to different kinds of knowledge. The answer to our question will, therefore, largely turn on the relative importance of the different kinds of knowledge: those more likely to be at the disposal of particular individuals and those which we should with greater confidence expect to find in the possession of an authority made up of suitably chosen experts. If it is today so widely assumed that the latter will be in a better position, this is because one kind of knowledge, namely, scientific knowledge, occupies now so prominent a place in public imagination that we tend to forget that it is not the only kind that is relevant. It may be admitted that, as far as scientific knowledge is concerned, a body of suitably chosen experts may be in the best position to command all the best knowledge available – though this is of course merely shifting the difficulty to the problem of selecting the experts. What I wish to point out is that, even assuming that this problem can be readily solved, it is only a small part of the wider problem.

Today it is almost heresy to suggest that scientific knowledge is not the sum of all knowledge. But a little reflection will show that there is beyond question a body of very important but unorganized knowledge which cannot possibly be called scientific in the sense of knowledge of general rules: the knowledge of the particular circumstances of time and place. It is with respect to this that practically every individual has some advantage over all others because he possesses unique information of which beneficial use might be made, but of which use can be made only if the decisions depending on it are left to him or are made with his active co-operation. We need to remember only how much we have to learn in any occupation after we have completed our theoretical training, how big a part of our working life we spend learning particular jobs, and how valuable an asset in all walks of life is knowledge of people, of local conditions and of special circumstances. To know of and put to use a machine not fully employed, or somebody's skill which could be better utilized, or to be aware of a surplus stock which can be drawn upon during an interruption of supplies, is socially quite as useful as the knowledge of better alternative techniques. The shipper who earns his living from using otherwise empty or half-filled journeys of tramp-steamers, or the estate agent whose whole knowledge is almost exclusively one of temporary opportunities, or the *arbitrageur* who gains from local differences of commodity prices – are all performing eminently useful functions based on special knowledge of circumstances of the fleeting moment not known to others.

It is a curious fact that this sort of knowledge should today be generally regarded with a kind of contempt and that anyone who by such knowledge gains an advantage over somebody better equipped with theoretical or technical knowledge is thought to have acted almost disreputably. To gain an advantage from better knowledge of facilities of communication or transport is sometimes regarded as almost dishonest, although it is quite as important that society make use of the best opportunities in this respect as in using the latest scientific discoveries.

This prejudice has in a considerable measure affected the attitude towards commerce in general compared with that towards production. Even economists who regard themselves as definitely immune to the crude materialist fallacies of the past constantly commit the same mistake where activities directed towards the acquisition of such practical knowledge are concerned – apparently because in their scheme of things all such knowledge is supposed to be 'given'. The common idea now seems to be that all such knowledge should as a matter of course be readily at the command of everybody, and the reproach of irrationality levelled against the existing economic order is frequently based on the fact that it is not so available. This view disregards the fact that the method by which such knowledge can be made as widely available as possible is precisely the problem to which we have to find an answer.

If it is fashionable today to minimize the importance of the knowledge of the particular circumstances of time and place, this is closely connected with the smaller importance which is now attached to change as such. Indeed, there are few points on which the assumptions made (usually only implicitly) by the 'planners' differ from those of their opponents as much as with regard to the significance and frequency of changes which will make substantial alterations of production plans necessary. Of course, if detailed economic plans could be laid down for fairly long periods in advance and then closely adhered to, so that no further economic decisions of importance would be required, the task of drawing up a comprehensive plan governing all economic activity would be much less formidable.

It is, perhaps, worth stressing that economic problems arise always and only in consequence of change. As long as things continue as before, or at least as they were expected to, there arise no new problems requiring a decision, no need to form a new plan. The belief that changes, or at least day-to-day adjustments, have become less important in modern times implies the contention that economic problems also have become less important. This belief in the decreasing importance of change is, for that reason, usually held by the same people who argue that the importance of economic considerations has been driven into the background by the growing importance of technological knowledge.

Is it true that, with the elaborate apparatus of modern production, economic decisions are required only at long intervals, as when a new factory is to be erected or a new process to be introduced? Is it true that, once a plant has been built, the rest is all more or less mechanical, determined by the character of the plant, and leaving little to be changed in adapting to the ever-changing circumstances of the moment?

The fairly widespread belief in the affirmative is not, as far as I can ascertain, borne out by the practical experience of the businessman. In a competitive industry at any rate – and such an industry alone can serve as a test – the task of keeping costs from rising requires constant struggle, absorbing a greater part of the energy of the manager. How easy it is for an inefficient manager to dissipate the differentials on which profitability rests, and that it is possible, with the same technical facilities, to produce with a great variety of costs, are among the commonplaces of business experience which do not seem to be equally familiar in the study of the economist. The very strength of the desire, constantly voiced by producers and engineers, to be allowed to proceed untrammelled by considerations of money costs, is eloquent testimony to the extent to which these factors enter into their daily work.

One reason why economists are increasingly apt to forget about the constant small changes which make up the whole economic picture is probably their growing preoccupation with statistical aggregates, which show a very much greater stability than the movements of the detail. The comparative stability of the aggregates cannot, however, be accounted for – as the statisticians occasionally seem to be inclined to do – by the 'law of large numbers' or the mutual compensation of random changes. The number of elements with which we have to deal is not large enough for such accidental forces to produce stability. The continuous flow of goods and services is maintained by constant deliberate adjustments, by new dispositions made every day in the light of circumstances not known the day before, by B stepping in at once when A fails to deliver. Even the large and highly mechanized plant keeps going largely because of an environment upon which it can draw for all sorts of unexpected needs: tiles for its roof, stationery for its forms, and all the thousand and one kinds of equipment in which it cannot be self-contained and which the plans for the operation of the plant require to be readily available in the market.

This is, perhaps, also the point where I should briefly mention the fact that the sort of knowledge with which I have been concerned is knowledge of the kind which by its nature cannot enter into statistics and therefore cannot be conveyed to any central authority in statistical form. The statistics which such a central authority would have to use would have to be arrived at precisely by abstracting from minor differences between the things, by lumping together, as resources of one kind, items which differ as regards location, quality and other particulars in a way which may be very significant for the specific decision. It follows from this that central planning based on statistical information by its nature cannot take direct account of these circumstances of time and place and that the central planner will have to find some way or other in which the decisions depending on them can be left to the 'man on the spot'.

If we can agree that the economic problem of society is mainly one of rapid adaptation to changes in the particular circumstances of time and place, it would seem to follow that the ultimate decisions must be left to the people who are familiar with these circumstances, who know directly of the relevant changes and of the resources immediately available to meet them. We cannot expect that this problem will be solved by first communicating all this knowledge to a central board which, after integrating all knowledge, issues its orders. We must solve it by some form of decentralization. But this answers only part of our problem. We need decentralization because only thus can we insure that the knowledge of the particular circumstances of time and place will be promptly used. But the 'man on the spot' cannot decide solely on the basis of his limited but intimate knowledge of the facts of his immediate surroundings. There still remains the problem of communicating to him such further information as he needs to fit his decisions into the whole pattern of changes of the larger economic system.

F. A. von Hayek 23

How much knowledge does he need to do so successfully? Which of the events which happen beyond the horizon of his immediate knowledge are of relevance to his immediate decision, and how much of them need he know? There is hardly anything that happens anywhere in the world that *might* not have an effect on the decision he ought to make. But he need not know of these events as such, nor of *all* their effects. It does not matter for him *why* at the particular moment more screws of one size than of another are wanted, *why* paper bags are more readily available than canvas bags, or *why* skilled labour or particular machine tools have for the moment become more difficult to obtain. All that is significant for him is *how much more or less* difficult to procure they have become compared with other things with which he is also concerned, or how much more or less urgently wanted are the alternative things he produces or uses. It is always a question of the relative importance of the particular things with which he is concerned, and the causes which alter their relative importance are of no interest to him beyond the effect on those concrete things of his own environment.

It is in this connection that what I have called the 'economic calculus' (or the Pure Logic of Choice) helps us, at least by analogy, to see how this problem can be solved, and in fact is being solved, by the price system. Even the single controlling mind, in possession of all the data for some small, self-contained economic system, would not – every time some small adjustment in the allocation of resources had to be made – go explicitly through all the relations between ends and means which might possibly be affected. It is indeed the great contribution of the Pure Logic of Choice that it has demonstrated conclusively that even such a single mind could solve this kind of problem only by constructing and constantly using rates of equivalence (or 'values' or 'marginal rates of substitution'), that is, by attaching to each kind of scarce resource a numerical index which cannot be derived from any property possessed by that particular thing, but which reflects, or in which is condensed, its significance in view of the whole means–ends structure. In any small change he will have to consider only these quantitative indices (or 'values') in which all the relevant information is concentrated; and, by adjusting the quantities one by one, he can appropriately rearrange his dispositions without having to solve the whole puzzle *ab initio* or without needing at any stage to survey it at once in all its ramifications.

Fundamentally, in a system in which the knowledge of the relevant facts is dispersed among many people, prices can act to co-ordinate the separate actions of different people in the same way as subjective values help the individual to co-ordinate the parts of his plan. It is worth contemplating for a moment a very simple and commonplace instance of the action of the price system to see what precisely it accomplishes. Assume that somewhere in the world a new opportunity for the use of some raw material, say, tin, has arisen, or that one of the sources of supply of tin has been eliminated. It does not matter for our purpose – and it is significant that it does not matter – which of these two causes has made tin more scarce. All that the users of tin need to know is that some of the tin they used to consume is now more profitably employed elsewhere and that, in consequence, they must economize tin. There is no need for the great majority of them even to know where the more urgent need has arisen, or in favour of what other other needs they ought to husband the supply. If only some of them know directly of the new demand, and switch resources over to it, and if the people who are aware of the new gap thus created in turn fill it from still other sources, the effect will rapidly spread throughout the whole economic system and influence not only all the uses of tin but also those of its substitutes and the substitutes of these substitutes, the supply of all the things made of tin, and their substitutes, and so on; and all this without the great majority of those instrumental in bringing about these substitutions knowing anything at all about the original cause of these changes. The whole acts as one market, not because any of its members survey the whole field, but because their limited individual fields of vision sufficiently overlap so that through many intermediaries the relevant information is communicated to all. The mere fact that there is one price for any commodity – or rather that local prices are connected in a manner determined by the cost of transport, etc. – brings about the solution which (it is just conceptually possible) might have been arrived at by one single

F. A. von Hayek 25

mind possessing all the information which is in fact dispersed among all the people involved in the process.

We must look at the price system as such a mechanism for communicating information if we want to understand its real function – a function which, of course, it fulfils less perfectly as prices grow more rigid. (Even when quoted prices have become quite rigid, however, the forces which would operate through changes in price still operate to a considerable extent through changes in the other terms of the contract.) The most significant fact about this system is the economy of knowledge with which it operates, or how little the individual participants need to know in order to be able to take the right action. In abbreviated form, by a kind of symbol, only the most essential information is passed on and passed on only to those concerned. It is more than a metaphor to describe the price system as a kind of machinery for registering change, or a system of telecommunications which enables individual producers to watch merely the movement of a few pointers, as an engineer might watch the hands of a few dials, in order to adjust their activities to changes of which they may never know more than is reflected in the price movement.

Of course, these adjustments are probably never 'perfect' in the sense in which the economist conceives of them in his equilibrium analysis. But I fear that our theoretical habits of approaching the problem with the assumption of more or less perfect knowledge on the part of almost everyone has made us somewhat blind to the true function of the price mechanism and led us to apply rather misleading standards in judging its efficiency. The marvel is that in a case like that of a scarcity of one raw material, without an order being issued, without more than perhaps a handful of people knowing the cause, tens of thousands of people whose identity could not be ascertained by months of investigation, are made to use the material or its products more sparingly; that is, they move in the right direction. This is enough of a marvel even if, in a constantly changing world, not all will hit it off so perfectly that their profit rates will always be maintained at the same even or 'normal' level.

I have deliberately used the word 'marvel' to shock the reader out of the complacency with which we often take the working of this mechanism for granted. I am convinced that if it were the result of deliberate human design, and if the people guided by the price changes understood that their decisions have significance far beyond their immediate aim, this mechanism would have been acclaimed as one of the greatest triumphs of the human mind. Its misfortune is the double one that it is not the product of human design and that the people guided by it usually do not know why they are made to do what they do. But those who clamour for 'conscious direction' – and who cannot believe that anything which has evolved without design (and even without our understanding it) should solve problems which we should not be able to solve consciously – should remember this: the problem is precisely how to extend the span of our utilization of resources beyond the span of the control of any one mind; and, therefore, how to dispense with the need of conscious control and how to provide inducements which will make the individuals do the desirable things without any-one having to tell them what to do.

The problem which we meet here is by no means peculiar to economics but arises in connection with nearly all truly social phenomena, with language and with most of our cultural inheritance, and constitutes really the central theoretical problem of all social science. As Alfred Whitehead has said in another connection, 'It is a profoundly erroneous truism, repeated by all copy-books and by eminent people when they are making speeches, that we should cultivate the habit of thinking what we are doing. The precise opposite is the case. Civilization advances by extending the number of important operations which we can perform without thinking about them.' This is of profound significance in the social field. We make constant use of formulas, symbols and rules whose meaning we do not understand and through the use of which we avail our-selves of the assistance of knowledge which individually we do not possess. We have developed these practices and institutions by building upon habits and institutions which have proved successful in their own sphere and which have in turn become the foundation of the civilization we have built up.

The price system is just one of those formations which man

has learned to use (though he is still very far from having learned to make the best use of it) after he had stumbled upon it without understanding it. Through it not only a division of labour but also a co-ordinated utilization of resources based on an equally divided knowledge has become possible. The people who like to deride any suggestion that this may be so usually distort the argument by insinuating that it asserts that by some miracle just that sort of system has spontaneously grown up which is best suited to modern civilization. It is the other way round: man has been able to develop that division of labour on which our civilization is based because he happened to stumble upon a method which made it possible. Had he not done so, he might still have developed some other, altogether different, type of civilization, something like the 'state' of the termite ants, or some other altogether unimaginable type. All that we can say is that nobody has yet succeeded in designating an alternative system in which certain features of the existing one can be preserved which are dear even to those who most violently assail it – such as particularly the extent to which the individual can choose his pursuits and consequently freely use his own knowledge and skill.

It is in many ways fortunate that the dispute about the indispensability of the price system for any rational calculation in a complex society is now no longer conducted entirely between camps holding different political views. The thesis that without the price system we could not preserve a society based on such extensive division of labour as ours was greeted with a howl of derision when it was first advanced by von Mises twenty-five years ago. Today the difficulties which some still find in accepting it are no longer mainly political, and this makes for an atmosphere much more conducive to reasonable discussion. When we find Leon Trotsky arguing that 'economic accounting is unthinkable without market relations'; when Professor Oskar Lange promises Professor von Mises a statue in the marble halls of the future Central Planning Board; and when Professor Abba P. Lerner rediscovers Adam Smith and emphasizes that the essential utility of the price system consists in inducing the individual, while seeking his own interest, to do what is in the general interest, the differences can indeed no longer be ascribed to political prejudice. The remaining dissent seems clearly to be due to purely intellectual, and more particularly methodological, differences.

A recent statement by J. A. Schumpeter (1942) in his *Capitalism, Socialism and Democracy* provides a clear illustration of one of the methodological differences which I have in mind. Its author is pre-eminent among those economists who approach economic phenomena in the light of a certain branch of positivism. To him these phenomena accordingly appear as objectively given quantities of commodities impinging directly upon each other, almost, it would seem, without any intervention of human minds. Only against this background can I account for the following (to me startling) pronouncement. Professor Schumpeter argues that the possibility of a rational calculation in the absence of markets for the factors of production follows for the theorist 'from the elementary proposition that consumers in evaluating ("demanding") consumers' goods *ipso facto* also evaluate the means of production which enter into the production of these goods' (Schumpeter, 1942, p. 175).[1]

Taken literally, this statement is simply untrue. The consumers do nothing of the kind. What Professor Schumpeter's '*ipso facto*' presumably means is that the valuation of the factors of production is implied in, or follows necessarily from, the valuation of consumers' goods. But this, too, is not correct. Implication is a logical relationship which can be meaningfully asserted only of propositions simultaneously present to one

1. Professor Schumpeter is, I believe, also the original author of the myth that Pareto and Barone have 'solved' the problem of Socialist calculation. What they, and many others, did was merely to state the conditions which a rational allocation of resources would have to satisfy and to point out that these were essentially the same as the conditions of equilibrium of a competitive market. This is something altogether different from showing how the allocation of resources satisfying these conditions can be found in practice. Pareto himself (from whom Barone has taken practically everything he has to say), far from claiming to have solved the practical problem, in fact explicitly denies that it can be solved without the help of the market. See Pareto (1927, pp. 233–4). The relevant passage is quoted in an English translation at the beginning of my article on 'Socialist calculation: the competitive "solution"' (von Hayek, 1940, p. 125).

and the same mind. It is evident, however, that the values of the factors of production do not depend solely on the valuation of the consumers' goods but also on the conditions of supply of the various factors of production. Only to a mind to which all these facts were simultaneously known would the answer necessarily follow from the facts given to it. The practical problem, however, arises precisely because these facts are never so given to a single mind, and because, in consequence, it is necessary that in the solution of the problem knowledge should be used that is dispersed among many people.

The problem is thus in no way solved if we can show that all the facts, *if* they were known to a single mind (as we hypothetically assume them to be given to the observing economist), would uniquely determine the solution; instead we must show how a solution is produced by the interactions of people each of whom possesses only partial knowledge. To assume all the knowledge to be given to a single mind in the same manner in which we assume it to be given to us as the explaining economists is to assume the problem away and to disregard everything that is important and significant in the real world.

That an economist of Professor Schumpeter's standing should thus have fallen into a trap which the ambiguity of the term 'datum' sets to the unwary can hardly be explained as a simple error. It suggests rather that there is something fundamentally wrong with an approach which habitually disregards an essential part of the phenomena with which we have to deal: the unavoidable imperfection of man's knowledge and the consequent need for a process by which knowledge is constantly communicated and acquired. Any approach, such as that of much of mathematical economics with its simultaneous equations, which in effect starts from the assumption that people's *knowledge* corresponds with the objective *facts* of the situation, systematically leaves out what is our main task to explain. I am far from denying that in our system equilibrium analysis has a useful function to perform. But when it comes to the point where it misleads some of our leading thinkers into believing that the situation which it describes has direct relevance to the solution of practical problems, it is high time that we remember that it does not deal with the social process at all and that it is no more than a useful preliminary to the study of the main problem.

References

PARETO, V. (1927), *Manuel d'économie pure*, Giard, Paris, 2nd edn.
SCHUMPETER, J. A. (1942), *Capitalism, Socialism and Democracy*, Harper & Row.
VON HAYEK, F. A. (1940), 'Socialist calculation: the competitive "solution"', *Economica*, vol. 7 (new series), pp. 125–49.

2 Oskar Lange

On the Economic Theory of Socialism

Excerpt from Oskar Lange, 'On the economic theory of Socialism',
in B. E. Lippincott (ed.), *On the Economic Theory of Socialism*, University
of Minnesota Press, 1938, pp. 57–90. (First published in a slightly
different form in *Review of Economic Studies*, vol. 4, 1936–7, nos. 1 and 2.)

The present state of the debate

Socialists have certainly good reason to be grateful to Professor
von Mises, the great *advocatus diaboli* of their cause. For it was
his powerful challenge that forced the Socialists to recognize
the importance of an adequate system of economic accounting
to guide the allocation of resources in a Socialist economy. Even
more, it was chiefly due to Professor von Mises's challenge that
many Socialists became aware of the very existence of such a
problem. And although Professor von Mises was not the first to
raise it and although not all Socialists were as completely
unaware of the problem as is frequently held, it is true, nevertheless, that, particularly on the European Continent (outside
of Italy), the merit of having caused the Socialists to approach
this problem systematically belongs entirely to Professor von
Mises. Both as an expression of recognition for the great service
rendered by him and as a memento of the prime importance of
sound economic accounting, a statue of Professor von Mises
ought to occupy an honorable place in the great hall of the
Ministry of Socialization or of the Central Planning Board of the
Socialist State. I am afraid, however, that Professor von Mises
would scarcely enjoy what seems the only adequate way to repay
the debt of recognition incurred by the Socialists, and it is
difficult to blame him for not doing so. First, he might have to
share his place with the great leaders of the Socialist movement,
and this company might not suit him. And then, to complete
the misfortune, a Socialist teacher might invite his students in a
class on dialectical materialism to go and look at the statue,
in order to exemplify the Hegelian *List der Vernunft* which

made even the staunchest of bourgeois economists unwittingly serve the proletarian cause.

Since the clear and distinct formulation of a problem is certainly a major contribution to science, the economist will have to join the Socialists in their recognition of Professor von Mises's work on economic calculation in a Socialist economy. As Professor von Hayek has put it, to Professor von Mises belongs 'the distinction of having first formulated the central problem of Socialist economics in such a form as to make it impossible that it should ever again disappear from the discussion' (von Hayek, 1935, p. 32).[1]

But, unfortunately, besides formulating the problem, Professor von Mises has also claimed to have demonstrated that economic calculation is impossible in a Socialist society. The economist will scarcely find it possible to accept this claim. From the economist's point of view, he would have done better to confine himself to the formulation of the problem, as Pierson did; though, if he had done so, he probably would not have merited the great recognition of the Socialists. For it was exactly Professor von Mises's denial of the possibility of economic accounting under Socialism that provided his challenge with such force and power. Thus the Socialist and the economist will view the achievement of Professor von Mises differently – a strange instance of the divergence of their opinions, which, as Professor von Mises thinks, must be always the rule.

A solution of the problem, different from that advanced by Professor von Mises, was suggested by Pareto as early as 1897 (pp. 364ff.; see also 1910, pp. 362–4) and was later elaborated by Barone (1908).[2] The further discussion of the problem, with one exception, which will be mentioned later, has scarcely gone beyond what is already contained in Barone's paper.

Professor von Mises's contention that a Socialist economy

1. The reader's attention is called to the first English translation of von Mises's work *Die Gemeinwirtschaft*, published under the title *Socialism* late in 1937. The translation, made by J. Kahane, is based on the revised 1932 edition of the German work.

2. This paper has also been published in English, under the title "The ministry of production in the collectivist State," as an appendix to the volume on *Collectivist Economic Planning*, edited by von Hayek.

cannot solve the problem of rational allocation of its resources is based on a confusion concerning the nature of prices. As Wicksteed has pointed out, the term 'price' has two meanings. It may mean either price in the ordinary sense, i.e. the exchange ratio of two commodities on a market, or it may have the generalized meaning of 'terms on which alternatives are offered'. Wicksteed (1933, p. 28) says, '"Price", then, in the narrower sense of "the money for which a material thing, a service, or a privilege can be obtained", is simply a special case of "price" in the wider sense of "the terms on which alternatives are offered to us".'[3] It is only prices in the generalized sense which are indispensable to solving the problem of allocation of resources. The economic problem is a problem of *choice* between alternatives. To solve the problem three data are needed: (a) a preference scale which guides the acts of choice; (b) knowledge of the 'terms on which alternatives are offered'; and (c) knowledge of the amount of resources available. Those three data being given, the problem of choice is soluble.

Now it is obvious that a Socialist economy may regard the data under (a) and (c) as given, at least in as great a degree as they are given in a Capitalist economy. The data under (a) may either be given by the demand schedules of the individuals or be established by the judgement of the authorities administering the economic system. The question remains whether the data under (b) are accessible to the administrators of a Socialist economy. Professor von Mises denies this. However, a careful study of price theory and of the theory of production convinces us that, the data under (a) and under (c) being given, the 'terms on which alternatives are offered' are determined ultimately by the technical possibilities of transformation of one commodity into another, i.e. by the production functions. The administrators of a Socialist economy will have exactly the same knowledge, or lack of knowledge, of the production functions as the Capitalist entrepreneurs have.

But Professor von Mises seems to have confused prices in the

3. Similarly Schumpeter has stated that the term 'exchange ratio' may be used in a wider sense to indicate the alternatives available, so that production may be regarded as an 'exchange' *sui generis*. See Schumpeter (1908, pp. 50ff.).

narrower sense, i.e. the exchange ratios of commodities on a market, with prices in the wider sense of 'terms on which alternatives are offered'. As, in consequence of public ownership of the means of production, there is in a Socialist economy no market on which capital goods are actually exchanged, there are obviously no prices of capital goods in the sense of exchange ratios on a market. And, hence, Professor von Mises argues, there is no 'index of alternatives' available in the sphere of capital goods. But this conclusion is based on a confusion of 'price' in the narrower sense with 'price' in the wider sense of an index of alternatives. It is only in the latter sense that 'prices' are indispensable for the allocation of resources, and on the basis of the technical possibilities of transformation of one commodity into another they are also given in a Socialist economy.

Professor von Mises argues that private ownership of the means of production is indispensable for a rational allocation of resources. Since, according to him, without private ownership of the means of production no determinate index of alternatives exists (at least in the sphere of capital goods), the economic principles of choice between different alternatives are applicable only to a special institutional set-up, i.e. to a society which recognizes private ownership of the means of production. It has been maintained, indeed, by Marx[4] and by the historical school (in so far as the latter recognized any economic laws at all) that all economic laws have only historico-relative validity. But it is most surprising to find this institutionalist view supported by a prominent member of the Austrian school,[5] which

4. With regard to Marx this statement requires certain qualifications. [See the appendix to *On the Theory of Socialism*.]

5. I am, of course, perfectly aware that Professor von Mises does not regard himself as an institutionalist and that he has stated explicitly the universal validity of economic theory (see von Mises, 1933, pp. 27–8). But there is a spectacular contradiction between this statement and his assertion that private ownership of the means of production is indispensable for a rational allocation of resources. For if this assertion is true, economics as the theory of allocation of resources is applicable only to a society with private ownership of the means of production. The implications of the denial of the possibility of rational choice in a Socialist economy are plainly institutionalist.

did so much to emphasize the universal validity of the funda-mental principles of economic theory.

Thus Professor von Mises's denial of the possibility of econ-omic calculation in a Socialist system must be rejected. However, Professor von Mises's argument has been taken up recently in a more refined form by Professor von Hayek and Professor Rob-bins. They do not deny the *theoretical* possibility of a rational allocation of resources in a Socialist economy; they only doubt the possibility of a satisfactory *practical* solution of the problem. Discussing the solution offered by Barone, Dickinson and others, Professor von Hayek (1935, p. 207) says that 'it must be admitted that this is not an impossibility in the sense that it is logically contradictory'. But he denies that the problem is capable of a practical solution in a society without private ownership of the means of production (von Hayek, 1935, pp. 208 ff.).

The issue has been put very clearly by Professor Robbins (1934, p. 15):

On paper we can conceive this problem to be solved by a series of mathematical calculations. . . . But in practice this solution is quite unworkable. It would necessitate the drawing up of millions of equations on the basis of millions of statistical data based on many more millions of individual computations. By the time the equations were solved, the information on which they were based would have become obsolete and they would need to be calculated anew. The suggestion that a practical solution of the problem of planning is possible on the basis of the Paretian equations simply indicates that those who put it forward have not grasped what these equations mean.

Thus Professor von Hayek and Professor Robbins have given up the essential point of Professor von Mises's position and retreated to a second line of defense. In principle, they admit, the problem is soluble, but it is to be doubted whether in a Socialist community it can be solved by a simple method of *trial and error*, as it is solved in the Capitalist economy. The significance of the private ownership of the means of production and of an actual market for capital goods has shifted. Theoreti-cally prices in the generalized sense of 'terms on which alterna-tives are offered' are admitted to be given also without an actual market. The function of the market is, according to them, a different one, namely, to provide a method of allocating resources by trial and error. And it is this function a Socialist economy would be deprived of.

The position taken by Professor von Hayek and by Professor Robbins is a significant step forward in the discussion of the problem. It promises a much more fruitful approach than Professor von Mises's wholesale denial of the possibility of economic accounting under Socialism. Whether by having taken this step they, too, will merit an honourable statue, or at least a memorial tablet, in the building of the Ministry of Socialization or of the Central Planning Board is yet to be seen. The great importance of the problem makes it quite possible.

Barone has already pointed to the fact that the equations of economic equilibrium must be solved also in a Socialist society by trial and error.[6] He regarded such a solution as possible but failed to indicate how it would be achieved. However, the way in which a Socialist economy would solve the problem by a method of trial and error has been indicated quite clearly by Fred M. Taylor in a paper published in 1929. This paper provides in substance the answer to Professor von Hayek's and Professor Robbins's argument, and it is the first contribution which really goes beyond what is contained in Barone's paper. But the great importance of the argument of von Hayek and Robbins necessitates a more detailed investigation of the problem. It is, therefore, the purpose of the present essay to elucidate the way in which the allocation of resources is effected by trial and error on a competitive market and to find out whether a similar trial and error procedure is not possible in a socialist economy.

The determination of equilibrium on competitive market

Let us see how economic equilibrium is established by trial and error on a competitive market. By a competitive market we mean a market in which (a) the number of individuals is so great that no one of them can influence prices appreciably by varying his demand or supply and, therefore, is forced to regard prices as constant parameters independent of his behavior; (b) there is free entry into and exodus from each trade or industry.

6. See von Hayek (1935, pp. 286–9).

The conditions of equilibrium are twofold:

1. All individuals participating in the economic system must attain their maximum positions on the basis of equilibrium prices.

2. The equilibrium prices are determined by the condition that the demand for each commodity is equal to its supply.

We may call the first the *subjective,* and the latter the *objective,* condition. These two conditions, however, do not determine equilibrium unless there is added a third condition which expresses *the social organization of the economic system.* In our case this condition states that:

3. The incomes of the consumers are equal to their receipts from selling the services of the productive resources they own, plus entrepreneurs' profits (which are zero in equilibrium).[7]

This condition is no equilibrium condition in the strict sense, for it holds independently of whether the economic system is in equilibrium or not.[8] Notwithstanding, it is necessary to make equilibrium determinate. Let us analyse these three conditions, 1, 2 and 3; 1 and 2 being the equilibrium conditions *sensu stricto.*

Condition 1. The subjective condition of equilibrium is carried out by the 'individuals'[9] maximizing their utility, profit or income from the ownership of productive resources.
(i) The consumers maximize the total utility they derive from their income by spending it so that the marginal utility of the amount obtainable for a unit of income (expressed in money) is equal for all commodities. Their incomes and the prices being given (the latter are necessary to determine what is the amount of a commodity obtainable for a unit of income), the demand for consumers' goods is determined.

7. Such profits as do not vanish in equilibrium, because of entrepreneurial ability being a scarce factor of production, may be conveniently regarded as receipts from selling productive resources (i.e. entrepreneurial abilities).

8. To put it in mathematical terms: this condition is an identity and not an equation.

9. The term 'individual' is used here in the broad connotation of *Wirtschaftssubjekt* so as to include also collective units (i.e. family households and joint-stock companies).

(ii) The producers maximize their profit. The process of maximizing profit is composed of two parts: (a) the determination of the optimum combination of factors and (b) the determination of the optimum scale of output. The first is attained by combining the factors of production in such proportion as to equalize the marginal productivity of the amount of each factor which can be purchased for a unit of money.[10] The prices of the factors being given, so that it is possible to determine what is the amount of each factor obtainable for a unit of money, this condition determines the minimum cost curve of the producer. This curve being given, the optimum scale of output is attained when the marginal cost is equal to the price of the product (which is given on the market). Thus the output of the single producer and his demand for factors of production are determined. This determination is based entirely on the first property of the competitive market, namely, that the prices of the product and of the factors are independent of the scale of output and of the combination of factors chosen by the producer (because of the large number of competing producers). The determination of the total output of an industry is based on the other property of the competitive market, i.e. on the free entry of producers into, or their exodus from, any industry. This makes the total output of an industry such that the price of the product is equal to the average cost[11] of production. The output and

10. This statement has to be corrected if limitational factors are used in production. There are two kinds of limitational factors, according to whether the amount of the limitational factor which must be used in production is a function of the quantity of product we wish to obtain, or of the amount of another factor used. If limitational factors of the first kind are used the statement in the text holds for the substitutional factors, the amount of limitational factors necessary being determined by the scale of output chosen. If limitational factors of the second kind are used the marginal productivity of the substitutional factors must be proportional to their prices *plus* the marginal expenditure for the limitational factors which are a function of the substitutional factor in question; the amount of the limitational factors necessary is then determined by the amount of the substitutional factors used. As to limitational factors of the first kind, see Georgescu-Roegen (1935, pp. 40–49). Dr Tord Palander has drawn my attention to the existence of the second kind of limitational factors.

11. As used throughout this paper, average cost means average cost per unit of output.

demand for factors of production by each producer and the total output of an industry being given, the total demand for factors by an industry is determined, too. Thus, the prices of the products and of the factors being given, the supply of products and the demand for factors are determined.

(iii) The owners of the ultimate productive resources (labor, capital and natural resources) maximize their income by selling the services of these resources to the highest bidder. The prices of the services of these resources being given, their distribution between the different industries is determined.[12]

Condition 2. The subjective condition of equilibrium can be carried out only on the basis of a *given* set of prices and of consumers' incomes. The prices are regarded by the individuals as constants independent of their behavior. For each set of prices and of consumers' incomes we get different quantities of commodities demanded and supplied.

Condition 3 states that the incomes of the consumers are equal to their receipts from selling the services of the ultimate productive resources they own, plus entrepreneurs' profits. In virtue of this condition incomes of consumers are determined by prices of the services of ultimate productive resources and by profits so that, finally, prices alone remain as the variables determining demand and supply of commodities. By assuming different sets of prices we obtain the demand and supply schedules. Now, the objective condition of equilibrium serves to pick out a special set of prices as the only one which assures the compatibility of the subjective maximum positions of all individuals participating in the economic system. This con-

12. In order to simplify the exposition we disregard the fact that the amount of the resources available, instead of being constant, may depend on their price. Thus the total supply of labor may be a function of the wage rate. As to capital, its amount may be regarded in the short period as constant, whereas in the long run the rate of interest certainly affects saving. In long-period equilibrium the amount of capital is determined by the condition that the rate of its marginal *net* productivity is equal to the interest rate and to the time preference of the individuals (which may be, and probably is, zero). See Knight (1931, pp. 197ff.), Lange (1936, 1937) and von Hayek (1936).

dition means that the demand and the supply of each commodity have to be equal. Prices which satisfy this condition are the equilibrium prices. If the demand and supply schedules are all monotonic functions there exists only one set of prices which satisfies the objective equilibrium condition; otherwise, there may be a multiple solution, but some of the price sets obtained represent unstable equilibria.[13]

Such is the theoretical solution of the problem of equilibrium on a competitive market. Now let us see how the problem is solved actually by *trial and error*. The solution by trial and error is based on what may be called the *parametric function of prices*, i.e. on the fact that, although the prices are a resultant of the behavior of all individuals on the market, each individual separately regards the actual market prices as given data to which he has to adjust himself. Each individual tries to exploit the market situation confronting him which he cannot control. Market prices are thus parameters determining the behavior of the individuals. The equilibrium value of these parameters is determined by the objective equilibrium condition 2. As Walras has so brilliantly shown (1926, pp. 65, 132–3, 214–15, 217 ff., 259–60, 261 ff.), this is done by a series of successive trials (*tâtonnements*).

Let us start with a set of prices given *at random* (for instance, by drawing numbers from an urn). On the basis of this *random* set of prices (Walras's *prix criés par hasard*) the individuals fulfill their subjective equilibrium condition and attain their maximum positions. For each commodity a quantity demanded and a quantity supplied is established. Now the objective equilibrium condition comes into play. If the quantity demanded and the quantity supplied of each commodity happen to be equal, the entire situation is settled and the prices are the

13. If the demand and supply schedules are not monotonic functions the first must have an increasing, and the latter must have a decreasing, branch. Demand can be an increasing function of price in the case of competing commodities and, as Walras has shown, supply can be a decreasing function of price when the commodity in question has a personal utility for the seller. If either demand is an increasing, or supply is a decreasing, function of price there may be a multiple solution even if those functions are monotonic. However, these are quite exceptional cases.

equilibrium prices. If, however, the quantities demanded and the quantities supplied diverge, the competition of the buyers and sellers will alter the prices. Prices of those commodities the demand for which exceeds the supply rise, while the prices of the commodities where the reverse is the case fall. As a result we get a *new* set of prices, which serves as a new basis for the individuals' striving to satisfy their subjective equilibrium condition. The subjective equilibrium condition being carried out, we get a new set of quantities demanded and supplied. If demand and supply are not equal for each commodity, prices change again and we have *another* set of prices, which again serves as a basis for individual rearranging of choices; and thus we get a new set of quantities demanded and supplied. And so the process goes on until the objective equilibrium condition is satisfied and equilibrium finally reached.[14] Actually it is the *historically given* prices which serve as a basis for the process of successive trials.

We have to apologize to the reader for having occupied his attention with this textbook exposition of the elements of the theory of economic equilibrium. But the very fact that the possibility of determining prices (in the wider sense of 'terms on which alternatives are offered') in a Socialist economy has been denied seems to indicate that the meaning of these elements has not been fully grasped. Now let us see whether a similar method of trial and error cannot be applied in a Socialist economy.

14. Thus each successive set of prices is nearer to satisfying the objective equilibrium condition than the preceding one. However, since a change of the quantity supplied generally requires a period of time, some qualification must be made. In industries where changes of output can be effected in a more or less continuous way, by varying some factors of production and leaving the others unchanged, and by extending, as time goes on, the number of factors which are made variable, the process of adaptation is determined by a family of short-period supply (and cost) curves. With this type of adaptation, which may be termed Marshallian, each successive price is nearer to the equilibrium price. But where output can be varied only by jerks, as in the case of crops, the mechanism described by the cobweb theorem comes into action and successive trials approach equilibrium only under special conditions. However, the Marshallian type of adaptation of supply seems to be the dominant one.

The trial and error procedure in a Socialist economy

In order to discuss the method of allocating resources in a Socialist economy we have to state what kind of Socialist society we have in mind. The fact of public ownership of the means of production does not in itself determine the system of distributing consumers' goods and of allocating people to various occupations, nor the principles guiding the production of commodities. Let us now assume that freedom of choice in consumption and freedom of choice of occupation are maintained and that the preferences of consumers, as expressed by their demand prices, are the guiding criteria in production and in the allocation of resources. Later we shall pass to the study of a more centralized Socialist system.[15]

In the Socialist system as described we have a genuine market (in the institutional sense of the word) for consumers' goods and for the services of labor. But there is no market for capital goods and productive resources outside of labor.[16] The prices of capital goods and productive resources outside of labor are thus prices in the generalized sense, i.e. mere indices of alternatives available, fixed for accounting purposes. Let us see how economic equilibrium is determined in such a system. Just as in a competitive individualist régime, the determination of equilibrium consists of two parts.

1. On the basis of *given* indices of alternatives (which are market prices in the case of consumers' goods and the services of labor and accounting prices in all other cases) both the individuals participating in the economic system as consumers

15. In pre-war literature the terms 'Socialism' and 'Collectivism' were used to designate a Socialist system as described above and the word 'Communism' was used to denote more centralized systems. The classical definition of Socialism (and of Collectivism) was that of a system which socializes production alone, while Communism was defined as socializing both production and consumption. At the present time these words have become political terms with special connotations.

16. To simplify the problem we assume that all means of production are public property. Needless to say, in any actual socialist community there must be a large number of means of production privately owned (e.g. by farmers, artisans, and small-scale entrepreneurs). But this does not introduce any new theoretical problem.

and as owners of the services of labor and the managers of production and of the ultimate resources outside of labor (i.e. of capital and of natural resources) make decisions according to certain principles. These managers are assumed to be public officials.

2. The prices (whether market or accounting) are determined by the condition that the quantity of each commodity demanded is equal to the quantity supplied. The conditions determining the decisions under 1 form the *subjective*, while that under 2 is the *objective*, equilibrium condition.

3. Finally, we have also a condition 3, expressing the social organization of the economic system. As the productive resources outside of labor are public property, the incomes of the consumers are divorced from the ownership of those resources and the form of condition 3 (social organization) is determined by the *principles of income formation adopted*.

The possibility of determining condition 3 in different ways gives to a Socialist society considerable freedom in matters of distribution of income. But the necessity of maintaining freedom in the choice of occupation limits the arbitrary use of this freedom, for there must be some connection between the income of a consumer and the services of labor performed by him. It seems, therefore, convenient to regard the income of consumers as composed of two parts: one part being the receipts for the labor services performed and the other part being a social dividend constituting the individual's share in the income derived from the capital and the natural resources owned by society. We assume that the distribution of the social dividend is based on certain principles, reserving the content of those principles for later discussion. Thus condition 3 is determinate and determines the incomes of the consumers in terms of prices of the services of labor and social dividend, which, in turn, may be regarded as determined by the total yield of capital and of the natural resources and by the principles adopted in distributing this yield.[17]

17. In formulating condition 3 capital accumulation has to be taken into account. Capital accumulation may be done either 'corporately' by deduct-

Condition 1. Let us consider the subjective equilibrium condition in a Socialist economy.

(i) Freedom of choice in consumption being assumed,[18] this part of the subjective equilibrium condition of a competitive market applies also to the market for consumers' goods in a socialist economy. The incomes of the consumers and the prices of consumers' goods being given, the demand for consumers' goods is determined.

(ii) The decisions of the managers of production are no longer guided by the aim of maximizing profit. Instead, certain rules are imposed on them by the Central Planning Board which aim at satisfying consumers' preferences in the best way possible. These rules determine the combination of factors of production and the scale of output.

One rule must impose the choice of the combination of factors which minimizes the average cost of production. This rule leads to the factors being combined in such proportion that the marginal productivity of that amount of each factor which is worth a unit of money is the same for all factors.[19] This rule is addressed to whoever makes decisions involving the problem of the optimum combination of factors, i.e. to managers responsible for running existing plants and to those engaged in building new plants. A second rule determines the scale of output by stating that output has to be fixed so that marginal cost is equal to the price of the product. This rule is addressed to two kinds of persons. First of all, it is addressed to the managers of plants and thus determines the scale of output of each plant

---

ing a certain part of the national income before the social dividend is distributed, or it may be left to the savings of individuals, or both methods may be combined. But 'corporate' accumulation must certainly be the dominant form of capital formation in a Socialist economy.

18. Of course there may be also a sector of socialized consumption the cost of which is met by taxation. Such a sector exists also in Capitalist society and comprises the provision not only of collective wants, in Cassel's sense, but also of other wants whose social importance is too great to be left to the free choice of individuals (for instance, free hospital service and free education). But this problem does not represent any theoretical difficulty and we may disregard it.

19. See, however, the correction for limitational factors in footnote 10.

and, together with the first rule, its demand for factors of production. The first rule, to whomever addressed, and the second rule when addressed to the managers of plants, perform the same function that in a competitive system is carried out by the private producer's aiming to maximize his profit, when the prices of factors and of the product are independent of the amount of each factor used by him and of his scale of output.

The total output of an industry has yet to be determined. This is done by addressing the second rule also to the managers of a whole industry (e.g. to the directors of the National Coal Trust) as a principle to guide them in deciding whether an industry ought to be expanded (by building new plants or enlarging old ones) or contracted (by not replacing plants which are wearing out). Thus each industry has to produce exactly as much of a commodity as can be sold or 'accounted for' to other industries at a price which equals the marginal cost incurred *by the industry* in producing this amount. The marginal cost incurred by an industry is the cost to that industry (not to a particular plant) of doing whatever is necessary to produce an additional unit of output, the optimum combination of factors being used. This may include the cost of building new plants or enlarging old ones.[20]

Addressed to the managers of an industry, the second rule performs the function which under free competition is carried out by the free entry of firms into an industry or their exodus from it: i.e. it determines the output of an industry.[21] The

20. Since in practice such marginal cost is not a continuous function of output, we have to compare the cost of each additional *indivisible input* with the receipts expected from the additional output thus secured. For instance, in a railway system as long as there are unused carriages the cost of putting them into use has to be compared with the additional receipts which may be obtained by doing so. When all the carriages available are used up to capacity, the cost of building and running additional carriages (and locomotives) has to be compared with the additional receipts expected to arise from such action. Finally, the question of building new tracks is decided upon the same principle. Cf. Lerner (1937, pp. 263–7).

21. The result, however, of following this rule coincides with the result obtained under free competition only in the case of constant returns to the industry (i.e. a homogeneous production function of the first degree). In this case marginal cost incurred by the industry equals average cost. In all other cases the results diverge, for under free competition the output of an industry

second rule, however, has to be carried out irrespective of whether average cost is covered or not, even if it should involve plants or whole industries in losses.

Both rules can be put in the form of the simple request to use always the method of production (i.e. combination of factors) which minimizes average cost and to produce as much of each service or commodity as will equalize marginal cost and the price of the product, this request being addressed to whoever is responsible for the particular decision to be taken. Thus the output of each plant and industry and the total demand for factors of production by each industry are determined. To enable the managers of production to follow these rules the prices of the factors and of the products must, of course, be given. In the case of consumers' goods and services of labor they are determined on a market; in all other cases they are fixed by the Central Planning Board. Those prices being given, the supply of products and the demand for factors are determined.

The reasons for adopting the two rules mentioned are obvious. Since prices are indices of terms on which alternatives are offered, that method of production which will minimize average cost will also minimize the alternatives sacrificed. Thus the first rule means simply that each commodity must be produced with a minimum sacrifice of alternatives. The second rule is a necessary consequence of following consumers' preferences. It means that the marginal significance of each preference which is satisfied has to be equal to the marginal significance of the alternative preferences the satisfaction of which is sacrificed. If the second rule was not observed certain lower preferences would be satisfied while preferences higher up on the scale would be left unsatisfied.

(iii) Freedom of choice of occupation being assumed, laborers

---

is such that average cost equals the price of the product, while according to our rule it is marginal cost (incurred by the industry) that ought to be equal to the price. This difference results in profits being made by the industries whose marginal cost exceeds average cost, whereas the industries in which the opposite is the case incur losses. These profits and losses correspond to the taxes and bounties proposed by Professor Pigou in order to bring about under free competition the equality of private and social marginal net product. See Pigou (1929, pp. 223–7).

offer their services to the industry or occupation paying the highest wages. For the publicly owned capital and natural resources a price has to be fixed by the Central Planning Board with the provision that these resources can be directed only to industries which are able to 'pay', or rather to 'account for', this price. This is a consequence of following the consumers' preferences. The prices of the services of the ultimate productive resources being given, their distribution between the different industries is also determined.

Condition 2. The subjective equilibrium condition can be carried out only when prices are *given*. This is also true of the decisions of the managers of production and of the productive resources in public ownership. Only when prices are given can the combination of factors which minimizes average cost, the output which equalizes marginal cost and the price of the product, and the best allocation of the ultimate productive resources be determined. But if there is no market (in the institutional sense of the word) for capital goods or for the ultimate productive resources outside of labor, can their prices be determined objectively? Must not the prices fixed by the Central Planning Board necessarily be quite arbitrary? If so, their arbitrary character would deprive them of any economic significance as indices of the terms on which alternatives are offered. This is, indeed, the opinion of Professor von Mises (see von Hayek, 1935, p. 112). And the view is shared by G. D. H. Cole, who says (1935, pp. 88, 183–4):

A planless economy, in which each entrepreneur takes his decisions apart from the rest, obviously confronts each entrepreneur with a broadly given structure of costs, represented by the current level of wages, rent and interest. . . . In a planned Socialist economy there can be no objective structure of costs. Costs can be imputed to any desired extent. . . . But these imputed costs are not objective, but *fiat* costs determined by the public policy of the State.

This view, however, is easily refuted by recalling the very elements of price theory.

Why is there an objective price structure in a competitive market? Because, as a result of the parametric function of prices, there is generally only *one* set of prices which satisfies the objective equilibrium condition, i.e. equalizes demand and supply of each commodity. The same objective price structure can be obtained in a Socialist economy if the *parametric function of prices* is retained. On a competitive market the parametric function of prices results from the number of competing individuals being too large to enable any one to influence prices by his own action. In a Socialist economy, production and ownership of the productive resources outside of labor being centralized, the managers certainly can and do influence prices by their decisions. Therefore, the parametric function of prices must be imposed on them by the Central Planning Board as an *accounting rule*. All accounting has to be done *as if* prices were independent of the decisions taken. For purposes of accounting, prices must be treated as constant, as they are treated by entrepreneurs on a competitive market.

The technique of attaining this end is very simple: the Central Planning Board has to fix prices and see to it that all managers of plants, industries and resources do their accounting on the basis of the prices fixed by the Central Planning Board, and not tolerate any use of other accounting. Once the parametric function of prices is adopted as an accounting rule, the price structure is established by the objective equilibrium condition. For each set of prices and consumers' incomes a definite amount of each commodity is supplied and demanded.

Condition 3 determines the incomes of the consumers by the prices of the services of ultimate productive resources and the principles adopted for the distribution of the social dividend. With those principles given, prices alone are the variables determining the demand and supply of commodities.

The condition that the quantity demanded and supplied has to be equal for each commodity serves to select the equilibrium prices which alone assure the compatibility of all decisions taken. *Any price different from the equilibrium price would show at the end of the accounting period a surplus or a shortage of the commodity in question.* Thus the accounting prices in a Socialist economy, far from being arbitrary, have quite the same objective character as the market prices in a régime of competition. Any mistake made by the Central Planning Board in fixing prices would announce itself in a very objective way – by a physical shortage or surplus of the quantity of the commodity or resources in question – and would have to be corrected in order to keep production running smoothly. As there is generally only one set of prices which satisfies the objective equilibrium condition, both the prices of products and costs[22] are uniquely determined.[23]

Our study of the determination of equilibrium prices in a Socialist economy has shown that the process of price determination is quite analogous to that in a competitive market. The Central Planning Board performs the functions of the market. It establishes the rules for combining factors of production and choosing the scale of output of a plant, for determining the output of an industry, for the allocation of resources and for the parametric use of prices in accounting. Finally, it fixes the prices so as to balance the quantity supplied and demanded of each commodity. It follows that a substitution of planning for the functions of the market is quite possible and workable.

Two problems deserve some special attention. The first relates to the determination of the best distribution of the social dividend. Freedom of choice of occupation assumed, the distribution of the social dividend may affect the amount of services of labor offered to different industries. If certain occupations received a larger social dividend than others, labor would be

22. Von Hayek maintains that it would be impossible to determine the value of durable instruments of production because, in consequence of changes, 'the value of most of the more durable instruments of production has little or no connection with the costs which have been incurred in their production' (1935, p. 227). It is quite true that the value of such durable instruments is essentially a capitalized quasi-rent and therefore can be determined only after the price which will be obtained for the product is known (cf. ibid., p. 228). But there is no reason why the price of the product should be any less determinate in a Socialist economy than on a competitive market. The managers of the industrial plant in question have simply to take the price fixed by the Central Planning Board as the basis of their calculation. The Central Planning Board would fix this price so as to satisfy the objective equilibrium condition, just as a competitive market does.

23. However, in certain cases there may be a multiple solution. Cf. page 41 above.

diverted into the occupations receiving a larger dividend. There-fore, the distribution of the social dividend must be such as not to interfere with the optimum distribution of labor services between the different industries and occupation. The optimum distribution is that which makes the differences of the value of the marginal product of the services of labor in different industries and occupations equal to the differences in the marginal disutility[24] of working in those industries or occupa-tions.[25] This distribution of the services of labor arises auto-matically whenever wages are the only source of income. *Therefore, the social dividend must be distributed so as to have no influence whatever on the choice of occupation.* The social dividend paid to an individual must be entirely independent of his choice of occupation. For instance, it can be divided equally per head of population, or distributed according to age or size of family or any other principle which does not affect the choice of occupation.

The other problem is the determination of the rate of interest. We have to distinguish between a short-period and a long-period solution of the problem. For the former the amount of capital is regarded as constant, and the rate of interest is simply determined by the condition that the demand for capital is equal to the amount available. When the rate of interest is set too low the socialized banking system would be unable to meet the demand of industries for capital; when the interest rate is set too high there would be a surplus of capital available for

24. It is only the *relative* disutility of different occupations that counts. The absolute disutility may be zero or even negative. By putting leisure, safety, agreeableness of work, etc., into the preference scales, all labor costs may be expressed as opportunity costs. If such a device is adopted each industry or occupation may be regarded as producing a joint product: the commodity or service in question *and* leisure, safety, agreeableness of work, etc. The services of labor have to be allocated so that the value of this marginal *joint* product is the same in all industries and occupations.

25. If the total amount of labor performed is not limited by legislation or custom regulating the hours of work, etc., the value of the marginal product of the services of labor in each occupation has to be *equal* to the marginal disutility. If any limitational factors are used, it is the marginal *net* product of the services of labor (obtained by deducting from the marginal product the marginal expenditure for the limitational factors) which has to satisfy the condition in the text.

Oskar Lange 51

investment. However, in the long period the amount of capital can be increased by accumulation. If the accumulation of capital is performed 'corporately' before distributing the social dividend to the individuals, the rate of accumulation can be determined by the Central Planning Board *arbitrarily*. The Central Planning Board will probably aim at accumulating enough to make the marginal *net* productivity of capital zero,[26] this aim being never attained because of technical progress (new labor-saving devices), increase of population, the discovery of new natural resources and, possibly, because of the shift of demand toward commodities produced by more capital-intensive methods.[27] But the rate, i.e. the *speed*, at which accumulation progresses is arbitrary.

The arbitrariness of the rate of capital accumulation 'corporately' performed means simply that the decision regarding the rate of accumulation reflects how the Central Planning Board, and not the consumers, evaluate the optimum time-shape of the income stream. One may argue, of course, that this involves a diminution of consumers' welfare. This difficulty could be overcome only by leaving all accumulation to the saving of individuals.[28] But this is scarcely compatible with the organization of a Socialist society.[29] Discussion of this point is postponed to a later part of this essay.

Having treated the theoretical determination of economic equilibrium in a Socialist society, let us see how equilibrium can be determined by a method of *trial and error* similar to that in a competitive market. This method of trial and error is based on the *parametric function of prices*. Let the Central Planning

26. Cf. Wicksell (1934, p. 241).

27. These changes, however, if very frequent, may act also in the opposite direction and diminish the marginal *net* productivity of capital because of the risk of obsolescence due to them. This is pointed out by Lerner (1936, p. 72).

28. This method has been advocated by Barone (see von Hayek, 1935, pp. 278–9).

29. Of course, the consumers remain free to save as much as they want out of the income which is actually paid out to them, and the socialized banks could pay interest on savings. As a matter of fact, in order to prevent hoarding they would have to do so. But *this* rate of interest would not have any necessary connection with the marginal *net* productivity of capital. It would be quite arbitrary.

Board start with a given set of prices chosen *at random*. All decisions of the managers of production and of the productive resources in public ownership and also all decisions of individuals as consumers and as suppliers of labor are made on the basis of these prices. As a result of these decisions the quantity demanded and supplied of each commodity is determined. If the quantity demanded of a commodity is not equal to the quantity supplied, the price of that commodity has to be changed. It has to be raised if demand exceeds supply and lowered if the reverse is the case. Thus the Central Planning Board fixes a new set of prices which serves as a basis for new decisions, and which results in a new set of quantities demanded and supplied. Through this process of trial and error equilibrium prices are finally determined. Actually the process of trial and error would, of course, proceed on the basis of the prices *historically given*. Relatively small adjustments of those prices would constantly be made, and there would be no necessity of building up an entirely new price system.

This process of trial and error has been excellently described by the late Professor Fred M. Taylor. He assumes that the administrators of the Socialist economy would assign provisional values to the factors of production (as well as to all other commodities). He continues (1929):

If, in regulating productive processes, the authorities were actually using for any particular factor a valuation which was too high or too low, that fact would soon disclose itself in unmistakable ways. Thus, supposing that, in the case of a particular factor, the valuation . . . was too high, that fact would inevitably lead the authorities to be unduly economical in the use of that factor; and this conduct, in turn, would make the amount of that factor which was available for the current production period larger than the amount which was consumed during that period. In other words, too high a valuation of any factor would cause the stock of that factor to show a surplus at the end of the productive period.

Similarly, too low a valuation would cause a deficit in the stock of that factor. 'Surplus or deficit – one or the other of these would result from every wrong valuation of a factor' (Taylor, 1929). By a set of successive trials the right accounting prices of the factors are found.

Thus the accounting prices in a Socialist economy can be determined by the same process of trial and error by which prices on a competitive market are determined. To determine the prices the Central Planning Board does not need to have 'complete lists of the different quantities of all commodities which would be bought at any possible combination of prices of the different commodities which might be available' (see von Hayek, 1935, p. 211). Neither would the Central Planning Board have to solve hundreds of thousands (as Professor von Hayek expects, 1935, p. 212) or millions (as Professor Robbins thinks, 1934, p. 151) of equations. The only 'equations' which would have to be 'solved' would be those of the consumers and the managers of production. These are exactly the same 'equations' which are 'solved' in the present economic system and the persons who do the 'solving' are the same also. Consumers 'solve' them by spending their income so as to get out of it the maximum total utility; and the managers of production 'solve' them by finding the combination of factors that minimizes average cost and the scale of output that equalizes marginal cost and the price of the product. They 'solve' them by a method of trial and error, making (or imagining) small variations *at the margin*, as Marshall used to say, and watching what effect those variations have either on the total utility or on the cost of production. And only a few of them have been graduated in higher mathematics. Professor von Hayek and Professor Robbins themselves 'solve' at least hundreds of equations daily, for instance, in buying a newspaper or in deciding to take a meal in a restaurant, and presumably they do not use determinants or Jacobians for that purpose. And each entrepreneur who hires or discharges a worker, or who buys a bale of cotton, 'solves equations' too. Exactly the same kind and number of 'equations', no less and no more, have to be 'solved' in a Socialist as in a Capitalist economy, and exactly the same persons, the consumers and managers of production plants, have to 'solve' them.

To establish the prices which serve the persons 'solving equations' as parameters no mathematics is needed either. Neither is there needed any knowledge of the demand and supply functions. The right prices are simply found out by watching the quantities demanded and the quantities supplied and by raising the price of a commodity or service whenever there is an excess of demand over supply and lowering it whenever the reverse is the case, until, by trial and error, the price is found at which demand and supply are in balance.

As we have seen, there is not the slightest reason why a trial and error procedure, similar to that in a competitive market, could not work in a Socialist economy to determine the accounting prices of capital goods and of the productive resources in public ownership. Indeed, it seems that this trial and error procedure would, or at least could, work *much better* in a Socialist economy than it does in a competitive market. For the Central Planning Board has a much wider knowledge of what is going on in the whole economic system than any private entrepreneur can ever have and, consequently, may be able to reach the right equilibrium prices by a *much shorter* series of successive trials than a competitive market actually does.[30] The argument that in a Socialist economy the accounting prices of capital goods and of productive resources in public ownership cannot be determined objectively, either because this is theoretically impossible or, because there is no adequate trial and error procedure available, cannot be maintained. In 1911 Professor Taussig classified the argument that 'goods could not be valued' among the objections to Socialism that are 'of little weight' (Taussig, 1911, pp. xvi, 456–7). After all the discussions since that time, no reason can be found to change this opinion.

30. In reducing the number of trials necessary a knowledge of the demand and supply schedules derived from statistics, on which Dickinson wants to base the pricing of goods in a socialist economy, may be of great service, but such knowledge, although *useful*, is *not necessary* in finding out the equilibrium prices. However, if the Central Planning Board proceeds in fixing prices purely by trial and error and the managers of production adhere strictly to treating the prices fixed as constant, in certain branches of production the fluctuations described by the cobweb theorem might appear also in a Socialist economy. In such cases the Planning Board would have, in order to avoid such fluctuations, deliberately to use anticipations as to the influence of variations of output on the price of the product, and vice versa (i.e. a knowledge of demand and supply schedules) in fixing the accounting prices. Such deliberate use of demand and supply schedules is useful in all other cases, too, for it serves to shorten the series of trials and thus avoids unnecessary waste.

References

BARONE, E. (1908), 'Il ministerio della produzione nello stato collettivista', *Giornale degli Economisti e Rivista di Statistica*, vol. 37, pp. 267–93, 391–414.

COLE, G. D. H., *Economic Planning*, New York.

GEORGESCU-ROEGEN, N. (1935), 'Fixed coefficient of production and the marginal productivity theory', *Rev. econ. Stud.*, vol. 3, pp. 40–49.

KNIGHT, F.H. (1931), 'Professor Fisher's interest theory', *J. polit. Econ.* vol. 39, pp. 176–212.

LANGE, O. (1935), 'Formen der Angebotsanpassung und wirtschaftliches Gleichgewicht', *Zeitschrift für Nationalökonomie*, bd. VI, heft 3.

LANGE, O. (1936), 'The place of interest in the theory of production', *Rev. econ. Stud.*, vol. 3, pp. 159–92.

LANGE, O. (1937), 'Professor Knight's note on interest theory', *Rev. econ. Stud.*, vol. 4, pp. 231–5.

LERNER, A. P. (1936), 'A note on Socialist economics', *Rev. econ. Stud.*, vol. 4, pp. 72–6.

LERNER, A. P. (1937), 'Statics and dynamics in Socialist economics', *Econ. J.*, vol. 47, pp. 263–7.

PARETO, V. (1897), *Cours d'économie politique*, vol. 2, Rouge, Lausanne.

PARETO, V. (1910), *Manuel d'économie politique*, Giard, Paris.

PIGOU, A. C. (1929), *The Economics of Welfare*, Macmillan, 3rd edn.

ROBBINS, L. C. (1934), *The Great Depression*, Macmillan.

SCHUMPETER, J. A. (1908), *Das Wesen und der Hauptinhalt der theoretischen Nationalökonomie*, Duncker & Humblot, Leipzig.

TAUSSIG, F. W. (1911), *Principles of Economics*, vol. 2, Macmillan Co.

TAYLOR, F. M. (1929), 'The guidance of production in a Socialist state', *Amer. econ. Rev.*, vol. 19, pp. 1–8.

VON HAYEK, F. A. (ed.) (1935), *Collectivist Economic Planning*, Routledge & Kegan Paul.

VON HAYEK, F. A. (1936), 'Utility analysis and interest', *Econ. J.*, vol. 46, pp. 58–60.

VON MISES, L. (1933), *Grundprobleme der Nationalökonomie*, Fischer, Jena.

WALRAS, L. (1926), *Elements d'économie politique pure*, éd. déf., Pichon, Paris.

WICKSELL, K. (1934), 'Professor Cassel's system of economics', in L. Robbins (ed.), *Lectures on Political Economy*, vol. 1, Routledge & Kegan Paul.

WICKSTEED, P. H. (1933), *The Common Sense of Political Economy*, Routledge & Kegan Paul, 2nd edn.

Part Two **Two Traditions**

The shades of Jevons, Menger, Edgeworth, Wicksteed, Wicksell, Clark and Fisher may justifiably be offended by the attribution of modern price theory to two sources, Alfred Marshall and Léon Walras, but these two scholars have had far and away the most influence on twentieth-century thought. It is to Marshall that we owe the habit of asking what difference do small changes make (the habit of looking to the margin), measurement of responsiveness of quantities by elasticities of demand and supply, and analysis of short-run and long-run adjustments within situations of partial equilibria. In contrast with Marshall's down-to-earth struggle with the interpretation of the detailed working of the economy stands Walras's grand construction of general equilibrium. In a typical British or American textbook on price theory nine-tenths of the contents stem from Marshall's work, general equilibrium only getting notice in a last chapter or appendix. However, welfare economics, international trade theory and the theory of economic planning are all Walrasian, and the Walrasian tradition is likely to grow even further in importance now that W. Leontief has invented the means in input–output analysis to make general equilibrium analysis operational.

3 Ragnar Frisch

Alfred Marshall's Theory of Value[1]

Ragnar Frisch, 'Alfred Marshall's theory of value', *Quarterly Journal of Economics*, vol. 64, 1950, pp. 495–524.

Like all human work, Alfred Marshall's theory of value had its definite shortcomings. To mention but one: Marshall did not see that any optimalization procedure – that is, any problem of combining factors in the 'best' way – depends essentially on a system of prices or other kinds of value coefficients which the enterprise, or the industrial sector, or the nation, etc., that carries out the optimalization, must *assume* (as constants or functions of other parameters involved) in order that the optimalization shall have a precise meaning. He was apparently under the impression that the premises of the problem of the 'best' combination of factors could as a rule be formulated in purely technical terms, which, of course, is true only in the special case where all the factors are strictly limitational in their effects. Since Marshall's general line of reasoning was certainly not confined to this special case, much of what he said about optimalization turned out to be rather obscure.

Despite shortcomings such as this one, and despite all the changes in economic conditions and economic policies that have come about since Marshall wrote his theory of value, this theory still holds its own. It contains elements about which no economist can afford to be ignorant however 'modern' he claims to be.

1. The references apply to the *Principles of Economics*, Macmillan, 7th edn, 1916, and later reprints. In the references the first roman numeral denotes 'book', the second 'chapter' and the arabic numeral the section. The formulation of the present paper has been influenced by many stimulating discussions with students, particularly with Mr Sten Nilson, at that time a student of economics in Oslo University.

The various orders of change

A main point in Marshall's theory of value is the distinction between the various *orders* of change: firstly changes of very short duration, taking place within some days or at the most within a few weeks; secondly those requiring a somewhat longer period, from a few months to one year; and finally those extending over very long periods, several years (V. V. 8. p. 379). Corresponding to these orders of change, there are three distinct, separate parts of the theory dealing with:

1. Temporary equilibrium.

2. Normal equilibrium with reference to short periods.

3. Normal equilibrium with reference to long periods.

One could also speak of a fourth type of change requiring still longer periods, secular movements, but it is not necessary to deal with these latter movements separately, as they do not call for a *method of analysis* differing in principle from that of type 3. Between 1, 2 and 3 above, however, there is a distinct difference in Marshall's method of analysis, which will be discussed below.

Marshall mentions that, rigorously speaking, there is a *continuous* transition between the different periods of time involved in 1, 2 and 3. 'Of course there is no hard and sharp line of division between "long" and "short" periods' (V. V. 8. p. 378). Roughly speaking, however, it is possible to distinguish between those factors affecting price formation that *cannot* be changed in the short run or *actually do change* slowly, and others that change more rapidly. Therefore, as a matter of convenience one is led to use several types of theory, in which different sets of factors are assumed to be constant.

A mechanical analogy will illustrate this way of reasoning. Consider a system of three pendulums A, B and C, mutually connected (B is suspended from A and C is suspended from B) as shown in Figure 1. The top pendulum is the longest and heaviest, the bottom the shortest and lightest. It is difficult to study the movement of this system in an exact way – even with the help of mathematics. But one can get a useful *approximation* by first studying the movement of *each pendulum separately*.

We can study the motion of B, for instance, under the assumption that the pendulum above, A, does not move during a period of time which is relevant to the study of a swing of pendulum B, and under the further assumption that the lowest pendulum C is so small that its movement does not exert any appreciable influence on that of B. The position of the top pendulum A, will then represent a *normal level* to which the position of B is referred, and correspondingly B represents the normal level for C. When each pendulum is studied in this way, the composite

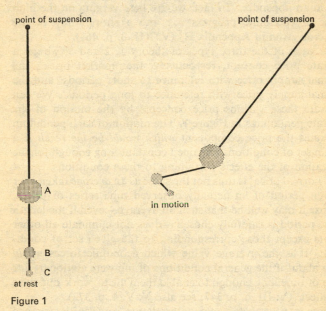

point of suspension

point of suspension

A

in motion

B

C

at rest

Figure 1

movement can be *built up* from the separate movements. The level which at first was assumed to be constant will then become variable. Of course, this only furnishes an approximation, but it might be sufficiently accurate for the purpose at hand. The greater the difference between the pendulums with respect to length and weight, the closer will be the approximation obtained by using this method of analysis. If on the other hand there is a *small* difference between the pendulums, the result will not be sufficiently exact. In this case the system must be seen as a whole and we must study specifically for instance how one pendulum, when swinging, acts as a *moving force* on the others. Translated to economic language this means that we have to deal with a truly dynamic analysis of economic *evolution*, a theory of *progress*.

The analysis of Marshall is mainly built on the possibility of splitting the problem into separate movements. He expressly renounces the full dynamic analysis, giving only an intimation of it in an appendix. 'In fact, we are here verging on the high theme of economic progress ... and a short study of the subject is given in Appendix H' (V. XII. 3. p. 461).

For each of the three types of theory 1, 2 and 3, we get a separate price concept, respectively, the 'market price', the 'normal supply price with reference to short periods' and the 'normal supply price with reference to long periods'. We can illustrate these various price concepts by the motion of the separate pendulums in Figure 1. The motion of each pendulum illustrates the price component *which would be the result* if a certain set of conditions remained constant long enough for the realization of the effects pertaining to these conditions.

A 'normal price' is thus not the same as an *average* taken over a given period of an actually observed time series of prices, because it may well be that such an average – even if the length of the period is carefully chosen – does not eliminate all other factors except those corresponding to the given set of conditions: 'It is the average value which economic forces *would* bring about if the general conditions of life were stationary for a run of time long enough to enable them all to work out their full effect' (V. III. 6. p. 347; see also V. V. 4. p. 372).

There is, nevertheless, a certain relation between the average and the normal. Since our classification of the price-determining factors in categories corresponds generally speaking to the degree of variability which we *actually* find in these factors in economic life, the average price taken over a period of considerable length frequently *approximates* the normal price produced by factors of the corresponding category of variability. Marshall's distinction between 'short' and 'long' periods is thus in a way related to the purely statistical *decomposition* of economic time series, that is, the breaking up of these series into short and long cyclical movements and possibly also an underlying secular trend.

We shall consider more closely the kind of conditions which Marshall keeps constant in the three different theories of price formation. In type 1 there is *no* change in the factors of production. The stock of goods on hand is assumed to be given by previous production. In type 2 there is a *partial* adaptation of the factors of production, viz., those that usually are called the 'variable' ones. In type 3 there is adaptation of all factors of production; the *plant* itself may be changed so that even the productive *capacity* becomes one of the variables in the problem. 'In the last chapter we looked at the affairs of only a single day; and supposed the stocks offered for sale to be already in existence' (V. III. 1. p. 337).

As regards *normal* prices, when the term Normal is taken to relate to *short* periods of a few months or a year, Supply means broadly what can be produced for the price in question with the existing stock of plant, personal and impersonal, in the given time. As regards *normal* prices, when the term Normal is to refer to *long* periods of several years, Supply means what can be produced by plant, which itself can be remuneratively produced and applied within the given time (V. V. 8. p. 379).

The temporary equilibrium then becomes a theory for purchase and sale. 'Holders will be willing to sell', 'buyers will be willing to buy' (V. II. 2. p. 333). The price-determining factors in this case include forecasts of the probable future price movements (the time-link between the markets), the demand for cash, etc. In some extreme cases this can give an almost vertical supply or demand schedule, but as a rule the demand schedule will be falling and the supply schedule rising in this type of market. Marshall's discussion of these cases is to be found in the short chapter (V. II).

The main part of Marshall's theory of value deals with 'normal equilibrium' and especially that of long periods. 'The remainder of the present volume is chiefly concerned with ... the normal relations of wages, profits, prices, etc., for rather long periods' (V. V. 8. p. 380). In order to bring out clearly, on the one hand, the difference between the two types of theory, and on the other hand, how they supplement one another and how they are related to more recent views on the theory of prices, we shall here also deal rather extensively with normal equilibrium with reference to short periods.

Normal equilibrium with reference to short periods

Occupying a central position in Marshall's theory of value is his conception of a *regular life cycle* for a private firm. The firm grows, culminates and decays like a tree in the forest (IV. XIII. 1. pp. 315–16). This is the regular cycle. There are, however, some firms that deviate from the rule. Depending upon the skill, energy and fortune of the owner, the firm may grow faster and reach higher than the others and the decline may be postponed.

If we study the supply of a certain commodity at a certain time, we will thus find *strong, weak* and *average* firms. They differ first and foremost in the extent to which they have been able to realize 'internal economies', i.e. cost reductions caused by conditions within the separate firm (IV. XIII. 1. p. 314).[2] Let us then for each firm examine how the *costs* vary with the volume of production under the condition that the productive plant and the marketing and administrative machinery is kept constant and only the short-period variable factors change. These variable factors, whose short-period quantities are functions of the volume of production within the same short period, are mainly raw materials, labor and that physical depreciation of plant which depends upon the intensity of production (some of the physical depreciation is independent of the extent and intensity of production). The expenses corresponding to these variable factors are the *variable* costs. When calculated per unit produced, their costs will here be called unit cost for the variable factors. This is what Marshall calls 'special, direct or prime cost' (V. IV. 5. p. 359). For its relation to the normal equilibrium with reference to short periods, see V. V. 6. p. 374. 'It is nearly always above, and generally very much above the special or prime cost for raw materials, labour and wear-and-tear of plant, which is immediately and directly

2. See also 'External and internal economies' in the Index to *Principles of Economics*.

involved by getting a little further use out of appliances which are not fully employed.'

That part of the costs which is independent of the short-period volume of production – i.e. the general cost of administration and sale, the general physical depreciation and the depreciation caused by the plant growing old – we call *fixed costs*. Calculated per unit produced we use the term unit cost for the fixed factors. This is what Marshall calls 'supplementary cost' (V. IV. 5. p. 359). The sum of these two unit costs we call the unit cost for all factors, which is the same as Marshall's 'total cost'. The marginal cost is the marginal increment of the total cost with respect to the quantity produced during the short period. This marginal cost is evidently the same whether it is calculated inclusive or exclusive of the fixed costs. (In calculating a marginal increment any additive constants drop out.) For each of the firms in the market we thus get three curves as shown in Figure 2. For reasons known from the theory of production, the minimum point of the unit cost curve will coincide with the marginal cost curve.

These are the short period *cost* curves. They are derived by determining the cost for each of a set of alternative short-period *volumes* of production. How can we now derive the *supply* schedule? This is a curve derived by taking alternative levels of the short period price as given, and for each such level finding out what the corresponding quantity supplied will be (in the case of the cost curves we did the opposite, for each quantity we determined a price). Marshall here distinguishes between two cases. One in which the price of the product is *high* (in relation to the cost structure of the enterprise) and the other where the price of the product is *low*. The reaction of the enterprise will be fundamentally different in the two cases. The borderline, we can say, is at the minimum of the unit cost curve for all factors. In the figure this is at a price of 43 cents. An expansion of production beyond this point will evidently not be advantageous unless the producer is compensated for the *marginal cost* (which under such an expansion is higher than the unit cost with all factors included). Marshall assumes that the firm in this upper range of prices in the normal short run acts as a quantity adaptor (to use a modern term). This means that the *supply schedule in this case will coincide with the marginal cost curve* (represented by the shaded curve in Figure 2) – '... in every case the cost of production is marginal' (V. V. 5. p. 373; see also V. V. 6. p. 374).

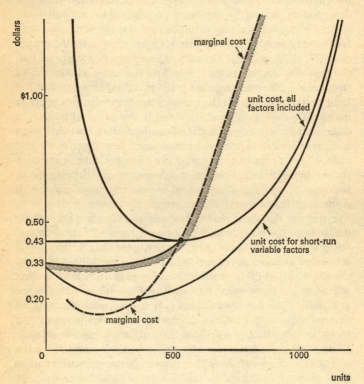

Figure 2

If the firm *considered only the immediate situation* it would still be profitable to follow the marginal cost curve downwards even if the price should fall below 43 cents. It would be profitable to follow the marginal cost curve down to the minimum point of the unit cost curve for the variable factors, i.e. in the figure, 20 cents. This part of the marginal cost curve passes through a range that in more recent price theory has been called the region of 'cut-throat competition'. In this region the firm will not have all of its fixed costs covered. It will have some of them covered, however, since the price in this region is somewhat higher than the unit cost for the variable factors. Below the lower limit at 20 cents, not even the variable costs are covered.

According to Marshall, the firms will not follow the marginal cost curve through the region of 'cut-throat competition', that is, between 43 cents and 20 cents. When the price falls below the point at which all costs are no longer covered, that is, below 43 cents, many of the firms will begin to react according to a different strategic type than that prevailing when they were above this critical point. Most firms will then, according to Marshall, consider a *stronger* curtailment of production than indicated by the marginal cost curve. If the price becomes appreciably lower than the minimum on the unit cost curve with all factors included (though still above the minimum on the unit cost curve for the variable factors), they may temporarily *cease* production. They will perhaps follow a course somewhat like the one indicated by the lower shaded curve in the figure which reaches a horizontal level at 33 cents. This horizontal part of the curve indicates the price at which the firm will temporarily cease production. The reason why the firm follows a curve of this type instead of the marginal cost curve is that 'each man fears to spoil his chance of getting a better price later from his own customers or if he produces for a large market ... fears the resentment of other producers ...' (V. V. 6. p. 374; see also V. XII. 3. p. 458–9 and V. XV. 1. p. 498).

The first of the considerations here mentioned by Marshall is what we now would call *supply orientated* demand and a time relationship in such a market. The second corresponds to a stronger or weaker, open or concealed, organization of the market. (Certain aspects of this problem can be analysed by means of *conjectural* elasticities.) It is, according to Marshall, especially in the case of production with large fixed costs (i.e. a large region of cut-throat competition) that we may get this restriction of supply with a view to supporting the price. In such cases the point at which the firm decides to cease production temporarily may be *far* above the lower unit cost minimum, i.e. in Figure 2 far above 20 cents. If it were not, the enterprise may cause a disaster:

In a trade which uses very expensive plant, the prime cost of goods is but a small part of their total cost; and an order at much less than their normal price may leave a large surplus above their prime cost. But if producers accept such orders in their anxiety to prevent their plant from being idle, they glut the market and tend to prevent prices from reviving. . . . They might ruin many of those in the trade, themselves perhaps among the number (V. V. 6. p. 375).

Thus, although nothing but prime cost enters *necessarily and directly* into the supply price for short periods, it is yet true that supplemen- costs also exert some influence indirectly (V. V. 6. p. 376).

When a firm does not follow the marginal cost curve between the two critical unit cost minima, but a curve such as the shaded one in Figure 2, we may say that it practices a *restrictive strategy* between these two points.

If the price is given and there are for instance three firms in the market, one strong, one average and one weak, we get a situation as indicated in Figure 3. The unbroken curves I and II for each firm represent respectively the unit cost curves for all factors and for the variable factors. The broken curves are the marginal cost curves. The shaded ones are the individual supply schedules. The supply schedule of the market (not drawn) is derived in the usual manner by horizontal addition of the individual supply curves (the shaded ones). In the short period normal market, neither the individual nor the market supply schedule can thus be falling. 'Here we see an illustration of the almost universal . . . law, that the term normal being taken to refer to a short period of time . . . *an increase in the amount demanded raises the normal supply price*' (V. V. 4. p. 370). And 'we expect the short-period supply price to increase with increasing output' (V. XII. 3. p. 460). The point of intersection between the supply schedule of the market and the demand schedule of the market determines the normal *equilibrium price* with reference to short periods.

Assume that this price is of the magnitude indicated by the horizontal line in Figure 3. This price is far above the unit cost minima of the strong firm. The strong firm will, therefore, according to Marshall's assumptions, act as a straightforward quantity-adaptor in this market situation. The little square in the figure shows at which point on the marginal cost curve of this firm the adaptation will take place. The strong firm will, at

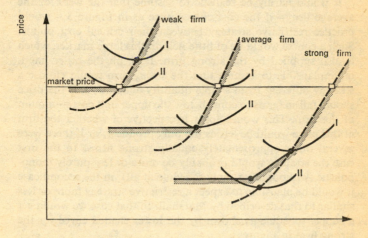

Figure 3

this price, earn more than needed to cover its fixed costs, it gets a net *quasi-rent* (for a definition of quasi-rent, see amongst others V. IV. 6, the note on p. 362 and V. VIII. 6. p. 412).

The average firm will have its costs – the fixed costs included – just covered (see the figure). We may, therefore, perhaps say that this firm is in a marginal position with respect to its own structure, while the strong firm is in a supermarginal position with respect to its own structure. In the case of the weak firm in the diagram, the price is just at the point where a further lowering of it would cause the firm to cease production. This firm is in a submarginal position with respect to its own structure, i.e. it will not get all its costs covered.

On the other hand we may say that the weak firm in Figure 3 is the marginal firm with respect to the market as a whole. It represents that part of the total production which would disappear with further decrease in price. Both the average and the strong firm are supermarginal with respect to the market, because they will not cease (only slightly curtail) production, if the price falls a little.

It would hardly be realistic to assume that the weak or the average firm – if the cost curves were as in Figure 3 – would practice restrictive strategy between their critical cost points. Such a course would be of little help in this large market, which is also supplied by the strong firm. It is, on the other hand, quite plausible to assume that the *strong* firm would choose a strategy different from simple quantity-adaptation, if the price should fall so far as to come below the upper unit cost minimum of this firm. This would apply irrespective of whether the firm at this price would be left as the only producer, or if there were several other approximately equally strong firms. In the first case the strategy would probably be more or less purely mono-polistic (without any supply schedule at all); in the second case it would be plausible to expect a restrictive strategy more or less similar to that described by Marshall. In that case we would get a supply schedule as shown by the lower shaded curve for the strong firm in Figure 3.

We might now examine more closely what Marshall means by 'the true marginal supply price for short periods' (V. V. 6. p. 374). When he employs this term to denote the ordinate of the supply schedule of the market, he uses it in another sense than we do when we compare *marginal* cost and *unit* cost. The differ-ence between these latter curves can be formulated in the following manner: the unit cost curve is of such a nature that the *rectangle* through a point on the curve – for instance the rectangle $OABC$ in Figure 4 – represents the total cost, while the marginal cost curve is of such a nature that the area underneath the curve – the shaded area $OAEF$ – represents the total cost which is in excess of the fixed costs. This is the same as to say that marginal cost equals the rate of increase of the total cost with respect to the volume of production. For each point on the abscissa in Figure 4, these areas must be of the same size when there are no fixed costs. Otherwise, there must be a constant difference equal to the fixed costs. This is only an expression for the relation that exists by definition between marginal cost and unit cost. If the unit cost curve includes a given sum for fixed costs, its ordinate will approach infinity as we approach the origin from the right (i.e. when the volume of production approaches zero). If it is exclusive of the fixed costs (or if there are no fixed costs), so that the rectangle drawn from the unit cost curve and the area below the marginal cost curve not only have a constant difference but are exactly equal, then the unit cost curve and the marginal cost curve must start from the same ordinate at their origin. This is the case in Figure 4.[3] Unit cost and marginal cost will be represented by one and the same curve when, and only when, the unit cost (and consequently also the marginal cost) is *constant*, i.e. does not vary with the volume of production. It is easy to see that in such a case the unit cost and the marginal cost curve will be coinciding horizontal lines.

When Marshall uses the term 'marginal supply price' for the ordinate of the supply schedule in the short-period normal market, it is *not* because this supply schedule is of such a kind that the area below the curve represents the total cost of producing the amount of the goods brought forth in the market (which would mean that the ordinate represents the rate of increase of total cost with respect to the volume of production). The meaning of the market supply curve which Marshall has here in mind, is such that the ordinate of the curve times the abscissa is equal to the total value of the goods sold in the market. The reason why Marshall nevertheless uses the term 'marginal' here and specifically speaks of a 'marginal supply price' is that he goes *behind* each point on this market curve and examines the separate firms and their reactions. Consider an individual firm which acts on the *assumption of a fixed price*. Its supply schedule for 'virtual displacements' around the given point will be identical with this firm's marginal cost curve, at least when the price is sufficiently high. If a great number of such firms adapt themselves in this manner to a given market price, they will all reach the *same* marginal cost, and *this common magnitude* may then be regarded as the marginal cost *of the market*. This magnitude is the ordinate of the market curve now

3. In Figure 2 we made no such assumption.

discussed. To each price (each ordinate of the curve), there corresponds a definite quantity of commodities exchanged in this market. As the price rises and falls this quantity will change. For each of these alternative quantities the corresponding market price may – when we momentarily look at a cross-section of the individual firm as above – be regarded as the marginal cost of the market. It is this conception that lies behind Marshall's 'marginal supply price'. And it is natural to include in this marginality concept also those variations in the market supply that are caused by individual firms being eliminated (V, V. 5. p. 373). It is, I believe, in this manner that his use of the word 'marginal' in the short-period normal market must be explained. When we deal with the normal equilibrium with reference to long periods this question will be further elaborated upon.

In connection with the diagram in Figure 4 we shall finally give a suggestion as to how it is possible graphically to illustrate

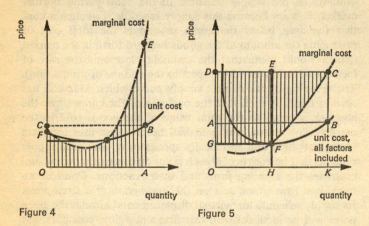

Figure 4   Figure 5

quasi-rent in the short-period normal market. For simplicity we consider aggregate net profit without splitting this sum up into individual components according to source. If H and K in Figure 5 are two arbitrary quantities, we may evidently always regard the quasi-rent at K as the quasi-rent at H plus the *change* in quasi-rent from *H* to *K*. The change in quasi-rent is however, the same as the change in the total product value (price times quantity) minus the change in total cost. If the horizontal line *DC* represents the price *OD* (assumed to be constant for this firm), the rectangle *HKCE* will be the increase in total product value between *H* and *K*. And the increase in total cost will be the area beneath the marginal cost curve between *H* and *K*. The increase in the quasi-rent is in other words the nearly triangular shaded area to the right of the vertical *EH*. If the initial point *H* is taken to be just where the marginal cost curve intersects the unit cost curve for all factors, the quasi-rent at *H* will be the rectangle *GFED* (the profit per unit at *H* times the product quantity at *H*). The total shaded area is then the quasi-rent. As the price rises and the point C moves up along the marginal cost curve, the shaded area will increase. The line *GF* can be regarded as the bottom and *GD* and *FC* as the sides of a vessel that is gradually being filled with, say, water. The amount of water illustrates the magnitude of the quasi-rent, the level of the surface represents the price. The quasi-rent at *K* may evidently also be represented by the rectangle *ABCD* (profit per unit multipled by the quantity produced). This rectangle must in other words be equal to the shaded area, irrespective of the position of the point *K*.

Normal equilibrium with reference to long periods

When an equilibrium with reference to short periods has been established, the question naturally arises whether it will *persist* for a long time or if it contains forces that will *change* the situation. If so these forces must in one way or another change the assumptions on the basis of which we analysed the equilibrium with reference to short periods. So long as these assumptions remain unchanged, the point of equilibrium can, of course, not change. If such forces exist, what will be the course of the development resulting from them? Specifically, will we approach a new equilibrium, one that will be more durable? And if so, what price and volume of production will characterize this new durable equilibrium? These are the main questions Marshall attempts to answer in his theory of 'long-run normal equilibrium'.

There are two fundamental concepts in this analysis, which are typical of his way of thinking. They are the '*representative firm*' and '*normal profit*'. These two concepts together with the 'long-period normal supply price' constitute a logical unity. If we accept two of them, it is not difficult to give a precise definition of the third. Implicitly, therefore, these concepts define one another. But it is not easy to give a precise and explicit definition of each one of them. To begin with we must therefore accept the concepts on the strength of a more or less loose description, and then trust that the *relations* between them, to be introduced as we proceed in our analysis, will serve to define them more precisely. It is this procedure that has been followed by Marshall, and it is hardly possible to do it in any other way, even though one could wish to make the presentation rather more systematic than Marshall has made it.

To bring out the meaning of the concepts we must examine more closely the categories in which the costs are divided. The unbroken curves in Figures 2 and 3 show how unit cost varies over short periods. But the very distinction between the upper and the lower curve of the individual firm is based on long-period reasoning. A part of what is included in the upper curve is in a sense not cost in the short run, only in the long run. This applies particularly if we interpret the term 'cost' as *something that must be covered if production is going to be maintained*. How large a portion of the upper cost in this sense must be left out of the short-period cost concept depends on whether the firm in the short run is a pure quantity-adaptor or, to a smaller or larger degree, practices a restrictive strategy or possibly some type of power-strategy. In any case there is a part of the upper cost that does not determine supply in the short run. In the long run, on the other hand, all costs must determine supply.

Prime costs relatively to long periods become supplementary relatively to short . . . (V. IX. 3. p. 420).

To sum up then as regards short periods. . . . The supply of specialized skill and ability, of suitable machinery . . . has not time to be fully adapted to demand. . . . Variations in the particular income derived from them do not *for the time* affect perceptibly the supply. . . . The income is a surplus of total receipts over total cost, that is, it has something of the nature of a rent. . . . But unless it is sufficient to cover in the long run a fair share of the general costs of the business, production will gradually fall off. In this way a controlling influence over . . . supply price during short periods is exercised by causes in the background which range over a long period (V. V. 7. p. 377).

Among the costs determining supply in the long run is also included a 'normal profit'.

. . . the supply price of business ability and energy . . . and the supply price of that organization by which the appropriate business ability and the requisite capital are brought together . . . we may call . . . gross earnings of management (IV. XII. 12. p. 313).

The normal supply price of any amount of a commodity may be taken to be its normal expenses of production, including *gross* earnings of management (V. III. 5. p. 343).

Marshall's entire analysis of long-period price formation is in its essentials only an extension of this division of the cost elements. By introducing the concept 'normal profit' (or 'normal earnings') he acquires a theoretical tool for studying any actually realized profit in relation to the normal, and *he is able to formulate a law* that can tell us how the situation will change according as the actual profits are larger or smaller than the normal ones.

Such a comparison between something 'normal' and something 'actual' we also find in other economic theories, for instance in Knut Wicksell's theory on the difference between the 'normal rate of interest' and the 'market rate of interest'. The similarity between the theories of Marshall and Wicksell is more than formal. I shall not here deal with Wicksell's theory in detail, but only mention that Wicksell's 'normal rate of interest' is equal to his 'rate of productivity' when the capital market is in equilibrium, and both concepts are closely related to the concept of normal profits. An analysis built on the gap between a 'normal' and an 'actual' profit we also find in Lord Keynes's *A Treatise on Money* of 1930.

To formulate Marshall's law of disequilibrium, that is, his law concerning the gap between the 'normal' and the 'actual' profit, we go back to Figure 2. That the *actual* profit is greater than the *normal* for a firm which has adapted itself in the short period normal market means that, at the given market price, this firm will get an *extra* profit (a net profit) over and above the normal. This again means that the adaptation has taken place at a point where the market price is higher than the ordinate of the upper unit cost curve at the point which corresponds to the quantity supplied to the market by this firm. From Figure 2 we see that this will occur when the market price is *above* the minimum of the upper unit cost curve. Let us assume that this is the case for the *majority* of the firms in the market, and that this situation will last long enough for the long period effects to develop. These effects will manifest themselves *by changing the life-cycles of the various firms*. The firms that are progressing will experience a growth that is 'more rapid than normal', those that are declining will have their decline slowed down, and the motive for energetic businessmen to go ahead with new enterprises will be 'stronger than normal'. All this pulls in the direction of an adaptation of those factors that were constant in the short-period market, namely an adaptation in a direction which will make the total volume of production gradually *larger* than it was in the short-period equilibrium. 'A price higher than this would increase the growth of the rising firms and slacken ... the decay of falling firms with the net result of an increase in the aggregate production' (V. III. 5. p. 343). When 'sellers receive more than is sufficient ... there is at work an active force tending to increase the amount brought forward for sale' (V. III. 6. p. 345). This way of reasoning on a 'tendency towards the normal' has been typical of the classics since Adam Smith.

How *large* will this increase in the volume be? Probably the development will approach a *stationary situation*. And the question is: what will be the characteristics of this new situation? The volume of production in the stationary situation must evidently be equal to that which can be *sold* at the price which will then reign. It is probable that this is not the price of the initial situation, since the amount produced will have increased during the process of long-period adaptation. How high the price will be, we cannot as yet determine with certainty, since it depends upon that interaction between supply and demand which we are trying to uncover. For the same reason we cannot as yet say anything definite about the amount that will be bought and sold. For the time being we must, therefore, consider a series of *alternatives* for the stationary situation, which we are anticipating, and study each alternative separately. Then we must later examine the extent to which each of these alternatives will make for equality between supply and demand. In this manner we can finally decide which one of the alternatives will be realized.

The various alternatives for the stationary situation can be described in different ways. On the supply side the alternative can most conveniently be described by indicating the aggregate quantity which will be sold per unit of time '. . . in real life . . .' (V. XII. 1. p. 457 note). In other words, we consider a *scale of stationary situations,* one in which there is sold a total constant amount of, say, 100,000 units of produce per unit of time, one in which is sold a constant amount of 150,000 units, etc. (a 'unit of produce' may if necessary be defined by a volume index if the firms of the industry in question produce different types of commodities). To each alternative quantity produced (= sold) in the stationary situation corresponds a *typical form of the life-cycles of the firms*. If total long-run production is 150,000 units of produce per unit of time, the life-cycle will tend to make for *larger* individual firms than would be the case when the total long-run production was only 100,000 per unit of time. But regardless of whether the total production per unit of time is large or small, rising firms and falling firms will always be represented in such a proportion that the aggregate production is *constant*. Otherwise the situation would not be stationary.[4] '. . . the same amount of things . . . will have been produced . . . for many generations' (V. V. 2. p. 367). From this follows that, in the situation to which we are looking forward, there cannot be a majority of firms earning *more* than normal profit, because then the amount brought forth in the market

4. We may well imagine all figures reduced per unit of population, so that 'constant' only means 'constant per head'. The population and consequently also the absolute volume of production may then rise. This does not imply any appreciable difference in the analysis, but the presentation becomes a little more cumbersome. We shall therefore adhere to an analysis involving absolute numbers. See '. . . nearly all its distinctive features . . .' (V. V. 3. p. 368).

will begin to rise. Neither can there be a majority earning less than a normal profit. The two categories must be approximately equally represented ('equally' interpreted in relation to the effect on the aggregate amount produced), and as a rule there will then be some firms 'in the middle' earning just the normal profit.

What will be the unit cost for all factors in the new situation? Since the individual firms on the whole will have become larger than in the initial situation, they must generally have realized some '*internal economies*'. Furthermore, the increase in the aggregate amount in the market must have entailed *external economies* (IV. IX. 7. p. 266). The two effects are different in character (V. XII. 2. p. 457). Thus, there are two reasons why the firms in the new situation generally will have *lower unit costs* than they had in the initial situation. There may also be circumstances working in the opposite direction. For instance the supply of one or more factors of production may be physically limited and this fact will raise their prices. In this case we may find that the unit cost in the new stationary situation visualized will be unchanged or even higher than in the initial situation. We assume that during the process of adaptation to the new stationary situation, new inventions or technical advances of a more extensive nature do not appear – 'We exclude from view any economies that may result from substantive new inventions; but we include those which may be expected to arise naturally out of adaptations of existing ideas' (V. XII. 3. p. 460; see also V. XV. 1. p. 497). Which of the two tendencies – the one making for rising or the one making for falling unit cost – will prevail, depends upon the technical conditions as a whole in the branch of industry under consideration and upon the conditions of competition (the strategic types), because these will influence the distribution of the size of the firms. When these elements are given, the distribution of the firms according to unit cost will also be given. And this will hold for any hypothetical volume of the final stationary total production – which in our example is taken to be larger than the total production in the initial situation.

If, in the initial situation, a majority of the firms earned *less* than normal profits, the development would take a direction opposite to the one described above, i.e. toward a stationary situation in which the total quantity produced is *smaller* than initially. But otherwise the analysis would be the same. To every hypothesis about the magnitude of the final aggregate volume of production, there corresponds a certain distribution of the firms according to life-cycles and consequently according to unit cost.

In order to describe in a *shorter* way this reaction of supply in the process of long-period adaptation, and at the same time to extend the analysis in certain respects, Marshall introduces a concept which he calls the *representative firm*. 'It is just here that our device of a representative firm comes to our aid' (V. XII. 3. p. 459). The representative firm is to give a miniature illustration of the supply side, in the sense that if we want to know how total supply will react, *we may simply study how the representative firm will react*. The characteristics of the representative firm must be defined in accord with this aim. In general terms we can say that it must not be 'some new producer just struggling into business', nor 'a firm with . . . a vast business and huge well-ordered work-shops . . .', but 'one . . . with a fairly long life and fair success, which is managed with normal ability and which has normal access to the economies external and internal which belong to that aggregate volume of production' (IV. XIII. 2. p. 317). If we should try to formulate the definition in a more quantitative manner, we might say that the volume of production of the representative firm must vary *parallel* to the aggregate volume of production in the market, its unit cost must represent the average unit cost in the market, etc. The representative firm is in other words a *construction of the mind,* a device by which to reason quickly and conveniently on the evolution of the market as a whole. It is not certain that there will always be an actual firm in the market which may be picked out as representative. But if there are many firms in the market and each of them develops through a typical life-cycle, several of them will at some time or other in their development pass through a stage in which for a while they are *similar* to the representative firm. The size of the representative firm depends upon the size of the long-period aggregate production which we consider.

Now let us see how the analysis of the long-period adaptation will appear when formulated in terms of the representative firm. Marshall does not concern himself particularly with the representative firm in the analysis of the short-period adaptation; he has introduced the concept specifically for the study of the long-period adaptation. However, in order to bring out the relationship between the two types of price formation, it will be of interest to pay some attention to the reactions of the representative firm in the short-period market. It is essential to remember throughout that the reaction of the representative firm is characterized by two quantity parameters: $x =$ the short-period volume of production of the representative firm, and $y =$ the long-period volume of production of the representative firm (compare the expressions in terms of partial derivatives at the end of this article). For simplicity in the graphical representation we may sometimes measure both x and y along the same axis, but it must always be remembered that these magnitudes are two distinct variables. Furthermore it must be remembered that the concept of the representative firm is constructed in such a way that the reaction of this firm is a *miniature representation of the reaction of the market*. The supply curve of this firm may therefore – with the proper interpretation of a scale coefficient along the quantity axis – be looked upon as the supply curve *of the market*. At first sight it may seem a little confusing to mix up in this way ideas that pertain to a firm with ideas that pertain to the market as a whole, but on closer scrutiny the reasoning will, I think, be found quite consistent. It is, I believe, only in this way that it is possible to give a correct presentation of Marshall's theory.

Let us first consider what determines the *size* of the representative firm. In the stationary state dealt with above, the rise of some firms and the decline of others will counterbalance each other so that the aggregate volume of production in the market will remain constant. A firm that is to be representative in such a situation must naturally be one that is also characterized by a constant volume of production. This means that *this* firm is not subject to the same typical law of development as the individual, actually existing firms. Even if the market price, the total volume of commodities in the market and all other factors relevant to price formation remain *constant*, the individual firms will first go through a period of growth during which they expand and in so doing increase their internal economies (but if the situation is stationary with respect to the market as a whole, the external economies are unchanged). This period is followed by a period of decline during which the internal economies of these individual firms disappear. On the other hand, the representative firm, subject to the constant external environment, will remain unchanged and permanently enjoy the same internal economies. Its external economies also remain unchanged so long as the external environment is the same. And both these types of economies correspond to the 'average' for the market. '... in our stationary state ... firms rise and fall, but ... the "representative" firm remains always of about the same size, as does the representative tree of a virgin forest' (V. V. 2. p. 367). The 'average' in this context cannot be interpreted simply as the elementary arithmetical average. The median would possibly be more correct, but even this might not be adequate. The only decisive consideration is that the representative firm must have such a *type of reaction* to the given conditions of the market, that the firm may be regarded as representative of the total supply side when we study the price formation. From this point of view we can establish as a primary characteristic that it must keep its volume of production constant under stationary market conditions.

What should its profits be under such conditions? The only plausible definition of this will follow immediately if for a moment we look at the short-period adaptation (see Figure 3). If a majority of the firms during a considerable period of time earn more than a normal profit, this will, as we have seen, start a long-period development toward a large volume of production, and vice versa. If the representative firm is to describe the reaction of the supply side, we must assign to it the characteristic that it reacts with increase, decrease or constancy of its volume of production, depending upon whether its actual profits are larger, smaller or equal to the normal profit. In a stationary market situation, it must in other words earn just a normal profit. The normal profit thus becomes a long-period cost element for the representative firm in the sense that this profit must be covered by the market price, if the supply is to be maintained.

This gives a composition of the long-period unit cost curve of the representative firm which may be described as follows: we consider a series of alternative situations, each of which is stationary and characterized by a *given magnitude* of the aggregate volume of production in the market (and consequently also characterized by a given constant magnitude of the production of the representative firm). For each of these situations we examine what the unit cost will be for a firm which is representative of the given branch of industry at this volume of production. It depends upon the factors already mentioned: the average extent of internal and external economies at the given volume of production, and whether or not there are factors of production that are limited in quantity. *The unit cost thus determined, considered as a function of the volume of production of the representative firm, represents the long-period unit cost curve.*

The curve describing this relationship plays an important role in Marshall's analysis, and he takes pains to describe it as clearly as possible and to specify a number of the elements included in its ordinate. He uses as an illustration 'a person well acquainted with the woollen trade . . .' (V. III. 5. p. 343). The expressions in the adjoining footnote (p. 344) show clearly that we deal here with the *unit* cost, *not* the *marginal* cost in the sense of the rate of increase of the total market value with respect to the volume of production, '. . . when an amount OM of cloth . . . the wool . . . which would be consumed in making it . . . that amount . . . which is employed in making a yard . . . where there is an aggregate production of OM yards'. He stresses that it is the *normal costs with reference to long periods* that are to be included, and in his concretization of this point he makes a remark which shows that, despite the difference in principle between the concepts 'normal' and 'average with respect to time', there is nevertheless a relationship between them in practice. 'Again in estimating the *normal* supply price of wool, he would take *the average of several past years*' (V. V. 1. p. 365 – Frisch's italics).

We shall proceed to study the *market equilibrium*. The long-period unit cost curve may, as we have seen, rise or fall with an increase in the volume of production, '... or may even alternately increase or diminish' (V. III. 5. p. 344). The *demand*, on the other hand, Marshall maintains, must always be represented by a declining curve: '... in every case the more of a thing is offered for sale in a market, the lower is the price at which it will find purchasers' (V. III. 4. p. 342). This is hardly correct as a general rule without exceptions, but it does undoubtedly apply in the great majority of cases. On the whole, Marshall's analysis of demand is far less extensive than his analysis of supply, possibly owing to the strong classical influence. For demand, he makes no fundamental distinction between 'temporary', 'short normal' and 'long normal' equilibrium, and therefore has no different types of demand theories in these three markets. It is true that he remarks that 'the shorter the period which we are considering the greater must be the share of our attention which is given to the influence of demand on value' (V. III. 7. p. 349). But this is in effect a remark on *supply*. What Marshall wants to stress is that the shorter the period under consideration, the smaller is the number of factors of production that can be varied, the smaller is consequently the elasticity of supply, therefore, the smaller is the extent to which we can say that supply is *price determining*. He also mentions that the variations in demand may be of shorter or longer duration, as for instance in the excellent 'Illustration from the fishing trade' (V. V. 4. p. 369); but even here the different orders of variations of demand are included mainly to illustrate how the difference between short and long periods will affect *supply*. In any case Marshall presents *conceptually* the same type of demand schedule in all markets. It is a 'buyers will be willing to buy' curve (V. II. 2. p. 333). We accept, then, such a curve and confront it with the long period unit cost curve of the representative firm as shown in Figure 6. To each point of the abscissa in Figure 6 corresponds a given magnitude of the representative firm, as explained above. Interpreting the cost curve in Figure 6, we must again remember that the reaction of the representative firm is meant to give a picture of the reaction of the market as a whole. At least in *one* sense, therefore, the long period unit cost curve of the representative firm – with the application of the proper scale coefficient along the horizontal axis – may be considered a long period supply curve of the market, namely, in this sense: if the market price is maintained at such and such a level (for a sufficiently long period), then the volume of output of the representative firm (and hence of the market as a whole) will *stabilize itself* at such and such a level. With this interpretation we can show that the *intersection* of the (long-period) demand curve and the long-period unit cost curve of the representative firm will determine the equilibrium point towards which the market tends in the long run.

When we study the interaction between these two curves, we must clearly realize that the unit cost curve of the representative firm is *not* a supply curve in the sense of 'the individual firm will be willing to sell so much at this price'. Marshall's expression 'supply price' in this connection may be misunderstood. The unit cost curve in Figure 6 is not a supply curve in the same sense as the supply curve Marshall deals with in his discussion of 'temporary equilibrium'. The supply curve he uses in *that* connection is a 'holders will be willing to sell' curve (V. II. 2. p. 333), and shows the amount of commodities the sellers will bring forth in the market if the price is given. In our terminology we can say that it is the curve of quantity-adaptation. The unit cost curve in Figure 6, on the other hand, shows what the cost (in the long run) will be if the (long-run) volume of production is given. This is the *definition* of the curve. From this definition of the curve as a cost curve we can however deduce that it must also have a specific significance in describing supply. In this respect the reasoning is similar to that applied to the individual firm in the short period: although its marginal cost curve in the short period is *defined* by computing what the marginal cost would be at different levels of output, the marginal cost curve of the individual firm also gets a significance in the analysis of supply in the range of high levels of the price.

The choice between price or volume as the independent variable in the present case is more than a formality. If all the data are available, a cost (total, unit or marginal) can be computed as a *single valued* function of the price. This applies to the functional relationship represented by the unbroken curve in Figure 6. On the other hand this curve does *not* give the volume of production as a single valued function of the price. Since the curve at first falls and then rises – as Marshall expressly has said it does – the volume will be a *multiple valued function* of the price. This is another advantage of *defining* the curve as a cost curve.

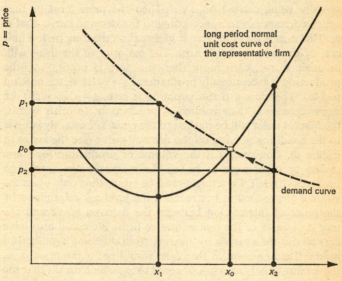

Figure 6

$x =$ quantity per unit of time

There is also another fact showing that the curve of the representative firm in Figure 6 is not a supply curve in the 'holders will be willing to sell' sense. If it were, this curve and the demand curve ought to be symmetrically placed in the analysis. In a pure exchange market, for instance, the demand and supply curves are only two branches of a common curve. Depending upon the price, each person could be either a buyer or a seller. In such a case it might be convenient to merge the demand and supply curve of the market into *one* curve which shows *net* demand or supply. The two curves in Figure 6 are *not symmetrical* and cannot be merged in this way. This lack of symmetry is characteristic of Marshall's use of the curves. In his analysis of the curves, Marshall considers the possibility of a situation in which the point (p, x) characterizing the market does *not* lie on the unit cost curve. According to his analysis, it must, however, *always* lie on the demand curve. His argument is as follows: assume that the volume of production for some reason or other is x_1, '. . . the rate at which production is actually being carried on. . . .' Then the price must be that which corresponds to x_1 according to the demand curve, that is p_1. This means that the price is higher than the long period unit cost of the representative firm. The majority of the firms will, in other words, earn more than the normal profit, '. . . the production is exceptionally profitable . . .' (V. III. 6. the note on p. 346). Therefore – if this situation is lasting – they will take steps to *increase* their volume of production. In other words, the market point will be pushed to the *right* – constantly subject to the condition of lying on the demand curve (see the arrow in Figure 6). Conversely: if the volume of production for some reason or other were to be x_2, the market point would be pushed to the left. Equilibrium will be established only when the volume of production has reached the level x_0, determined by the point of intersection between the demand curve and the unit cost curve of the representative firm. We could also have carried out the analysis by starting from different hypothetical *prices*. The argument in that case would be: if the price is p_1, there must be sold an amount equal to x_1, which means that the firms earn more than a normal profit, etc.

When the equilibrium is determined by a mechanism as indicated above, it must evidently be *stable* so long as the unit cost curve of the representative firm (regardless of whether it is rising, falling or horizontal) intersects the demand schedule from *below*, but unstable in the opposite case. To say that an equilibrium is stable means that if it is disturbed, there will be generated a force tending to re-establish it (V. III. 6. p. 345). Conversely in the case of an unstable equilibrium.

The relationship between short-period normal and long-period normal equilibrium

Figure 7 indicates how the long-period theory and the short-period theory can be brought together. The essential point in interpreting this figure is to remember the distinction between x = short-period volume of production and y = long-period volume of production. When moving along the large U-shaped curve in Figure 7 we think of the reaction of the representative

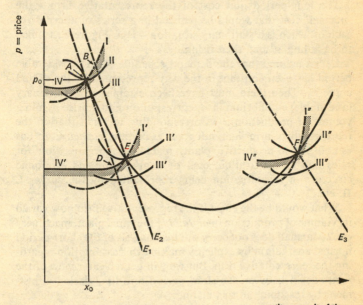

Figure 7

firm (and hence of the market as a whole) when long-period conditions change. Under such a variation the horizontal axis must be looked up as a y-axis. When moving along the small curves – for instance along those around the point A – we think of the reactions of the representative firm (and hence of that of the market as a whole) in the short period. Under such a variation the horizontal axis must be looked upon as an x-axis. This is only a trick applied in order to make it possible to draw the figure *on a flat sheet of paper*. If we had wanted to use a three-dimensional representation, we might have drawn the small curves around the point A on a separate sheet of paper orientated, say, perpendicularly to the plane on which Figure 7 is drawn and having its horizontal axis marked x. Similarly for the small curves around E and around F.

The long-period unit cost of the representative firm – the 'normal' cost that would be realized in a series of alternatives each of which is a stationary situation – is in Figure 7 assumed to be falling at first, then rising.

Let us assume that the demand schedule for a considerable period has been constant in the way represented by the dotted curve E_1. Then there must have been established a stationary (and stable) equilibrium in A, corresponding to a price p_0 and a volume of production x_0. Corresponding to this situation the representative firm had adopted a certain *capacity*; it has established a productive plant, machinery, organization for sales and administration, etc., of a given size, its economic structure in this situation being represented by the curves I, II, etc.

What would be the effect if the representative firm now varied its volume of production, *maintaining* the same plant, machinery etc.? Marshall does not carry out his analysis of the short-period normal adaptation by explicitly making this assumption regarding the representative firm. But we will get a clearer view of the relationship between the short-period and long-period adjustment by reasoning in this manner.

If the representative firm varies its short-period volume of production, it will have a marginal cost curve as indicated by the broken curve I, an upper unit cost curve as shown by II and a lower unit cost curve as shown by III in the area around A. The shaded curve IV indicates the short-period *supply schedule* in the area around A. The *interrelationships* of these short-period curves are those discussed above in the short-period analysis. But what will their position be in relation to the long-period unit cost curve? First of all it is evident that the upper short-period unit cost curve, II, must pass through the point A, because in the original stationary equilibrium, the firm earned just a normal profit. Not only this; we can also say which particular point on II coincides with A. It must be the minimum of II, because A evidently must lie on the short-period *supply schedule* (the shaded curve) and there is only one point common to II and the short-period supply schedule, viz. the minimum point (see the analysis of the short-period adaptation). Since the short-period unit cost curve II has its minimum in A, the short-period *marginal* cost curve must also pass through A. In other words, the price in A may at the same time be regarded: (a) as a long-period unit cost, (b) as a short-period unit cost, (c) as a short-period marginal cost, (d) as a short-period supply price and (e) as an average over time of the costs that actually are paid under the assumed stationary conditions. 'In a rigidly stationary state . . . the normal expenses of production, the marginal expenses and the average expenses (rent being counted in) would be the same thing for long periods and for short' (V. XV. 1. p. 497). By 'average' expenses Marshall means unit cost ['the average expenses could be deduced by dividing out the amount of the commodity' (App. H. 4. p. 810)].

Let us now assume that the demand schedule is shifted upward, say, to E_2. The immediate effect will be a shift of the equilibrium point to the point of intersection, B, with the short-period marginal cost curve, since the capacity of the representative firm is unchanged in the short run, and its supply schedule will accordingly coincide with the short-period marginal cost curve when the volume of production is expanded. The price will temporarily rise and the representative firm will earn more than a normal profit. If, however, this new increased demand lasts for a sufficiently long period, there will be time for an increase in the capacity of the representative firm (and hence of the industry), bringing us to the point of intersection E with the long-period unit cost curve. It lies below A, since the long-period unit cost curve is declining in this interval (internal and external economies, accompanying the expansion of production, counterbalance possible adverse factors such as increased scarcity of land). If the representative firm has based its plant on this new total volume of production, its short-period cost curves will be as shown by I', II' and III' in the area around E. And the short-period supply curve corresponding to the new plant will be the shaded curve IV'. It is drawn as it would appear, if the representative firm practiced a restrictive strategy in the area between the upper and lower short-period unit cost minimum.

The point D on this restrictive supply curve would be the market equilibrium if the demand schedule for a relatively short time should revert to its original position. This, in other words, would lead to a *further* lowering of the price. Should the demand for a *long* period revert to its original level E_1, the equilibrium would in principle revert to A. In actual practice, however, we have to introduce a modification at this stage; the development along the long-period curve is not completely *reversible*. As a rule, *all* the 'economies' gained during the expansion of production will not be lost during the subsequent contraction. For the contraction back from E there will be a long-period unit cost curve coinciding with the former curve in E, but being somewhat lower towards the left '. . . would have to be replaced by a lower schedule . . . these economies are not readily lost' (App H. 3. p. 808). In the terminology of the theory of production we may say that the *production function* that applies will be different under a contraction and an expansion.

If the demand schedule is shifted upward to the position E_3, a completely new long-period equilibrium will be established in F. Here the long-period unit cost is approximately the same as in E, but higher than in the interval of the long-period volume of production at the centre of the diagram. The reason may be that the amounts of certain factors of production are physically limited or can only be produced with increasing costs in the long run. In the area around F there will be short-period curves analogous to those around A and around E.

Such a set of short-period curves *may be drawn around every point on the long-period unit cost curve*. Each set of these short-period curves will apply under the condition that the capacity of the plant of the representative firm (and hence of the industry) in the long run is adapted to a volume of production of just the magnitude indicated by the corresponding point on the long-period unit cost curve. The whole analysis must thus be carried through with two independent quantities as variables, the short-period volume for the representative firm and the long-period volume for the representative firm.

One must interpret the use Marshall makes of the word 'marginal' in the long-period analysis in the light of this relationship between the short-period and the long-period schedules. On the face of it there is a contradiction in his terminology on this point. On the one hand it is evident that the long-period 'supply curve' of the representative firm is a unit cost curve (see the remarks above in connection with the quotation from the note in V. III. 5. p. 344). On the other hand, Marshall calls this curve, the curve of 'the true long-period marginal cost' (V. XII. 3. p. 460). And he says on the different *order* of short-period and long-period analysis: '. . . in every case the cost of production is marginal, that is, it is the cost of production of those goods which are on the margin of not being produced at all, and which would not be produced if the price to be got for them were expected to be lower' (V. V. 5. p. 373). The inconsistency disappears if one takes into consideration the equality between the various quantities (intersection of curves), for instance at the point *A* in Figure 7 or at the point *E* or *at any other point* on the long period unit cost curve. When Marshall calls the cost 'marginal', it is a way of expressing the fact that the point representing the cost lies on the short-period marginal cost curve and may be subjected to a *virtual* shift along this curve. When he says that the cost – in certain cases – will fall when the volume of production increases, he expresses the fact that the point may move along the long-period unit cost curve. In other words: the 'marginality' is *defined* with respect to the short-period variation, and the magnitude thus defined is studied in its relationship partly to the short-period variation and partly to the long-period variation, particularly the latter. That this is what he means is made evident by the remark:

We thus get at the true long-period marginal cost, falling with a gradual increase of demand. . . . We do not expect it to fall immediately in consequence of a sudden increase in demand. On the contrary we expect the short period supply price to increase with increasing output (the movement from *A* to *B*). But we also expect a gradual increase in demand to increase gradually the size and the efficiency of this representative firm [the movement from *A* to *E*] (V. XII. 3. p. 460).

And perhaps even more clearly: 'the term "margin" . . . may be used . . . with regard to short and quick fluctuations . . . because in relation to such fluctuations the production of those commodities ... conforms to the law of diminishing and not increasing return' (the movement from A to B). But for the movement *along* the long-period unit cost curve 'the term "margin" should be avoided' and 'there is no clearly defined marginal product' (App. H. 1. p. 805). Correctly interpreted there is good logic in this.

A little mathematical symbolism will immediately put the matter straight: the total cost b is regarded as a function of two variables, the short-period volume of production x and the long-period volume of production y. We therefore write this cost $b(x, y)$. 'Marginal cost' is defined as $b' = \{\partial b(x, y)\}/\partial x$. This quantity, like b, is a function of x and y, and we write it $b'(x, y)$. 'We do not expect, etc.' means first that $b'(x, y) > b'(y, y)$ when $x > y$ and secondly that $b'(y, y)$ – which is a function of one variable – in many cases decreases with increasing y. 'The term margin should be avoided' means that $\{db(y, y)\}/dy$ should *not* be called marginal cost.

This presentation has sought to outline and systematize the reasoning in Marshall's Book V. Only its general features have been considered. To appreciate the wealth of detail one must study the book itself. What is most valuable in Marshall's work is the way in which he succeeded in combining the theoretical and the concrete.

4 Gustav Cassel

The Mechanism of Pricing

Gustav Cassel, 'The mechanism of pricing', in *The Theory of Social Economy*, translated by S. L. Barron, Ernest Benn, 1932, pp. 137–64.

Arithmetical treatment of the problem of equilibrium

In the preceding chapter [not included here] we ascertained that the principles governing pricing in any exchange economy are necessary consequences of the general economic principle. The reader who has grasped these principles is thus now able to form an accurate idea of the general nature of pricing and has a safe foundation for the treatment of most of the problems of theoretical economics. The science, however, also sets problems which require a profounder examination of the mechanism of pricing. These relate mainly, on the one hand, to the controversial nature of the causal sequence in the pricing process and, on the other hand, to an important problem of monetary theory, with which we shall deal later – the degree of definiteness of the problem of pricing. In order to illustrate clearly the mechanism of pricing, it is necessary to present the relation between the various factors in the price-fixing process in mathematical form. This is not to be understood as meaning that it is necessary to represent the pricing process by difficult mathematical expressions which are beyond the grasp of persons of average education. The essentials of the mechanism can be grasped by anyone with a general acquaintance with equations with several unknown quantities. The mathematical presentations of facts in the first two sections of this chapter need, therefore, deter nobody from reading them.

The work is, however, so arranged that these paragraphs may be omitted without interrupting the general connection. The reader, in that case, will simply have to put aside any thought of a deeper study of the problems just mentioned.

In conformity with the conclusions drawn in the preceding

chapter, we have to consider here a self-contained community based on exchange, in which the determination of prices is governed entirely by the principle of scarcity and the principles incidental to it. It is immaterial for the purposes of our present inquiry how such a state of affairs is brought about. We know that prices can be fixed in this way in economies which are very differently organized, and particularly that our existing economy approximately effects this by widely varying methods. In this section we shall first assume that, with regard to cost of production, there is no indefiniteness and that the principle of scarcity is therefore sufficient for the complete determination of prices (see Cassel, 1899).

Let us first consider the simple case where the influence of production does not affect the problem, and the quantities of goods available to consumers in a particular period are given; which is equivalent to assuming that production is invariable and fixed once for all. Let us call these quantities the supply of the particular commodities, and represent them by $S_1, S_2, ..., S_n$, where n is the number of different commodities.

We shall assume that consumers and producers are different individuals. Where a producer consumes part of his own product, we shall consider him in his capacity of consumer as a separate individual. Thus any consumption on the part of producers is not to be deducted beforehand from the supply, but is to be compared with the total supply in the same way as consumption in any other form.

We first assume that the quantity of money which every consumer expends on the satisfaction of his wants in the period under consideration is fixed in advance. Given such conditions, it is obvious that the demand of each consumer for the different commodities during the period is fixed, once the prices of these commodities are fixed.

The relation between the demand for and the price of a commodity is most effectively shown where, as independent variable, the price of the commodity is chosen. If we then vary the price, we can determine how much of the particular commodity an individual will buy at any particular price or, in other words, how individual demand varies with the price. The result of this inquiry can be expressed in tabular form; or else individual demand – the quantity of a commodity which an individual will buy at a given price – can be conceived of as a function of price, the form of this function expressing the personal valuation.

The advantage of this way of expressing individual demand is emphasized when one wishes to deal with the demand of several individuals together. We then have a common independent variable, the price, and we know the demand of any particular consumer at every value of this variable. These demands are each represented by a number which expresses how many units of the particular commodity the consumer in question wishes to buy. These quantities can, therefore, be added together; in this way we get the conception of the total demand for the particular commodity. This, too, can be shown in the form of a table giving the total quantity of the commodity which is demanded at any given price; or we can represent this aggregate demand as a function of the price.

If, however, we examine the demand function rather more closely, we find that it also includes, as variables, the prices of all other commodities. The demand of the individual consumer for a certain commodity is not fixed until the prices of all commodities which can be the object of his demand are given. Not until this is done has he all the data which influence him in regulating his consumption within the limits imposed by his means; only then is he in a position to determine his demand for any particular commodity.

The demand of the individual consumer, and hence also the total demand of consumers in the aggregate, for any particular commodity is thus determined by the prices of the n commodities. If we represent the total demand for the n commodities in the given period by $D_1, D_2, ..., D_n$, we can then express these magnitudes as functions of the n prices, thus:

$$D_1 = F_1(p_1, ..., p_n),$$
$$D_2 = F_2(p_1, ..., p_n),$$
$$\vdots$$
$$D_n = F_n(p_1, ..., p_n),$$

1

where $p_1, ..., p_n$ are the prices of the n commodities.

Now, the demand for any particular commodity, given a state of equilibrium, must coincide with the supply of it, since the fixing of prices, in accordance with the principle of scarcity, must be such as to restrict demand so as to satisfy it with the available supply of commodities. It follows therefore that:

$$D_1 = S_1, D_2 = S_2, ..., D_n = S_n,$$
and hence, according to **1**:
$$F_1(p_1, ..., p_n) = S_1,$$
$$F_2(p_1, ..., p_n) = S_2,$$
$$\vdots$$
$$F_n(p_1, ..., p_n) = S_n. \qquad\qquad\qquad\qquad\qquad\qquad\qquad \textbf{2}$$

To solve the pricing problem in the simple case considered here, we have therefore only to regard the *n* prices as the unknowns in the problem and to assume them according to the usual mathematical method to be given. We are then in a position to express the demand for the *n* goods at these prices in conformity with equations **1**, whence equations **2** follow as a consequence of the principle of scarcity. This series of equations contains *n* equations for determining the *n* unknown prices; which is, in general, sufficient for determining the *n* unknown quantities. In the present case, where the money expenditure of consumers is given beforehand, prices, too, are obviously fixed at their absolute level. As soon as the prices are known, however, the demand of the individual consumer, and also the aggregate demand, for any particular commodity can be calculated. Since the demand is satisfied at the prices so calculated, the whole problem of the distribution of the commodities available for consumers is solved.

That the problem of pricing for each separate commodity cannot be dealt with in isolation is seen to be due to the fact that the demand for a commodity depends not upon the price of that particular commodity alone, but upon the prices of all commodities in general. It is this fact which necessitates the representation of the pricing process by a series of simultaneous equations, such as our series **2**. The homogeneity of the pricing process cannot be adequately conveyed in any other way.

We have assumed here that the supply is fixed, i.e. that during the particular period commodities are available, or will be provided by production, in unvarying quantities, fixed in advance. Let us now abandon this assumption and introduce the whole question of production into the pricing problem. As we intend in this section to consider a pricing process based entirely on the principle of scarcity, we shall assume that the cost of production of any particular commodity is clearly determined by the prices of the factors of production.

In our discussion of the present problem we must consider a continuous process of production, and must present in arithmetical form the conditions of equilibrium in a society with unvarying prices. We shall first deal with the simplest case – that of a stationary society.

The limits to the production of new commodities are imposed by the scarcity of the factors of production. The restriction upon the satisfaction of wants is simply referred back, through production, to the scarcity of the factors of production. The general nature of the factors of production, too, was indicated in the third section [not included here]. Here, where we are particularly concerned with the mechanism of pricing, we must assume the quantities of the factors of production as given. To provide a concrete foundation for our inquiry, we may take as types of the factors of production, labour, the raw materials provided by nature, and the services of durable goods already in existence. The answer to the question as to how far these factors of production may be regarded as primary, or are themselves reproducible, must be reserved for the next Book [not included here], as must also the complete and final analysis of the factors of production. There we shall be able to deal with the question of how far the factors of production, although not reproducible, are nevertheless subject in another way, varying in degree according to the quantities available, to the influence of the pricing process. Here we must be content merely to assume a series of factors of production to be primary factors, and available in given quantities. Let r be the number of these factors of production, and $R_1, R_2, ..., R_r$, the quantities of them which are available in a given period. This period, which we may call the 'income period' or, if we select a unit of time for the purpose, the 'unit period', may, if the productive process is sufficiently uniform, be made as short as we choose; it may, according to the nature of the problem in hand, represent, for example, a day, a week or a year.

With the help of these factors of production, commodities of n different kinds are produced. To produce the unit quantity of commodity 1, quantities $a_{11}, ..., a_{1r}$ of the factors of production may be necessary; for the unit quantity of commodity 2, quantities $a_{21}, ..., a_{2r}$ of the same factors of production may be necessary, and so on; finally, for the unit quantity of commodity n, the quantity $a_{n1}, ..., a_{nr}$. These quantities may be called 'technical coefficients'. They represent the technical conditions of production. As we have assumed these conditions to be fixed, the technical coefficients are to be regarded as given magnitudes in the problem. Obviously, several a may be equal to zero, since not all the factors of production are necessary for the production of any particular commodity.

With regard to the significance of these technical coefficients, the following observation may be made: the production of a unit quantity of a commodity requires in general the use of factors of production belonging to a whole series of different unit periods. Production is only completed, and the finished product made available for consumption, in the last of these periods. Our a designate primarily the total quantity of the factors of production of each particular kind which are required in this way for the production of the unit quantity of any commodity. As such they are aggregates of quantities of factors of production of different unit periods. In the stationary state, however, production is maintained at a constant level. The manufacture of a commodity of a certain kind is therefore repeated in every unit period. In order that the unit quantity of a commodity shall result from this continuous productive process in each unit period, there must be available in each such period a definite quantity of factors of production. The demands which the continually repeated production of finished goods imposes on the factors of production in a given period are totalled and determine this quantity. It is, therefore, obviously the same as the quantity of factors of production of different unit periods which is necessary for the production of a definite unit quantity of the commodity. Our a thus designate the quantities of factors of production defined both in the first and in the second way.

The necessary limitation of demand, according to the principle of scarcity, must now be secured by uniform prices; that is to say, there must be one price for every single factor of production as well as for every finished article. We now take the prices of the different factors of production as the unknowns in the pricing problem. Let us for the moment assume these unknowns to be given, and let us represent them by $q_1, ..., q_r$. The price of each of the n finished goods can now be calculated:

$$a_{11}q_1 + a_{12}q_2 +, ..., + a_{1r}\,q_r = p_1,$$
$$a_{21}q_1 + a_{22}q_2 +, ..., + a_{2r}q_r = p_2,$$
$$\vdots$$
$$a_{n1}q_1 + a_{n2}q_2 +, ..., + a_{nr}q_r = p_n. \hspace{3em} \textbf{3}$$

Once the prices of the finished goods are known, however, then, according to what has just been said, the aggregate demand for each commodity in each unit period is known and can be calculated by means of the following series of equations:

$$D_1 = F_1(p_1, ..., p_n),$$
$$D_2 = F_2(p_1, ..., p_n),$$
$$\vdots$$
$$D_n = F_n(p_1, ..., p_n). \hspace{3em} \textbf{4}$$

In accordance with the principle of scarcity, when prices are in equilibrium every demand must be satisfied by the supply, and we thus get

$$D_1 = S_1, D_2 = S_2, ..., D_n = S_n, \hspace{3em} \textbf{5}$$

where S_1, S_2, S_n are the quantities of each of the different commodities produced within a unit period.

Thus we now know the quantities of the particular commodities which are to be produced in each unit period. From this we can calculate the demands which are made upon the factors of production of a particular unit period, let us say the present, as follows. In order constantly to produce in each unit period a unit of commodity 1, we require quantities $a_{11}, ..., a_{1r}$ of these factors of production. For the quantity S_1 we therefore require quantities $a_{11}S_1, ..., a_{1r}\,S_1$. The same thing holds in the case of the remaining products. In all, therefore, for the continuous production of quantities $S_1, ..., S_n$, we require

the quantity $a_{11}S_1 + a_{21}S_2 +, \ldots, + a_{n1}S_n$
of factor of production 1,
the quantity $a_{12}S_1 + a_{22}S_2 +, \ldots, + a_{n2}S_n$
of factor of production 2,
$\vdots$
the quantity $a_{1r}S_1 + a_{2r}S_2 +, \ldots, + a_{nr}S_n$
of factor of production r.   **6**

These quantities thus represent the indirect demand of consumers for the factors of production needed in each unit period in the continuous stationary society. In accordance with the principle of scarcity, this demand for each factor of production must be equal to the quantity of that factor available within the particular unit period, since it is the task of pricing to limit demand as far as is necessary for this purpose. Therefore

$$R_1 = a_{11}S_1 + a_{21}S_2 +, \ldots, + a_{n1}S_n$$
$$R_2 = a_{12}S_1 + a_{22}S_2 +, \ldots, + a_{n2}S_n$$
$$\vdots$$
$$R_r = a_{1r}S_1 + a_{2r}S_2 +, \ldots, + a_{nr}S_n \quad\quad\quad \textbf{7}$$

The S, in conformity with the series of equations **5** and **4**, are here functions of the p, and therefore, from equations **3**, functions of the q. The series of equations **7** thus contains as unknowns the r prices of the factors of production. It also contains r equations, and the series is thus in general sufficient for determining the unknowns. Once the prices of the factors of production are known, the prices of the products can be calculated in accordance with the series of equations **3**. Similarly, the demand for each of the finished commodities in each unit period is obtained from the series of equations **4**. Consequently, we can calculate the demands which are made on production. Equations **5** show how much of each particular commodity must be produced in each unit period which determines the distribution of the factors of production among the various branches of production. The requirements which the continuous demand, regulated by these prices, makes of the different factors of production available in a particular unit period are to be calculated according to formulae **6**. The coincidence of these requirements with the available quantity of factors of production is guaranteed by equations 7. The pricing problem is thus completely solved for the case considered here.

Our equations reveal the true nature of pricing, and the pricing process cannot be accurately presented in any simpler form. The demand for a product represents an attempt to attract certain factors of production to a particular use. Conflicting with this attempt are similar attempts in the form of demands for the other products. There arises in this way a struggle for the relatively scarce factors of production, which is decided in the exchange economy by placing uniform prices on the factors, which prices in turn determine the prices of the products and thus form a means of effecting the necessary restriction of demand. The demand for a particular factor of production arising from the continuous demand for each particular product is totalled for each unit period, to form a total demand for that factor of production, which is represented by the right-hand side of equations 7, and which must, in a state of equilibrium, equal the given quantity of the factor of production. An equation of this kind must be applicable to each factor.

There has been a great deal of discussion as to what are the factors determining price. This question can now be answered. The determining factors of price are the different given coefficients of our equations. These coefficients may be classified in two main groups, which we may call the objective and the subjective factors determining price. The objective factors are partly the quantities of the factors of production (R) and partly the so-called technical coefficients (a). The subjective factors are the coefficients of equations 4, which show the dependence of demand upon prices. All these factors are essential in determining prices. An 'objective' or 'subjective' theory of value, in the sense of a theory that would attribute the settlement of prices to objective or subjective factors alone is, therefore, absurd; and the whole of the controversy between these theories of value, which has occupied such a disproportionately large place in economic literature, is a pure waste of energy.

The system of equations 7 states that the indirect demand, made by continuous consumption, for the different factors of production in each period must be covered by the quantities of those factors of production available in that period, and that prices must be at such a level that demand is regulated in agreement with this condition. We can, therefore, say that prices are determined by the scarcity of the factors of production relatively to the indirect demand of consumers for them. The scarcity of the factors of production, in accordance with our assumptions, is a given factor in the problem. Demand, on the other hand, is itself a function of the prices of finished goods, and hence also, in conformity with equations 3, a function of the prices of the factors of production, and cannot, therefore, be regarded as a factor determining them. What is, on this side, a given factor determining prices is the way in which the functions of demand are dependent on the prices of the factors of production, i.e. the form of these functions or the aggregate of their coefficients which characterize the nature of the demand for the factors of production. If we thus give the scarcity of the factors of production and the nature of the demand for them as the two price-determining factors, it at once becomes clear that there can be no question at all of the priority of one or the other of these factors. They are both, in the full sense of the word, essential determining factors of price.

The solution of the pricing problem is general in so far as it also embraces the previously considered case where commodities, which are directly demanded, are not reproducible at will, but are available in given quantities. These commodities are on a level with the factors of production only in our general solution of the problem. That a commodity is reproducible only means, of course, that its scarcity can be ascribed to the absolute scarcity, from the viewpoint of production, of other commodities. These absolutely scarce commodities we call the primary factors of production. The solution of the pricing problem is accordingly uniform for all kinds of goods. The attempts that are sometimes made to construct different theories of prices for reproducible and non-reproducible goods are thus both superfluous and misleading.

We have reduced the pricing problem to factors which, for the moment at least, we may regard as given factors of the problem. We often find indicated, however, as factors determining prices, factors which, in effect, are themselves variables in the problem just as prices are, and which can only be determined by the given factors we have described. That demand represents such a variable has already been shown. How far each particular demand both for factors of production and for finished products can be satisfied and, therefore, who the marginal purchaser is or which is the last need to be satisfied and, consequently, how great the 'marginal utility' is, are all questions which can be answered only in connection with the determination of prices through our series of equations. What we call 'marginal utility' – if we now wish to introduce this conception – thus occupies exactly the same place as an unknown in the problem as does price, and it is, therefore, obviously absurd to cite 'marginal utility' as a factor explaining price.

Much the same as we have said about demand may be said of the 'cost of production' of a commodity, which likewise is usually given as an independent factor determining price. The cost of production of our commodities is given by equation 3, and is thus not known until the prices of the factors of production, which represents the unknowns of the problem, are known. If we wish to quote the 'technical cost of production' as a co-determining factor of price, we must simply understand by this the 'technical coefficients' a. Cost is essentially an economic conception, chiefly originating from the fact that demand must be restricted through prices on account of the scarcity of the means for satisfying wants.

The cost of production of a commodity is not, as is sometimes supposed, an isolated phenomenon. The factors of production which are used for producing a commodity can generally also be used for producing other commodities and are, as regards the consumption of those commodities, subject to a demand which emphasizes their relative scarcity. The prices of these factors of production and thus, too, the cost of production of the first commodity, are also dependent on this demand. For instance, as long as the waterfalls of Scandinavia were used only for the production of mechanical power, chiefly for the timber and iron industries, natural water horse-power was very cheap, if not valueless, in many districts, and the industries which used this power scarcely needed, as a rule, to reckon it, in its natural state, among the costs of production. Now that there has arisen a demand for water power for the production of electrical energy, however, this demand has in many cases raised the price of natural water power, and this must be taken into account in calculating costs of production in the timber and iron industries.

This dependence of the cost of production of a commodity upon the demand for other commodities is the counterpart of the dependence of the demand for a commodity upon the prices of other commodities, to which we referred previously. It is this general interdependence of the unknowns in the pricing problem, as was shown in the simple cases above where production does not enter into the question, that makes any isolated treatment of the pricing problem for a single commodity impossible; it is this that shows that the pricing problem is essentially a single problem extending over the whole of the exchange economy and gives the pricing process an intrinsic consistency which can only be expressed by a system of simultaneous equations.

To get this clearest possible presentation of the essential homogeneity of the pricing process, it was necessary to make a number of assumptions in order to simplify matters. Our main assumptions were that the sums of money to be spent by consumers are fixed beforehand, that the technical coefficients are of given fixed magnitudes and that the primary factors of production are available in given quantities. If we wish to make a closer approximation to reality, we must forgo these assumptions at every stage. The magnitudes which we assumed to be given now appear as variables which are themselves dependent upon prices and must be conceived of as functions of the prices of the factors of production for the purposes of our present treatment of the pricing problem. It may here be objected – and misunderstanding in this direction has often arisen – that we are now arguing in a circle. Prices of the factors of production, together with all other prices, are first ascribed to certain constants which must, therefore, be taken as the natural determinants of price. It is then said that these constants are, in fact, not constants at all, but are themselves dependent upon prices. Further consideration of the matter, however, shows that there is no contradiction here, but a gradual extension of the causal connection we are considering. If a series of factors which were previously treated as constants are now conceived of as functions of the prices of the primary factors of production, then the form of these functions, i.e. the nature of the dependence which we have now recognized, represents a new independent determinant of price. In place of the factors which, in our first treatment of the problem, we assumed to be given, there emerge new constants which mark this dependence. The whole of the pricing process is, in this way, traced back by degrees to remote factors which, for the purpose of economic analysis, may be assumed to be given. We have in effect already been proceeding in this way. At the beginning of this section we assumed the quantity of finished goods available for consumers to be given, and on this assumption, which greatly simplified matters, we found a solution of the pricing problem which provides a very useful introduction to the essential nature of the pricing process. But we subsequently dropped this assumption. We recognized that the quantities of commodities themselves depend upon prices and, in place of these constants, we took more remote factors as fixed determinants of prices. By this means our survey of the pricing process was materially extended. We must now continue in this way, by substituting certain dependent factors step by step for constants. We shall now do this with direct reference to the amounts of money to be spent by consumers. The substitution of certain dependent factors for the fixed technical coefficients is done in section 17 [not included here]. The corresponding extension of our treatment of the pricing process with reference to the quantities of factors of production, which we at first took as given, is a very extensive task, which will be one of the main objects of Book II [not included here].

We first assumed, as we said, that the sum of money which every consumer expends for the satisfaction of his wants in the unit period is fixed in advance. On this assumption, a knowledge of the prices of the finished goods is obviously adequate to determine the demand of each individual consumer for those goods. The aggregate demand for various goods can then be calculated by means of our series of equations 4. If, finally, prices are calculated by means of equations 7, they are fixed relatively to the aggregate money expenditure of consumers which we assumed as given. We can, therefore, conclude that prices, by means of the series of equations 7, are fixed absolutely and not merely relatively to one another.

The assumption that the money expenditure of consumers on the purchase of finished goods for satisfying their wants is fixed in advance must now be dropped. The money payments of a consumer are clearly determined by his income. At least, this is generally the case if we consider payments and income over rather longer periods. Payments need not, therefore, be equal to income in every period. The consumer can, of course, save part of his income. In certain cases too, he may spend more than his income, by borrowing money to purchase commodities and leaving his debts unpaid for a time. Both saving and consumption in excess of one's income may be influenced by the prices current at any moment. If, however, all prices are given, we must assume that the extent of the total payments of each individual consumer, and their distribution among the various classes of commodities, are determined by his income. These payments are constant in the case of the stationary state and, as no saving takes place in that society on the whole, are also equal to the income. For the sake of simplicity, we may assume the same in the case of each individual.

The income of the individual is, however, determined by the prices of the factors of production which he sells in the course of the productive process. The various incomes of the members of the exchange economy are thus determined by the pricing process, and neither these incomes nor the payments made with them should, therefore, be regarded as magnitudes, fixed in advance, in the pricing problem. Not until we regard income, too, as one of the unknowns in the pricing problem are we in a position to deal with the pricing problem in a way which accurately reflects our exchange economy, shows that consumers are at the same time producers, and indicates how much of the final product the individual producer is in a position to acquire in exchange for his productive labour. The pricing problem, thus given a general application, contains in itself the problem of economic distribution. The problem of distribution is, therefore, not an independent problem of economic science, but is to be regarded essentially as a special aspect of the general problem of prices. Incidentally, the solution of the problem of distribution, viewed in this way, is included in our series of simultaneous equations. This, of course, does not mean that the practical problem of distribution cannot be regarded from other angles; indeed, it must be thus regarded. The character of economic distribution always lies in the prices fixed by our system of equations for the factors of production co-operating in the social productive process, and the shares of the various members of society in the social products are thus necessarily determined by the relative scarcity of those factors of production which are at their disposal. Only a study of pricing conceived in these general terms can give us a complete and harmonious picture of the processes within the exchange economy.

Our new assumptions do not alter anything in the outward form of the series of equations which serve to determine prices. But the content of equations **4** is now changed. Previously, these equations stressed the dependence upon commodity prices, on the assumption that the aggregate payments of consumers were given. Now we have to start from the prices of the factors of production, provisionally assumed to be known, and by means of them to calculate the incomes of the individuals. In conformity with our assumption, these incomes, in conjunction with commodity prices which, too, are calculated from the prices of the factors of production, determine the aggregate payments for consumption made by the individual; and, therefore, we can construct equations **4** in the same way as before. But these equations no longer include the total payments which we previously assumed to be given as constants. Now, however, the coefficients of the functions $F_1, \ldots, F_n$ are functions of the prices of the factors of production. But the variables $p_1, \ldots, p_n$ are themselves, in accordance with the system of equations **3**, functions of the unknowns $q_1, \ldots, q_r$. Thus the functions $F_1, \ldots, F_n$ now include, beside the variables $q_1, \ldots, q_r$, only constants which must be taken as given in the problem, and which represent the dependence of demand on the general price position and on the division of income fixed by that price position.

So far, we have conducted our analysis on the assumption of a stationary society. We must now take into consideration the society which is progressing at a uniform rate. In it, the quantities of the factors of production which are available in any period, that is our $R_1,\ldots,R_r$, are subject to a uniform increase. We shall represent by c the fixed rate of this increase, and of the uniform progress of the society generally. If we assume the prices of the factors of production to be given, then the money incomes, which are received by selling those factors and which thus increase in the same percentage c, are fixed. Part of this income is saved; the rest is spent on the purchase of finished goods. In the uniformly progressive state, however, the degree of saving is constant and the sums of money which are available in every period for consumption increase likewise in the percentage c. By means of technical coefficients a, the prices of the finished goods are determined in accordance with equations **3** in the same way as in the previous case. Since these prices remain constant, demand, with its continually growing purchasing power, can be satisfied to an increasing extent. In the uniformly progressing economy, we must, therefore, assume that our $D_1,\ldots,D_n$ all increase together in the fixed percentage c. The same must then also be true of our $S_1,\ldots,S_n$.

The continuous production of these steadily increasing quantities of goods, however, makes special demands upon the factors of production $R_1,\ldots,R_r$ that are available in a given unit period. Outwardly, equations **7** remain unchanged; but the coefficients a must be replaced by others. As we have already seen, the a are sums of other constants, which show how much of them refers to each unit period; that is, how much of each factor of production in each unit period is taken into account for the production of a definite unit quantity of each finished commodity. As production is now assumed to increase uniformly, there must be substituted, for these unit quantities, other quantities which steadily increase in the percentage c. Therefore, the corresponding constants also increase in the same ratio. That is, if a series of successive unit periods are considered, they must be multiplied by ascending powers of a constant factor, which is clearly determined by c. The constants thus determined must be added again to sums which have to replace the a in equations 7.

The essential thing is, however, that these new coefficients contain, in addition to the elements of the old 'technical coefficients', only the rate of progress c and they are, therefore, to be regarded as given quantities in the pricing problem under discussion, if the prices of the factors of production are taken as known. Thus the equations 7 retain their character and suffice, as in the previous case, to fix the prices of the factors of production so that the whole pricing problem is solved.

The demands which a steadily increasing production makes upon the factors of production during a present unit period are naturally greater than those which a stationary production, corresponding to the present supply of finished goods, would make. The income of the present unit period, determined by the prices of the factors of production, also exceeds, in the same proportion, the total value of the available finished goods in that period. This income falls into two parts, one of which is used to buy finished goods and the other to buy the increase of real capital during the period in question. The first part is used to pay for those factors of production which are needed for the production of finished goods, including the maintenance of the existing real capital. The second part is used to pay for the remaining factors of production, which are devoted to the increase of real capital. The ratio between the two parts determines the degree of saving and the rate of progress c. The special significance which the rate of interest has in this connection will be considered in a later section.

It is clear that the functions $F_1, \ldots, F_n$ must be of the same form, and that they will remain unchanged if all the q expressed in the money unit are multiplied by any multiplier whatever. For, in an exchange economy that is in a state of constant equilibrium, the demand can only be determined by the relative prices. The same equilibrium could be preserved just as well if, let us say, the prices were doubled, since the income would then be twice as great; and the distribution of the income among the various means for satisfying wants can only depend upon the ratio between the prices of goods and income, when there is a stable equilibrium, and not upon the absolute amounts themselves.

That the result would be different if the equilibrium were altered, since regard must be had to a price position other than that of the moment, will have to be borne in mind when we consider the theory of money.

We can see, too, in other ways, that the functions $F_1,\ldots,F_n$ must have this characteristic. It is well known that in modern physics the calculation of the dimensions of the different magnitudes discussed in the science plays an important part. Theoretical economics can make use of the same method. Price, reckoned in money, is one of the fundamental economic measuring-rods and can be called the measure of value. Now, the demand for a particular commodity is expressed by the number of units of the commodity desired and this can be expressed as a length (so many yards of cloth, for example), or as a weight (so many pounds of sugar), and so forth. It clearly does not include the value measurement; with regard to value, its dimension is nil. This is equivalent to saying that a multiplication of all the q expressed in the money unit, which now alone represent the measurement of value in the demand functions F, by one and the same factor, does not influence these functions.

A multiplication of all the prices q by any factor whatever has, therefore, no influence upon the equations 5 and 7. As the latter, which fixes the prices q, has this attribute, it must also be realized by a system of prices q, in which all the q, expressed in the money unit, are multiplied by any factor we please to choose. Hence the systems of equations is indeterminate, in that it determines the prices in question only up to a multiplicative factor; or, as it is popularly expressed, determines only the relative and not the absolute prices. In order to obtain the absolute prices, a new condition must be introduced; for example, the price of a commodity or of a group of commodities must be given. This condition was fulfilled so long as the total expenditure of the consumer, reckoned in money terms, was taken for granted. In the general pricing problem, a multiplicative factor of all prices remains undetermined. The determination of this factor and, consequently, the final solution of the pricing problem, belongs to the theory of money.

The pricing factors

By the study we have just made, we have answered in principle the question as to which are the determining factors of prices. The essential subjective factors in prices are inherent in the dependence of the demand for finished products upon prices. The objective factors, even if the principle of scarcity alone is taken into consideration, are the technical conditions of production, on the one hand, and the supplies of the available factors of production, on the other. In cases where the supplementary principles of pricing also apply, these pricing factors are modified in part and replaced by others. The differential principle, for example, introduces, as an objective factor of pricing, the nature of the dependence of the technical conditions of production upon the extent of production. The principle of substitution likewise takes into account the nature of the connection between the quantities of the factors of production, each of which may partly replace the other.

We call these three groups of factors the immediate price-determining factors. Up to the present in our treatment of the pricing problem, these factors have been regarded as given. But they themselves depend upon a variety of different elements of the economic and general social aspects of human life. If we want to study the influence of these elements on prices, we have first to study their influence on the immediate pricing factors. It is only through them that remote factors can affect prices. Hence all such inquiries bring us back to our solution of the pricing problem. The causal link which connects prices and their direct determinants, the real nature of which we have now learned, remains always the clearest and most precise explanation of the problem.

Important factors which thus influence prices externally are, for example, changes in the size of the population or its composition regarding age, sex, civil status, classes and occupations, migration within the economic area in question, changes in economic organization, in the legal order, in taxation, in the economic customs of the people (in regard to saving, or to the general conception of the requirements of one's social position, for instance), the destruction of things by war, the exhaustion of natural resources or discoveries of new sources and opening-up of new regions and, finally, progress in technical processes – in a word, all the factors which give mobility and vitality to economic life. In so far as these movements affect prices, and are in turn affected by them, we have to deal with dynamic problems of pricing. These dynamic problems of pricing have, of course, a considerably larger content than the static problem of pricing, in which the immediate pricing factors are taken for granted and in which all we have to do is to explain how they determine prices and what direction production takes in a state of equilibrium. It would be a mistake, however, to imagine that the solution of the static problem is without any significance for the dynamic problems. On the contrary, all questions relating to the dynamic problems of pricing are converted first into questions as to the effect of certain movements and changes upon the immediate pricing factors, and consequently as to the fixing of prices by those factors in accordance with the causal sequence already described. It is true that the conditions of our solution of the pricing problem are very often not realized, particularly when violent economic changes occur. In such a case there may be a period when, for example, goods which were produced at the old cost have to be sold at the new and lower prices, the principle of cost thus remaining unfulfilled. But as soon as the transitional stage is over, the fixing of prices in any system which fulfils, in some degree, the requirements of a sound progressive economic organization will closely follow the principle of cost, and will, therefore, be elucidated substantially by our solution of the pricing problem. This solution is also very significant in connection with all the dynamic problems of theoretical economics. Nevertheless, we must always bear in mind that the conditions of a period of transition considerably influence the conditions of the normal settlement of prices which follow: they may, for instance, permanently alter the composition of the population, or the quality of the labour of certain groups of the population.

How remoter causes affect the direct pricing factors is a question which must naturally be answered separately for each particular case. However, it does not fall within the scope of a general economic theory. Here, we have only to show how variations in the direct pricing factors affect pricing, and also the problem which is bound up with this, namely, the determination of the direction of production. We have already made the formal side of the problem clear. It is, however, unnecessary for us to examine in what respect the influence of these particular changes, also, will actually be realized, or whether the actual changes in certain of the given factors have a greater significance in the pricing process, so that these problems need not be dealt with. In this case, a more or less substantial simplification of the whole theory of pricing, which various schools of economic thought have attempted to achieve, would perhaps be possible. We have essayed an answer to these questions in relation to each of the three principal groups of direct pricing factors.

In connection with the subjective factors, which show the dependence of the demand for finished goods upon the prices of them, we notice, above all, that a change in the demand only influences prices when it affects either the demand for the factors of production or the methods of production. Given these two groups of factors, the prices of finished goods are also determined according to our assumptions.

Consequently, it is appropriate to estimate the effect that a change in the demand for finished goods has on the demand for factors of production. A change in the direction of demand frequently simply means that the factors of production are applied in other ways, without thereby causing any alteration in the total demand for any particular factor. We need not go very far to see that this is theoretically possible, since a given supply of factors of production can quite easily be put to many different uses. If, for example, the taste of bread-consumers alters in such a way that wheaten-bread partially displaces rye-bread, all that this really means is that a little more arable land and agricultural labour will be devoted to wheat growing, and a little less of each to rye. A change in the total demand for arable land or for agricultural labour need not take place on account of this. If the land can be used for wheat growing just as well as for rye, then the price of this factor of production need not alter at all. All that happens in this case is that the change in the demand results in the factor of production being put to a partly different use. With regard to actual industrial products, such a condition is fairly general. Whether the demand for knives or for skates is relatively the greater is, in the long run, a matter of indifference to the prices of these articles, since the labour and particularly the material used in the production of knives can just as easily be used, as a whole, in the production of skates. In all such cases it depends only upon the quantities of the appropriate factors of production necessary to produce the one or the other article. As the changes in the demand for these articles do not affect the demand for the factors of production, the prices of these factors may be assumed to be fixed, and it can then be asserted that the prices of the articles vary in direct proportion to their costs of production. One would arrive, therefore, at a 'cost of production theory' for a limited circle of commodity prices.

But under no circumstances may we conclude from this that the subjective factors, in such cases, have completely lost their significance in the pricing process and that prices may finally be reduced to purely objective factors. It can well be a matter of indifference to pricing whether the demand changes in the direction of one or another of a specific group of goods, so long, that is, as the total demand for the different factors required to produce these goods remains unaltered. This total demand for a factor of production, arising as it does out of the whole group of goods is, however, not without importance for the price of the factor. The existence of this total demand is, clearly, an essential condition of the maintenance of the price of the factor of production and, through this, of the entire pricing process. As long as this total demand remains constant, it has naturally no tendency to alter the price of the factor of production. But it can change, however, and such a change must obviously affect pricing.

It is plainly undeniable that the supply of many of the most important materials in the generation preceding the Great War maintained an approximately equal pace with the growing demand for special finished products and that no very substantial changes in the relative scarcity of these materials have occurred since. It is undeniable, too, that, in so far as this is true, the great changes in demand have not had much influence on the pricing process and that the control of prices through the technical costs of production has become of the first importance. This steadily uniform provision of materials, is however, in no way a usual phenomenon. It is, for instance, indisputable that the continually growing demand for new houses, and the building activity engendered by this, materially enhances the prices of the wood used for building purposes. The great strides made in general literacy during the last decade have led to a very marked demand for newspapers which, in turn, has had a definitely increasing influence on the prices of wood-pulp and consequently on those of forests. In such cases, the demand obviously exerts a powerful influence on the scarcity-values of the materials and thus on the whole pricing process.

The steadily increased provision of certain types of raw materials, sufficient to meet growing requirements, was, moreover, only possible at a time when the progressive economic development of the world constantly provided new possibilities of catering for the increasing need for the most varied materials. We naturally cannot assume that the supply of material as will keep a steady pace with each growing demand in the future, too. Without indulging in pessimistic reflections as to the possibilities of providing for a growing world population, we can and must keep the truth constantly before us that, in the case of certain materials, an acute shortage is to be expected in the future. This fact is now generally recognized. Since the Great War, world politics have been strongly influenced by a fear of an approaching scarcity of certain materials such as fertilizers and, above all, petroleum. This, too, is well known. However, as soon as the limitation to our material resources becomes more marked, it will undoubtedly be proved that the development and growth of demand exercise a real and active influence on pricing.

A special case in which a change in the demand for a finished article exercises a direct and active effect on the pricing process is that of joint products. Our fourth supplementary principle shows that the prices of joint products must be fixed in such a way that a market is found for them all. If the demand for one of the products increases, then, as a rule, its price must also increase, because the increase in the total production that would be necessitated would unduly lower the prices of the remaining joint products (for which the possibility of a bigger market has not been realized). For example, since central-heating came into general use, municipal gas-works have obtained prices for their coke often much higher than would otherwise have been the case.

Furthermore, a change in the subjective factors of pricing can also influence the costs of production and, in consequence, the pricing process. Theoretically, the nature of these effects has already been made clear by the construction of the first two supplementary principles. In certain cases, an increased demand may mean a rise in the prices of the products; in other cases, a fall. A rise in price occurs when, in order to satisfy the increased demand, new firms, with higher costs of production, enter the market, in which case the differential principle comes into force. An example of this is the increase which takes place in the price of milk or firewood in a growing city which, already large, must satisfy the need for those commodities out of supplies coming from increasingly distant sources. A fall in price occurs, on the other hand, when production is carried on under conditions of decreasing costs. The extraordinary increase in the demand for bicycles, for example, has made a very cheap mass production possible, resulting in substantially lower prices to buyers.

The foregoing account should be sufficient to show that those pricing factors which we have called subjective also have a real, and in no way a merely passive, influence on prices.

Most variations in prices, however, and usually the most substantial ones, are produced by changes in the technical conditions of production. At all events, this is the case in the period of progressive industrialism when revolutionary changes in the methods of production continually create new foundations for pricing. As usual, we must regard transport as a stage in the productive process. The transformation in the technical methods of production has been of particularly great importance for the whole pricing process. The facts with which we have to deal here are so well known as to make it unnecessary to quote examples. The reaction of the pricing process on the selection of the methods of production has already been illustrated during the construction of the supplementary principles of pricing.

Finally, when we come to the factors of production, there remains no doubt that their supply in the exchange economy, according as it is more or less ample, exercises a fundamental influence on pricing. This influence makes itself directly felt as soon as considerable changes occur in the supply of these factors.

The relevancy of such changes is plain, without further consideration, from a study of actual economic life, particularly with regard to the raw materials provided by nature. Changes in the quantities of the available factors of production affect pricing, partly directly through their influence on the relative scarcity of the factors but also partly indirectly through that on the selection of the methods of production. When two factors of production compete with each other and when, therefore, the principle of substitution comes into force, an intensified shortage of one factor can be more or less completely modified by an increased use of the second. The effect on pricing extends, in this case, too, to the second factor but, in regard to the product, will become much attenuated, sometimes even absolutely reduced to zero. This latter, of course, can be particularly the case if the quantity of the second factor is increased simultaneously. A considerable number of changes can, therefore, take place in the exchange economy, having only a relatively small, or sometimes absolutely nil, effect upon the pricing of finished goods. The possibility of satisfying one and the same need in several different ways exercises, on the whole, a stabilizing effect upon prices. We can take as an example, the satisfaction of the need for lighting; a growing scarcity of petroleum, let us say, will not necessarily influence the price of illumination, since so many substitutes are available to fill the gap. The price of petroleum cannot be increased excessively. Such cases where changes in the supply of the factors of production have only a slight effect upon prices should not, however, hide the fact that our supply of them, according as it is more or less plentiful, still constitutes a fundamental and, usually, very active pricing factor.

Thus we observe that the three groups of pricing factors discussed, to wit, the demand of the consumers, the technique of production and the supply of factors of production, have collectively a fundamental significance in the pricing process in actual economic life. It is obvious, too, that none of them can be omitted by constructing an even more elementary and simplified theory of pricing. But if all three groups of factors must be taken into account, then the theory of pricing is in full accord with our solution. And besides this solution, there can be no other theory of pricing which is descriptive and explanatory of the actual conditions of an exchange economy.

In our analysis of the pricing process we have so far taken for granted the quantities of the primary factors of production available – that is, we have assumed them to be determined by external circumstances and, consequently, to be objective factors independent of the pricing process. This assumption is only justified in a preliminary survey of the problem. In any case, it is really only a first approximation and is only realized within certain limits of the fluctuation of prices. The prices of the factors of production have, in fact, an influence on the supply of them to the exchange economy. This influence may be latent in normal circumstances but may be very active under other conditions. The analysis, therefore, must be carried further on this point.

Implicit in our conception of the primary factors of production is the fact that they cannot be produced and, therefore, cannot be increased by production. Thus, on the one hand, we have to find to what extent what are usually called primary factors of production really satisfy this strict requirement or are capable of being increased by some activity which must be looked upon as productive. On the other hand, the supply of a factor of production may conceivably depend upon the price, even when there is no possibility of producing it. Our task, therefore, will be to discover the nature of this dependence.

When we drop the assumption that the factors of production are available in fixed quantities, a certain change in our idea of scarcity takes place. The scarcity of a factor of production is then no longer determined by an invariable quantity of itself, but is due rather to the way in which the quantity of the factor offered depends upon the price. The scarcity makes itself felt in the slowness with which the increase of the factor of production follows a rise in the price. This makes the pricing problem somewhat complicated but is of very little importance in the theoretical treatment of it. The fixing of prices on the more general assumption referred to above can be dealt with entirely within the limits of our analysis of the mechanism of pricing. The dependence of the supply of the factors of production upon their prices is really only the antithesis of the dependence of the demand for the finished products upon their prices, which we have already considered. It, therefore, offers no new obstacle to our survey of the general mechanism of pricing.

However, the way in which the supply of some of the principal factors of production depends upon the prices of them must be made the subject of a special study. As the same condition holds good for the demand, the task which now confronts us can be formulated as follows: we have to study the effect of the prices of the factors of production upon the supply of, and demand for, them.

The next Book [not included here] will be devoted to this work, which is of the greatest importance in theoretical economics.

Reference

CASSEL, G. (1899), 'Grundriss einer elementaren Preislehre', *Zeitschrift für die gesamte Staatswissenschaft.*

Part Three Demand

The theory of consumers' choice was developed to explain
the properties and interdependence of market demand
functions (demand curves). This theory, which consists of an
examination of the logic of choice, has shown its power in
many contexts beyond the traditional boundaries of
economics. One of the points where the theory spills over into
psychology, politics and decision theory is in the analysis of
choices involving risk, and Armen Alchian explains the main
concepts used. The other two Readings in this part are
concerned with demand at the market level, and with the
possibilities and problems of estimating demand relationships.

5 Armen Alchian

The Meaning of Utility Measurement[1]

Armen Alchian, 'The meaning of utility measurement', *American Economic Review*, vol. 42, 1953, pp. 26–50.

Economists struggling to keep abreast of current developments may well be exasperated by the resurgence of measurability of utility. After all, the indifference curve analysis was popularized little over ten years ago amidst the contradictory proclamations that it eliminated, modified and strengthened the role of utility. Even yet there is confusion, induced partly by careless reading and exposition of the indifference curve analysis and partly by misunderstandings of the purposes and implications of utility measurement. This paper attempts to clarify the role and meaning of the recent revival of measurement of utility in economic theory and of the meaning of certain concepts and operations commonly used in utility theory.

Measurement in its broadest sense is the assignment of numbers to entities. The process of measurement has three aspects which should be distinguished at the outset. First is the purpose of measurement, second is the process by which one measures something, i.e. assigns numerical values to some aspect of an entity, and the third is the arbitrariness, or uniqueness, of the set of numerical values inherent in the purpose and process. In the first part of this paper we briefly explore the idea of arbitrariness or uniqueness of numbers assigned by a measurement process. In part 2 we state some purposes of utility measurement. In part 3 we examine a method of

1. The author wishes to acknowledge gratefully the aid of Norman Dalkey and Harry Markowitz, both of the R AND Corporation. The patient explanations of Dalkey in answering innumerable questions overcame early impulses to abandon the attempt to understand recent utility literature. Markowitz detected several ambiguities and errors in earlier drafts of this exposition. Since neither has seen the final draft they must be relieved of responsibility for remaining errors and ambiguities.

measuring utility, the purpose of the measurement and the extent to which the measurement is unique. In part 4 we look at some implications of the earlier discussion.[2]

1. Degree of measurability

The columns of Table 1 are sequences of numbers illustrating the concept of the 'degree of measurability'. The entities, some aspect of which we wish to measure, are denoted by letters. Later we shall discuss the meaning of these entities. Our first task is to explain the difference between monotone transformations and linear transformations.

We shall begin with monotone transformations and then come to linear transformations via two of its special cases, additive and multiplicative constants.

Monotone transformations

Let there be assigned a numerical magnitude (measure) to each entity concerned. For example in Table 1, for the ten entities, A–J, listed in the extreme left-hand column, nine different sets of numbers are utilized to assign nine different numbers to each of the entities. If two sets of numbers (measures) result in the same ranking or ordering of the entities (according to the numbers assigned), then the two sets are *monotone transformations* of each other. In Table 1 it will be seen that all nine measures give the same ranking, thus all nine measures are monotone transformations of each other. If this property holds true over the entire class of entities concerned, then the two measures are monotone transformations of each other for that class of entities. The possible set of monotone transformations obviously is very large.

2. The explanation assumes no mathematical background and is on an elementary level. This paper is not original in any of its ideas, nor is it a general review of utility and demand theory. It is merely a statement of some propositions that may help the reader separate the chaff from the wheat. It may even make clear to the reader, as it did to the writer, one meaning of utility. Most of the material presented here is contained in Marschak (1950), an article written for the mathematically mature. A bibliography is included, to which those who might wish to read more deeply should refer. Excellent starting points are Friedman and Savage (1948) and Marschak (1951).

Table 1 Illustration of Types of Measurement

	Alternative measures of 'utility'								
Entities	1	2	3	4	5	6	7	8	9
A	1	2	6	11	2	6	5	6	3
B	2	4	7	12	4	12	7	10	7
C	3	5	8	13	6	18	9	14	13
D	4	8	9	14	8	24	11	18	21
E	5	11	10	15	10	30	13	22	31
F	7	14	12	17	14	42	17	30	43
G	11	22	16	21	22	66	25	46	57
H	14	28	19	24	28	84	31	58	73
I	16	33	21	26	32	96	35	66	91
J	17	34	22	27	34	102	37	70	111

Linear transformations: additive constants

We shall approach the linear transformation by considering two special forms. Look at the numbers in column 3. They are the same as those in 1 except that a constant has been added, in this case 5, i.e. they are the *same* '*up to*' (except for) an *additive constant*. The measure in column 4 is equivalent to that in column 1 with 10 added. Columns 1, 3 and 4 are *transforms* of each other 'up to' (by means of) *additive constants*. This can also be expressed by saying they are equivalent except for an additive constant. The term 'up to' implies that we may go through some simpler types. For example, all the transforms up to an additive constant are also contained in the larger, less restricted class of possible transforms known as monotone transforms. An additive constant is a quite strong restriction, even though it may not seem so at first since there is an unlimited number of available constants. But relative to the range of possibilities in the general linear transformations this is very restrictive indeed.

Linear transformations: multiplicative constants

Now look at column 5. It is equivalent to column 1 except for multiplication by a constant, in this case, 2. Column 5 is a monotone transform of column 1, and it is also a 'multiplicative by a constant' transform of column 1. Column 6 is column 1 multiplied by 6. Thus, while columns 1, 5 and 6 are monotone transforms of each other, they are also a more particular type of transform. They are transforms up to a multiplicative constant. These are special cases of linear transformations which we shall now discuss.

General linear transformations

The numbers of column 7 are equivalent to column 1 except for multiplication by 2 and addition of 3. Letting y denote the numbers of 'measures' in column 7 and x those of column 1, we have $y = 2x+3$. Column 8 is derived similarly from column 1; the multiplier is 4 and the added constant is 2. Column 8 is given by $4x+2$, but a little inspection will show that column 8 can be derived from column 7 by the same process of multiplying and adding. In this case column 8 is obtained from column 7 by multiplying by 2 and adding -4. Columns 1, 7 and 8 are thus 'linear transforms' of each other. This is also expressed by saying that they are the same measures 'up to a linear transformation'; that is, any one of these measures can be obtained from any other one by simply selecting appropriate constants for multiplication and addition.

There is a particular property of the linear transformation that has historical significance in economics. Look at the way the numbers change as one moves from entity to entity. For example, consider columns 1 and 7. The numerical change from entity E to entity F has a value of 2 in the measure of column 1, while in the measure of column 7, it has a numerical value of 4. From F to G the change is 4 in measure 1, and in measure 7 it is 8. If the increment is positive, it will be positive in all sequences which are linear transforms of this particular sequence. But this is true also for all monotone transformations – a much broader class of transformations or measures. Of greater significance, however, is the following attribute of linear transforms: if the differences between the numbers in one of the sequences increases (or decreases) from entity to entity, then the differences between the numbers of these same entities in all of its *linear* transformations will also be increasing (or decreasing). In general, the property of increasing or decreasing increments is not affected by switching from one sequence of numbers to any linear transformation of that given sequence. In mathematical terms, the sign of the second differences of a sequence of numbers is invariant to linear transformations of that sequence.[3] The significance of invariance will be discussed later, but we should note that this property of increasing (or decreasing) differences between the numbers assigned to pairs of entities is nothing but increasing marginal utility – if one christens the assigned numbers 'utilities'.

2. Purpose of measurement

Order

In the nine columns of Table 1 are nine 'different' measures of some particular aspect of the entities denoted A, B, C, ..., J. How different are they? We have already answered this. Which is the 'right' one? This depends upon what one wants to do with the entities and the numbers. It would be more useful to ask which one is a *satisfactory* measure, for then it is clear that we must make explicit for what it is to be satisfactory.[4] For example, if my sole concern were to predict which of the entities would be the heaviest, the next heaviest, etc., I could, by successively comparing pairs in a balancing scale, completely order the entities. Having done so, I could then assign the numbers in *any* one of columns 1 through 9 so long as I assign the biggest number to the heaviest, and so on down. This means that for the purpose of indicating *order*, any one of the monotone transforms is acceptable.

The remaining task is to determine whether the order is 'correctly' stated; the fact that the order is the same, no matter which one of the above transforms is used, does not imply that the order is correct. What do we mean by 'correctly'? We mean that our stated or predicted order is matched by the order

3. In monotonic transformations the sign of the *first* differences only are necessarily left undisturbed.

4. A pause to reflect will reveal that there is a second problem besides that of deciding what 'satisfactory' means. This second problem, which we have so far begged, is: 'How does one assign numbers to entities?' It is deferred to the following section.

revealed by some other observable ordering process. You could put the entities on some new weighing scales (the new scales are the 'test'), and then a matching of the order derived from the new scales with our stated order is a verification of the correctness (predictive validity) of our first ordering. Any monotone transform of one valid ordering number sequence is *for the purpose* in this illustration *completely equivalent* to the numbers actually used. That is, any one of the possible monotone transformations is just as good as any other.

We may summarize by saying that, given a method for validly ordering entities, any monotone transformation of the particular numerical values assigned in the ordering process will be equally satisfactory. We may be technical and say that 'all measures of order are equivalent up to (except for being) monotone transformations'. Or, in other words, a method of validly denoting *order* only, is not capable of uniquely identifying a particular set of numbers as *the* correct one. Any monotonic transformation will do exactly as well. The degree of uniqueness of an ordering can also be described by saying it is only as unique as the set of monotone transformations. Thus, we often see the expression that 'ordering is unique up to a monotone transformation'.

Ordering groups of entities

But suppose our purpose were different. Suppose we want to be able to order *groups* of entities according to their weights. More precisely, suppose we want to assign numbers to each of the component objects so that when we combine the objects into sets or bundles we can order the weights of the composite bundles, knowing only the individually valid numbers assigned to each component, by *merely adding* together the numbers assigned to each component. And we want to be able to do this for any possible combination of the objects. Fortunately man has discerned a way to do this for weights. The numbers which are assigned by this discovered process are arbitrary up to a multiplicative constant (of proportionality), so that the numbers could express either pounds, ounces, tons or grams. That is, we can arbitrarily multiply all the numbers assigned to the various components by any constant we please, without destroying the validity of our resulting numbers for this particular purpose. But we cannot use any monotone transformation as we could in the preceding case where our purpose was different.

If we were to add an arbitrary constant to each component's individually valid numerical (weight) value we would not be able to add the resulting numbers of each component in order to get a number which would rank the composite bundles. Thus, the numbers we can assign are rather severely constrained. We cannot use any linear transformation, but we can use a multiplicative constant, which is a special type of linear transformation. And if we were to 'measure' lengths of items so as to be able simply to 'add' the numbers to get the lengths of the items laid end to end, we would again find ourselves confined to sequences (measures) with a multiplicative constant as the one available degree of arbitrariness.

Utility and ordering of choices

The reader has merely to substitute for the concept of weight, in the earlier example about weight orders, the idea of 'preference' and he is in the theory of choice or demand. Economics goes a step further and gives the name 'utility' to the numbers. Can we assign a set of numbers (measures) to the various entities and predict that the entity with the largest assigned number (measure) will be chosen? If so, we could christen this measure 'utility' and then assert that choices are made so as to maximize utility. It is an easy step to the statement that 'you are maximizing your utility', which says no more than your choice is predictable according to the size of some assigned numbers.[5] For analytical convenience it is customary to postulate that an individual seeks to maximize something subject to some constraints. The thing – or numerical measure of the 'thing' – which he seeks to maximize is called 'utility'. Whether or not utility is some kind of glow or warmth or happiness, is here irrelevant; all that counts is that we can assign numbers to entities or conditions which a person can

5. The difficult (impossible?) psychological, philosophical step of relating this kind of utility to some *quantity of satisfaction, happiness, goodness* or *welfare* is not attempted here.

strive to realize. Then we say the individual seeks to maximize some function of those numbers. Unfortunately, the term 'utility' has by now acquired so many connotations, that it is difficult to realize that for present purposes utility has no more meaning than this. The analysis of individual demand behavior is mathematically describable as the process of maximizing some quantitive measures, or numbers, and we assume that the individual seeks to obtain that combination with the highest choice number, given the purchasing power at his disposal. It might be harmless to call this 'utility theory'.[6]

Three types of choice predictions

Sure prospects. Before proceeding further it is necessary to indicate clearly the types of choice that will concern us. The first type of choice is that of selecting among a set of alternative 'riskless' choices. A riskless choice, hereafter called a sure prospect, is one such that the chooser knows exactly what he will surely get with each possible choice. To be able to predict the preferred choice means we can assign numbers to the various entities such that the entity with the largest assigned number is the most preferred, the one with the second largest number is the next most preferred, etc. As said earlier, it is customary to christen this numerical magnitude with the name 'utility'.

An understanding of what is meant by 'entity' is essential. An entity denotes any specifiable object, action, event, or set or pattern of such items or actions. It may be an orange, a television set, a glass of milk, a trip to Europe, a particular time profile of income or consumption (e.g. steak every night, or ham every night, or steak and ham on alternate nights), getting married, etc. Identifying an entity exclusively with one single event or action would lead to unnecessary restrictions on the scope of the applicability of the theorem to be presented later (see e.g., Malinvaud, 1952; Manne, 1952; Samuelson, 1952; Wold, 1952).

6. The author, having so far kept his opinions submerged, is unable to avoid remarking that it would seem 'better' to confine utility 'theory' to attempts to explain or discern why a person chooses one thing rather than another – at equal price.

Groups of sure prospects. A second problem of choice prediction would be that of ordering (predicting) choices among riskless *groups* of entities. A riskless group consists of several entities all of which will be surely obtained if that group is chosen. The problem now is to predict the choice among riskless groups knowing only the utilities assigned to the individual entities which have been aggregated into groups. Thus if in Table 1 we were to assemble the entities A through J into various groups, could we predict the choice among these groups of entities knowing only the utility numbers that were assigned to the component entities for the purpose of the preceding choice problem? Of course we ask this question only on the assumption that the utilities previously assigned to the component entities were valid predictors of choice among the single sure prospects.[7]

Uncertain prospects. A third type of problem is that of ordering choices among risky choices, or what have been called uncertain prospects. An uncertain prospect is a group of entities, only one entity of which will be realized if that group is chosen. For example, an uncertain prospect might consist of a fountain pen, a radio and an automobile. If that uncertain prospect is chosen, the chooser will surely get one of the three entities, but which one he will actually get is not known in advance. He is not completely ignorant about what will be realized, for it is assumed that he knows the probabilities of realization attached to each of the component entities in an uncertain prospect. For example the probabilities might have been 0·5 for the fountain pen, 0·4 for the radio and 0·1 for the automobile. These probabilities sum to 1·0; one and only one of these entities will be realized. An uncertain prospect is very much like a ticket in a lottery. If there is but one prize, then the uncertain prospect consists of two entities, the prize or the loss of the stake. If there are several prizes, the uncertain prospect consists of several entities – the various prizes and, of course, the loss of the stake (being a loser).

But there is another requirement that we want our prediction process to satisfy. Not only must we be able to predict the choices, but we want to do it in a very simple way. Specifically,

7. For an illustration of this problem of rating a composite bundle by means of the ratings of the components, see Manne (1952).

we want to be able to look at each component separately, and then from utility measures assigned to the elements, as if they were sure prospects, we want to be able to aggregate the component utility measures into a group utility measure predicting choices among the uncertain prospects. For example, suppose the uncertain prospects consisted of a pen, a radio and an automobile as listed in Table 2.

Are there utilities which can be assigned to the pen, the radio and the automobile, so that for the purpose of comparing these four uncertain prospects the same numbers could be used in arriving at utility numbers to be assigned to the uncertain prospects? In particular, can we assign to the pen, the radio and the automobile numbers such that when multiplied by the associated probabilities in each uncertain prospect they will yield a sum (expected utility) for each uncertain prospect, and such that these 'expected utilities' would indicate preference?

Table 2 Examples of Uncertain Prospects

Uncertain prospect	Probabilities of getting		
	Pen	*Radio*	*Automobile*
1	0·5	0·4	0·1
2	0·58	0·30	0·12
3	0·85	0·0	0·15
4	0·0	0·99	0·01

Before answering we shall briefly indicate why choices among uncertain prospects constitute an important class of situations. Upon reflection it will be seen to be the practically universal problem of choice. Can the reader think of many cases in which he *knows* when making a choice, the outcome of that choice with absolute certainty? In other words, are there many choices – or actions – in life in which the *consequences* can be predicted with absolute certainty? Even the act of purchasing a loaf of bread has an element of uncertainty in its consequences; even the act of paying one's taxes has an element of uncertainty in the consequences involved; even the decision to sit down has an element of uncertainty in the consequence. But to leave the trivial, consider the choice of occupation, purchase of an automobile, house, durable goods, business investment, marriage, having children, insurance, gambling, etc., *ad infinitum*. Clearly choices among uncertain prospects constitute an extremely large and important class of choices.

3. Method of measurement

So far we have discussed the meaning and purpose of measurement. We turn to the method of measurement recognizing that for each type of choice prediction the method of measurement must have a rationale as well as a purpose. For a moment we can concentrate on the rationale which is properly stated in the form of axioms defining rational behavior.

Sure prospects

Let us start with a rationale for the first type of choice. We postulate that an individual behaves consistently, i.e. he has a consistent set of preferences; that these preferences are transitive, i.e. if B is preferred to A, and C to B, then C is preferred to A; and that these preferences can be completely described merely by attaching a numerical value to each. An implication of these postulates is that for such individuals we can predict their choices by a numerical variable (utility). Asking the individual to make pairwise comparisons we assign numbers to the sure prospects such that the choice order will be revealed by the size of the numbers attached. The number of pairwise comparisons that the individual must make depends upon how fortunate we are in selecting the pairs for his comparison. If we are so lucky as first to present him with a series of pairs of alternatives of sure prospects exactly matching his preference order, the complete ordering of his preferences will be obtained with the minimal amount of pairwise comparisons. Any numbering sequence which gives the most preferred sure prospect the highest number, the second preferred sure prospect the second highest number, etc., will predict his choices according to 'utility maximization'. But any other sequence of numbers could be used so long as it is a *monotone transformation* of the first sequence. And this is exactly the meaning of the statement that utility is *ordinal* and not cardinal. The transitivity postulate enables this pairwise comparison to reveal the complete order of preferences, and the consistency postulate means he would make his choices according to the prediction. Thus if he were to be presented with any two of ten sure prospects, we would predict his taking the one with the higher utility number. If our prediction failed, then one of our postulates would have been denied, and our prediction method would not be valid. A hidden postulate is that the preferences, if transitive and consistent, are stable for the interval involved.[8] Utility for this purpose and by this method is measurable up to a monotonic transformation, i.e. it is ordinal only.

Groups of sure prospects

The second type of choice, among *groups* of sure prospects, can be predicted using the same postulates only if we treat each group of sure prospects as a sure prospect. Then by presenting pairs of 'groups of sure prospects' we can proceed as in the preceding problem. But the interesting problem here is that of predicting choice among groups of sure prospects (entities) only by knowing valid utility measures for choices among the component sure prospects. Can these utility numbers of the component entities of the group of sure prospects, which are valid for the entities by themselves, be aggregated to obtain a number predicting choice among the groups of sure prospects? In general the answer is 'no'. Hence, although utility was measurable for the purpose of the kind of prediction in the preceding problem, it is not measurable in the sense that these component measures can be aggregated or combined in any known way to predict choices among *groups* of sure prospects. Utility is 'measurable' for one purpose but not for the other.[9]

8. Some problems involved in this assumption and in its relaxation are discussed by Georgescu-Roegen (1950).

9. It is notable that the usual indifference curve analysis is contained in this case. Any *group* of sure prospects (point in the xy plane of an indifference curve diagram) which has more of each element in it than there is in another group of two sure prospects, will be preferred to the latter. And further, if one group of sure prospects has more of one commodity than does the other group of sure prospects, the two groups can be made indifferent by sufficiently increasing the amount of the second commodity in the other group

Uncertain prospects

We want to predict choices among uncertain prospects. And we want to make these predictions solely on the basis of the utilities and probabilities attached to the elements of the uncertain prospects.

Without going into too many details an intuitive idea of the content of the axioms used in deriving this kind of measurability will now be given.[10] For expository convenience the statement that the two entities A and B are equally desirable or indifferent will be expressed by $A = B$; if however A is either preferred to or indifferent to B, the expression will be $A \geqslant B$.

1. For the chooser there is a transitive, complete ordering of all the alternative possible choices so far as his preferences are concerned. That is if $C \geqslant B$ and $B \geqslant A$, then $C \geqslant A$.

2. If among three entities, A, B and C, $C \geqslant B$, and $B \geqslant A$, then there is some probability value p, for which B is just as desirable as the uncertain prospect consisting of A and C, where A is realizable with probability p, and C with probability 1-p. In our notation: if $C \geqslant B$ and $B \geqslant A$, then there is some p for which $B = (A, C; p)$, where $(A, C; p)$ is the expression for the uncertain prospect in which A will be realized with probability p, and otherwise, C will be realized.

3. Suppose $B \geqslant A$, and let C be any entity. Then $(B, C; p) \geqslant (A, C; p)$ for any p. In particular, if $A = B$, then the prospect comprising A and C, with probability p for A and 1-p for C, will be just as desirable as the uncertain prospect comprised of B and C with the same probability p for B, and 1-p for C.

---

of sure prospects. The indifference curve (utility isoquant) approach does not assign numbers representing utility to the various sure prospects lying along either the horizontal or the vertical axis and then from these numerical values somehow obtain a number which would order choices among the groups of prospects inside the quadrant enclosed by the axes.

10. This is the method developed by von Neumann and Morgenstern (1944). A very closely analogous method was suggested in 1926 by Ramsey (pp. 166–90). The neatest, but still very difficult, exposition is by Marschak (1950). Still another statement of essentially the same set of axioms is in Friedman and Savage (1948).

4. In the uncertain prospect comprising A and B with probability p for A, it makes no difference what the process is for determining whether A or B is received, just so long as the value of p is not changed. Notationally,

$$\{(A, B;\ p_1), B;\ p_2\} = (A, B;\ p_1\ p_2).$$

To help understand what these axioms signify we give an example of behavior or situation that is inconsistent with each, except that I can think of no totally unreasonable behavior inconsistent with the first axiom. Behavior inconsistent with the second axiom would be the following: suppose C is two bars of candy, B is one bar of candy and A is being shot in the head. Form an uncertain prospect of C and A with probability p for C. If there is no p, however small or close to zero, which could possibly make one indifferent between the uncertain prospect and B, the one bar of candy, he is rejecting axiom 2. Are such situations purely hypothetical?

The third axiom, sometimes called the 'strong independence assumption', has provoked the most vigorous attack and defense. So far no really damaging criticism has been seen. It takes its name from the implication that whatever may be the entity, C, it has no effect on the ranking of the uncertain prospects comprised of A or C and B or C. This kind of independence has nothing whatever to do with independence or complementarity among groups of commodities. Here one does not receive both A and C, or B and C. He gets either A or C in one uncertain prospect, or he gets either B or C in the other. Even if A and C were complements and B and C were substitutes, the ordering would not be affected – this is what the postulate asserts (see Malinvaud, 1952; Manne, 1952; Samuelson, 1952; Wold, 1952).

Axiom 3 is inconsistent with a situation in which the utility of the act of winning itself depends upon the probability of winning, or more generally if probability itself has utility. For example, at Christmas time, one does not want to know what gift his wife is going to give him; he prefers ignorance to any hints or certainty as to what his gift will be. This is a type of love for gambling. Conversely, one may be indifferent to whether he gets roast beef or ham for dinner, but he does want to know which it will be purely for the sake of knowing, not because it will affect any prior or subsequent choices.

Axiom 4 is inconsistent with a concern or difference in feeling about different ways of determining which entity in an uncertain prospect is actually received even though the various systems all have the same probability. For example, suppose an uncertain prospect had a probability of 0·25 for one of the entities. It should make no difference whether the probability is based on the toss of two successive coins with heads required on both, or whether it is based on the draw of one white ball from an urn containing one white and three black. But consider the case of the slot machine. Why are there three wheels with many items on each wheel? Why not one big wheel and why are the spinning wheels in sight? One could instead have a machine with covered wheels. Simply insert a coin, pull the handle and then wait and see what comes out of the machine. Does seeing the wheels go around or seeing how close one came to nearly winning affect the desirability? If observation or knowledge of the number of steps through which the mechanism must pass before reaching the final decision makes any difference, even if the fundamental probability is not subjectively or objectively affected, then axiom 4 is denied.

Implied in the stated axioms is a method for assigning numerical utility values to the various component entities. The method is perhaps explained best by an illustration of the method using the entities of Table 1. Take one entity, A, and one other, say B, as the two base entities. Between these two entities you choose B as preferable to A. Now I *arbitrarily* assign (i.e. choose any numbers I wish so long as the number for B exceeds that for A) the number 2 to B and some smaller number, say 1, to A. You then consider entity C, which you assert you prefer to A and to B. The next step is rather involved; I now form an uncertain prospect consisting of C and A. You are now offered a choice between B, a sure prospect, and the uncertain prospect comprised of 'A or C', where you get A or C depending upon the outcome of a random draw in which the probability of A is *p*, otherwise you get C.

You are asked to, and you do, select a value of *p* which when contained in the uncertain prospect leaves you indifferent between B and the uncertain prospect, 'A or C'.[11] If p were set at nearly zero, you would choose the uncertain prospect, since C is assumed here to be preferred to A; choosing the uncertain prospect would mean that you would almost surely get C. The converse would be the outcome if p were set at nearly 1. Therefore, some place in between there is a value of p which would leave you indifferent between B and the uncertain prospect of 'A or C'. After you indicate that value of p, I assign to the uncertain prospect the same number, 2, I did to B since they are equally preferred by you.

Now we may determine a number for C by the following procedure. Treat the probability p, and its complement $1-p$, as weights to be assigned to the numbers for A and C such that the weighted sum is equal to the number 2, which has been assigned to the uncertain prospect. If, for example, you were indifferent when p was equal to 0·6, then we have the following definitional equation, where we let $U(A)$ stand for the number assigned to A, $U(B)$ for the number assigned to B, and $U(C)$ for the number assigned to C:

$$U(B) = p \times U(A) + (1-p) \times U(C)$$
$$\frac{U(B) - p \times U(A)}{(1-p)} = U(C) = 3·5$$

Using this convenient formula we can assign numbers to the entities D, E, F by appropriately forming uncertain prospects and letting you determine that value of p which produced indifference. These revealed numbers will completely order the entities. If E has a larger number than G, E will be preferred over G. This assignment of numerical value is made without ever comparing E and G directly. Each has been compared with a base entity. A brief pause to reflect will reveal that in this paragraph we have been specifying a convenient method for manipulating, or combining the 'utilities' or 'choice indicator numbers' as well as specifying a process of attaching numbers (utilities) to the entities.

It happens that if we insist on using the simple formula above,

11. It is important to notice that the sure prospect must not be preferred to both of the components of the uncertain prospects, for in that event no probability value would induce indifference.

rather than some more complicated one, the numerical magnitudes assigned by this process are unique up to a linear transformation. For example, suppose that by our process of assigning numbers we obtained the set of numbers in column 3 of Table 1 for entities A to J. Now, instead of assigning 7 and 6 to B and A, had we decided in the first place to assign a value of 7 to entity B and a value of 5 to entity A, we could have obtained instead the sequence in column 7. Column 7 is a linear transformation of column 3. In other words, we may arbitrarily, at our complete discretion, assign numbers to *two* of the entities; once that has been done, our method will determine the remaining unique numbers to be assigned. But all the various *sets* of numbers (utilities) that could have been obtained, depending upon the two initial numerical values, are linear transformations of each other. Thus, our measurement process is unique 'up to' a linear transformation.

If the preceding method of assigning numbers does predict correctly the choice a person actually makes among uncertain prospects, then we have successfully assigned numbers as indicators of choice preferences. We have successfully measured utility and have done it with the convenient computational formula above. Furthermore, every linear transformation of our predicting numbers, 'utilities', would be equally valid – or invalid.

In summary, (a) we have found a *way* to assign numbers; (b) for the way suggested, it so happens that the assigned numbers are unique up to linear transformations; (c) the numbers are convenient to manipulate. All this was implicit in our set of postulates. Before asking whether the numbers predict actual behavior, we shall discuss some side issues.

Diminishing or increasing marginal utility

Recalling our earlier exposition of the mathematical properties of linear transformations, we see that in all of the columns (except 2 and 9 which are not linear transformations of the others) the pattern of *increments* between the numbers assigned to entities is similar. For example, between pair H and I on scale 7 the increment is 4 and between pair I and J it is 2. Moving from H through I to J we have a diminishing increment in the numerical magnitudes assigned. In more familiar terminology we have diminishing marginal utility among H, I and J.[12] Similarly, all the linear transforms of scale 7 will retain this diminishing marginal utility over the range of entities H, I and J. And the suggested way of assigning numbers to the component entities assigns numbers (utilities) which are equivalent up to a linear transformation; that is, any one of the linear transformations will be just as good – for our purposes – as any other of them. By implications we can determine whether there is diminishing or increasing marginal utility.

Maximization of expected utility

By this method of assigning utilities we have ordered all the entities. However, our purpose was more than this; otherwise the uniqueness of the numbers up to a linear transformation would have been an unnecessary restriction. As we know, any monotonic transformation would leave order unaffected. The linear transformation restriction is imposed by our desire to predict choices among uncertain prospects from the utilities and probabilities of the component entities and to do it in a convenient form, viz., according to maximization of expected utility.[13]

Implied in our set of postulates is not only the preceding method of assigning numbers for utilities but also (in fact the two are merely two aspects of the same implication) a method for combining the utilities of the component entities into a utility number for the uncertain prospect.

This method is based on the implication that a person who behaves according to the axioms will choose among uncertain prospects according to expected utility. Expected utility is merely the sum of the weighted utilities of the components of the uncertain prospects where the weights are the probabilities associated with each component. In symbolic form

$$U(A \text{ or } B, p) = pU(A) + (1-p)U(B)$$

12. More strictly we should also have some scale for measuring the amount of H, I and J, either in weight or volume, etc. While the process for assigning these scales also is a complex one, we may pass over it in order to concentrate upon the 'utility' measure.

13. It is not dictated by any nostalgia for diminishing marginal utility.

where the expression $U(A$ or $B, p)$ denotes the utility of the uncertain prospect of entities A and B in which A will be received with probability p, and B otherwise. For example, we could from any one of our measures in Table 1 (except columns 2 and 9) predict what one would do when faced with the following choice: he is presented first with an uncertain prospect containing entities B and C. If he chooses this prospect, his probability of getting B is one-half; otherwise, he will get C. The other uncertain prospect which he is offered contains entities A and E, and if he chooses this prospect his probability of getting E is one-fourth – otherwise, he gets A. Our individual will choose the first prospect, no matter which of our acceptable measures we use. We obtain this prediction by multiplying (weighting) the 'utility' measures of each entity in each prospect by the probability of that entity. If we use the utility measure of column 8, we have for the first prospect $(\frac{1}{2} \times 14) + (\frac{1}{2} \times 10) = 12$, and for the second prospect, $(\frac{3}{4} \times 6) + (\frac{1}{4} \times 22) = 10$. The first prospect has the larger expected 'utility' and will be chosen.[14] How can we justify this procedure of adding the products of probabilities and 'measures of utilities' of entities in an uncertain prospect and calling the result 'the utility' of the uncertain prospect? The axioms of human behavior on which it is based are those which earlier gave us the procedure for 'measuring utility' up to a linear transformation.[15]

Another way to express this implication that a rational

14. If column 9 had been used, the chooser would have been declared indifferent, i.e. the two combinations have equal utility. This is inconsistent with the utility value and predictions derived from the measures in the other columns.

15. If our task is merely to order choice among the uncertain prospects, we could, after obtaining the expected utility of the prospect, obviously perform any monotonic transformation on it without upsetting the order of choices among the uncertain prospects. However, there seems little point in doing so, and there is good reason not to do so. In particular one might wish to predict choices among groups of uncertain prospects where, in each group of prospects, the entities are themselves uncertain prospects. This combination of several uncertain prospects into one resultant uncertain prospect is a consistent operation under the preceding postulates, and the utility measures attached to it will have an implied validity if the utility measures attached to the component prospects, derived in the manner indicated earlier, are valid.

person chooses among uncertain prospects so as to maximize expected utility is in terms of the implied shapes of indifference curves in the plane of *probabilities* of the various components of the uncertain prospects.

Suppose that I am indifferent between receiving a watch and receiving $30. In Figure 1 (a), the horizontal scale measures the probability with which I will get $30 and the vertical axis measures the probability with which I will get the watch. The

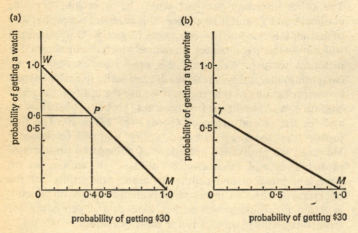

Figure 1

origin represents the point at which I am sure to get nothing. The point W on the vertical axis presents the situation in which I am sure to get the watch and not get the $30. The point M on the horizontal axis represents the situation in which I am sure to get the money and am sure not to get the watch. A straight line drawn from W to M represents all the various uncertain prospects in which I might get the watch or I might get the money, where the probabilities are given by the horizontal distance for the money and the vertical distance for the watch. Thus, the point P represents the prospect in which I will get the watch with probability $\frac{2}{3}$ or otherwise the money (with probability $\frac{1}{3}$). The preceding axioms imply that this straight line is an indifference line or utility isoquant. In other words, the utility isoquant is a *straight* line in the space of probabilities, in this case a straight line from one sure prospect (the watch with certainty) to the other equally sure prospect (the $30 with certainty).

The straight line utility isoquants need not go from sure prospect to sure prospect, as can be seen from a second example. Suppose that I am indifferent between receiving $30 with certainty (sure prospect of $30) and the uncertain prospect in which I will get a particular typewriter with probability 0·6 and nothing with probability 0·4. In Figure 1(b), this latter uncertain prospect is *T* on the vertical axis. Since I am indifferent between this uncertain prospect *T* and the $30 with certainty (point *M*) a straight line, *TM*, is a utility isoquant, and all prospects represented by the points on that line are indifferent to me – have the same utility. In summary, in any such figure, a straight line through any two equally preferred prospects will also contain all prospects (certain and uncertain) that are equally preferred to the first two. This can be generalized into three and more dimensions in which case the straight line becomes a plane surface in three or more dimensions.

The additivity of the simple weighted (by probabilities of the components of the entities) 'utilities' enables us to call this composite utility function a linear utility function. This means that the measure of 'utility' of uncertain prospects (in a probability sense) of entities is the sum of the 'expectation' of the 'utilities' of the component entities; it does not mean that our numerical numbers (measuring utility) assigned to the entities are linear functions of the physical amounts (e.g., weights or counts) of the magnitude entities. Here linearity means that the utility of the uncertain prospects is a linear function of the utility of the component entities; incidentally the utility function is also a linear function of the probabilities of the entities.

4. Validity of measurement

Has anyone ever succeeded in assigning numbers in this way and did the sequence based on past observations predict accurately the preferences revealed by an *actual* choice among new and genuinely available prospects? The only test of the validity of this whole procedure, of which the author is aware, was performed by Mosteller and Nogee (1951).

The essence of the Mosteller–Nogee experiment was to subject approximately twenty Harvard students and National Guardsmen to the type of choices (indicated above on pages 137–8) required to obtain a utility measure for different entities. In the experiment, the entities were small amounts of money, so that what was being sought was a numerical value of utility to be attached to different amounts of money. After obtaining for each individual a utility measure for various amounts of money, Mosteller and Nogee predicted how each individual would choose among a set of uncertain prospects, where the entities were amounts of money with associated probabilities. Although some predictions were incorrect, a sufficiently large majority of correct predictions led Mosteller and Nogee to conclude that the subjects did choose among uncertain prospects on the basis of the utilities of the amounts of money involved and the probabilities associated with each, i.e. according to maximized expected utility. Perhaps the most important lesson of the experiment was the extreme difficulty of making a really good test of the validity of the implications of the axioms about behavior.

Whether this process will predict choice in any other situation is still unverified. But we can expect it to fail where there are pleasures of gambling and risk taking, possibly a large class of situations. Pleasures of gambling refers not to the advantages that incur from the possibility of receiving large gains, but rather to the pleasure of the act of gambling or act of taking an extra risk itself. There may be an exhilaration accompanying sheer chance taking or winning *per se* as distinct from the utility of the amount won. Even worse, the preference pattern may change with experience.

5. Utility of income

We can conclude our general exposition with the observation that although the preceding discussion has referred to 'entities' we could have always been thinking of different amounts of income or wealth. The reason we did not was that we wanted to emphasize the generality of the choice problem and to emphasize that utility measures are essentially nothing but choice indicators. However, it is useful to consider the utility of income. How do the numerical values (utilities) assigned by the preceding method vary as income varies? Now this apparently sensible question is ambiguous, even after our preceding discussion which we presume to have eliminated confusion about the meaning of 'measurability of utility'. For the question still remains as to whether the utility measure assumes (a) a utility curve that stays put and along which one can move up and down as income varies; or (b) a utility curve whose shape is definable only on the basis of the current income as a reference point for change in levels of income. The former interpretation emphasizes dependence of utility on levels of income, while the latter emphasizes the dependence of utility on the changes in income around one's present position.

The most common type of utility curve has been one whose shape and position is independent of the particular income actually being realized at the time the curve of utility of income is constructed. For example, Friedman and Savage (1948) draw a utility curve dependent primarily upon levels of income rather than upon changes in income, and it is presumed that individuals choose as if they were moving along that curve. The generic shape of the curve postulated by Friedman and Savage is shown in Figure 2.[16] This shape is supposed to explain the presence of both gambling and insurance. How does it do this?

Reference back to our method of predicting choices among uncertain prospects reminds us that choices will be made so as to maximize expected utility. A graphic interpretation is very simple. In Figure 2, let the income position now existing be A; let the individual be faced with a choice of staying where he is, or of choosing the uncertain prospect of moving to income position B with probability 0·999 or of moving to income position C with probability 0·001. Position A represents paying fire insurance, while positions C and B form the uncertain prospect where C is the position if a fire occurs with no insurance and B is the position if no fire occurs with no insurance.

16. The utility curve is unique up to a linear transformation.

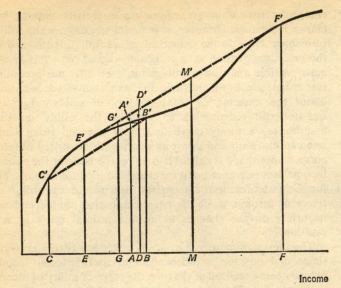

Income

Figure 2

Will he choose the uncertain prospect or the sure position A?
The basis for the choice as implied in our postulates can be
described graphically as follows: from point B' draw a straight
line to point C'. This straight line gives the expected utility of all
uncertain prospects of the incomes B and C as the probability
attached to C varies from zero to one. The point on this straight
line yielding the expected utility of our uncertain prospect can
be found by computing the expected *income*, D, and then rising
vertically to point D' on the straight line $B'C'$. The ordinate
DD' is the expected utility of the uncertain prospect. If the length
of DD' is less than AA', as it is in our example, where AA'
denotes the utility of the income after taking insurance, then the
person will choose the insurance and conversely.

It is apparent that if the utility curve were always convex as in
the first and last part of the curve in Figure 2, a person would
never choose an uncertain prospect whose expected income was
no greater than the insured income position. And if the curve
were concave, a person would always choose the uncertain

prospect where the expected income was at least equal to the present insured position.

If the curve has the shape postulated by Friedman and Savage, it is possible to explain why a person will take out insurance and will at the same time engage in a gamble. To see how the latter is possible, suppose a person were at position A. At the same time that he might be willing to take out insurance he may also be willing to gamble by choosing an uncertain prospect of ending up at E or F, despite its lower expected income at G, because the expected utility GG' of the uncertain prospect is larger than the utility AA' of position A. Friedman and Savage tentatively attempt to lend some plausibility to this shape of utility curve by conjecturing that economic society may be divisible into two general income level classes, the lower one being characterized by the first convex part of the curve and the higher one by the upper convex section. An intermediate group is in the concave section.

Markowitz (1952) has pointed out certain unusual implications of the Friedman–Savage hypothesis. A person at the point M would take a fair bet with a chance to get to F. This seems unlikely to be verified by actual behavior. Secondly, if a person is at a position a little below F, he will not want insurance against small probabilities of large losses. Further, any person with income greater than F will never engage in any fair bet. But wealthy people do gamble. Is it solely the love of risk taking? To overcome these objections, Markowitz postulates that utility is related to *changes* in the level of income and that 'the utility function' has three inflection points. The middle one is at the person's 'customary' income level, which except in cases of recent windfall gains and losses is the present income. The income interval between the inflection points is a non-decreasing function of income. The curve is monotonically increasing but bounded; it is at first concave, then convex, then concave and finally convex.

Markowitz's hypothesis is consistent with the existence of both 'fair' (or slightly 'unfair') insurance and lotteries. The same individual will both insure and gamble. The hypothesis implies the same behavior whether one is poor or rich.

Markowitz recognizes that until an unambiguous procedure

is discovered for determining when and to what extent current income deviates from customary income, the hypothesis will remain essentially nonverifiable because it is not capable of denying any observed behavior. The Markowitz hypothesis reveals perhaps more forcefully than the Friedman–Savage hypothesis, that utility has no meaning as an indicator of a level of utility. Utility has meaning only for changes in situations. Thus while I might choose to receive an increase in income rather than no increase, there is no implication that after I have received it for a while I remain on a higher utility base – however interpreted – than formerly. It may be the getting or losing, the rising or the falling that counts rather than the actual realized position. In any event Markowitz's hypothesis contains no implications about anything other than changes in income.

Our survey is now completed. We started with developments after the Slutsky, Hicks, Allen utility position in which utility is measured up to monotone transformations only. This meant exactly no more and no less than that utility is ordinal. In other words, the numerical size of the increments in the numbers in any one measure (column of numbers in Table 1) is without meaning. Only their signs have significance. Utility translation: marginal utility has meaning only in being positive or negative but the numerical value is meaningless, i.e. *diminishing* or *increasing* marginal utility is completely arbitrary since one can get either by using the appropriate column.[17]

The first post-war development was the von Neumann and Morgenstern axioms which implied measurability utility up to a linear transformation, thus reintroducing diminishing or increasing marginal utility,[18] and which also implied a hypothesis or maxim about rational behavior. This was followed by the Friedman and Savage article (1948) and Marschak's paper (1950). These papers are essentially identical in their postulates and propositions although the presentation and exposition are

17. It is a simple task – here left to the reader – to find the current textbooks and articles – which will be left unnamed – stating that the indifference curve analysis dispenses with the concept of utility or marginal utility. Actually it dispenses only with *diminishing* or *increasing* marginal utility.

18. Incidentally, the *Theory of Games* of von Neumann and Morgenstern is completely independent of their utility discussion.

so different that each contributes to an understanding of the other. The Friedman and Savage paper, however, contains an added element: they attempt to prophesy the shape of the curve of utility of income that would be most commonly revealed by this measurement process. Mosteller and Nogee (1951) then made a unique contribution in really trying to verify the validity and applicability of the postulates. Most recently, Markowitz (1952) criticized the Friedman and Savage conjecture about the shape of utility of income curve, with his own conjecture about its dependence upon income changes. And that is about where matters stand now.

A moral of our survey is that to say simply that something is, or is not, measurable is to say nothing. The relevant problems are: (a) can numerical values be associated with entities and then be combined according to some rules so as to predict choices in stipulated types of situations, and (b) what are the transformations that can be made upon the initially assigned set of numerical values without losing their predictive powers (validity)? As we have seen, the currently proposed axioms imply measurability up to a linear transformation. Choices among uncertain prospects are predicted by a simple probability-weighted sum of the utilities assigned to the components of the uncertain prospect, specifically from the 'expected utility'.

And now to provide emotional zest to the reader's intellectual activity the following test is offered. Imagine that today is your birthday; a friend presents you with a choice among three lotteries. Lottery A consists of a barrel of 2000 tickets of which two are marked $1000 and the rest are blanks. Lottery B consists of another barrel of 2000 tickets of which twenty are marked $100 and the rest are blanks. Lottery C consists of a barrel of 2000 tickets of which one is marked $1000 and ten are marked $100. From the chosen barrel one ticket will be drawn at random and you will win the amount printed on the ticket. Which barrel would you choose? Remember there is no cost to you, this is a free gift opportunity. In barrel A the win of $1000 has probability 0·001 and the probability of getting nothing is 0·999; in barrel B the probability of winning $100 is 0·01 and getting nothing has probability 0·99; in barrel C $1000 has probability 0·0005, $100 has probability 0·005 and winning nothing has probability 0·9945. For each barrel the mathematical expectation is $1. The reader is urged to seriously consider and to make a choice. Only after making his choice should he read the footnote.[19]

Conclusion

1. Some readers may be jumping to the conclusion that we really can use *diminishing* or *increasing* marginal utility and that the 'indifference curve' or 'utility isoquant' technique has been superfluous after all. This is a dangerous conclusion. The 'indifference curve' technique is more general in not requiring measurability of utility up to a linear transformation. But its greatest virtue is that unlike the earlier 'partial' analysis of demand of a single commodity the indifference curve analysis by using an extra dimension facilitates intercommodity analyses – the heart of price analyses. But does the more 'precise' type

19. Only the reader who chose C should continue, for his choice has revealed irrationality or denial of the axioms. This can be shown easily. He states he prefers C to A and to B. First, suppose he is indifferent between A and B; he doesn't care whether his friend chooses to give him A or B just so long as he gets one or the other. Nor does he care how his friend decides which to give. In particular if his friend tosses a coin and gives A if heads come up, otherwise B, he is still indifferent. This being so, a fifty/fifty chance to get A or B is equivalent to C, as one can see by realizing that C is really equivalent to a 0·5 probability of getting A and a 0·5 probability of getting B. Thus if A and B are indifferent there is no reason for choosing C.

Second, the reader choosing C may have preferred A over B. We proceed as follows. Increase the prize in B until our new B, call it B′, is now indifferent with A. Form the uncertain prospect of A and B′ with probability of 0·5 for A. This is better than C since C is nothing but an uncertain prospect composed of A and the old B, with probability of 0·5 for A. Where does this leave us? This says that the new uncertain prospect must be preferred to C. But since the new uncertain prospect is composed of 0·5 probability for A and 0·5 for B′, the chooser of C must be indifferent between the uncertain prospect and A. (In axiom 3 let A and B be indifferent, and let C be identically the same thing as A. In other words, if the two entities in the uncertain prospect are equally preferred, then the uncertain prospect is indifferent to one of the entities with certainty.) The upshot is that A is just as desired as the new uncertain prospect which is better than C. Thus A is preferred to C, but the chooser of C denied this. Why? Either he understood and accepted the axioms and was irrational in making a snap judgement, or else he really did not accept the axioms. He may now privately choose his own escape. This example is due to Harry Markowitz.

of measurement give us more than the ordinal measurement gives? Yes. As we have seen, measurability 'up to a linear transform' both implies and is implied by the possibility of predicting choices among uncertain prospects, the universal situation.

2. Nothing in the rehabilitation of measurable utility – or choice-indicating numbers – enables us to predict choices among groups of sure prospects. The 'utility' of a group of sure prospects is not dependent on *only* the utility (assigned number) of the *entities* in the combination. It is dependent upon the particular *combination of entities*, i.e. we do not postulate that the utility of one sure element in a group of sure things is independent of what other entities are included. We think it obviously would not lead to valid predictions of actual choices. Therefore, it must be realized that nothing said so far means that we could measure the total utility of a market basket of different entities by merely adding up the utilities of the individual component entities. No method for aggregating the utilities of the component entities for this purpose has been found; therefore, for this purpose we have to say that utility is not measurable.

3. Is the present discussion more appropriate for a journal in psychology or sociology? If economists analyse the behavior of a system of interacting individuals operating in field of action – called the economic sphere – by building up properties of the system from the behavior aspects of the individuals composing the system, then the economists must have some rationale of behavior applicable to the individuals. An alternative approach is to consider the whole system of individuals and detect predictable properties of the system. The classic example of this distinction is in physics. One approach postulates certain laws describing the behavior of individual molecules, or atom particles, while the other starts with laws describing the observable phenomena of masses of molecules. Apparently, most economists have relied upon the former approach, the building up from individuals – sometimes referred to as the aggregation of microeconomic analysis into macroeconomic analysis. On the other hand, those who are skeptical of our

ability to build from individual behavior find their haven in postulates describing mass behavior. The current utility analyses aid the former approach.

4. The expression 'utility' is common in welfare theory. For demand theory and the theory of prediction of choices made by individuals, measurability of the quantity (called 'utility') permits us to make verifiable statements about individual behavior, but there is as yet no such happy development in welfare theory. 'Measurability up to a linear transformation' does not provide any theorems for welfare theory beyond those derivable from ordinality. I mention this in order to forestall temptations to assume the contrary. The social welfare function as synthesized by Hicks and Scitovsky, for example, does not require the 'utility' (choice-ordering numbers) of each individual to be measurable up to a linear transformation. It is sufficient that the individual's utility be measurable up to a monotone transformation – or, in other words, that it have merely ordinal properties. Ordinal utility is adequate in this case because orderings are made of positions or states in which, as between the two states compared, everyone is better off in one state than in the other. The welfare function does not enable a ranking of two states in one of which some people are worse off.[20] This would require an entirely different kind of measure of utility for each person because of the necessity of making interpersonal aggregations of utilities. As yet no one has proposed a social welfare function acceptable for this purpose, not has anyone discovered how, even in principle, to measure utility beyond the linear transformation. Even more important, the various elements in the concept of welfare (as distinct from utility) have not been adequately specified. In effect the utility whose measurement is discussed in this paper has literally nothing to do with individual, social or group welfare, whatever the latter may be supposed to mean.

5. A brief *obiter dictum* on interpersonal utility comparisons may be appropriate. Sometimes it is said that interpersonal

20. Absolutely nothing is implied about taxation. For example, justification of progressive income taxation by means of utility analysis remains impossible. The best demonstration of this is still Fagan (1938).

utility comparisons are possible since we are constantly declaring that individual A is better off than individual B. For example, 'a rich man is better off than a poor man'. But is this really an interpersonal utility comparison? Is it not rather a statement by the declarer that he would prefer to be in the rich man's position rather than in the poor man's? It does not say that the rich *man* is happier or has more 'utility' than the poor *man*. Even if the rich man has a perpetual smile and declares himself to be truly happy and the poor man admits he is sorrowful, how do we know that the rich *man* is happier than the poor *man*, even though both men prefer being richer to being poorer? If I were able to experience the totality of the poor man's situation and the rich man's, and preferred the rich man's, it would not constitute an interpersonal comparison; rather it would be an *intrapersonal*, intersituation comparison.

It is hoped that the reader now has at his command enough familiarity with the meanings of measurability to be able to interpret and evaluate the blossoming literature on utility and welfare, and that this exposition has made it clear that welfare analysis gains nothing from the current analysis, and conversely.

References

FAGAN, E. D. (1938), 'Recent and contemporary theories of progressive taxation', *J. polit. Econ.*, vol. 46, pp. 457–98.
FRIEDMAN, M., and SAVAGE, L. J. (1948), 'The utility analysis of choices involving risk', *J. polit. Econ.*, vol. 56, pp. 279–304.
GEORGESCU-ROEGEN, N. (1950), 'The theory of choice and the constancy of economic laws', *Quart. J. Econ.*, vol. 64, pp. 125–38.
MALINVAUD, E. (1952), 'Note on Neumann–Morgenstern's strong independence axiom', *Econometrica*, vol. 20, pp. 661–79.
MANNE, A. S. (1952), 'The strong independence assumption – gasoline blends and probability mixtures', *Econometrica*, vol. 20, pp. 665–8.
MARKOWITZ, H. (1952), 'The utility of wealth', *J. polit. Econ.*, vol. 60, pp. 151–8.
MARSCHAK, J. (1950), 'Rational behavior, uncertain prospects and measurable utility', *Econometrica*, vol. 18, pp. 111–41.
MARSCHAK, J. (1951), 'Why "should" statisticians and businessmen maximize "moral expectation"?', *Proceedings, 2nd Berkeley Symposium on Mathematical Statistics and Probability*, University of California Press, pp. 493–506.
MOSTELLER, F., and NOGEE, P. (1951), 'An experimental measurement of utility', *J. polit. Econ.*, vol. 59, pp. 371–404.

RAMSEY, F. (1926), *The Foundations of Mathematics and Other Logical Essays*, Humanities Press, 1950.

SAMUELSON, P. (1952), 'Probability, utility and the independence axiom', *Econometrica*, vol. 20, pp. 670–78.

VON NEUMANN, J., and MORGENSTERN, P. (1944), *The Theory of Games and Economic Behavior*, Princeton University Press.

WOLD, H. O. A. (1952), 'Ordinal preferences or cardinal utility?' *Econometrica*, vol. 20, pp. 661–3.

6 Richard Stone

A Dynamic Model of Demand

Richard Stone, 'A dynamic model of demand', in *Mathematics in the Social Sciences and Other Essays*, Chapman & Hall, 1966, pp. 179–89. (First published in *Przeglad Statystyczny*, vol. 7, 1960, no. 3.)

1. Introduction

In any empirical science, theory must lead to statements about the actual world which are not merely truisms, and these statements can be tested by comparing them with actual observations. For example, in its simplest form the theory of consumers' behaviour suggests that the amount demanded of any commodity will depend, given the tastes and habits of consumers, largely on their income and the structure of relative prices. Attempts to test this theory by the analysis of time series and of cross-section data, as in Stone *et al.* (1954), prove abundantly that it is a good starting point and, indeed, that many important conclusions about the behaviour of consumers can be established on this comparatively simple basis.

But the simplest models, though easy to work with, suffer from their very simplicity. It is our task as scientists to explain the phenomena we study and to do so in as simple terms as we can. But we must always be on our guard against oversimplification and so when we have got a model which provides a good approximation in many situations we must try to improve it so that it extends to a still wider range of situations; that is, it is more general. This process of going from simple models (first approximations) to more general ones (second and later approximations) is in fact the only way in which we can gain and extend useful knowledge. To refuse to consider simple models in a new subject because, after all, the world is a very complicated place, is sheer nihilism and if persisted in effectively brings any branch of science to a standstill.

The particular generalization which I shall consider in this paper is concerned with the adaptation of consumers to changing circumstances. The simple models of consumers' behaviour are static, which means that consumers are supposed to adjust themselves to changing circumstances instantaneously and do not become involved in processes of adjustment that take time. This is in many cases a reasonable assumption, particularly when it is remembered that our observations relate to years or quarters and not to days or hours. But in some cases we may believe that the period of adjustment is important and in these we should like a model which would enable us to take into account the rate at which consumers try to adjust themselves to changing circumstances.

In the next section a dynamic model is given in terms of the demand for a durable good. In the third section various generalizations of this model are given from which it is clear that it can easily be adapted to an analysis of the demand for perishable goods and indeed can provide a basis for the simultaneous analysis of the whole structure of consumption. Section 4 relates to various problems of calculation and section 5 exemplifies the practical working of the model in terms of applications that have already been made. The paper ends with a brief concluding section.

2. A dynamic model of the demand for a durable good

The following account relates to a dynamic model which Mr Rowe and I put forward (1957) though we had previously used a very similar model in studying the aggregate consumption function (1956). For the moment I shall concentrate on the economics of the model and leave questions of calculation and estimation until later.

Let q denote the quantity of some durable good which is bought in some period, say a year. These purchases all go either to maintaining the stock of the good existing at the beginning of the year or to increasing that stock. If we denote the use of the year (consumption) by u and the net addition to the stock by v, then

$$q \equiv u + v. \tag{1}$$

The next equation provides a definition of consumption, u. It is assumed that the good lasts indefinitely but that each year it depreciates on account of use according to a reducing-balance depreciation formula. For example, suppose that the annual depreciation rate is 20 per cent. Then out of 100 new units the equivalent of 20 will be used up in the first year and the corresponding stock at the end of that year will be equivalent to 80 new units. The equivalent of 16 will be used up in the second year and the stock at the end of that year will be equivalent to 64 new units. In the third year, the use will be 12·8 units and the closing stock will be 51·2 units and so on indefinitely. Thus it is assumed that goods gradually wear out through use but are never actually scrapped. It is perfectly possible to allow for scrapping, as will be seen below, but this involves a knowledge of the survival characteristics of the good which is frequently not available.

If s denotes the stock at the beginning of the year, measured in the equivalent number of new units, and if $1/n$ is the rate of depreciation, then evidently the consumption of the year is at least as large as s/n. But in fact it is larger because some use is obtained from the purchases of the year, q. If these purchases were entirely concentrated at the beginning of the year, then the corresponding use would be q/n but in fact they are spread in some way through the year and so the use is equal to q/m where $m \geqslant n$. Thus

$$u \equiv \frac{s}{n} + \frac{q}{m}. \qquad\qquad 2$$

If it is assumed that purchases are spread evenly through the year then we shall see that m is related to n in quite a simple way.

These relationships are truisms in the sense that we choose to define our variables so that they hold in all circumstances. The next relationship is not a truism but is a hypothesis about consumers' behaviour. It is based on the concept of an equilibrium stock, s^* say, which if attained in any given situation would leave consumers content, in the sense that they would wish neither to increase not to diminish it. If s^* is different from s it is assumed that consumers will take steps to bring the two variables into equality, increasing their stock if $s^* > s$ and diminishing it if $s^* < s$. It is assumed that in general they cannot close the gap immediately and that what they actually do is to close a proportion of it, r say, in a period. Thus

$$v = r(s^* - s). \qquad\qquad 3$$

Now s^* is not directly observable whereas all the other variables are either observable or can be calculated from the definitions. It is assumed therefore that s^* depends on income and the price structure: for example, we might have

$$s^* = \alpha + \beta\left(\frac{\mu}{\pi}\right) + \gamma\left(\frac{p}{\pi}\right) \qquad\qquad 4$$

where μ is money income, p is the price of the good and π is an index of all other goods and services bought by consumers. Unless the good (or group of goods) being analysed is important in the consumers' total budget, π will usually be indistinguishable from an index of retail prices.

By combining **1**, **2** and **3** we can express purchases and consumption in terms of equilibrium stocks and actual stocks. Thus

$$q = k\{rns^* + (1 - rn)s\} \qquad\qquad 5$$

where $k \equiv m/n(m-1)$; and

$$u = k\{r^*s^* + (1 - r^*)s\} \qquad\qquad 6$$

where $r^* \equiv rn/m$. Thus both purchases and consumption are proportional to certain weighted averages of actual and equilibrium stocks. These variables, q and u, can be expressed in terms of observable variables by substituting for s^* from **4** into **5** and **6**.

We can now see that this model is indeed a generalization of the static model. For if $rn = 1$ the second term on the right-hand side of **5** disappears and q is proportional to s^*, that is to say it depends in a static way on income and the price structure.

But there are now two additional possibilities. First, $rn < 1$; in this case the opening stock s, exerts a positive influence on q. Second, $rn > 1$; in this case s exerts a negative influence on q. The interpretation of these cases will be clear when we have examined the expressions for long- and short-term responses.

The ultimate level of purchases, $q*$ say, associated with a given level of $s*$ is equal to the level of consumption, $u* = ks*$ say, which is associated with $s*$ since, when $s = s*$, $v = 0$. So the long-term partial derivative of purchases with respect to income is

$$\frac{\partial q*}{\partial \mu} = \frac{k\beta}{\pi} \qquad\qquad 7$$

while the corresponding short-term derivative can be seen from **5** to be

$$\frac{\partial q}{d\mu} = \frac{rnk\beta}{\pi} \qquad\qquad 8$$

So the ratio of the short- to the long-term response is

$$\frac{\partial q}{\partial q*} = rn. \qquad\qquad 9$$

Thus if $rn > 1$ the immediate effect of a change in $s*$ is greater than the long-term effect, and conversely if $rn < 1$. So if the ratio of the rate of adjustment to the rate of depreciation is greater than one, a change in $s*$ will have a larger effect immediately than in the long run. The reason is that, given n, consumers are in this case trying to adjust quickly and so add rapidly to their stocks with the consequence that they buy more in the short run that will be ultimately needed merely to maintain their new stocks. In the converse case they will adjust slowly, starting by buying very little and ultimately increasing their purchases to the level needed to maintain their new level of stocks.

Clearly there is no difficulty in restating these results in terms of elasticities.

It is frequently convenient in demand analysis to express the static equation in a log-linear rather than a simple linear form. In this case **4** takes the form

$$s* = \alpha \left(\frac{\mu}{\pi}\right)^{\beta} \left(\frac{p}{\pi}\right)^{\gamma}, \qquad\qquad 10$$

in which case it is convenient to change **3** to

$$v = \frac{ms}{n}\left[\left(\frac{s^*}{s}\right)^{r^*} - 1\right],$$ **11**

from which it follows that

$$u = ks^{*r^*}s^{1-r^*}$$ **12**

and

$$q = kms^{*r^*}s^{1-r^*} - \frac{ms}{n}.$$ **13**

By comparing **6** and **12** we see that a geometric average has replaced an arithmetic average, and comparing **5** with **13** we see that the expression for q is a little more complicated than in the linear case.

3. Generalizations

A number of generalizations follow easily from what has been said in the last section; let us look at some of these.

The case of perishable goods

These goods correspond to the limiting case in which $n \to 1$. It is shown in Stone and Rowe (1957) that

$$\lim_{n \to 1} ks = E^{-1}q$$ **14**

where E is an operator such that $E^{-\theta}q_t \equiv q_{t-\theta}$. Thus, for example, ks in **5** and **6** is replaced by $E^{-1}q$, that is by the purchases of the preceding period.

Time lags in the determining variables

In **4** it is assumed that s^* is determined by the current value of income and the price structure. In practice consumers may adjust in terms of some average of past incomes or even of some kind of income projection. Such considerations may easily be incorporated in the model. Thus let $\mu/\pi \equiv \rho$. Then in place of p in **4** we might substitute

$$\rho^* \equiv \eta\rho + (1-\eta)E^{-1}\rho.$$ **15**

If we use **3** as an estimating equation the regression estimators would relate to $r\alpha$, $r\beta\eta$, $r\beta(1-\eta)$, $r\gamma$ and r, from which we could estimate $\beta\eta$ and $\beta(1-\eta)$ and therefore β and so η.

A variable rate of adjustment

Again assume, as will normally be the case, that **3** is used as an estimating equation. Since r is a factor of the right-hand side of **3**, it follows that, if x is an observable variable, we can make r a function of x by replacing s^* and s by xs^* and xs. Two examples of this useful device may be given.

First, suppose we wish to allow for hire-purchase conditions, that is to say the possibility of paying only a proportion, ξ say, of the purchase price at the time of purchase plus a number of regular instalments spread over τ time periods. Then we might define hire-purchase conditions x, as

$$x \equiv \xi + \frac{1-\xi}{\tau}. \qquad\qquad 16$$

If we wished to allow x to influence the equilibrium stock we could do this by dividing p/π in **4** into two parts: xp/π and $(1-x)p/\pi$ and treating these as separate variables. If we wished to allow x to influence the rate of adjustment we could replace r by r^{**}/x where r^{**} is a constant. From **3** it follows that in this case

$$xv = r^{**}(s^*-s) \qquad\qquad 17$$

provides a satisfactory estimating equation. In practice, to keep **3** and **17** comparable, it is convenient to take $xv/\bar{x}$, where $\bar{x}$ is the mean value of x, as the dependent variable.

Second, we may have to analyse the demand for a comparatively new commodity which consumers are only gradually learning to appreciate. In this case consumers are finding out the potentialities of the good and only a limited number, the pioneers, are seriously in the market. Accordingly the average rate of adjustment will be low because even if the pioneers are adjusting in the way that the whole community will eventually come to adopt, they are, initially, only a small, though growing part of the whole consuming public. In this case we might wish to make the rate of adjustment dependent on the proportion of the population which already possessed the new good.

Allowance for scrapping

In section 2 it was assumed that durable goods last for ever but are subject to a continuous depreciation through use so that the contribution of an individual unit to the total stock follows, through time, an exponential decay curve. This is, in a sense, a limiting assumption. We might equally well have assumed that a good does not depreciate at all through use; that is an old good is just as satisfactory as a new one except for the fact that it is more likely to fall to pieces and so be unusable. The reason why this alternative assumption was not made in section 2 is that to make use of it we need to know the specific mortality rate of goods in each year of their life. Typically we do not have this information but if we had it we could proceed as follows.

Let λ denote the mortality rate in the period in which the good is bought and let l denote a vector of mortality rates for goods bought last year, the year before that and so on. Then we might define consumption as

$$u \equiv l's + \lambda q, \qquad\qquad 18$$

where s denotes a vector of stocks of different ages existing at the beginning of the period. If 2 is replaced by 18 we have what may be called a replacement model rather than a depreciation model. But now we need not two parameters, m and n, but a larger number, λ and l, depending on the survival characteristics of the good. Typically, survival rates will follow, approximately, a logistic decay curve; that is to say in the early years of life most units will survive, in middle life there will be a sharp decline in survival rates from year to year, and finally survival rates will tend to zero.

In fact we can combine the depreciation and replacement models so as to give a better approximation to reality. In this case we define consumption as follows. In the first place it is equal to the amount scrapped out of current purchases plus the depreciation of the period on the amount bought in the period which survives. This component is $\{\lambda+(1-\lambda)/m\}q$. From a written-down stock at the beginning of the period, which we might denote by $\hat{w}s$ (w being a vector which embodies any depreciation formula), the total mortality in the year is $l'\hat{w}s$. The depreciation of the year on units in the written-down value of the stock at the beginning of the year is $d'(I-\hat{I})\hat{w}s$, where I denotes the unit matrix. So this component is $l'\hat{w}s+d'(I-\hat{I})\hat{w}s$. Thus for this model

$$u \equiv \{l'+d'(I-\hat{I})\}\hat{w}s+\{\lambda+\delta(1-\lambda)\}q, \qquad\qquad 19$$

where $\delta \equiv 1/m$. Consideration will show that 19 generalizes the models based on 2 and 18.

A system of demand relationships

We have so far considered a single demand equation but for some purposes we may wish to consider a consistent system of demand relationships. A means of doing this is set out in Stone (1954). This system can be made dynamic by allowing the basic equation to determine equilibrium consumption rather than actual consumption. The characteristics of this system, which will not be described here, can be found in Stone and Croft-Murray (1959).

The aggregate consumption function

The relationship of consumers' total expenditure to their income is important for many purposes of economic policy. An attempt to investigate it with the help of an early version of the system just mentioned is given in Stone and Rowe (1956, parts 1 and 2).

A generalization of the input–output model of Leontief

The dynamic system just referred to generalizes the input–output model of Leontief since, in principle, it could be applied to every sector of a Leontief input–output matrix. If this were done every sector would respond to the price structure as well as to its revenue. Some thoughts on such a model are contained in Stone (1955). But the estimation procedure used there is inefficient and for the proper procedure reference should be made to Briggs (1957).

4. Calculations

The model described in this paper gives rise to numerous problems of calculation and estimation which must be faced if it is to be applied. Let us look at some of these.

The calculation of stocks from past purchases

If we look at equations **1** and **2** we see that there are six symbols q, u, v, s, n and m. Let us assume that n is given; we shall see shortly that this enables us to calculate m. In addition we may assume that q is given. Thus we have three unknowns, u, v and s, and only two equations. So we need a third equation before the unknowns can be calculated.

This equation is an identity connecting stocks and flows, namely

$$Es \equiv s+v, \qquad\qquad 20$$

that is, stocks at the end of the year equal stocks at the beginning plus net investments in the year. From **1**, **2** and **20**

$$Es \equiv s+q-u$$
$$\equiv \left(\frac{n-1}{n}\right)s+\left(\frac{m-1}{m}\right)q$$
$$\equiv as+bq \qquad\qquad 21$$

say, where $a \equiv (n-1)/n$ and $b \equiv (m-1)/m$. If **21** is multiplied by the operator E^{-1} and if a continuous substitution is made for $E^{-\theta}s$, $\theta = 1, 2, \ldots$, there results

$$s \equiv \frac{b}{a}\sum_{\theta=1}^{\infty} a^{\theta}E^{-\theta}q$$

$$\equiv \frac{b}{a}\sum_{\theta=1}^{\tau} a^{\theta}E^{-\theta}q + a^{\tau}E^{-\tau}s \qquad\qquad 22$$

if the calculation has to be started with an assumed stock, $E^{-\tau}s$, available τ time periods ago.

The relationship of m to n

If it is assumed that purchases are spread evenly through each period, then the relationship of m to n is given in Stone and Rowe (1957). In a slightly different form, this may be written as

$$m = \frac{\sum_{\theta=1}^{\infty} (1/\theta n^{\theta})}{\sum_{\theta=2}^{\infty} (1/\theta n^{\theta})}. \qquad 23$$

This expression converges rapidly to the value $2n - \frac{1}{3}$ as n increases.

The time taken for a good to depreciate through use to 10 per cent of its original amount

Let n^* denote the number of time periods that must elapse before a good with depreciation rate $1/n$ is 90 per cent depreciated. Then, as shown in Stone and Rowe (1957),

$$n^* = \frac{2\cdot3}{\sum_{\theta=1}^{\infty} (1/\theta n^{\theta})}$$

$$= 2\cdot3n - 1\cdot2 \qquad 24$$

approximately. Thus for example if $n = 5$, $n^* = 10\cdot3$ approximately.

Internal estimates of 1/n

It has been shown by Nerlove (1960) that the depreciation rate can be estimated from the observations. The procedure is as follows. By combining 1, 2 and 20 we see that

$$q = \frac{m-1}{m}\left[Es - \left(\frac{n-1}{n}\right)s \right] \qquad 25$$

$$= k\{1 + (n-1)\Delta\}Es.$$

where $\Delta \equiv 1 - E^{-1}$. Thus

$$\Delta q = k\{1 + (n-1)\Delta\}v \qquad 26$$

$$= k\Omega v$$

say. Thus, by applying the transformation Ω to the variables on which s^* depends, we obtain a suitable estimating equation. By trying different values of n we can then select that one which gives the highest correlation in the regression equation. Some results will be found in Stone and Rowe (1960).

The combination of data with different time units

We may wish to combine data with different time units; for example in Britain we have quarterly data for the post-war period but only annual data for the pre-war period. If we want to combine these observations we have to solve an aggregation problem. This is done for a linear model in Stone and Rowe (1957). This solution provides a linear approximation for non-linear models.

5. Applications

It may be of interest to indicate some of the results obtained from the model discussed in this paper.

Analyses for individual groups of durable goods

In Stone and Rowe (1957) analyses were given for clothing and for household durable goods. These were carried out for the inter-war period and for it and the post-war years to 1955 combined. A log-linear model was used and variables were transformed to first differences. The calculations were carried out with several different values of the depreciation rate. The highest correlations were obtained with $n = 1$ for clothing and $n = 4$ for household durable goods. When short- and long-term elasticities were calculated it was found that the long-term income elasticities were very similar to those obtained from household budgets collected in 1937–9. In other respects the basic features of demand responses appeared quite similar in the inter-war and post-war periods.

More recently a further analysis has been made of the two major categories of household durable goods: furniture and floor coverings, and radio and electrical goods. In each case it was assumed that $n = 4$. Quarterly data for the years 1953 through 1958 were used and the model was a linear one exactly as set out in this paper. The main purpose of these new analyses was to test the importance of hire-purchase in the ways suggested in the earlier part of this paper. The main results can be summarized in the following table.

From this table we see that income is a very important influence both in the short and long run whereas price has very little influence for the group as a whole. We also see that by introducing hire-purchase we improve the analysis but that having introduced it in one way or the other we cannot easily decide which formulation is the better. The main effect of introducing hire-purchase in either way is to reduce the high

Table 1 Demand Elasticities for Furniture and Floor Coverings, United Kingdom, 1953–8

| | Income elasticities | | Price elasticities | | Proportion of the variance of purchases accounted for |
	Short-term	Long-term	Short-term	Long-term	
No allowance for hire-purchase	4·70	1·90	0·05	0·02	0·86
Hire-purchase affecting equilibrium stock	3·01	2·13	−0·26	−0·18	0·92
Hire-purchase affecting the rate of adjustment	3·51	2·03	0·14	0·08	0·93
Hire-purchase affecting both	2·82	2·11	−0·08	−0·06	0·94

value of the short-term income elasticity which appears if it is left out. It is interesting to note that according to the budget investigations of 1937–9 the income elasticity for this group was about 2·4.

Comparison of pre-war and post-war demand structures

In Stone and Rowe (1958) a number of analyses are given for both the inter-war and post-war periods. It is found that in many cases the structural parameters are quite close. It appears to be generally true that the rate of adjustment is relatively low (of the order of 0·3 in annual terms) for durable goods and relatively high (of the order of 1 in annual terms) for perishable goods. In these analyses a successful attempt was made to trace the influence of temperature and rainfall on the demand for certain goods.

Dynamic systems of demand relationships

In Stone and Croft-Murray (1959) an account is given of the first attempt to work with a complete dynamic system of relationships. The results are encouraging and in fact give quite a good account of observed variations in the seven commodity groups among which personal consumption is subdivided. At the time when this study was made it was not possible to handle more than seven commodity groups and the two-stage iterative computing procedure was not in a technically efficient form. These difficulties have now been overcome to some extent: we can now handle up to thirteen groups and the computer program has been radically improved.

The analysis in Stone and Croft-Murray (1959) gives for the first time a complete matrix of elasticities of substitution which is symmetric (that is satisfies the Slutsky condition). It shows that with the relatively large groups used the substitution effects of changes in the price structure are relatively small. It also suggests that a large part of consumers' expenditure is, as one might expect, in a sense committed in advance. This in turn suggests that large, sudden changes in consumption patterns are not very likely to occur on a broad front, and this is in accordance with historical observations.

An analysis of thirteen commodity groups has just been completed with the help of the new program. The results are interesting but have not yet been fully analysed.

6. Summary and conclusions

I have tried to summarize some recent work in dynamic demand analysis which is giving good results but which is still at a comparatively early stage of development. I have concentrated on a formulation of the basic model which emphasizes the economic assumptions involved and have indicated some generalizations which readily suggest themselves and which illustrate the potentialities of the model. I have described some calculations which are useful and may not be immediately obvious, but I have not gone in any detail into statistical and computing techniques. These are all well known so far as the simple models are concerned and extremely difficult and by no means fully solved for the complete system of demand equations. Finally I have outlined the main results which have so far been obtained.

References

BRIGGS, F. E. A. (1957), 'On problems of estimation in Leontief models', *Econometrica*, vol. 25, pp. IX–X.

NERLOVE, M. (1960), 'The market demand for durable goods: a comment', *Econometrica*, vol. 28, pp. 132–42.

STONE, R. (1954), 'Linear expenditure systems and demand analysis: an application to the pattern of British demand', *Econ. J.*, vol. 64, pp. 511–27.

STONE, R. (1955), 'Transactions models with an example based on the British national accounts', *Account. Res.*, vol. 6, pp. 202–26.

STONE, R., and CROFT-MURRAY, G. (1959), *Social Accounting and Economic Models*, Bowes & Bowes.

STONE, R., and ROWE, D. A. (1956), 'Aggregate consumption and investment functions for the household sector considered in the light of British experience', *Nationaløkonomisk Tidsskrift*, vol. 94.

STONE, R., and ROWE, D. A. (1957), 'The market demand for durable goods', *Econometrica*, vol. 25, pp. 423–43.

STONE, R., and ROWE, D. A. (1958), 'Dynamic demand functions: some econometric results', *Econ. J.*, vol. 68, pp. 256–70.

STONE, R., and ROWE, D. A. (1960), 'The durability of consumers' goods', *Econometrica*, vol. 28, pp. 407–16.

STONE, R., *et al.* (1954), *The Measurement of Consumers' Expenditure and Behaviour in the United Kingdom, 1920–38*, vol. 1, Cambridge University Press.

7 E. J. Working

What Do Statistical 'Demand Curves' Show?[1]

E. J. Working, 'What do statistical "demand curves" show?',
Quarterly Journal of Economics, vol. 41, 1927, pp. 212–25.

Many questions of practical importance hinge upon the elasticity of demand, or of demand and supply. The economist can answer them only in a vague and indefinite manner, because he does not know the nature of the demand curve. What will be the effect of a five-million-bushel increase in the corn crop upon the price of corn and of hogs? What will be the effect of a tariff on imports and prices; on the protected industry; on the balance of international payments? How large an indemnity can Germany pay? The answers all depend in greater or less measure upon the elasticity of demand of the various commodities in question.

Such are the needs of the theorist, and in recent years a great deal of attention has been turned to the construction of statistical demand curves. Beef, corn, cotton, hay, hogs, pig iron, oats, potatoes, sweet potatoes, sugar and wheat are on the list of commodities for which we have statements of the 'law of demand'. Many economists have been skeptical, while others have been enthusiastic, on the significance of such demand curves. In consequence of this divergence of opinion, it may be well to consider some of the theoretical aspects of what the demand curves constructed by our statistical experts may be expected to show. Do they correspond to the demand curves of economic theory? If so, it would seem that they represent some-

1. The author is indebted to those who have read the manuscript while it was in various stages of completion. The criticisms of Professors Allyn A. Young, F. W. Taussig and W. L. Crum of Harvard University, of Dr C. O. Hardy of the Institute of Economics and of Dr H. Working of the Food Research Institute, have been particularly helpful. The original charts were drawn by Mr R. P. Ward of the Institute of Economics.

thing tangible by which our theories may be tested and turned to better account.[2]

Among the statistical studies of demand that have been made, there are cases in which the same commodity has been studied by more than one investigator, and their results indicate varying degrees of elasticity of demand. But despite this, in all but one of the cases the demand curves have been negatively inclined – they have been in accord with Marshall's 'one general *law of demand*'.[3]

In the case of pig iron, however, Professor H. L. Moore (1914, p. 114) finds a 'law of demand' which is not in accord with Marshall's universal rule. He finds that the greater the quantity of pig iron sold, the higher will be the prices. If this is the nature of the statistical demand curve for pig iron, surely statistical demand curves must be of a very different sort from the demand curves of traditional economic theory!

Professor Moore holds that the statistical 'law of demand' at which he arrives is a *dynamic* law, while that of theory is a *static* law. He says in part: 'The doctrine of the uniformity of the demand function is an idol of the static state – the method of *ceteris paribus* – which has stood in the way of the successful treatment of dynamic problems.' If it be true that statistical demand curves and the demand curves of theory differ so utterly from each other, of what value is statistical analysis to the theorist – of what value is economic theory to the statistical analyst? It would seem that so far as the study of demand is concerned, the statistical analyst and the economic theorist are on paths so divergent as to be wholly out of touch with each other. Before we accede to such a discouraging thought,

2. Among the leading discussions of the subject, the following may be noted: Lehfeldt (1914), Moore (1914, 1917, 1919, 1922, 1925, 1926), Schultz (1925) and Working (1925).

In this list no attempt is made to include the many studies of demand of specific articles. A bibliography of the latter is given by Working (1925, pp. 539–43).

3. 'There is then one general *law of demand*: the greater the amount to be sold, the smaller must be the price at which it is offered in order to find purchasers; or, in other words, the amount demanded increases with a fall in price and diminishes with a rise in price' (Marshall, 1890, p. 99 of 1920 edn).

let us examine a little more closely the nature of statistical demand curves as they may be viewed in the light of economic theory.

Let us first consider in what way statistical demand curves are constructed. While both the nature of the data used and the technique of analysis vary, the basic data consist of corresponding prices and quantities. That is, if a given quantity refers to the amount of a commodity sold, produced, or consumed in the year 1910, the corresponding price is the price which is taken to be typical for the year 1910. These corresponding quantities and prices may be for a period of a month, a year or any other length of time which is feasible; and, as has already been indicated, the quantities may refer to amounts produced, sold or consumed. The technique of analysis consists of such operations as fitting the demand curve and adjusting the original data to remove, in so far as is possible, the effect of disturbing influences. For a preliminary understanding of the way in which curves are constructed, we need not be concerned with the differences in technique; but whether the quantities used are the amounts produced, sold, or consumed is a matter of greater significance, which must be kept in mind.

For the present, let us confine our attention to the type of study which uses for its data the quantities which have been sold in the market. In general, the method of constructing demand curves of this sort is to take corresponding prices and quantities, plot them, and draw a curve which will fit as nearly as possible all the plotted points. Suppose, for example, we wish to determine the demand curve for beef. First, we find out how many pounds of beef were sold in a given month and what was the average price. We do the same for all the other months of the period over which our study is to extend, and plot our data with quantities as abscissas and corresponding prices as ordinates. Next we draw a curve to fit the points. This is our demand curve.

In the actual construction of demand curves, certain refinements necessary in order to get satisfactory results are introduced.[4] The purpose of these is to correct the data so as to

4. Instead of using actual prices and quantities, percentage changes or link relatives of prices and quantities may be used. In footnote 2 will be found

remove the effect of various extraneous and complicating factors. For example, adjustments are usually made for changes in the purchasing power of money, and for changes in population and in consumption habits. Corrections may be made directly by such means as dividing all original price data by 'an index of the general level of prices'. They may be made indirectly by correction for trends of the two time series of prices and of quantities. Whatever the corrections and refinements, however, the essence of the method is that certain prices are taken as representing the prices at which certain quantities of the product in question were sold.

With this in mind, we may now turn to the theory of the demand-and-supply curve analysis of market prices. The conventional theory runs in terms substantially as follows (see Marshall, book 5, ch. 2; Taussig, 1911, ch. 10, 1921, p. 204). At any given time all individuals within the scope of the market may be considered as being within two groups – potential buyers and potential sellers.[5] The higher the price, the more the sellers will be ready to sell and the less the buyers will be willing to take. We may assume a demand schedule of the potential buyers and a supply schedule of the potential sellers which express the amounts that these groups are ready to buy and sell at different prices. From these schedules supply and demand curves may be made. Thus we have our supply and demand curves showing the market situation at any given time, and the price which results from this situation will be represented by the height of the point where the curves intersect.

This, however, represents the situation as it obtains at any given moment only. It may change; indeed, it is almost certain to change. The supply and demand curves which accurately represent the market situation of today will not represent that of a week hence. The curves which represent the average or aggregate of conditions this month will not hold true for the

references to various discussions of the details of statistical procedure used in the consideration of demand curves and also of the theory of statistical analysis of demand curves.

5. This does not mean that the same individual may not be in both groups. He may be a potential seller at any price above a certain level and a potential buyer at any price below.

corresponding month of next year. In the case of the wheat market, for example, the effect of news that wheat which is growing in Kansas has been damaged by rust will cause a shift in both demand and supply schedules of the traders in the grain markets. The same amount of wheat, or a greater, will

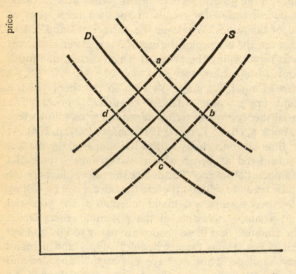

Figure 1

command a higher price than would have been the case if the news had failed to reach the traders. Since much of the buying and selling is speculative, changes in the market price itself may result in shifts of the demand and supply schedules.

If, then, our market demand and supply curves are to indicate conditions which extend over a period of time, we must represent them as shifting.[6] A diagram such as the following, Figure 1, may be used to indicate them. The demand and supply curves may meet at any point within the area *a, b, c, d,* and over a

6. Cf. Taussig (1921, p. 204). This article illustrates a somewhat different way of representing market conditions. It represents the curves as being of uncertain conformation rather than as shifting.

period of time points of equilibrium will occur at many different places within it.

But what of statistical demand curves in the light of this analysis? If we construct a statistical demand curve from data of quantities sold and corresponding prices, our original data consist, in effect, of observations of points at which the demand and supply curves have met. Although we may wish to reduce our data to static conditions, we must remember that they originate in the market itself. The market is dynamic and our data extend over a period of time; consequently our data are of changing conditions and must be considered as the result of shifting demand and supply schedules.

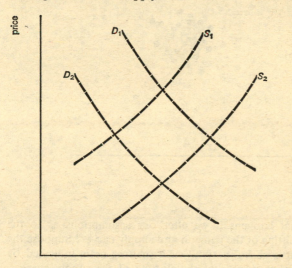

Figure 2   quantity

Let us assume that conditions are such as those illustrated in Figure 2, the demand curve shifting from D_1 to D_2, and the supply curve shifting in similar manner from S_1 to S_2. It is to be noted that the chart shows approximately equal shifting of the demand and supply curves.

Under such conditions there will result a series of prices which may be graphically represented by Figure 3. It is from data such as those represented by the dots that we are to construct a demand curve, but evidently no satisfactory fit can be obtained. A line of one slope will give substantially as good a fit as will a line of any other slope.

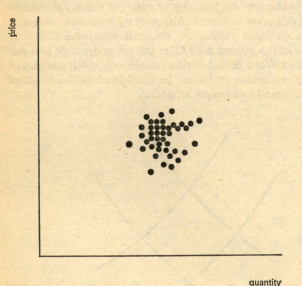

price

quantity

Figure 3

But what happens if we alter our assumptions as to the relative shifting of the demand and supply curves? Suppose the supply curve shifts in some such manner as is indicated by Figure 4, that is, so that the shifting of the supply curve is greater than the shifting of the demand curve. We shall then obtain a very different set of observations – a set which may be represented by the dots of Figure 5. To these points we may fit a curve which will have the elasticity of the demand curve that we originally assumed, and whose position will approximate the central position about which the demand curve shifted. We may consider this to be a sort of typical demand curve, and from it we may determine the elasticity of demand.

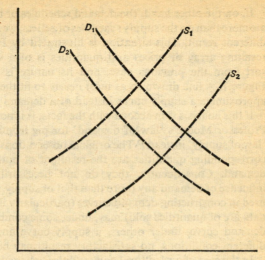

Figure 4

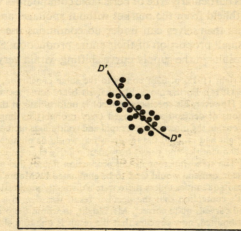

Figure 5

If, on the other hand, the demand schedules of buyers fluctuate more than do the supply schedules of sellers, we shall obtain a different result. This situation is illustrated by Figure 6. The resulting array of prices and quantities is of a very different sort from the previous case, and its nature is indicated by Figure 7. A line drawn so as most nearly to fit these points will approximate a supply curve instead of a demand curve.

If this analysis is in accord with the facts, is it not evident that Professor Moore's 'law of demand' for pig iron is in reality a 'law of supply' instead?[7] The original observations of prices and corresponding quantities are the resultant of both supply and demand. Consequently, they do not necessarily reflect the influence of demand any more than that of supply. The methods used in constructing demand curves (particularly if the quantity data are of quantities sold) may, under some conditions, yield a demand curve, under others, a supply curve and, under still different conditions, no satisfactory result may be obtained.

In the case of agricultural commodities, where production for any given year is largely influenced by weather conditions, and where farmers sell practically their entire crop regardless of price, there is likely to be a much greater shifting of the supply schedules of sellers than of the demand schedules of buyers. This is particularly true of perishable commodities which cannot be withheld from the market without spoilage, and in case the farmers themselves can under no conditions use more than a very small proportion of their entire production. Such a condition results in the supply curve shifting within very wide limits.

7. Wright (1915, p. 638) comes to the same conclusion, in a review of Moore (1914). Furthermore, his analysis bears some resemblance to that above. However, his specific argument is unfortunate in that he says 'the conditions of demand are changed (very probably by improved business conditions) in the direction of a rapid and continuous increase'. Apparently Mr Wright had in mind the results which would be obtained by the use of absolute quantities and prices instead of relative changes in quantities and prices. The trend inherent in the production figures due to a continuous increase in demand would tend to be eliminated by Moore's use of *relative* changes in quantities unless there were a distinctly progressive increase. Mr Wright's contention that the peculiar result was due to a shifting of the demand curve is quite correct. Mr Wright, to whom the present paper has been submitted, now concurs that the result is due to a shifting back and forth rather than to a continuous shift of the demand curve to the right.

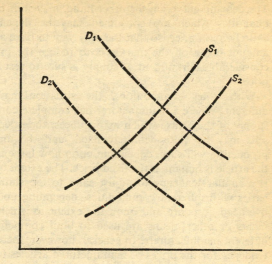

price

D_1

D_2

S_1

S_2

Figure 6

quantity

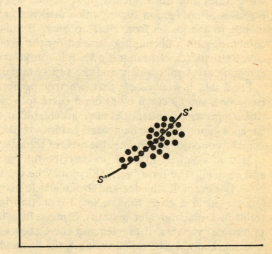

price

S'

S''

Figure 7

quantity

The demand curve, on the other hand, may shift but little. The quantities which are consumed may be dependent almost entirely upon price, so that the only way to have a much larger amount taken off the market is to reduce the price, and any considerable curtailment of supply is sure to result in a higher price.

With other commodities, the situation may be entirely different. Where a manufacturer has complete control over the supply of the article which he produces, the price at which he sells may be quite definitely fixed, and the amount of his production will vary, depending upon how large an amount of the article is bought at the fixed price. The extent to which there is a similar tendency to adjust sales to the shifts of demand varies with different commodities, depending upon how large overhead costs are and upon the extent to which trade agreements or other means are used to limit competition between different manufacturers. In general, however, there is a marked tendency for the prices of manufactured articles to conform to their expenses of production, the amount of the articles sold varying with the intensity of demand at that price which equals the expenses of production. Under such conditions, the supply curve does not shift greatly, but rather approximates an expenses-of-production curve, which does not vary much from month to month or from year to year. If this condition is combined with a fluctuating demand for the product, we shall have a situation such as that shown in Figures 6 and 7, where the demand curves shift widely and the supply curves only a little.

From this, it would seem that, whether we obtain a demand curve or a supply curve by fitting a curve to a series of points which represent the quantities of an article sold at various prices, depends upon the fundamental nature of the supply and demand conditions. It implies the need of some term in addition to that of elasticity in order to describe the nature of supply and demand. The term 'variability' may be used for this purpose. For example, the demand for an article may be said to be 'elastic' if, at a given time, a small reduction in price would result in a much greater quantity being sold, while it may be said to be 'variable' if the demand curve shows a tendency to shift markedly. To be called variable, the demand curve should have the tendency to shift back and forth, and not merely to shift gradually and consistently to the right or left because of changes of population or consuming habits.

Whether a demand or a supply curve is obtained may also be affected by the nature of the corrections applied to the original data. The corrections may be such as to reduce the effect of the shifting of the demand schedules without reducing the effect of the shifting of the supply schedules. In such a case the curve obtained will approximate a demand curve, even though the original demand schedules fluctuated fully as much as did the supply schedules.

By intelligently applying proper refinements, and making corrections to eliminate separately those factors which cause demand curves to shift and those factors which cause supply curves to shift, it may be possible even to obtain both a demand curve and a supply curve for the same product and from the same original data. Certainly it may be possible, in many cases where satisfactory demand curves have not been obtained, to find instead the supply curves of the articles in question. The supply curve obtained by such methods, it is to be noted, would be a market supply curve rather than a normal supply curve.

Thus far it has been assumed that the supply and demand curves shift quite independently and at random; but such need not be the case. It is altogether possible that a shift of the demand curve to the right may, as a rule, be accompanied by a shift of the supply curve to the left, and vice versa. Let us see what result is to be expected under such conditions. If successive positions of the demand curve are represented by the curves D_1, D_2, D_3, D_4 and D_5 of Figure 8, while the curves S_1, S_2, S_3, S_4 and S_5 represent corresponding positions of the supply curves, then a series of prices will result from the intersection of D_1 with S_1, D_2 with S_2, and so on. If a curve be fitted to these points, it will not conform to the theoretical demand curve. It will have a smaller elasticity, as is shown by D' D'' of Figure 8. If, on the other hand, a shift of the demand curve to the right is accompanied by a shift of the supply curve to the right, we shall obtain a result such as that indicated by

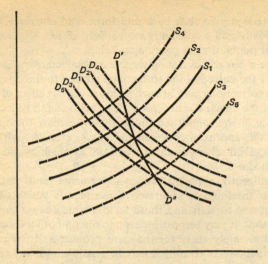

Figure 8

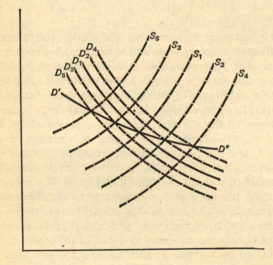

Figure 9

D' D'' in Figure 9. The fitted curve again fails to conform to the theoretical one, but in this case it is more elastic.

Without carrying the illustrations further, it will be apparent that similar reasoning applies to the fitted 'supply curve' in case conditions are such that the demand curve shifts more than does the supply curve.

If there is a change in the range through which the supply curve shifts, as might occur through the imposition of a tariff on an imported good, a new fitted curve will result, which will not be a continuation of the former one – this because the fitted curve does not correspond to the true demand curve. In case, then, of correlated shifts of the demand and supply curves, a fitted curve cannot be considered to be the demand curve for the article. It cannot be used, for example, to estimate what change in price would result from the levying of a tariff upon the commodity.

Perhaps a word of caution is needed here. It does not follow from the foregoing analysis that, when conditions are such that shifts of the supply and demand curves are correlated, an attempt to construct a demand curve will give a result which will be useless. Even though shifts of the supply and demand curves are correlated, a curve which is fitted to the points of intersection will be useful for purposes of price forecasting, provided no new factors are introduced which did not affect the price during the period of the study. Thus, so long as the shifts of the supply and demand curves remain correlated in the same way, and so long as they shift through approximately the same range, the curve of regression of price upon quantity can be used as a means of estimating price from quantity.

In cases where it is impossible to show that the shifts of the demand and supply curves are not correlated, much confusion would probably be avoided if the fitted curves were not called demand curves (or supply curves), but if, instead, they were called merely lines of regression. Such curves may be useful, but we must be extremely careful in our interpretation of them. We must also make every effort to discover whether the shifts of the supply and demand curves are correlated before interpreting the results of any fitted curve.

In assuming that we are dealing with quantities actually sold in the market, and in disregarding the fact that for many commodities there is a whole series of markets at various points in the marketing chain, we have simplified our problem. But it has been more than mere simplification, for the interpretation which is to be placed on statistical demand curves depends in large measure upon these matters. Whether the demand curve is a 'particular' or a 'general' demand curve, depends upon whether or not we use quantities sold. Whether it represents consumer or dealer demand, depends upon the point in the marketing chain to which the quantities sold refer.

Most theorists are acquainted with the concept of the general demand curve as it is presented by Wicksteed (1914, p. 1) and Davenport (1913, pp. 47–51). Briefly, the idea is that demand should be considered as including not merely the quantities that are bought, but rather all those in existence. The general demand curve, then, includes the possessors of a commodity as having a demand for it at any price below their reservation price, even if they are prospective sellers. Instead of showing the amounts that will be brought at various prices, it shows the marginal money valuation which will be placed upon varying quantities of an existing supply.

Wicksteed even indicates that the supply curve ought not to be considered at all. The following gives an intimation of his viewpoint:

But what about the 'supply curve' that usually figures as a determinant of price, coordinate with the demand curve? I say it boldly and baldly: there is no such thing. When we are speaking of a marketable commodity, what is usually called a supply curve is in reality a demand curve of those who possess the commodity; for it shows the exact place which every successive unit of the commodity holds in their relative scale of estimates. The so-called supply curve, therefore, is simply a part of the total demand curve (Wicksteed, 1914, p. 13).

Thus the general demand curve is an expression of the relation between the supply of a commodity and its valuation. In other words, to put it in more familiar terms, it expresses the marginal valuation of different supplies. It is the same sort of thing as a curve of marginal utility, except that it uses monetary valuations instead of abstract 'satisfactions' as its ordinate. This raises the question, if, instead of quantities sold, we use quantities produced (or total supply) when we construct a statistical demand curve, do we not obtain a general demand curve, and does not this preclude the possibility of obtaining a supply curve? Let us examine the matter a little further.

As it is usually applied, the idea of the general demand curve refers to valuations of an existing stock of durable goods, such as paintings, diamonds or hats. If it is applied to a stock of non-durable goods, it is of less significance; and in case this stock is replenished periodically, the demand curve must be considered as changing greatly from period to period. For example, in the case of wheat the stock varies greatly, being large just after harvest and gradually dwindling until it becomes very small just before the next harvest. The general demand curve, as applied to an existing stock, would exhibit correspondingly large shifts.

An idea similar to that of the general demand curve is that which is used in regard to *rate* of supply. If, instead of using the rates at which quantities are sold in the market, we use rate of production, which we relate to the unit value of the commodity, we obtain a curve which is analogous to the general demand curve. It gives the marginal valuation which would be placed upon various rates of supply, that is, of supplies produced, not of supplies sold. This sort of a demand curve has been called a 'general' demand curve, but it is to be noted that the general demand curve which uses total stocks as its abscissa cannot be placed as coordinate with a supply curve; whereas the demand curve which uses as abscissa total quantities produced can be used in connection with a supply curve of quantities produced.

The use of quantities produced, then, does not give us a general demand curve in the usual sense of the word. Instead, it gives us a demand curve which we may consider as being coordinate with a supply curve, though we must keep in mind that our supply curve in this case is of supplies produced rather than of supplies sold in the market. The demand curve is of demand for storage and consumption by producers as well as for storage and consumption by buyers. There is no reason why we may not obtain a supply curve instead of a demand curve, even though we use quantities produced. To do so requires only that shifts in the demand curve be very large relative to those of the supply curve, and that amounts sold differ but little from amounts produced. The scatter of the points will, of course, be greater than if amounts sold had been used.

The question of the difference between consumer and dealer demand presents a problem somewhat analogous to that just discussed. The amount of a commodity sold at one point in the marketing chain may differ from that sold at another in much the same way that the amount produced may differ from the amount sold. This is particularly true if monthly data are used. A case in point would be the demand for eggs. The amount of eggs sold by farmers in the spring of the year is greatly in excess of the amount sold by retail dealers, while in the winter months it is much less. Since differentials between the prices received by farmers and those received by retail dealers remain fairly constant, very different demand curves would be obtained. The consumers' demand curve would be very much less elastic than that of the dealers who buy from farmers.

Differences between dealer demand and consumer demand are largely dependent upon whether we are considering short or long periods. Over long periods of time, dealer demand tends to conform to consumer demand. This difference, however, is not a thing which depends upon the length of period over which the data extend, but of the length of period to which the individual observations of prices and quantities refer. In the case of eggs, if yearly data were used, the principal difference which would be found between the elasticity of consumer and dealer demands would be due to price differentials alone.

The question whether statistical demand curves are static or dynamic is a perplexing one and rather difficult to deal with. This is largely due to uncertainty as to just what is meant by the terms 'static' and 'dynamic'. Moore (1914, pp. 64–7, 113) holds that his 'laws of demand' are dynamic, and that this is an eminently desirable feature. Schultz, while considering it most desirable to obtain both a static and a dynamic law by means of multiple correlation, holds that the statistical devices of relative changes and of trend ratios give a static 'law of demand' (Schultz, 1925, pp. 498–502).

Conditions are often defined as being static or dynamic on

two different grounds. They may be called static if they refer to a point of time; or else they may be said to be static if all other things are held equal. Statements such as these, however, lack much in clarity and accuracy. How can a statement be made as to prices at which different quantities of a commodity will sell at a *point* of time? Is it really supposed that *all* other things must be held equal in order to study the demand of the commodity? Rather, the real supposition, though it may not be accurately expressed, is that the relationships between the various economic factors should be the same as those which exist at a given point of time, or that the relationships between these factors should remain constant.

The data used in a statistical study of demand must, of course, extend over a period of time, but they may in effect conform to conditions at a point of time if trend is removed and if there is no other change in the relationship between quantity and price. Of course, the shifting of the demand and supply curves constitutes a change in the relationship between the quantity and price, but the process of curve-fitting corresponds to that of averaging. Consequently, the fitted curve may be considered to depict the average relationship between quantity and price. This amounts to the same thing as representing the relationship at a point of time which is typical for the period studied. In this sense, then, of relating to a point of time, Moore's 'laws of demand' are static instead of dynamic.

Holding 'all other things equal,' however, is a different matter. Schultz (1925, pp. 498-9) states the difficulty in the following manner:

In *theory* the law of demand for any one commodity is given only on the assumption that the prices of all other commodities remain constant (the old *ceteris paribus* assumption). This postulate fails in the case of commodities for which substitutes are available. Thus when the price of beef is changed markedly, the prices of such rival commodities as mutton, veal and pork cannot be supposed to remain constant. Likewise, the price of sugar cannot be increased beyond a certain point without affecting the prices of glucose, corn sugar and honey.

Marshall (1890, p. 100 of 1920 edn) makes similar restrictions as to the need for other things to be held equal, and suggests that in some cases it may be best to 'group together commodities as distinct as beef and mutton', in order to obtain a demand curve which will not be too restricted because of other things being equal.

The question arises, however, whether it is desirable to hold all other things equal in any case. Is it not better to have a demand curve for beef which expresses the relation between the price and quantity of beef while the prices of pork, mutton and veal, vary as they normally do, with different prices of beef? Furthermore, may not this be called a static condition? The point can perhaps be made clearer if we take an extreme example. If we are studying the demand for wheat, it would be almost meaningless to get the demand curve for no. 2 winter wheat while holding the price of all other grades of wheat constant. Other grades of wheat can be so readily substituted that the demand would be almost completely elastic. The difference between this and holding the prices of pork, mutton and veal constant, while the price of beef varies, is only one of degree – a difference which depends upon the ease with which substitutes can be used in place of the article whose demand is being studied.

All other things being held equal is not a condition represented by a statistical law of demand or, strictly interpreted, of any useful demand curve theory. Some of the things that are correlated with the price of the commodity in question may be held equal, but it is impossible for all things to be held equal. However, a statistical law of demand represents a condition under which the relationships between factors may be considered to have remained the same or, to put it more accurately, a condition which is an average of the relationships during the period studied.

In conclusion, then, it is evident that the mere statement that the demand for a commodity has a given elasticity is meaningless. As with the results of all other statistical analysis, statistical demand curves must be incorporated in the light of the nature of the original data and of the methods of analysis used. There are four questions, the answers to which it is particularly important to know. They concern (a) whether the supply or demand curve is more variable, (b) the market to which the price and quantity data refer, (c) the extent to which 'other things are held equal' and (d) whether the shifting of the supply and demand curves is correlated or random.

For precision, it is preferable that the data of price and quantity should refer to the same market. Yet this may be out of the question. In a study of the demand for wheat, for example, if we want to obtain a demand curve of the quantity demanded by the entire country, we cannot use prices for all different points and for all different grades. Instead, the price at one market and for one grade may be used as representative, and the demand of the entire country determined for various prices at the one marketplace. If the price at any other market or for any other grade were used, the elasticity of demand might be different.

Furthermore, the point in the market chain must be specified and the results interpreted accordingly. As is the case with geographical points, it is preferable that the quantities and prices should refer to the same stage in the marketing process. If this is not the case, the interpretation should be made with the situation in view.

It is to be expected that the methods used in constructing statistical demand curves should be such as to give a demand curve which represents a point of time, that is, that trends in both quantities and prices are removed, or else multiple correlation is used to effect the same result. If, in addition to this, other things are held constant, the fact should be noted and the elasticity of demand should be stated as referring to a condition where these other things are held constant.

The matter of correlation between shifts of the demand and supply curves is a more difficult problem to deal with. Every effort should be made to discover whether there is a tendency for the shifting of these to be interdependent. In case it is impossible to determine this, it should be carefully noted that the demand curve which is obtained is quite likely not to hold true for periods other than the one studied, and cannot be treated as corresponding to the demand curve of economic theory.

References

DAVENPORT, H. J. (1913), *Economics of Enterprise*, Macmillan Co.

LEHFELDT, R. A. (1914), 'The elasticity of demand for wheat', *Econ. J.*, June, pp. 212–17.

MARSHALL, A. C. (1890), *Principles of Economics*, Macmillan, 8th edn, 1920.

MOORE, H. L. (1914), *Economic Cycles: Their Law and Cause*, Macmillan Co.

MOORE, H. L. (1917), *Forecasting the Yield and Price of Cotton*, Macmillan Co.

MOORE, H. L. (1919), 'Empirical laws of demand and supply and the flexibility of prices', *Polit. Sci. Quart.*, vol. 34, pp. 546–67.

MOORE, H. L. (1922), 'Elasticity of demand and flexibility of prices', *J. Amer. Stat. Assn*, vol. 18, pp. 8–19.

MOORE, H. L. (1925), 'A moving equilibrium of demand and supply', *Quart. J. Econ.*, vol. 39, pp. 357–71.

MOORE, H. L. (1926), 'Partial elasticity of demand', *Quart. J. Econ.*, vol. 50, pp. 393–40.

PERSONS, W. M. (1910), 'The correlation of economic statistics', *Pub. Amer. Stat. Assn*, pp. 287–322.

SCHULTZ, H. (1925), 'The statistical law of demand as illustrated by the demand for sugar: part 1', *J. polit. Econ.*, vol. 33, pp. 481–504; 'part 2', ibid., vol. 33, pp. 577–637.

TAUSSIG, F. W. (1911), *Principles of Economics*, Macmillan Co.

TAUSSIG, F. W. (1921), 'Is market price determinate?', *Quart. J. Econ.*, vol. 35, pp. 394–411.

WICKSTEED, P. H. (1914), 'The scope and method of political economy in the light of the "marginal" theory of value', *Econ. J.*, vol. 24, pp. 1–23.

WORKING, H. (1925), 'The statistical determination of demand curves', *Quart. J. Econ.*, vol. 39, pp. 503–43.

WRIGHT, P G. (1915), 'The contest in congress between organized labor and organized business', *Quart. J. Econ.*, vol. 29, pp. 235–61.

Part Four Costs

Cost theory is twice blessed. It must be true as a matter of logic, and hence it can be shown to be true as a matter of fact. Empirical verification is often complicated because most production functions involve a large number of factors of production which are usually not so divisible as the theorist would wish. L. Cookenboo, Jr, analyses a cost situation which fits snugly into the theorists' categories and so provides examples of actual isoquants and total product curves (Reading 8). Om P. Tangri (Reading 9) reworks the theory of total product curves to explain the symmetrical relationships within the law of variable proportions. Armen Alchian (Reading 10) comprehensively classifies the relationships between costs and outputs, making a place for gains from learning and clarifying the nature of economies of scale.

8 L. Cookenboo, Jr

Costs of Operation of Crude Oil Trunk Lines

L. Cookenboo, Jr, 'Costs of operation of crude oil trunk lines', in
Crude Oil Pipe Lines and Competition in the Oil Industry,
Harvard University Press, 1955, pp. 8–32.

This chapter will be concerned with a discussion of long-, short-
and intermediate-run costs of operating crude oil pipe lines. For
the benefit of the reader not conversant with economic jargon,
it might be well to begin with a description of the three cost
categories.

First, it is necessary to distinguish between the various types
of costs that may be considered under any of these three
categories. 'Total' cost (be it long-, short- or intermediate-run)
is the total expenditure necessary for producing a given output.
'Average' cost is the cost per unit of producing a given output;
it is equal to total cost divided by output. For example, if the
total expenditure for an output of 100 units is $1000, then total
cost is $1000 and average cost (per-unit cost) is $10 per unit
($1000 divided by 100 units). 'Marginal' cost is the change in
total cost associated with changes in output. If 100 units cost
$1000 and 101 units cost $1008, then 'marginal' cost is $8 (the
change in total cost divided by the change in output). 'Fixed'
and 'variable' costs are simply parts of total (or average) cost.
Fixed costs are those incurred even when no output is produced,
for example, interest on the money borrowed to buy machinery,
pay taxes, and so forth. Variable costs (out-of-pocket costs) are
expenditures that would not be necessary were no output
produced, for example, expenditures for labor and raw materials. Total cost is equal to the sum of total fixed cost and total
variable cost. Average cost is equal to the sum of average fixed
cost and average variable cost.

A 'short-run' cost curve shows the cost of producing various
outputs with a given amount of fixed capital equipment. In
other words, it is the cost curve for a given size of plant, the

output of which can be changed simply by using more or less labor and raw materials. Changes in short-run costs with changes in output represent changes in expenditures for items of variable cost *only*; no extra machinery or other capital equipment is needed to increase output.

A long-run cost curve (also called a 'planning' curve) is an

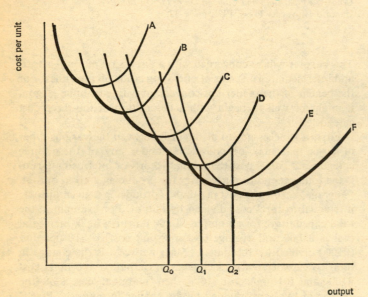

Figure 1 Long- and short-run average cost curves

'envelope' of all possible short-run curves. It shows the least possible expenditure for producing any output. That is, it takes into account all individual plant cost curves in order to determine which plant can produce each output for the least amount possible (relative to all other plants). This is illustrated in Figure 1.

This diagram shows per-unit cost plotted against output (the short-run cost curves) for each of six possible plants (A to F) that might be used to produce some product. The long-run average cost curve is the envelope of these short-run curves (the heavy, wavy line). (If there were an infinite number of plants possible, then the long-run curve would be continuous, not wavy.) It shows the least possible expenditure for any given output in the range of outputs under consideration. Output Q_0 might be produced with either plant A, B, C, D, E or F. However, D's short-run cost curve lies beneath all the others at Q_0; therefore its cost is the least possible for producing Q_0, and it may be said to be the 'optimum' plant for producing that output. In the range of outputs where its cost curve lies beneath all others, its short-run cost is equal to long-run cost. A long-run cost curve such as that in Figure 1 is called a 'planning' curve because it shows the least amount that could be spent to produce various outputs if a firm had the option of choosing from several sizes of plants. Such a long-run cost curve would be of value when building a new plant or when contemplating entering an industry. Once a plant is built, it is the short-run curve for this plant which shows what the firm would spend in order to produce various outputs.

Note the paradox in Figure 1 that D is *not* the optimum plant for the output at which it itself is most efficient (Q_1). Its most efficient output is the output which it produces at the least possible cost per unit that *it* is capable of achieving. In Figure 1, plant E could produce D's optimum output (Q_1) more cheaply than could D; hence E is the optimum plant at D's optimum output. It is a question of optimum *plant* relative to all *other* plants, versus optimum *output* for a *given* plant (without consideration of others) once that plant is built. Because of this paradox, any plant in Figure 1, say D, would be built originally to produce an output less than its own optimum output. Hence, it could subsequently increase its output, should it so desire, and thereby achieve a lower per-unit cost. Indeed, it could increase its output to Q_2 before average costs became higher than they were at the design output. It might be asked why a firm would ever consider producing Q_2 with D when E and F can produce it for less. If the need for Q_2 had been foreseen before any plant was built, then plant E would probably have been built. However, if the original output was desired was Q_0, the correct choice would have been D. A subsequent expansion to Q_2 could then be made with plant D. This would be done instead of building a new plant if the cash costs of operating plant D at Q_2 were less than the total costs of operating plant F at Q_2.

One other 'paradox' should be pointed out in Figure 1. Note that the short-run average costs decrease and then rise, even though the long-run cost curve falls throughout the range of outputs. Consequently a U-shaped short-run average cost curve may occur for each plant while long-run average costs decline continuously.

In the range of outputs where long-run average costs decrease (in this case throughout the range), there are said to be 'economies of scale'. That is, by producing larger amounts conglomerately in larger plants, it is possible to achieve lower per-unit costs, better known as 'mass-production economies'. If the long-run average cost curve declines throughout the range of outputs, then no plant can achieve the least possible (long-run) cost of producing the product, unless there is some size of plant, say F, which is the largest possible for one reason or another. However, something approaching the least possible long-run cost can be had with the large plants, for example, E and F in Figure 1, since the average cost curve declines more and more slowly as output rises. From the point of view of both society and the firm, plants in an industry having costs such as those shown in Figure 1 should be as large as possible in order to achieve as low average costs as possible – apart from any political or sociological disadvantages of large business.

In the case of pipe lines it is also necessary to utilize the concept of 'intermediate-run' costs. If the curves labeled A to F in Figure 1 were the basis of a planning curve for pipe lines, they would be called not 'short-run', but 'intermediate-run' pipe-line cost curves, each representing a given line size carrying various 'throughputs'. (Pipe-line output is called 'throughput' – the volume of liquid carried per unit of time.) In some industries the output of individual plants can be expanded above the original output simply by adding more labor or raw materials; these may be described with short-run cost curves. However, in the case of pipe lines, throughput can be increased above the designed capacity only by the addition of more capital equipment (pumping stations), along with extra labor and fuel. Short-run cost curves which allow for a fixed amount of capital equipment are 'reversible'. That is, when output is decreased (by laying off workers and buying smaller amounts of raw materials), the short-run curve shows the appropriate cost for the lower output. On the other hand, intermediate-run cost curves which include costs of varying amounts of capital equipment are not reversible. If pipe line D (again referring to Figure 1, this time as a series of intermediate-run curves) were built for throughput Q_0, then the costs of carrying throughputs less than Q_0 in line D would *not* be shown by the curve labeled D; these costs would be higher for all throughputs less than Q_0. Why? The curve D would be based, for planning purposes, on the proper (minimum possible) number of pumping stations for each throughput. It takes more stations of a given size to push larger throughputs through a given size pipe. Consequently, the number of stations built on line D for throughput Q_0 would be larger than needed for lesser throughputs. If throughput is cut below Q_0 the number of stations cannot be cut (as could the number of workers in some other industry), since stations represent fixed capital invest-ments – investments which incur costs even if the stations are not needed. In short, too many pumping stations would be present for any lower throughput; consequently there would be higher average costs than if the line had been designed for the lower throughput with the minimum number of stations required for that throughput. Hence, the necessity of the hybrid term 'intermediate-run' in the pipe-line case. In this case the long-run curve is the envelope of the intermediate-run curves, not of the short-run curves.

With this digression into the principles of economics in mind, it is possible to proceed with the discussion of pipe-line costs. The costs computed for this study were determined primarily by the method of engineering estimation, not by the use of actual historical costs. Where engineering estimation is feasible for cost studies it should be used, since actual costs may be subject to any number of erratic variations arising from construction or operating conditions unique to particular cases. In the case of the majority of the cost items, the process of computation involved a physical determination of the amount of equipment or services required, followed by the pricing of this amount from current price quotations furnished by suppliers and/or pipe-line companies. In some cases where particular items did not readily lend themselves to *a priori* engineering estimation, it was necessary to use historical costs. One example of this is the construction materials cost of pumphouses, for which actual costs obtained from a pipe-line company were used as the basis of computation. This particular item also illustrates the dangers of using historical costs. The stations were built in a period of unusually bad weather; hence the labor costs were much higher than would be the case normally. The materials costs were usable, but the labor costs had to be estimated from other sources. The notable exceptions where actual costs were used as the principal basis for computation include costs of surveying the right-of-way, main-line valves, office operation, site improvements at stations and the pipe-line communications system. Since the details of this cost study are reported elsewhere (Cookenboo, 1954), it will not be necessary to engage here in an extended discussion of such problems as optimum operating pressure, safety factor, wall thickness of pipe, centrifugal versus reciprocating pumps, diesel engines versus electric motors, and so forth. However, it is necessary to discuss in summary form certain points about pipe-line technology and the results of the cost study, since this information is all-important for the subsequent discussion.

Production function

In order to determine costs by engineering estimation, it is necessary to compute an 'engineering production function' relating the factors of production (the goods and services used to produce a product) and output. Such a function shows the possible combinations of the factors of production which can be used to produce various levels of output.

A basic choice between two 'factors of production' exists in the determination of the optimum line diameter for carrying any particular throughput. A given size of line may be used for several different throughputs by applying different amounts of power (hydraulic horse-power) to the oil carried – the more horse-power, the more throughput (but less than proportionately more). Conversely, any given throughput can be achieved by the use of several possible sizes of lines with the proper amount of horse-power applied. There are, in short, variable physical proportions of these two basic factors of production, 'line diameter' and 'horse-power', which may be used to develop any given throughput. As a result, the management of a pipe-line company is forced to choose between several sizes of line when planning to develop a given throughput. Furthermore, the long-run cost of carrying crude oil might vary with throughput, as did the long-run costs in Figure 1. Larger throughputs might cost less or more per barrel. Managements, then, not only have the option of several sizes of line for each throughput, they also may have the option of choosing throughputs having different costs per barrel. Other things being equal, a pipe-line company planning to build a line should select the cheapest combination of line diameter and horse-power for the throughput which can be carried at the least cost per barrel.

A production function relating line diameter, horse-power, and throughput can be derived for crude oil pipe lines. Indeed, many such functions could be derived, depending on the density and viscosity of the oil carried, the wall thickness of pipe used, and so forth. However, for the purposes of this monograph one function will suffice. The only differences among the cost curves derived from different functions are in absolute dollars per barrel-mile for each throughput, not in the relative positions of the intermediate-run cost curves for each line. The latter is the important point for public policy considerations. A crude oil trunk pipe-line production function is shown in Figure 2. This chart assumes a more or less typical Mid-Continent (60 SUS viscosity, 34°; API gravity) crude, ¼ inch pipe throughout the lines, lines 1000 miles in length with a 5 per cent terrain variation (giving 1050 miles of pipe), and no net gravity flow in the line (there may be hills as long as there are offsetting valleys). The production function covers throughputs of 25, 50, 75, 100, 125, 200, 250, 300, 350 and 400 thousand barrels per day; this encompasses the range of throughputs for crude oil trunk lines which have yet been built. The curves in the chart show the amounts of horse-power required for the several line sizes which

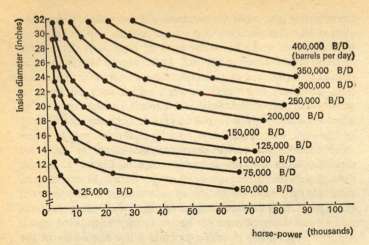

Figure 2 Production function for crude oil trunk pipe lines: line diameter versus horse-power versus throughput – 1000 mile lines[1]

might be used for a given throughput; each curve applies to one of the throughputs listed. The line sizes used are $8\frac{5}{8}$, $10\frac{3}{4}$, $12\frac{3}{4}$, 14, 16, 18, 20, 22, 24, 26, 30 and 32 inches (outside diameter) all having $\frac{1}{4}$ inch walls. This covers all line sizes used for recent crude lines. (Standard line pipe is only available in these sizes in the 8 to 32 inch range.) It will be noted that this is in reality a three-dimensional function, with line diameter and horse-power on a plane and with the throughput axis rising perpendicularly to this plane. The production function was computed by the use of a hydraulic formula for computing required horse-powers for various volumes of liquid flow in pipes of the sizes just noted, with appropriate constants for oil of the type used. This formula, simplified, is:

$$T^{2\cdot735} = (H)\,(D^{4\cdot735}) \div (0\cdot01046),$$

where T = throughput,
$\quad\quad\quad H$ = horse-power and
$\quad\quad\quad D$ = inside diameter of pipe.

1. Assumptions: 60 SUS, 34° API crude; no influence of gravity on flow; 5 per cent terrain variation (equalized up and down hill); $\frac{1}{4}$ inch pipe throughout.

200 Costs

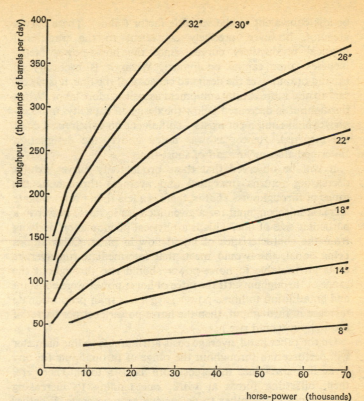

Figure 3 Vertical cross section of production function: horse-power versus throughput – line diameter held constant

Figure 3 shows vertical cross sections of the production function drawn perpendicular to the line-diameter axis. These are intermediate-run physical productivity curves which show the amount of horse-power that must be used with any given line size for various throughputs. They are analogous to traditional physical productivity curves of economic theory. Such a physical productivity curve in the textbooks might show the amount of wheat that can be produced from an acre of land by the use of varying numbers of workers, where line diameter is equivalent to the fixed factor (land) and horse-power is more or less equivalent to the variable factor (labor). These curves are not, however, precisely equivalent to the traditional physical productivity curves, since the horse-power factor includes some capital equipment. When it is necessary to expand output over the designed capacity of the line, it is necessary to add more capital equipment as well as more labor. When throughput is decreased below the designed capacity, unnecessary capital equipment exists – equipment on which fixed costs are incurred. Hence, as was noted above, the designation 'intermediate-run' instead of short-run.

It will be observed that these productivity curves exhibit decreasing returns (marginal and average) throughout the range of throughputs. That is, there is a less than proportionate increase in throughput for a given increase in horse-power in a particular size of line. This is a physical phenomenon deriving from the characteristics of liquid flow in pipes. Other things being equal, this would mean that intermediate-run average costs attributable to horse-power should rise throughout the range of throughputs. (If the price of horse-power were constant and an addition to horse-power gave a less than proportionate increase in throughput, then the horse-power cost per barrel of throughput would rise.)

On the other hand, average costs attributable to line diameter will perforce fall throughout the range of throughputs for any given line size, since these costs are fixed in total. There are, then, offsetting forces at work, one tending to increasing average costs, the other to decreasing average costs. Whether aggregate average costs would rise, fall or both, depends on the relative magnitudes of the horse-power and line diameter costs. In this case it will be seen that U-shaped intermediate-run average cost curves result. That is, average costs fall at first, but then level off and rise as more and more horse-power is added to a given line. (The initial fall is accentuated by the fact that the price of horse-power falls somewhat as total horse-power used on a given line increases, thereby offsetting to some extent the decreasing physical returns.)

Figure 4 shows vertical cross sections of the production function drawn perpendicular to the horse-power axis, as opposed to those in Figure 3 which are drawn perpendicular

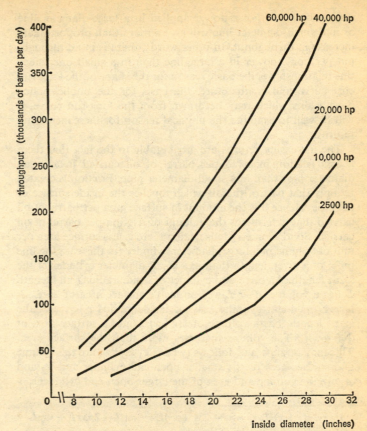

Figure 4 Vertical cross section of production function: line diameter versus throughput for selected horse-powers

to the line-diameter axis. These cross sections indicate what happens when horse-power is held constant and additional throughput is obtained by the use of more line diameter (a long-run movement over the production function surface that is possible only when planning the line, not after the line is built). It will be observed that these curves exhibit *increasing* physical returns (average and marginal) to scale. This means that the same amount of horse-power applied in a large-diameter line as in a small-diameter line will give a more than proportionate increase in throughput. In other words, there is more throughput per horse-power in a large line than in a small one. Since this relationship is the basic reason for the shape of the long-run cost curve and is, therefore, the basis for the public policy conclusions which may be drawn from the long-run curve, it will be well to examine the physical reason for these increasing returns.

The increasing returns are attributable to the fact that there is less friction incurred per barrel of oil carried in a large-diameter pipe than in a small-diameter pipe. Friction is created by only that part of the oil which touches the inside surface of the pipe. Hence it is the amount of surface area per barrel of oil carried that determines the amount of friction per barrel of oil carried. Solid geometry tells us that there is less surface area per unit of volume in a large-diameter cylinder (in this case the line pipe) of a given length than in a small-diameter cylinder of the same length. An open-end cylinder of inside radius r and length L has a volume of $\pi r^2 L$ and an inside surface area of $2\pi r L$. A larger open-end cylinder, say of inside radius $r+x$, and the same length, has a volume of $\pi(r+x)^2 L$ and a surface area of $2\pi(r+x)L$. The volume increases more than the surface area. This may be shown as follows (where V_1 and A_1 are the volume and surface area of the smaller open-end cylinder and V_2 and A_2 are the volume and area of the larger open-end cylinder):

$$V_1 = \pi r^2 L$$
$$V_2 = \pi(r+x)^2 L = \pi(r^2+2xr+x^2)L = \pi r^2 L + 2\pi xrL + \pi x^2 L$$
$$\Delta V = V_2 - V_1 = 2\pi xrL + x^2 \pi L$$
$$A_1 = 2\pi rL$$
$$A_2 = 2\pi(r+x)L = 2\pi rL + 2\pi xL$$
$$\Delta A = A_2 - A_1 = 2\pi xL.$$
Since $2\pi xrL + x^2 \pi L > 2\pi xL,$
$$\Delta V > \Delta A.$$

The volume increased by $(2\pi xrL + x^2 \pi L)$, while the surface area increased only by $2\pi xL$. It may be concluded that there is more volume per unit of surface area in a large than in a small pipe. This means that more oil can be transported per unit of surface

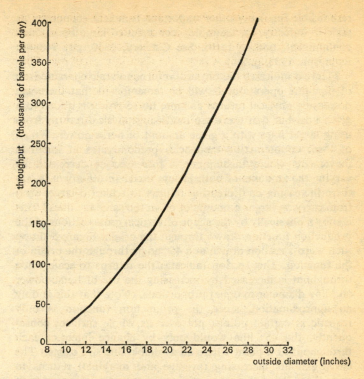

Figure 5 Physical returns to scale. Vertical cross section of production function through origin (45° angle)

area touched in a large than a small pipe. Since the amount of friction generated depends on the amount of surface area touched, it follows that more oil can be carried per given amount of friction developed in a large than in a small pipe. Therefore, the horse-power required to overcome a given amount of friction will propel more oil per day through a large pipe than through a small pipe. In short, because of the volume area relationship it is possible to develop more throughput per horse-power applied in large pipes than in small ones. (It is interesting to note that the volume–area relationship is

L. Cookenboo, Jr 205

responsible for many other important technical economies of scale in industry, for example, economies of large tanks, heat containment, and so forth. See Chenery, 1950, pp. 140–41; Robinson, 1935, p. 29.)

Figure 5 indicates the physical returns to scale characteristic of pipe-line operation. It will be remembered that there are decreasing physical returns as more horse-power is added to a given line, but that there are increasing physical returns from using larger lines with a given amount of horse-power. Which of these counteracting tendencies predominates in long-run movements where throughput is increased or decreased by varying the amounts of both factors used? In other words, are there increasing or decreasing returns to scale (to larger size) from carrying larger amounts of oil in the same facilities? This is shown physically by the shape of vertical cross sections of the production function drawn through the origin. Figure 5 shows such a cross section drawn at a 45° angle through the origin of the function. This section indicates the returns to scale when throughput is increased by increasing the use of horse-power and line diameter in equal proportions. (Note that this is only an approximation, since the production function is only realistic at certain points, not over its whole surface; consequently, the 45° line would only by chance intersect each throughput at a point where an available line size exists.) The curve exhibits increasing (average and marginal) returns to scale throughout the range of throughputs. In other words, if the amounts of horse-power and line diameter used are increased in equal proportions, then there would be a more than proportionate increase in throughput. This indicates that on an *a priori* basis it would be expected that long-run decreasing average costs would characterize pipe-line operation. Only if the price of one or both of the factors should increase sufficiently with the amount of the factor used to offset the increasing returns, would the long-run cost curve turn up. Actually, the price of horse-power decreases somewhat with the amount used, and the price of line diameter does not fluctuate sufficiently with the amount used to offset the physical relationship.

Lest the reader object to drawing these general conclusions only on the basis of an example where expansion is by increased utilization of the factors in equal proportions, it should be pointed out that this is a 'homogeneous' production function. Homogeneous production functions exhibit the same type of returns to scale on all parts of the surface. The function used reduces to (see page 200):

$$T^{2 \cdot 735} = (H)(D^{4 \cdot 735})(C),$$

or

$$T = (H^{\frac{1}{2 \cdot 735}})(D^{\frac{4 \cdot 735}{2 \cdot 735}})(C) = (H^{0 \cdot 37})(D^{1 \cdot 73})(C).$$

This is a function of the form,

$$T = H^m D^n C.$$

Such a function is homogeneous if $(m+n)$ is a constant, as it is in this case, where $(m+n) = 2 \cdot 1$. This also indicates that there are marked increasing returns to scale, since the function is of order 2 (constant returns to scale are implied from a function having an order of one).

The discussion of the technological relationships peculiar to pipe-line transportation of oil may now be summarized. A basic physical relationship may be deduced for the purpose of computing pipe-line costs. This relationship shows that there will be markedly increasing long-run physical returns to scale if larger and larger throughputs are carried. In the intermediate-run physical returns decrease. It follows, assuming that factor prices are more or less constant with the amount of the factor used, that there will be long-run decreasing costs (economies of scale) for pipe-line operation. Intermediate-run costs might rise, fall or both – since the increasing average costs attributable to horse-power are counteracted by fixed costs attributable to line diameter. Under such conditions, U-shaped curves are feasible. These cost conclusions are based solely on the physical relationships discussed and are independent of the cost determination to be considered next. The conclusions would be invalidated only if the price of one or both of the factors rose sufficiently with increases in the amount of the factor used to offset the increasing physical returns to scale. This is not the case. (This may also be predicted to a considerable extent apart from actual cost determination, since the amounts of the most important single cost items included in each factor are proportional to the amounts of the factors used.)

Costs

Pipe-line costs may be divided into three basic categories: (a) those variant with line diameter; (b) those variant with horse-power; (c) those variant only with throughput or length of line (a relatively small part of total cost). Since there is a choice for any given throughput among several possible combinations of line diameter and horse-power (as is shown in the production function in Figure 2), in order to be able to compute a long-run cost curve it is necessary to determine which of several possible combinations is least expensive for any throughput. This is done for each throughput by determining the total cost of each possible combination on, say, an annual basis. That combination whose total cost is least for a given throughput is the optimum combination for that throughput. Note that it is only the costs of line diameter and horse-power which must be so manipulated, since the other costs are irrelevant to the choice of the optimum combination of these two. The other costs are, of course, incurred and cannot be ignored; but they do not influence the choice of the proper size line for a given through-put.

Annual total intermediate-run costs are shown in Figure 6; these are derived by plotting annual total cost against through-put for each line diameter covered in the study. The shaded envelope of the intermediate-run cost curves is the long-run total cost curve. Figure 7 shows intermediate-run costs per barrel per 1000 miles (that is, average costs). This is a chart analogous to Figure 1 above. Its envelope is the long-run average cost curve. In the range of throughputs where the average cost curve of a given line size lies below all other average cost curves, that line is the optimum line for the throughputs covered. For example, the 30 inch line lies beneath all others between about 225,000 and 325,000 barrels per day; hence, it is the optimum line for throughputs between those limits.

The intermediate-run cost curves also show what it would cost to carry larger quantities of oil than the design throughput

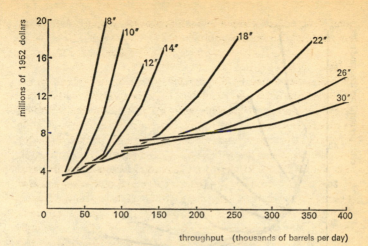

Figure 6 Annual total costs of operating crude oil trunk pipe lines.
(From Cookenboo, 1954, table 19)

if stations were added subsequent to the building of the line.
(Pipe lines cannot be operated at throughputs greater than the
designed capacity without the additions of more stations, since
the design capacity would require the highest operating
pressures permitted by the safety factor.) Remember that the
intermediate-run curve does *not* show the costs of throughputs
less than the design throughput.

While, as was pointed out above, the details of the cost study
lying behind the totals in Figures 6 and 7 are discussed at
length in Cookenboo (1954), a word or two should be said
about the assumptions involved in the engineering-type cost
determination. The principal items involved in the cost of line
diameter are all represented by initial outlays made during the
construction of the line. The most important line costs are the
service costs of laying the line, and the material costs of steel,
pipe coating, line block valves, corrosion protection, and so
forth. The assumptions of the characteristics of the lines, listed
above, were 1000 miles of ¼ inch pipe having fifty miles of
terrain variation (with no net gravity flow). This means that the
line costs include the material and service costs of laying 1050

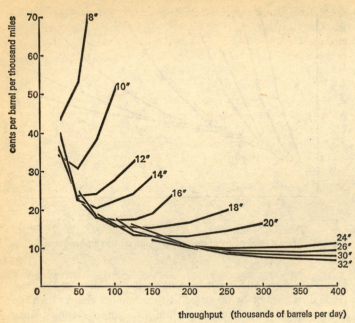

Figure 7 Costs per barrel of operating crude oil trunk pipe lines.
(From Cookenboo, 1954, table 19)

miles of pipe (coated in accord with the best coating practice
and protected by magnesium anodes).

The principal items involved in the costs of horse-power are
the annual expenditures for electric power and labor (and of
less importance, maintenance) to operate the pumping stations.
This category also includes the initial cost of the stations; this
represents the most difficult, time-consuming part of a pipe-line
cost computation (even though station costs are not too
important in relation to total costs). The stations used on the
pipe lines described in Figures 6 and 7 are semiautomatic,
equipped with centrifugal pumps and electric motors. Stations
pumping over 100,000 barrels per day are equipped with three
full-size pumps and motors (one motor per pump) which
together deliver the capacity throughput, and one half-size

210 Costs

pump and motor. This provides flexibility of operation which would otherwise be unattainable with constant speed electric motors. (With, as they say, $3\frac{1}{2}$ pumps, seven stages of operation are possible: no pumps, $\frac{1}{2}$ pump, $1\frac{1}{2}$, 2, $2\frac{1}{2}$ and 3 for capacity.) Stations pumping less than 100,000 barrels per day utilize two full-size pumps and one half-size pump. Each station utilizes in-and-out piping to permit the bypassing of any one pump without shutting down the whole station. The labor force required for such semiautomatic stations is two men per shift (regardless of the level of operation), unless the stations are very large; none used in this study was large enough to require extra operators. (In a semiautomatic pumping station the principal tasks of the operators are to watch the controls, shut off motor-operated valves when necessary, and maintain the equipment.)

The principal costs involved in the 'other' category are the initial costs of (a) tankage (the lines in this study have twelve and a half days' supply of storage capacity along the line), (b) surveying the right-of-way, (c) damages to terrain crossed, and (d) a communications system (here assumed to be a twelve-channel micro-wave system). It should be noted that while these costs vary either with throughput or with length of line, they are *proportional* to either throughput or length of line as the case may be. There are no significant per-barrel costs of a pipe line which change with length. The only such costs are those of a central office force; these are inconsequential in relation to total. Hence, it is possible to state that costs per barrel-mile for a 1000 mile trunk line are representative of costs per barrel-mile of any trunk line (those, say, seventy-five or a hundred miles in length and longer).

It will be observed in Figure 7 that there are economies of scale (decreasing long-run average costs) throughout the range of throughputs covered. The analysis was only carried through 32 inch lines and 400,000 barrels per day. However, if larger lines could be had at a constant price per ton of steel (the only price per unit of material likely to change with larger amounts than those used), then the long-run average cost curve would fall even farther. On the other hand, pipe much larger than 34 or 36 inches might well require the creation of special pipe-making facilities and, consequently, might command a higher price per ton than the pipe sizes used in this study. In this case, the long-run average cost curve might turn up near, say, 500,000 barrels per day. In any event, the rate of decrease of the average cost curve has declined appreciably by the time a throughput of 400,000 barrels per day is reached. Consequently, the cost per barrel of carrying a throughput of 400,000 barrels per day is probably close to the minimum that can be achieved with present pipe-making facilities.

It may also be noted from Figure 7, especially in the case of the large-diameter lines, that throughput can be expanded

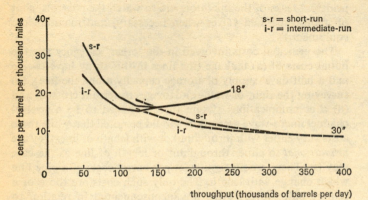

Figure 8 Short-run average costs of transporting crude oil in trunk lines. (*Note:* 18 inch line designed for 150,000 barrels per day; 30 inch line designed for 300,000 barrels per day)

appreciably over the design throughput before higher per-barrel costs than the original costs are incurred. (For a while, of course, there would actually be a decline in per-barrel costs.) For example, a 24 inch line built for 200,000 barrels per day could, if necessary, later be used for 300,000 barrels per day (after adding the required number of stations) without incurring increased costs per barrel.

Short-run cost curves could be computed for any of the possible combinations of line diameter and horse-power shown in Figure 2 – since each line would have a different short-run cost curve for each throughput it might carry. Building seven stations on an 18 inch line would yield one short-run curve. Building ten stations on an 18 inch line would yield another short-run curve. Building seven stations on a 20 inch line would yield yet another short-run curve – *ad infinitum*. To avoid the labor involved in computing short-run costs for every combination of line diameter and horse-power covered in the study (seventy-five in all), two were computed: one for an 18 inch line carrying 100,000 barrels per day, another for a 30 inch line carrying 300,000 barrels per day. The relative positions of short- and intermediate-run curves would be the same for any other combinations of line diameter and horse-power. These short-run average cost curves are shown in Figure 8.

Observe that short-run average costs are always higher than intermediate-run average costs for throughputs less than the designed throughput (the short-run curve does not exist for higher throughputs, since pipe lines cannot be operated over the designed capacity without violating the safety factor). The significance of this is that a line built to carry 250,000 barrels per day will incur higher costs than necessary if it consistently carries 200,000 barrels per day. If it had been designed for 200,000 barrels per day, then the intermediate-run cost for 200,000 barrels per day would be the cost incurred. This figure is less than the short-run cost of 200,000 barrels per day on a line with a capacity of 250,000 barrels per day.

This may be made clear by discussing briefly the process of computation of short-run costs. The only significant cost of a pipe line that is not fixed once the line is built is the cost of electric power. If the line is run below capacity, as many workers are still needed; and, of course, the same number of stations and the same amount of pipe exists. The only significant saving is in power costs. In order to compute short-run costs one simply subtracts the cost of the appropriate amount of electric power which is saved when throughput is cut to various levels from the intermediate-run cost at the designed output. This figure must be higher than intermediate-run costs of lesser throughputs because these costs are computed upon the basis of the proper (smaller) number of stations for the smaller throughputs. It should be noted that a given cut in throughput means a more than proportionate saving in power requirements, since electric power requirements vary with horse-power requirements. Remember that it takes a more than proportionate increase in horse-power to get a given increase in throughput; conversely, a decrease in throughput means a more than proportionate decrease in horse-power required – and hence a more than proportionate decrease in electric power required.

Summary

Intermediate-, long- and short-run costs for carrying crude oil were computed.

The long- and intermediate-run cost curves computed in a study of the engineering estimation type are of the same shape that would be predicted from the physical production functions for pipe-line transportation of crude (with no consideration of costs). The physical production function is homogeneous of order 2; under these conditions there will be marked economies of scale unless factor prices rise sharply with the amount of the factor used. This is not the case in the range of throughputs and line sizes covered.

The long-run average cost curve falls throughout the range of throughputs covered (see Figure 7), and it would continue to fall indefinitely if larger pipe could be obtained without paying a premium price. However, the rate of decline of long-run costs per barrel has slowed considerably by the time a throughput of 400,000 barrels per day is reached. Intermediate-run curves are U-shaped, but throughput can be increased appreciably over the designed level without increased per-barrel costs – especially in the case of large-diameter lines where the U is rather flat over wide ranges of throughputs.

Short-run costs are always greater than intermediate-run costs for a given line size. The only significant variable cost in pipeline operation is the cost of power (or fuel).

It may be concluded from these cost curves that the economies of scale characteristic of the operation of pipe lines require that oil must be carried conglomerately in as large quantities as is possible in large-diameter line. This gives the least transportation costs obtainable – the optimum situation from the point of view of both the firm and society. Furthermore, pipe lines should not be run at throughputs appreciably below capacity; otherwise higher (short-run) costs per barrel will be incurred than need be. Finally, the capacity of a large line can be expanded appreciably without increasing average costs; indeed, *decreased* average costs can be obtained with moderate expansions.

References

CHENERY, H. B. (1950), 'Engineering bases of economic analysis', unpublished doctoral thesis, Harvard University.
COOKENBOO, L., Jr (1954), 'Costs of operating crude oil pipe lines', *Rice Institute Pamphlet*, April, pp. 35–113.
ROBINSON, E. A. G. (1935), *Structure of Competitive Industry*, Nisbet.

9 Om P. Tangri

Omissions in the Treatment of the Law of Variable Proportions[1]

Om P. Tangri, 'Omissions in the treatment of the law of variable proportions', *American Economic Review*, vol. 56, 1966, pp. 484–93.

The purpose of this paper is to clarify two points with respect to the treatment of the Law of Variable Proportions (hereafter referred to as the Law) in most economics textbooks. The first concerns cost and product relationships in stage III, commonly called the 'irrational' region[2] of production, and the second deals with the symmetry of regions I and III.

Although stage III is an irrational area of production, it is not uncommon for firms lacking perfect knowledge actually to produce in that region, particularly in agriculture. As Bishop and Toussaint note (1958, p. 41),

evidence of production in region III is often noted. For example, during the late summer and fall months, we frequently have evidence of too many cattle on a given quantity of pasture, resulting in overgrazing of pastures and less production than could have been obtained with fewer cattle. Also, we find evidence of overcrowding of broilers and layers in poultry houses.[3]

Regardless of the empirical incidence, however, the chief reason for examining cost curves in stage III lies in presenting a complete and consistent treatment of the product–cost relationships in all three phases of the Law.

1. Martin Ulrich, a graduate student in my seminar, started me on this paper by expressing skepticism on the standard treatment of cost–product relationships. My thanks to him and to Surendra Kulshrestha, both of whom assisted me by running the necessary input–output computations (not included in the paper). Thanks also to the referee, my colleagues at the University of Manitoba and my brother at Wayne State University.

2. The terms 'stage', 'region' and 'phase' are used interchangeably in this paper.

3. For additional examples, see Heady (1952, pp. 94, 170).

Most of the textbooks on economics discuss the various product functions and their interrelationships for all three phases of the production function in considerable detail. However, the corresponding cost functions are derived only for the first two phases of the Law and the relationship between product and cost functions in stage III has been neglected, stated ambiguously, or misinterpreted.

The common practice is to draw a standard sigmoid-type total cost function and its corresponding average and marginal cost functions. This tends to leave the reader either wondering as to the product–cost relationships in the third phase or under the erroneous impression that the total, average and marginal cost functions as drawn are for all phases of the Law and that they continue to have a positive slope, even though the total product function assumes a negative slope in the third region.[4] The writer has found both undergraduate and graduate students curious and confused about this.

The cost–product diagram (Figure 1), reproduced from a recent textbook on agricultural economics by Snodgrass and Wallace (1964, p. 235), will show that the confusion is not confined to students alone. In providing a vivid illustration of the cost–product relationships, the authors completely overlook the point that the average variable cost (AVC) function cannot continue to rise with a positive slope, as shown in Figure 1, for the output beyond point C on the total physical product (TPP) function or on the marginal physical product (MPP) function, because from C onwards the TPP is falling and the MPP is negative. It is true that the authors recognize 'that the horizontal and vertical axes in each of the three figures [panels a, b and c, in Figure 1] . . . are not comparable on a quantitative basis [but] the importance is to show the relationship between various points on the physical product curves and the cost curves . . .' (Snodgrass and Wallace, 1964, p. 235). However, it is in this

4. Heady (1952, p. 94) is one of the few texts which advises the reader explicitly that the stages of increasing average and diminishing total returns are not drawn in subsequent chapters of the book. To the best of my knowledge, Vickrey (1964, pp. 159–60) is the only author who makes a brief reference to and draws very tiny portions of the backward-rising AVC and TVC functions. However, he does not show the complete interrelationships between various product and cost functions.

effort to show the relationship between various points on the product and cost functions that they either make the said error or at least fail to warn the reader anywhere in the book that such an error is due to the lack of exact quantitative correspondence between the horizontal and vertical axes of the three panels of the figure.

Interrelationships between product and cost functions

Figures 2 and 3 illustrate product–cost relationships for all phases of the Law. The product functions in Figure 2 are based on the production function:[5]

$$Y = 4 \cdot 0X + 0 \cdot 5X^2 - 0 \cdot 15X^3 \qquad\qquad 1$$

where Y represents total physical product, and X stands for the variable input which is being applied to a fixed amount of another input. This fixed input (not explicitly included in the production function) is assumed to be perfectly divisible and adaptable. The marginal physical product function, therefore, is given by

$$\frac{dY}{dX} = 4 + 1 \cdot 0X - 0 \cdot 45X^2. \qquad\qquad 2$$

In deriving cost functions (Figure 3) from product functions (Figure 2) it is assumed that the input market is perfectly competitive, so that the variable factor of production can be purchased at a constant price per unit of the input, irrespective of its quantity bought. The assumed input price, $Px = \$3$ per unit.

From Figures 2 and 3 it will be noted that when region III, the area of diminishing *total* returns, is included in the cost analysis, the various standard cost functions take on some peculiar attributes. In Figure 3, the total variable cost (TVC) function no longer remains single-valued; instead it becomes bi-valued. The TVC for all phases of the Law is denoted by OAB; the broken segment AB represents TVC for stage III. Notice that in this region, TVC continues to rise until point B,

5. This production is taken from Heady (1952, p. 39), except that the constant term, 40, has been dropped in order to keep our TPP function similar to the familiar textbook TPP which usually starts from the origin.

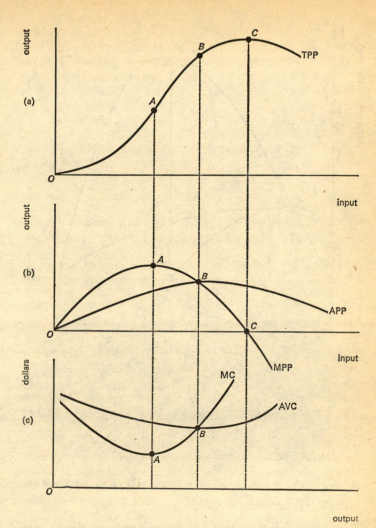

Figure 1 Product and cost curves. (From Snodgrass and Wallace, 1964, p.235)

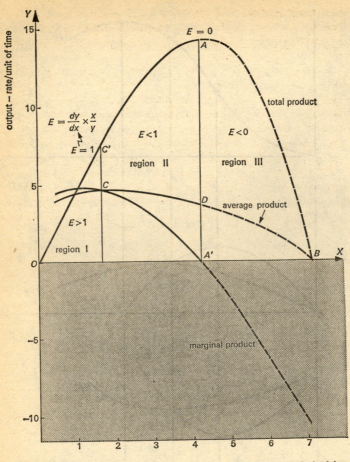

Figure 2 Factor–product relationships

a point representing a high positive cost but zero output, and has a negative slope because output is continuously falling, a phenomenon quite consistent with stage III.

The AVC function in Figure 3, represented by aDa', develops a cusp at D, a point representing the end of stage II and

beginning of stage III. After this point, the broken line *Da'*
denotes A V C for stage III. In this region, since output begins
to fall after point *D*, *Da'* assumes a negative slope. It is of the

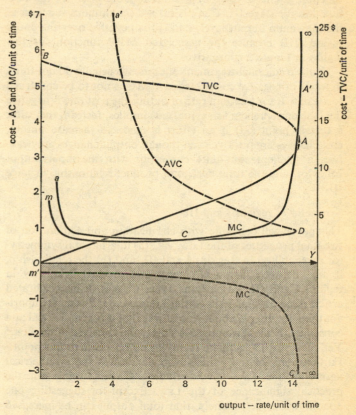

Figure 3 Cost–product relationships

same general shape as the A V C function, *aD*, in stages I and II,
but is at a higher cost level.

Again, diminishing *total* returns in production cause a
discontinuity in the marginal cost (M C) function. The complete
M C function for all regions of the Law is shown by *mCA'C'm'*

(Figure 3), where mCA' represents the M C function for stages I and II, and $C'm'$ denotes M C for stage III. It will be noted from Figure 3 that at point A' (maximum output), the M C function attains a value of $\pm\infty$. Therefore after A', the M C function for stage III, $C'm'$, is (a) a discontinuous function at the maximum output level, and (b) is negative over the entire region (III) because the associated M PP function for this region in Figure 2 is negative.

In our traditional treatment of costs, we usually do not think in terms of negative costs. Negative M C is not to be construed to mean that for a certain rate of output the cost rate is negative (i.e. the entrepreneur is saving) but implies, instead, that after a certain point (A') if an effort is made to increase output, cost changes are positive even though output changes are negative, a phenomenon quite consistent with the input–output behavior, and the total cost/total product relationship in stage III.

Symmetry of regions I and III

This paper will conclude with clarification and elaboration of two final properties of the Law, viz., (a) interfactoral symmetry[6] (or reversibility) in Regions I and III, and (b) the relationship, if any, between factor symmetry and product symmetry in regions I and III. As early as 1936, Cassels in his celebrated article (see p. 108 of 1946 edition) remarked: 'The most important thing to observe about this Law is that it is symmetrical and consequently the third phase is simply the converse of the first.' Yet, most textbooks make scanty or no reference to this point.[7] Furthermore, of the writers who do discuss the symmetrical nature of the Law, few, including Cassels, bring out the practical significance of the Law. Except for suggesting one operational aspect, namely, that total output can be increased in either region I or region III by reducing the relative intensity

6. The term 'symmetry' is used here to imply reversibility of factor proportions (or factor position) rather than strict mathematical symmetry.

7. Of some fifteen texts consulted, only a few, viz., Heady (1952, pp. 76-8), Leftwich (1958, pp. 116–21) and Stigler (1947, p. 125) discuss this point adequately. Even as good a text as Samuelson's (1964, pp. 518–19) devotes only five and a half lines to this point.

of the excessive factor, most of the writers leave the reader with the impression that symmetry of the Law is a mere theoretical nicety.

In our analysis of factor–product relations, Figure 2, it would be recalled that factor X (explicitly included in the production function) was treated as a variable factor of production. It was applied in equal incremental units to a given amount of some other factor (not explicitly included in the production function) which was treated as a fixed factor of production. Thus, in region I, where the ratio of the variable factor to the fixed factor is relatively low, the marginal physical product for the variable factor is positive and greater than the average physical product (until $MPPx = APPx$ at the outer boundary of region I).[8] In region III, however, where the ratio of the variable factor to the fixed factor is relatively high, MPP of the variable factor is negative and below the APP of this factor.

By reversing the positions of these factors, one can easily see that a low variable-fixed factor ratio in region I means a high fixed-variable factor ratio in the same region. Accordingly, when the MPP for our variable factor is positive in this region, it is negative for the other input in the same region. Likewise, in region III a high variable-fixed factor ratio means a low fixed-variable factor ratio in the same region. Thus, when the MPP for our variable factor is negative, it is positive for the other factor. In short, region I for one input is region III for some other input, and vice versa.[9]

The importance of factor reversibility lies not only in deciding *when* a particular factor of production should be decreased to increase production, but also in deciding *what* factor of production should be treated as variable or fixed in a given economic environment. These are not easy decisions. They confront not only entrepreneurs at the individual level but also policy makers at the national level whenever they are concerned

8. It is recognized that the location of the boundary between regions I and II at the point where MPP = APP holds true only when the production function is homogenous of the first degree. If either diminishing or increasing returns to scale are present, the boundary between regions I and II will not be marked by the equality of MPP and APP.

9. For an excellent graphic and tabular illustration of this point, see Leftwich (1958, pp. 116–21).

with optimum resource allocation. An example from Heady (1952, p. 77) will illustrate the point.

Within a cropping year, a farmer may consider hog numbers as fixed and corn as variable; he can either sell the year's corn crop or feed it in varying amounts to a given number of spring-farrowed pigs. Or, he can consider the corn crop as fixed and vary the number of hogs in proportion to it; the corn can be stored into the next year and opportunities will be open for farrowing more pigs. At the national level, food emergencies may arise which call for either feeding more or less grain to a given number of hogs within a year or storing the corn and increasing the number of hogs to which it might be fed. Which system will give greatest profits to the farmer or food to the nation?

Answers to such complicated problems can be determined only by an analysis of both the physical and economic relationships. The important point is that reversibility of the technical inputs not only allows the interchange of factor positions but also provides the necessary, though not sufficient, basis on which this choice is exercised. The usual textbook discussion of symmetry and optimum factor proportions then becomes meaningful.

The second point concerns the relationship, if any, between factor symmetry and product symmetry in regions I and III. Having read the class assignment on the symmetry of the Law in standard sources, many students ask: If regions I and III are symmetrical, why doesn't the TPP curve in region III have an inflection point corresponding to the inflection point in region I? In terms of the MPP function, why doesn't it achieve a maximum negative value in region III corresponding to the maximum positive value in region I, and reverse its direction toward zero (B in Figure 2) as it does toward the zero value (A' in Figure 2)?

These questions reveal a confusion between factor symmetry and product symmetry in regions I and III. Even though factor symmetry makes regions I and III the converse of each other, it does not necessarily mean that the *rate* of increase in total product in region I must be symmetrical to the *rate* of product loss in region III. Hence the difference in the exact behavior and shapes of the TPP and MPP curves in regions I and III.

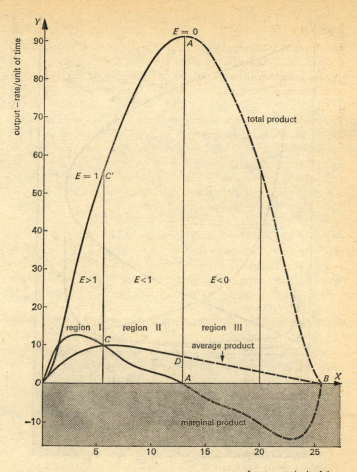

Figure 4 Factor–product relationships

The MPP curve in region III would achieve a maximum negative value and reverse its direction to join *B* only if the TPP curve in region III, under some special circumstances, were exactly symmetrical (used here in the mathematical sense) to the TPP curve in *both* regions I and II, i.e. if the TPP were

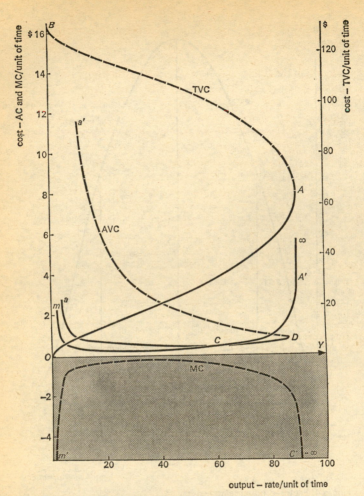

Figure 5 Cost–product relationships

symmetrical about the input value corresponding to the maximum **TPP** value. This is illustrated in Figure 4 where the **TPP** is symmetrical about input (X) value of 13. The **MPP** in region III, therefore, is an exact mirror image of the **MPP** in regions I and II. The corresponding cost functions are shown in Figure 5. Here the M C function in region III, corresponding to the M P P behavior, is also an exact mirror image of the M C function in the first two regions. But, this situation, as remarked earlier, is rather unusual. Theoretically, there is more reason to believe that the T P P curve would be nonsymmetrical than symmetrical. As Cassels stated (1936, p. 109 of 1946 reprint), 'since the *proportions* of the factors are less affected by each additional unit of the variable factor as we move to the right along the *X*-axis it is clear that *in general* the third phase must be more prolonged than the first'.

References

BISHOP, C. E., and TOUSSAINT, W. D. (1958), *Introduction to Agricultural Analysis*, Wiley.
CASSELS, J. M. (1936), 'On the Law of Variable Properties', in *Explorations in Economics: Notes and Essays Contributed in Honor of F. W. Taussig*, McGraw-Hill, pp. 223–36. Reprinted in *Readings in the Theory of Income Distribution*, vol. 3, 1946, American Economic Association.
HEADY, E. O. (1952), *Economics of Agricultural Production and Resource Use*, Prentice-Hall.
LEFTWICH, R. H. (1958), *The Price System and Resource Allocation*, Holt, Rinehart & Winston, 2nd edn.
SAMUELSON, P. A. (1964), *Economics: An Introductory Analysis*, McGraw-Hill, 6th edn.
SNODGRASS, M. M., and WALLACE, L. T. (1964), *Agriculture, Economics and Growth*, Appleton-Century-Crofts.
STIGLER, G. J. (1947), *The Theory of Price*, Macmillan Co., 2nd edn.
VICKREY, W. S. (1964), *Microstatics*, Harcourt, Brace & World.

10 Armen Alchian

Costs and Outputs

Armen Alchian, 'Costs and outputs', in *The Allocation of Economic Resources, Essays in Honor of B. F. Haley*, Stanford University Press, 1959, pp. 23–40.

Obscurities, ambiguities and errors exist in cost and supply analysis despite, or because of, the immense literature on the subject. Especially obscure are the relationships between cost and output, both in the long run and in the short run. Propositions designed to eliminate some of these ambiguities and errors are presented in this paper. More important, these suggested propositions seem to be empirically valid.

Costs

Costs will be defined initially as the change in equity caused by the performance of some specified operation where, for simplicity of exposition, the attendant change in income is not included in the computation of the change in equity. Suppose that according to one's balance sheet the present value of his assets were $100, and suppose that at the end of the operation one year later the value of his assets were expected to be $80, not counting the sale value of the product of the operation. The present value of $80 a year hence (at 6 per cent) is $75·47, which yields a cost in present capital value (equity) of $24·53. Because of logical difficulties in converting this present value concept into a satisfactory rate (per unit of time) concept, we defer a discussion of this problem and, for convenience, measure costs in units of present value or equity. Hereafter, the

1. Indebtedness to William Meckling of the RAND Corporation, who gave many long hours to discussion of the points raised herein, even before the first of several drafts, is very great. Although my egoism prevents sharing the authorship with him, I cannot absolve him from responsibility for any errors that still remain and likewise for any merit the paper may have.

unmodified expression 'costs' will always mean the present worth, capital value concept of cost, i.e. the change in equity.

Output

All the characteristics of a production operation can affect its cost. In this paper we want to direct attention to three characteristics:

1. The rate of output is typically regarded in economic analysis as the crucial feature. But it is only one feature, and concentration on it alone has led to serious error, as we shall see.

2. Total contemplated volume of output is another characteristic. Is a cumulated output volume of 10,000 or 100 or 1,000,000 units being contemplated? Whatever may be the rate of output, the total volume to be produced is a distinct feature with important effects on cost. Of course, for any rate of output, the larger the total cumulated volume to be produced, the longer the operation will continue. Hence, incorporated in this description of total output is the total time length of the programmed production. Will it span one month or one year, or (at the other extreme) is the contemplated total volume so large that at the rate of output an indefinitely long time is allowed to the production run?

3. The programmed time schedule of availability of output is a further characteristic. For a point output, the programmed date of the output availability is sufficient, but for outputs which continue over time, the time profile (delivery schedule) of the output replaces a single date. We shall call these three distinct aspects the output *rate*, the contemplated *total volume* and the programmed delivery *dates*.

These three characteristics can be summarized in the following definition, which also defines a fourth characteristic, *m*, the total length of the programmed schedule of outputs:

$$V = \sum_{T}^{T+m} x\,(t)\,dt.$$

In this expression *V* is the total contemplated volume of output, $x(t)$ the output rate at moment *t*, *T* the moment at which the first unit of output is to be completed and m the length of the interval over which the output is made available. Of these four features, only three are independently assignable; the fourth is then constrained. Unless specific exception is made, in the following we shall always discuss changes in only one of the features, V, $x(t)$ and T, assuming the other two to be constant and letting the full compensatory adjustment be made in m.[2]

Propositions about costs and output

Our task is now to make some propositions about the way costs are affected by changes in these variables. Letting C denote costs (i.e. the change in equity), we have

$$C = F(V, x, T, m)$$

subject to the definition of V, which constrains us to three degrees of freedom among the four variables.

Proposition 1

$$\left[\frac{\partial C}{\partial x(t)} \right]_{\substack{T = T_0 \\ V = V_0}} > 0. \qquad\qquad 1$$

The left-hand expression is the derivative of the costs with respect to x, when T and V are held constant, letting m make up the adjustment. It shows the change in costs when the rate of output is increased without increasing V and without changing the delivery date, but with an appropriate reduction of m. Proposition 1 states that the faster the rate at which a given volume of output is produced, the higher its cost. We emphasize that cost means the change in equity, not the *rate* of costs.

2. We note that time or dating enters in a multitude of ways: there is the date at which the delivery of output is to begin; there is the period of time used as a basis for the measure of the rate of output, i.e. so many units per day, per week or per year; and there is the total time over which the output is to be made available.

Proposition 2

$$\left[\frac{\partial^2 C}{\partial x^2}\right]_{\substack{V=V_0 \\ T=T_0}} > 0. \qquad\qquad 2$$

The increment in C is an increasing function of the output rate. This is a proposition about increasing marginal cost in present value measure, and is usually derived as an implication of efficient allocation of scarce heterogeneous resources among alternative uses.

Its validity, however, does not depend upon the validity of the premises of the classical model. For example, inventories need not increase in proportion to the rate of output if the variance of random deviations in output rates does not increase more than proportionally to the expected output rate. In this event, a sufficient condition for Proposition 2 as derived by the classical model would be upset. But destruction of sufficient conditions does not eliminate the possibility of all necessary conditions being fulfilled; thus, even if the classical model's assumptions are upset, the proposition could still be true. Whether or not it is, in fact, true cannot be settled by an examination of the model from which it is derived. For present purposes, Proposition 2 can be regarded, if one wishes, as a postulated proposition.[3]

Proposition 3

$$\left[\frac{\partial C}{\partial V}\right]_{\substack{x=x_0 \\ T=T_0}} > 0. \qquad\qquad 3$$

C increases with V for given x and date of initial output, T. At a constant output rate, for example, this will require a longer program of production, a larger m.

3. See Whitin and Peston (1954) for a longer discussion of some forces that could reverse the inequality of Proposition 2. Some of their suggested forces, e.g. relation between stocks of repairmen and number of machines, are circumvented by the ability to buy services instead of the agents themselves. Another weakness is the association of size of output with the number of independent random forces.

Proposition 4

$$\left[\frac{\partial^2 C}{\partial V^2}\right]_{\substack{x = x_0 \\ T = T_0}} < 0. \qquad\qquad 4$$

Increments in C diminishes as V increases, for any rate of output, x, and initial output date, T. Thus, for any constant rate of output, as the total planned output is increased by uniform increments, costs (changes in equity) will increase by diminishing increments. The 'reasons' for this proposition will be given later.

Proposition 4 also implies decreasing cost *per unit* of total volume, V. We shall state this as a separate proposition.

Proposition 5

$$\left[\frac{\partial C/V}{\partial V}\right]_{\substack{x = x_0 \\ T = T_0}} < 0. \qquad\qquad 4a$$

Graphic and numerical illustrations of Propositions 1 to 5

Graphic illustration

The above properties are shown by the cost surface in Figure 1. Proposition 1 describes the slope of a slice on the cost surface where the slice is parallel to the Cx plane. Proposition 2 states that the slope of the path of such a slice on the cost surface increases with x. Proposition 3 is portrayed by the slope of a slice along the surface parallel to the CV plane – going back into the page. The slope of this slice decreases as V increases. Proposition 4 describes the decreasing rate at which this surface of costs increases along this slice. Movements in other directions can be visualized. For example, one possible path is to start from the origin and move out some ray. This gives costs as a function of proportional increase in both the rate and the total output for a fixed interval of production, m, but the behavior of the cost slope of this slice, except for the fact that it is positive, cannot be derived from these propositions.

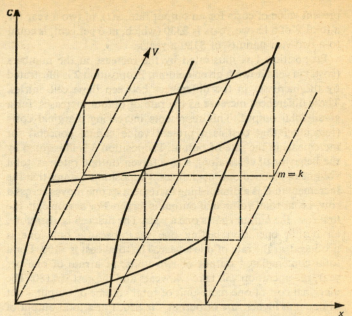

Figure 1 Cost surface as function of x and V

Tabular, arithmetic illustration

Table 1 Costs, Volume of Output and Rates of Output

Rate of output, x (per year)	Volume of output			
	1	2	3	4
1	100	180	255	325
2	120	195	265	330
3	145	215	280	340
4	175	240	300	355

For an output rate, x, of one per year, beginning at some specified T, production must continue for one year to get a total volume, V, of 1, for two years to get 2, three years for 3, etc. For a production rate of two per year, production must last one year to get 2 units, two years to get a total of 4, etc. The present value of costs for an output rate, $x(t)$, of two a year for a total V of 4 in two years is $330 (which, at 6 per cent, is equal to a two-year annuity of $180 a year).

Proposition 1 is illustrated by the increase in the numbers (costs) in cells down a given column. Proposition 2 is illustrated by the increases in the differences between these cell entries. These differences increase as the rate of output increases, for a given total output. This represents increasing marginal costs (remember that cost is a present value capital concept) for increments in the rate of output. Proposition 3 is illustrated by the behavior of costs along a row (given output rate) as total volume of planned output changes. Proposition 4 states that the increment in C is a diminishing increment as one moves across a row, i.e. as total volume of output is larger. For example, in the first row, the output *rate* is one a year. The first cell is, therefore, an output operation lasting one year, because only one is produced, at the rate of one a year. The total cost is $100. For a total contemplated output of two units, at a rate of one per year, the operation will take two years and the cost is $180. The marginal cost of one more unit of total volume of output – not of one unit higher *rate* of output – is $80. For a total output of three units in three years the cost is $255, an increment of $75, which is less than the previous increment of $80. Here the increments in cost are associated not with increments in rates of output, but with increments in total volume of output. Proposition 5 is illustrated by dividing the cell entries in a row by the output quantities at the head of each column. The quotient, cost per unit of output quantity, decreases as V increases.

Economic illustration

A comparison that could be made is the following: imagine a person to contemplate a total volume of output of one unit at the rate of one a year. But he subsequently revises his plans and produces one more in the next year at the rate of one a year, again planning to produce a total volume of just one unit. Compare the total costs of that operation with an operation in which two units of total output were initially planned at the rate of one a year. Both take two years, but the cost of the latter is $180 while the former's present value is $100 plus $100 discounted back one year at 6 per cent, or a total of $194. Thus it is cheaper to produce from a *plan* for a two-year output of two units at the rate of one a year than to produce two by repetition of methods which contemplate only one total unit of output at the same rate of one a year.

From this example it would appear that a reason for Proposition 4 is that better foresight enables one to see farther into the future and make more accurate forecasts; but this is not the reason, however helpful better foresight may be. A larger planned *V* is produced in a different way from that of a smaller planned *V*. A classic example is the printing press. To get three hundred copies of a letter in one day may be cheaper with mimeograph than with either typewriter or offset printing. The mimeograph method may be so much superior that, even if the rate of output were stepped up to 300 in an hour (instead of in a day), mimeographing might still be cheaper than typing. This does not deny that higher rates of output imply higher costs, as for example that 300 in an hour will cost more than 300 in two hours. The method of production is a function of the volume of output, especially when output is produced from basic dies – and there are few, if any, methods of production that do not involve 'dies'. Why increased expenditures on more durable dies should result in more than proportional increase of output potential is a question that cannot be answered, except to say that the physical principles of the world are not all linear (which may or may not be the same thing as 'indivisible').[4] Different methods of tooling, parts design and assembly is the usual explanation given in the production engineering literature.

Proposition 4 seems not to be part of current economic principles. Yet it may be the key to seeing the error in some attempts to refute Proposition 2, which applies to increased *rates* of output for constant total volume of output (or, as we shall see later, for perpetuity durations of output). Propositions 2 and 4 refer to two counterforces, rate of output and total planned volume of output. What would be the net effect of

4. Could it be that the term 'indivisibility' has been meant to cover this phenomenon? A yes or no answer to that question is impossible because of the extreme vagueness and ambiguity with which the term has been used. Furthermore, the question is probably of little, if any, significance.

increases in both cannot be deduced from the present propositions. All that can be said is that if the rate of output is increased for a given total contemplated volume of output, the increment in cost will be an increasing function of the rate of output. Proposition 4, on the other hand, implies diminishing increments as V increases, and it implies a lower per-unit cost for a larger total volume of output. Thus, we have the possibility that higher rates of production might be available at lower unit costs if they are associated with a larger volume of output, because this latter factor may be sufficient to overcome the effects of the higher output rate.

A larger volume of output could, of course, be obtained by both longer time and faster rates of production, but the relationship between time and volume should not be allowed to mask the fact that it is total contemplated volume of output – not the longer duration of output – that is here asserted (maybe erroneously) to be the factor at work in Propositions 3 and 4.

If both the *volume* and the *rate* of output change in the same direction, the two effects on costs are not in the same direction, and neither the net effect on the rate of change of *increments* in the cost nor even the effect on the costs per unit of total volume of output is implied by these or any other accepted postulates. It has been said, for example, that if some automobile manufacturer were to cut V, the volume of cars produced of a given year's model, from one million to half a million, costs per car would increase. This statement could refer either to a reduction in V achieved by producing for half the number of months at an unchanged monthly rate of output or to a simultaneous and parallel reduction in both V, the volume, and x, the monthly rate of output. If it refers to the former, it is a restatement of Proposition 5; if it refers to the latter, it is a statement that cannot be deduced from our propositions, which imply merely that costs would be lower if both V and x were reduced than if V alone were lowered.

Even returns to scale seem to have been confused with the effect of size of output. It is conjectured that a substantial portion of the alleged cases of increasing returns to scale in industries or firms is the result of ignoring the relation of costs to volume (rather than to rate) of output. The earlier discussions of automobile production and printing costs are simple illustrations of how this confusion can occur.

How many of the cases of alleged decreasing costs to *rates* of output are really decreasing costs to *volume* of output is an open question. Is it too much to expect that all of them can be so explained? Or that the realm of such cases can be greatly reduced by allowing for *V*, instead of letting *x* be the only variable? But that dirty empirical task is left for later and more ambitious efforts.

The observed concentration on a standardized model, e.g. four or five different sizes of tractors as distinct from a much greater possible range, is explained by the effect of volume of output on cost. Although an infinite range is possible, the concentration on a smaller set of fewer alternatives is more economical for most problems. The only way economic theory heretofore could explain this apparent anomaly was to invoke a falling cost curve for small output rates, in turn dependent upon some kind of unidentified indivisibility or returns to scale. Now the explanation may be contained in Propositions 4 and 9.

More Propositions

Four more propositions remain. Proposition 6 is given in a footnote because its implications will not be suggested in this paper.[5] Propositions 7 and 8 concern the effects of changes in *T*, the time between the decision to produce and the delivery of output.

Proposition 7

$$\left[\frac{\partial C}{\partial T}\right]_{\substack{x = x_0 \\ V = V_0}} < 0. \qquad\qquad 7$$

---

5. *Proposition 6*

$$\left[\frac{\partial^2 C}{\partial x \partial V}\right]_{T = T_0} < 0. \qquad\qquad 5$$

This says that the marginal present value-cost with respect to increased rates of output decreases as the total contemplated output increases. This can be regarded as a conjectural proposition, whose implications will

This is not shown in the graph or in the table, but it says that the longer the time between decision to produce and delivery of output, the less the cost.

If we think of a single output point, then T is relatively unambiguous. If the output is to be made available over a period of time, then T could be defined as the beginning moment of output. But many different output programs are possible, even when they all extend over the same interval. One might be tempted to use some sort of average T, say, the date of output weighted by the rate of output. However, such an average T cannot be used for our purposes, because any particular value of T can be identified with an infinite variety of output patterns. Since we are talking about partial derivatives, the whole problem is easily avoided. All we need do is to state that, if one moves any output program or schedule closer to the present (or

---

not be developed in this paper. And the same proposition can be re-expressed as

$$\left[\frac{\partial^2 C}{\partial V \partial x}\right]_{T = T_0} < 0. \qquad\qquad 6$$

This states that marginal present-value costs of increased quantity of output decrease as the rate of output increases.

Of interest is the relationship between these postulates and the implied shape of the production possibility function, where the rate and the volume of output are the two output alternatives. The cost isoquant with x and V as the arguments can be convex or concave. Usually a concave function is implied when rates of output of two different products are the arguments. However, J. Hirshleifer (1955) has pointed out that convex production possibilities are implicit in many engineering cost functions when quality and quantity are the alternative outputs. Hirshleifer, as it seems from his context, is really discussing cases where his quantity variable refers to volume and not to rate of output. Had he really meant rate of output rather than volume, his results might not have been so 'reasonable'. The convexity or concavity of the cost isoquant, it may be recalled, is given by the sign of

$$\frac{d^2 x}{dV^2} = \frac{F_{xx} F_y^2 - 2 F_{xv} F_x F_v + F_{vv} F_v^2}{F_v^3}.$$

Substituting our postulated conditions shows that the expression may be of any sign, hence the indeterminacy of the concavity or convexity property. However, concavity of the cost isoquant where the two arguments are rates of production for two different products is still implied.

farther into the future) by a simple time shift, T will have decreased (or increased). Whatever the shape of the output schedule, a reduction of the interval between the present moment and the beginning of the output date (a sort of uniform time-wise shifting) will increase cost. A more deferred output schedule (whatever its unchanged shape) will mean a lower cost.

Proposition 7 is really a corollary of Proposition 2. The slower the rate at which inputs are purchased, the lower their price because the lower are the costs to the seller, when Proposition 2 is applied to the seller.

Not only do the supply curves of inputs fall (or shift to the right) as more time is allowed, but the rates of shifting differ among inputs. The supply curves of some inputs are more elastic than those of others; and the rate at which the price elasticity of supply increases with T differs among inputs. Thus, while in an immediate period the price elasticity of supply of input x may be low relative to that of input y (and it may always be lower than that of y), the *ratio* of the costs of increments in y to the costs of increments in x may change with deferred purchase. If the ratio decreases, deferred purchases of y relative to purchases of x will be economical. In other words, it is not merely the slope of the supply curve or the price elasticity of supply that determines which inputs are going to be increased earliest. Rather, it is the rate at which these price elasticities *change* with deferred purchase that is critical. Thus, as stated earlier, the input x with a very low price elasticity of supply will vary more in the immediate period than the input of y with a higher price elasticity if the deferment of purchases by, say, a month would lower the cost of y more than that of x. As an extreme, if the supply curves of two inputs, x and y, were both horizontal, the input of one of them would be increased less if with deferred purchase the price or supply curve would become lower – though still horizontal. That input whose price would become lower with a deferred purchase would be increased in quantity later, with the relatively heavy present increase concentrated on that input whose deferred purchase price would not be as much lower.

Proposition 8

All the derivatives in Proposition 1 to 5 are diminishing functions of T, but not all diminish at the same rate. This proposition asserts a difference in the extent to which inputs will be varied in the immediate, the short and the longer period.

Short and long run. Statements to the effect that certain inputs are fixed in the short run are frequent and characteristic. In fact, there is no such fixed factor in any interval other than the immediate moment *when all are fixed*. Such statements may represent a confusion between revealed choice and technological constraints. There are no technological or legal restraints preventing one from varying any of his inputs. Even in Viner's (1931) classic statement of the short- and long-run cost curves, the short run is defined in terms of some *fixed* inputs and other inputs which can be varied as desired. He stated that the long run is the situation in which all the inputs are 'freely' variable. One need only ask, 'What do the desires to adjust depend upon in the short run?' and, 'What does "freely" variable mean?' The first is answered by 'costs' and potential receipts of the variations, and the second by noting that 'freely' does not mean that costs of changes are zero. The fact is that the costs of varying the inputs differ among inputs, and the ratios of these costs vary with the time interval within which the variation is to be made. At any *calendar* moment, T, the producer will choose which input to vary according to *economic costs* and not because of technical or legal fixities that prevent the changing of some inputs.[6]

Debate over definitions or postulates is pertinent only in the light of their purpose. The purpose of the short- and long-run distinction is, presumably, to explain the path of prices or output (x or V?) over time in response to some change in demand or supply. The postulate of fixed inputs, and others more variable with the passing of time, does imply a pattern of

6. The nearest, but still different, presentation of the immediate, short run and long run found by the author is that contained in Friedman's unpublished lecture notes. Other statements may exist; an exhausting search of the literature failed to clarify exactly what is meant by the long run and short run.

responses that seems to be verified by observable evidence. On that count, the falsity of the postulate is immaterial. But if there are other implications of such a postulate that are invalidated by observable evidence, the postulate becomes costly. The question arises, therefore, whether it is more convenient and useful to replace the fixity postulate by a more general one that yields all the valid implications that the former one did and more besides, while at the same time avoiding the empirically false implications. It appears that the proposed alternative is cheaper in terms of logical convenience, more general, and more valid in its implications. But that is a judgement which is perhaps best left to the reader.

The differences between a short-run (near T) and a long-run (distant T) operation imply differences in costs, and these costs are pertinent to an explanation of the path of prices or costs over time in response to a lasting change in demand or factor availabilities. For example, for a lasting increase in demand, the output made available at more distant dates is producible at a lower cost; this means that the supply at a given cost will be larger and the price lower in the more distant future as the longer-run operations begin to yield their output. These outputs, having been planned for a later T date, are lower in cost. Output will be larger for a given price, thus reducing price in the market. This longer-run lower cost is the phenomenon whose explanation has usually been sought by resort to fixity of some particular inputs in the short run. The above argument suggests that this phenomenon can be explained without the fixity assumption that in turn leads to other, empirically wrong, implications.

The implication of our proposition is worth emphasizing here. It is that we define a 'short run' and a 'long run' not as differing in the fixity of some inputs; instead, we use T as the length of the run, and then from Proposition 8 derive the implications that were sought by the fixity assumption.

Most important, however, Proposition 8 makes it clear that there is not both a 'long-run' and 'short-run' cost for any given output program. For any given output program there is only *one* pertinent cost, *not* two. Unambiguous specification of the output or action to be costed makes the cost definition unambiguous and destroys the illusion that there are two costs to consider, a short- and a long-run cost for any given output. There is only one, and that is the *cheapest* cost of doing whatever the operation is specified to be. To produce a house in three months is one thing, to produce it in a year is something else. By uniquely identifying the operation to be charged there results one cost, not a range of costs from immediate to short- to longer-run costs. There is a range of operations to be considered, but to each there is only *one* cost. The question is not, 'What are the long-run or short-run costs of some operation?' but instead, 'How do total, average and marginal costs vary as the T of the operation is changed?' Answer: 'They decrease as T increases, according to Propositions 7 and 8.'

The significance of this should be evident in the debate about marginal cost pricing policies for 'optimal' output. Also the use of short-run and long-run costs as alternatives in public utility pricing appears to be a ripe area for clarification of concepts.

What the relationship is between the presently suggested effects of T, which we have just called a short- or long-run effect, and the common short run or long run in the standard literature is not entirely clear. Rather vague and imprecise implications about short and long run are available. Hence, rather than assert that the T effect is here being proposed as a substitute for the standard short-run analysis, the reader is left free to supply his own interpretation of the conventional 'run' and to supplement or replace it, however he chooses, with the present proposition.

Proposition 9

The preceding propositions refer to costs of outputs for a given distribution of knowledge, F, at the present moment, to situations where technology is held constant.[7]

Proposition 9 is 'As the total quantity of units produced increases, the cost of *future* output declines.' The cost per unit may be either the average cost of a given number of incremental units of output or the cost of a specific unit. This is not

7. Technology, the state of distribution of knowledge, is different from techniques of production, which can be changed at any time, even with a constant technology.

identical with the earlier Proposition 4 referring to the effects of the larger planned V. There the effect was a result of varying *techniques* of production, not of changes in technology. Here we are asserting that knowledge increases as a result of production – that the cost function is lowered. It is not simply a matter of a larger V, but rather a lower cost for any subsequent V, consequent to improved knowledge. This distinction should not be attributed necessarily to all the explanations of the learning curve. Some describers of the learning curve bring in the effect of different techniques consequent to different-sized V. Others also mention that, as output is produced and experience acquired, improved knowledge is acquired. Thus, even if one continually planned to produce small batches of output, so the V was constant but repeated, the costs would nevertheless be falling. In the present presentation we have chosen to separate these two effects in logic and principle, attributing the first effect, that of technique, to changes in planned V but with a given state of knowledge (as in Proposition 4), while the second effect, that of increased knowledge consequent to accumulated production experience, is isolated in Proposition 9. A review of industrial and production management literature will show that both effects are adduced and incorporated in the learning curve discussion, contrary to our decision to separate them. This proposition about the rate of change in technology is accepted in industrial engineering. Usually the proposition is known as the 'learning curve' or 'progress curve'.[8]

Several factors have been advanced as a rationale for this proposition: job familiarization, general improvement in coordination, shop organization and engineering liaison, more efficient subassembly production, and more efficient tools. An extensive literature on this proposition has been developed, but it seems to have escaped integration with the rest of cost theory in economics.[9]

8. Sometimes the curve is called an 80 per cent progress curve, because it is sometimes asserted that the cost of the $2n$th item is 80 per cent of the cost of the nth item. Thus the fortieth plane would involve only 80 per cent of the direct man hours and materials that the twentieth plane did.

9. See Hirsch (1952). A less accessible, but more complete, reference to the published material is given in Asher (1956). But see Samuelson (1948, p. 473) where it is mentioned but left unincorporated.

Nevertheless, the proposition is a well-validated proposition and is widely used in industrial engineering. The significant implication of this proposition is that, in addition to rate of output, an important variable in determining total costs is the total planned output for two reasons: first, because of changes in technique via Proposition 4 and, second, because the larger is the planned and ultimately realized output, the greater is the accumulated experience (technology) and knowledge at any point in the future via Proposition 9. Thus, the average cost per unit of output will be lower, the greater is the planned and ultimately experienced output. A more complete discussion of the evidence for this proposition would require a separate paper.

On the advantages of the capital value measure

Use of capital values enables one to avoid misleading statements like 'We are going to operate at a loss in the near future, but operations will be profitable later', 'In the short run the firm may operate at a loss so long as receipts exceed variable costs', 'A firm operates with long-run rather than short-run objectives.' All of these statements are incorrect if liabilities or assets (other than money) are owned by the enterprise. What seems to be meant when a person talks about expecting to have losses for a while before getting profits is that cash flows will be negative for a while, but it is difficult to see how this in any relevant sense a situation of losses. And, similarly, when a person talks about expecting losses it appears that he means he expects future events to occur which are unfavourable; and in this case the changed belief about the future is immediately reflected in current values if not in current money flows – as many a stockholder has learned. Any periods during which expectation about future events becomes more favorable are periods of increasing equity (i.e. of profits), even though the period in which the more favorable events will occur is in the future. When a firm reports that it operated during the past quarter at a loss, it means simply that the net present value of assets decreased during that period, even though the future cash receipts and outlays have not yet been realized. The profits are in the present moment – the increase in equity – as some stockholders have joyously learned. The presently anticipated increase in *future* receipts relative to future outlays means an increase in *present* equity values, profits.

Statements to the effect that a firm would willingly and knowingly operate at a loss in the short run are consistent only with an identification of costs with money flows, and are certainly inconsistent with the postulates of seeking increased wealth (or utility) as a goal or survival attribute. Such identification of costs with money flows eliminates capital theory from the theory of the firm and from much of price theory. There is no cause to pay this price since it is just as easy not to abandon capital theory, and if one retains it more useful implications will be derived.

Yet, in economic texts costs are almost always measured as *time-rates,* and only rarely as capital values. At first blush this would seem to be an irrelevant or trivial distinction, since capital values are merely the present values of *receipt* or *outlay* streams. But what about going from capital values to time rates of *cost* streams? New problems arise in this effort. Suppose that the outlay stream for some operation is used as the basis for cost calculations. If, and only if, *no* other assets or liabilities are involved can money flows be identified with costs; otherwise they represent, in part, accumulations of assets or liabilities. As soon as assets and liabilities are admitted, money flows are not synonymous with costs, and changes in values of assets or liabilities must now be included. With the break between money outlays and costs, the measure of costs becomes the change in present value of net equity consequent to some action (ignoring receipts, for present purposes).

If a firm signed a contract and committed itself to produce some quantity of output, then the cost it has incurred in signing the contract and obligating itself to produce the output is its decrease in equity, say $E_a - E_b$. At moment a, prior to the contract, the equity or net wealth of the firm is E_a. At this moment the firm considers entering into some production plan. If it does so, what will happen to its equity at the end of the plan, or how will the equity change over that interval? If, for the moment, we ignore the receipts or income from that plan, the decrease of equity by moment b would be the measure of cost of the output operation which it is obligated to perform.

The difference, $E_a - E_b$, between the equity (E_a) at the beginning and the *present* value (E_a) of the equity (E_b) at the end of the operation, is the total cost, C, of the operation.

The *time-rate* of costs (of change in equity) is given by dE/dt, the slope of the line from E_a to E_t which is quite different from C. The former, dE/dt, is a derivative, a time rate of change. The latter, C, is the integral of the former. It is a finite difference, $E_a - E_t$, obtained from two different points on the E curve, while the former is the slope of the E curve and can be obtained only after an E curve is obtained. What is the meaning of the E *curve* in such a case? Presumably it means that, if the firm decided at any moment to stop further output, under this contract it would find itself with an equity indicated by the height of the line E_a E_t. Ignoring the contractual liability for obligation to produce according to the contract, the equity declines along the E line; but if one does regard the contract performance liability, the equity does not change as output is produced because there is an exactly offsetting reduction in contractual liability as output is produced. The equity of the firm stays constant over the interval if the outlays and asset values initially forecast were forecast correctly.

If the *rate* of cost, dE/dt, or if the E curve is plotted not against time, but against the *output rate*, we do not get a curve similar in interpretation to the usual total cost curve in standard cost curve analysis. The *rate* of cost, dE/dt can be converted to average cost per unit of rate of output by dividing the rate of cost, dE/dt, by the associated rate of output at that moment, and the marginal time-rate of cost is obtained by asking how the slope of the equity curve dE/dt is affected by changes in x, i.e. ($d^2E/dt\,dx$).

The difference between this curve, where dE/dt is plotted against x, and the usual time rate of cost curve analysis is that our current analysis is based on a larger set of variables, $x(t)$ and V, and hence dE/dt cannot be drawn uniquely merely against the rate of output, $x(t)$. A new curve must be drawn for each output operation contemplated; even worse, there is no assurance that such a curve of dE/dt drawn against the rate of output on the horizontal axis would have only one vertical height for each output rate. The curve might fold back on itself and be multivalued because one value of dE/dt might be associated with a particular rate of output early in the operation and another different value later in the operation, even though at both moments the output rate were the same.

The number of cost curves that could be drawn is greater by at least an extra factor, V. In fact, we have at least two families of curves, one for different values of V and one for different time profiles of $x(t)$, and it is not clear what is usually assumed about these in the standard cost curve analysis. One possibility is to assume that the length of the production run, m, or the contemplated total output, V, does not affect the rate at which equity changes for any given output rate. The difficulty with this position is not merely that it is logically wrong but that it leads to implications that are refuted by everyday events.

A kind of average or marginal cost can be defined on the basis of the approach suggested earlier. For any given contemplated operation, the change in equity implied can be computed and evaluated in present worths. If this cost is divided by the total contemplated volume of output, V, the result is present value cost per unit of product (not time rate per unit *rate* of output). If the same total output were to be produced at a higher output rate, x, and thus within a shorter time interval, m, the total cost (change in equity) would be greater, and so the cost per unit of total volume of output would be higher. As noted in the first part of this paper, the increases in total present value cost, $\partial C/x$ (not $d^2E/dt\ dx$), is the marginal cost, consequent to an increased rate of output. By varying the contemplated rates of output x for any given total output plan (V and T), one can get different total capital costs. These changes in total capital costs can be called the marginal capital costs. But it is important to note again that there are as many such marginal capital value cost functions as there are different possible total output patterns that can be contemplated, and these marginal capital costs are not time rates of costs.

Conclusion

Four features have been emphasized in the foregoing pages. First, the distinction between rate and quantity of output; second, changes in technology as distinct from changes in technique; third, the use of calendar time dates of output instead of technical fixity for distinguishing output operations; fourth, the use of capital value concepts instead of rates of costs.

The first and second features (and the ones that are emphasized in this paper) enable us to capture within our theory the lower costs attendant on larger quantities of output – not rates of output. Everyday experience where large rates of output are available at lower prices could be explained as a movement down the buyer's demand curve as the seller, in order to sell a larger amount, lowers price. But this seems to be incapable of explaining all such situations. Another explanation usually advanced is the economies of scale, where scale is related to *rate* of output. However, an alternative explanation suggested here is the lower cost resulting, not from higher *rates* of output per unit time, but from larger planned volume of total output quantities. An examination of the production management and engineering literature reveals much greater emphasis on batch or lot size as contrasted to the rate of output. Frequently the latter is not much of a variable in each particular firm's decision. This means that the extent to which rate of output *is* varied may be slight – not that it can't be varied or that its significance is slight. That there has been confusion between the rate of output and the batch size or quantity planned is sure. How much cannot be known.

The third feature – that of identifying each output operation with a calendar date and then postulating that the more distant the date the smaller the change in equity (the smaller the cost) – provides a way to escape the unnecessary bind imposed by the definition of short-run costs as that which results from fixed inputs. The ambiguous idea of two different costs, a short-run and a long-run cost for a given output, disappears and is replaced by one cost for each different program of output.

What must have been assumed in our present literature about the factors mentioned here? Was the rate of output profile assumed to be a constant rate extending into perpetuity? The answer could not be ascertained from an exhausting reading of the literature nor from analogically implied conditions. Certainly the standard cost curve analysis does not envisage a perpetuity output at some given rate, nor does it seem to specify the effects of shorter-length runs at any output. For example, Stigler, in his well-known paper on the effects of planning for variations in the rate of output, imagines one to be moving along a given cost curve appropriate to the case in which output varies. This desirable attempt to modify the cost curve analysis would have been more successful if the output had been further specified or identified in terms of V and T. Then the conventional curves would have disappeared, and many logical inconsistencies and ambiguities could have been removed from the standard analysis. But merely drawing the curve flatter and higher does not avoid the problems of appropriate interpretation of costs for unspecified values of the pertinent variables.

Finally, introduction of a new variable, V, complicates the equilibrium of demand and supply, for now there must be a similar element in demand which will determine the equilibrium size of V, if such there be. Suffice it to say here that even though consumers may not act or plan consciously in terms of V, their actions can be interpreted in terms of a resultant aggregative V. Producers, in contemplating the demand for their products, will be required to think of capital value or present value of income with the rate of output integrated into a V – possibly a break-even V – on the basis of which they make production plans. A simple rate of output, price relationships, will not be sufficient. But this remains to be developed later, only if the present propositions prove valid and useful.

References

ASHER, H. (1956), *Cost–Quantity Relationship in the Airframe Industry*, RAND Corporation.

HIRSCH, W. (1952), 'Manufacturing progress functions', *Rev. Econ. Stat.*, vol. 34, pp. 143–55.

HIRSHLEIFER, J. (1955), 'Quality *v.* quantity: cost isoquant and equilibrium', *Quart. J. Econ.*, vol. 64, pp. 596–606.

SAMUELSON, P. A. (1948), *Economics: An Introductory Analysis*, McGraw-Hill.

VINER, J. (1931), 'Cost curves and supply curves', *Zeitschrift für Nationalökonomie*, vol. 3, pp. 23–46.

WHITIN, T. M., and PESTON, M. H. (1954), 'Random variations, risks and returns to scale', *Quart. J. Econ.*, vol. 68, pp. 603–14.

Part Five **Markets**

There are broad markets, thin markets
Stable markets, big ones.
There are fish markets, flea markets
Gem markets and then some:
Gold markets, money markets
Flesh markets, gyrating ones;
Free markets, dope markets
Controlled markets, sloppy ones.
What a lot of markets there are!

There are black markets, grey markets
Job markets, sticky ones;
Shadow markets, ghost markets
Vice markets, baby ones!

There are bond markets, bill markets
Flexible markets, monopolized ones;
Stock markets, flow markets
Put-and-call markets, curb ones.

We could go on and on:

Auction markets, betting markets,
Markets made for barter;
Demand-determined, supply-determined
Markets run by charter.
Factor markets, supermarkets
Active markets, French ones
Futures markets, spot markets
Capital markets, resilient ones.

There are even markets for presidents.

R. A. Mundell, *Man and Economics*, McGraw-Hill, 1968

11 Joe S. Bain

Chamberlin's Impact on Microeconomic Theory

Joe S. Bain, 'Chamberlin's impact on microeconomic theory', in R. E. Kuenne (ed.), *Monopolistic Competition Theory: Studies in Impact*, Wiley, 1967, pp. 147–76.

Anyone setting out to appraise the impact of Chamberlin's major work on 'microeconomic theory' may quickly regret that the infelicitous terms 'micro' and 'macro' have been coined to dichotomize economic theory and have gained nearly universal acceptance. The terrain of economic theory is thus divided into two parts, although the subterritories of microstatics, microdynamics, macrostatics and macrodynamics are also recognized. And the part that could reasonably be viewed as 'micro' is very large. Theories of consumer behavior, of the firm and of both commodity and factor markets should be included offhand, bringing with them a part of capital theory, much of the theory of international trade, and the neoclassical theory of general equilibrium.

A comprehensive evaluation of the influence of *The Theory of Monopolistic Competition* (hereafter referred to as *Monopolistic Competition*) on contemporary microeconomic theory should not neglect any of these broad segments, but in this essay some arbitrary limits have been self-imposed. Because other contributors assess the impact of *Monopolistic Competition* on several designated areas of microeconomic theory and because it has had only a minor impact on some others, this essay considers only the influence of Chamberlin's work on the central system of microstatic theory that embraces the interrelated theories of the consumer, of the firm, and of individual commodity markets – on 'price theory' thus construed.

The general importance of the impact

What are the major impacts of *Monopolistic Competition* on this corpus of economic theory? Before trying to answer this question in detail, we should recognize the broader issue of whether it has had a major impact at all, for at present different economists or schools thereof evaluate the general importance of Chamberlin's work quite differently.

At the negative extreme, we find the opinion that *Monopolistic Competition* and subsequent theory in its tradition have added little of importance to microstatic theory. This view has several evident well-springs aside from laziness, a nostalgia for things past or a disrespect for any theory that isn't mathematically formulated. Most vigorously asserted is the belief that the systematic deviations from purely competitive market behavior that Chamberlin predicted for oligopolistic and product-differentiated markets *in fact* do not significantly affect the allocative efficiency of the actual price system, technical efficiency in production or income distribution. These deviations are in this view sufficiently unimportant that his theory explains the working of a market-controlled economy no better than a simpler theory of pure competition (supplemented by a theory of pure monopoly to take care of pathological situations). A sophisticated version of Marshall and Walras will do nicely. Right or wrong, this belief evidently rests on the ultimate in casual empiricism, as well as an odd standard of empirical relevance.

A related basis for discounting the importance of *Monopolistic Competition* is a genuine lack of interest in the empirical relevance of price theory, matched by a preoccupation with the refinement for its own sake of the theory of a purely competitive economy. For economists of this persuasion, microeconomic theory appears to be a logician's or mathematician's game, most readily played with a bare minimum of assumptions and of variables. Modern scholastic theorists simply aren't very interested, when considering microstatics, in Chamberlinian theory.

Another evident ground for neglecting Chamberlin's work also deserves mention. This is the fact that the centrally important Chamberlinian model of oligopoly does not generate unique general predictions of market performance. Unique predictions may be wrested from it only by introducing special institutional assumptions; otherwise, even a sophisticated theory of oligopoly at best yields probability judgements. To some theorists this 'deficiency' is fatal because the incorporation of oligopolistic markets into a system of microstatic theory precludes the deduction from very general assumptions of uniquely determined equilibria not only for one class of markets but also for the economy as a whole. Embracing the theory of oligopoly would frustrate the fulfillment of what they view as the essential purposes of a system of microstatic theory.

Those among contemporary price theorists who disparage or neglect the Chamberlinian type of theory are not a small minority, though their numerical importance is hard to judge. Price theory in general and microstatics in particular have not been the major preoccupation of economic theorists for some time, whereas a great deal of attention was given to price theory in the 1920s before Chamberlin's and Joan Robinson's works were published, and their books engendered a great flurry of writing in the two succeeding decades. The more recent comparative neglect of price theory seems attributable in large part to the wellknown shifting of fads or fashions in economics, which frequently sets off mass migrations to new territories before those recently occupied have been thoroughly explored, and in lesser part to the fact that after the easy gold in the vein opened by *Monopolistic Competition* had been panned, most theorists abandoned the mine. None the less, the considerable number of contemporary theorists who are detractors of Chamberlinian theory, who would like to forget about it or who have never really studied it, clearly poses an issue concerning its ultimate importance in the system of price theory.

A probable majority of theorists still accords to *Monopolistic Competition* and subsequent literature in its tradition a major role in the development of modern microstatic economic theory. It has been held that in *Monopolistic Competition* Chamberlin really introduced a new price theory with a vastly greater empirical relevance than that of pre-existing theory and with an immensely increased immediate or latent power to generate hypotheses concerning enterprise behavior in the actual economy. As an advocate of this general view, I have put the case as follows in an earlier brief essay on *Monopolistic Competition*:

Joe S. Bain 255

This work simultaneously did two very important things. It advanced expressly – really for the first time – the major and crucial theoretical construct in which an economy of enterprises was viewed as being made up of industries having a variety of distinctly different market structures, with market conduct and performance tending to differ significantly with differences in structure. And it implemented this construct by developing an uncomplicated but actually quite sophisicated classification of market structures. This classification reflected a remarkable insight into what in the world of markets was empirically relevant to price theory, was the evident parent of substantially all more elaborate market classifications which have been subsequently suggested, and provided the basic skeleton for all of them which have had appreciable merit. . . . Further, [its] identification of dimensions of market performance in addition to those involving price, production cost and output – that is, selling cost and product quality and variety – suggested an expanded range of matters deserving empirical [and, we might add here, theoretical] study within the sort of theoretical framework . . . established (Bain, 1964).

This view places major emphasis on Chamberlin's introduction into microstatic theory of an empirically relevant theory of markets, via the primary route of innovating an empirically relevant set of assumptions concerning varieties of market structures and the secondary route of recognizing some empirically important additional decision variables. In retrospect, this important global contribution clearly overshadows Chamberlin's accomplishments in 'grinding the deductive mill' to arrive at group equilibria, and also his specific predictions of market performance associated with various market structures and combinations of variables. For although *Monopolistic Competition* displayed considerable technical virtuosity for its time, it ran toward special rather than general solutions, failed to explore many significant implications of its general assumptions and generated only qualitatively ambiguous predictions concerning some sorts of equilibria in which ambiguity is not intrinsic.

Its detractors have made the most of these shortcomings, at the same time endeavoring to prove by vigorous assertion that the empirical relevance of the assumptions of a theory – and in particular a theory of pure competition – does not matter much as long as that theory generates (as it is held to do) reasonably accurate predictions concerning selected economic phenomena. There are two main objections to this position. First, it remains to be demonstrated on general grounds that a theory based on assumptions that are patently and significantly at odds with the relevant facts is likely, except by accident, to generate satisfactorily accurate predictions. Second, the predictive power of a Marshallian or other purely competitive theory has been alleged to be confirmed by empirical evidence generally by persons who exhibit a slight familiarity with and thoroughgoing disrespect for the mass of relevant evidence, or who in a purely *ex parte* spirit casually adduce selected scraps of evidence in support of their positions.[1] The major defense of Chamberlin's principal contribution rests on the methodologically sound proposition that an economic theory can only be as good as its assumptions, and on the observation that Chamberlin in his theory of markets replaced unrealistic with empirically relevant assumptions concerning both market structures and the number of evidently important decision variables.

Logically, the next issue in this overview of the importance of *Monopolistic Competition* for microstatic theory concerns the over-all significance of theorizing evidently engendered or inspired by Chamberlin's major work and extending its tradition. It seems appropriate, however, to withhold any initial broad statements on this question in order to turn at once to a more detailed consideration of the post-Chamberlinian literature, as the main question really is what and how much others have made of what Chamberlin began (through elaboration, extension, and revision) in striving for a more satisfactory price theory. This is a pressing question because although Chamberlin pointed the way to a revolutionary change in price theory and drew its broad outlines, he did not himself fully exploit the implications of his major conceptual discoveries. Although *Monopolistic Competition* made an unshakable

1. Koopmans states a related but more general objection to the methodological position, well summarized in the following remark: 'To state a set of postulates, and then to exempt a subclass of their implications from verification is a curiously roundabout way of specifying the content of a theory that is regarded as open to empirical refutation. It leaves one without an understanding of the reasons for the exemptions' (Koopmans, 1957, p. 139; see also pp. 132–42).

major contribution to price theory, it left an immense amount of work to be done if its potential were to be realized. Correspondingly, an assessment of microstatic theorizing inspired by Chamberlin necessarily involves considering criticisms of his work and revisionism as well as simple elaboration or gap-filling.

The succeeding pages consider several sorts of development of price theory that have extended or been inspired by Chamberlin's work and identify some potentially fruitful lines of theorizing that were suggested by *Monopolistic Competition* but have not been adequately explored. Considered successively are: (a) market classifications and the industry concept; (b) monopoly power under monopolistic competition; (c) the theory of oligopoly; and (d) equilibria involving product determination and selling costs.

Marketing classification and the industry concept

In *Monopolistic Competition* Chamberlin began by asserting that the assumption of nearly universal pure competition was unrealistic. He set out to repair things by assuming product differentiation to be pervasive, by resuscitating and reformulating a theory of oligopoly, and by developing or suggesting market equilibria especially for monopolistic competition (the large group with product differentiation) and also for oligopoly without and with product differentiation. The ink on the first edition was only well dried when a number of people realized that Chamberlin had suggested (deliberately or inadvertently) a system of price theory based on a classification of markets or industries in terms of market structures. This was discussed in print early in a short article by Machlup (1937, pp. 445 ff.), but the idea was in circulation before this presentation.

The rudimentary Chamberlinian classification, distinguishing markets according to numbers of sellers and whether or not their products were differentiated, naturally took the familiar form:

1. Markets with many sellers
(a) Pure competition
(b) Monopolistic competition

2. Markets with few sellers
(a) Pure oligopoly
(b) Heterogeneous oligopoly

3. Single-firm monopoly.

In recognizing this express or implied classification it was possible to grasp the systematic implications of Chamberlin's work and to see the possibility of exploiting them to revise and elaborate Marshallian particular equilibrium analysis as applied to industries. Also apparent was the intriguing possibility of generating empirically testable hypotheses concerning the relationships of the structure of industries to their market performance.

But had a classification of 'industries' really been suggested, and if it had been, was it theoretically valid and useful? Could or should Chamberlinian theory be used to rebuild a Marshallian particular equilibrium theory based on the industry as a unit? Chamberlin himself, intent on discrediting the unrealistic Marshallian concept of a world of isolated industries each with a homogeneous product that was a very distant substitute for every other product, had shied away from calling his competing or rivalrous groups of sellers 'industries'. He emphasized that 'groups' of close-but-imperfect substitute products might and probably would overlap, the product groups being only more distant substitutes *inter se*. Triffin (1940, pp. 88–9) holding that Chamberlin had none the less retained the industry concept, felt it improper for purposes of formal theorizing to accept both the assumption of pervasive and complex product differentiation and the concept of the industry at the same time, although he readily conceded that the industry was a valid and powerful organizing concept in applied price analysis. He therefore suggested the abandonment of particular-equilibrium price theory and called for but did not develop – nor has anyone since – a general-equilibrium theory incorporating Chamberlinian concepts. Heeding his counsel would evidently have insured the relegation of Chamberlinian theory to the category of a major curiosity and aborted any major exploitation of its potential.

The 'Chicago school' still holds a view akin to Triffin's.

Even in recent literature we find it popping away at Chamberlinian theory on the grounds that in employing such concepts as 'close substitutes' and 'substantial gaps in cross-elasticities' it 'introduces fuzziness and indefinable terms *into the abstract model where they have no place,* and serves only to make the theory analytically meaningless' (Friedman, 1961, p. 66; italics added). This stand is transparently ludicrous. It is argued that a price theory must be kept pristine and simple at any cost, even if empirically relevant assumptions won't let it stay that way. And it is by implication held that a modest and approximately accurate simplifying assumption – that firms in an admittedly product-differentiated economy are grouped into industries that are held together by close substitutability and separated by distant substitutability of their products – should be rejected in favor of the heroically and destructively unrealistic assumption that industries are as Marshall had them, purely competitive and isolated. An unrealistic assumption is involved in either case, but why stretch for the ultimate in unrealism, if assumptions are after all only the empirical generalizations from which a theory begins? We also wonder why Triffin could at once recognize the industry as a powerful organizing concept in applied Chamberlinian price theory and fail to perceive that it was an equally potent concept in a 'pure' Chamberlinian theory.

Triffin and Chicago notwithstanding, Chamberlinian theory has proved formally satisfactory, tractable and productive of meaningful hypotheses precisely when it has been adapted to particular-equilibrium analysis by assuming explicitly that the enterprise economy is made up of industries that are identified and separated by the value of cross-elasticities of demand among products, and by then classifying such industries according to their market structures. This assumption would have produced an unrealistic version of neo-Marshallian price theory if it had not indeed been true that in the real world products were clustered in close-substitute groups with gaps of distant substitution among them (intergroup cross-elasticities of demand being negligible or approaching zero), and if instead there were a single tangled mass of products related substitutionwise in a fashion so complex that industries could not be readily identified or separated. But the former and not the latter appears to be empirically the case, whatever may be the abstract possibilities, and this being so a Chamberlinian particular equilibrium theory is analytically meaningful, far more than the Marshallian one.

Flippant examples purportedly destructive of the industry concept in a product-differentiated economy (such as the alleged close substitution of nightclub admissions, pleasure cruises and cold showers) are not persuasive; for each of these there can be twenty queries such as those concerning the evident degree of substitutability between cigarettes and kitchen sinks, automobiles and roller skates, or concrete and gunpowder. A little serious endeavor to couple our powers of observation with our knowledge of the concept of cross-elasticity of demand might have shut off a great deal of pseudo-methodological quibbling over the acceptability and validity of the industry concept in a price theory that deals with a product-differentiated economy.

The classification of industries

Having incorporated the industry concept into a particular-equilibrium version of Chamberlinian theory, let us return to the classification of industries. Chamberlin did not build his market classification from a foundation of assumptions concerning cross-elasticities of demand between different products or sellers, and thus whatever he was effectively assuming concerning cross-elasticities was implicit rather than expressed. This omission on his part was the source of some of the earliest criticism of his model of group equilibrium in monopolistic competition, centered on the proposition that the monopoly power of the individual seller should fade toward the vanishing point as the number of sellers in the group increased, presuming that the cross-elasticity of demand as among pairs of products did not change or increase (see e.g. Kaldor, 1935, pp. 33 ff.). Discussion of this and related matters is reserved for the succeeding section, in which monopoly power under monopolistic competition is considered.

This sort of criticism engendered systematic attempts to define in terms of cross-elasticities of demand the rudimentary market classes suggested by Chamberlin. Triffin (1940, pp. 98–112) did an initially quite satisfactory job, the only evident flaw in which seems attributable to a slip or a typographical error. Some subsequent literature tended to obscure the issue because of mathematical misunderstandings until Bishop (1952, 1955) and Heiser (1955) analysed the definitional matter adequately and smoked out in the course of journal controversy (see Bishop, 1953; Chamberlin, 1953; Fellner, 1953) a special Chamberlinian assumption concerning the responsiveness of cross-elasticities between individual products to the number of products in a group or industry. Without reviewing the controversy, but taking sides to some extent (with the *general* position of Triffin, Bishop and Heiser), I suggest that the following propositions have emerged:

1. A formal classification of markets requires reference both to a conventional price cross-elasticity ($\delta q_j / \delta p_i$) $\times (p_i / q_j)$, designated by Bishop as E_{ji}) as a substitutability-of-products criterion, and either to an unconventional quantity cross-elasticity ($\delta p_j / \delta q_i$) $\times$ (q_i / p_j) (designated by Bishop as e_{ji}), or to some alternative measure, as a number-of-sellers or interdependence criterion.

2. Perfect substitutability of products in a market, regardless of the number of products or sellers in it, is denoted by the price cross-elasticity between every pair of products (E_{ji}) approaching infinity; 'symmetrical' product differentiation[2] in a market is denoted by E_{ji} for every pair being finite; and E_{ji} between products that are in different markets, industries, or groups will approach zero.

3. A large number of small sellers in a market, with or without product differentiation, is denoted (under symmetry assumptions) by a quantity cross-elasticity between every pair of sellers (e_{ji}) approaching zero; oligopolistic interdependence between any pair of sellers in a market is reflected in e_{ji} being finite.[3]

2. That is, product differentiation such that every product has the same degree of substitutability for every other product in the group (all intrapair substitutabilities thus being the same, and no pair of products being distant substitutes).

3. Except in the limiting case in which the own-price elasticity of the industry or group demand function is zero or nearly so.

In simple oligopoly (each of the few sellers having circular interdependence with all the others), e_{ji} will be finite for all pairs.

4. A market classification of the rudimentary Chamberlinian type can then under symmetry assumptions be described in cross-elasticity terms as seen in Table 1.

*Table 1*A Market Classification under Symmetry Assumptions

Market type	Cross-elasticities between each pair of members of the market E_{ji}	e_{ji}
Pure competition	$\rightarrow \infty$	$\rightarrow 0$
Monopolistic competition	finite	$\rightarrow 0$
Pure oligopoly	$\rightarrow \infty$	finite
Heterogeneous oligopoly	finite	finite

A single-firm monopolist would simply have an E_{ji} that approached zero with respect to every other product in the economy.[4]

This classification seems formally unassailable unless the notion of an infinite number of sellers in a competitive market is introduced (a mathematical possibility that is axiomatically excluded),[5] in which case some cross-elasticity terms would become indeterminate and a more complex system of formal criteria would be needed. Neglecting this possibility, we see that one really controversial issue has remained: whether additional attributes of monopolistic competition are (a) that the finite value of E_{ji} between every pair of products is small enough to insure that the own-price elasticity of demand of the individual seller $(\delta q_i / \delta p_i) \times (p_i/q_i)$, or E_{ii} in the symmetrical case is not extremely large (its sales curve is not approximately horizontal),

4. This definitional system fails to provide a distinction between single-firm monopoly and monopolistic competition in the event that the latter is construed as potentially incorporating values of E_{ji} which, though finite, approach zero. If it is so construed, then an added criterion referring to the own-price elasticities of the sales curves in the two situations must be introduced to distinguish pure monopoly.

5. In any real economy it is axiomatic that all populations (of persons, firms, etc.) are finite in number.

and (b) that as the number of sellers or products in a market becomes larger, the value of E_{ji} between every pair of products inevitably becomes proportionally smaller.

If E_{ji} is not small enough, the sloping *ceteris paribus* sales curve of the seller in monopolistic competition, which Chamberlin derived intuitively from product differentiation *cum* large numbers, will actually tend toward horizontality. If E_{ji} does not decrease or decreases less than proportionally as the number of sellers increase, E_{ii} tends to approach perfect elasticity with such an increase. These propositions are quickly evident in a simple model of fully symmetrical monopolistic competition (with all sellers producing equal outputs at the same price, and the value of E_{ji} the same for every pair of sellers), where obviously $E_{ii} = E_{ji} (n-1)$, when n is the number of sellers. They are capable of extension to more general cases.[6]

Alerted to these logical possibilities, Chamberlin (1953) has elected to defend the slope of the seller's demand curve in monopolistic competition by insisting that E_{ji} must be 'small enough' and must fall as n increases.[7] The validity or invalidity of these propositions, like that of the equally plausible counter-propositions that the finite value of E_{ji} might just as well be larger and in particular remain unchanged as n increases, cannot be proved on *a priori* grounds (unless we adopt as axiomatic the noticeable slope of Chamberlin's little *dd'* in monopolistic competition, and this is really not an axiom). Whether or to what extent the rejection of Chamberlin's postulates concerning the size of E_{ji} and its interaction with n deprives the large-

6. The two putative attributes of monopolistic competition (E_{ji} quite small and declining proportionally with increases in n) might be considered as formally interrelated and together require that with the smallest group (symmetrical heterogeneous duopoly) E_{ji} which would equal E_{ii} for each duopolist, does not exceed a critical value associated with a significantly sloping sales curve, and that with increases in the number of sellers in the group, from two through few to many, E_{ji} declines proportionally to maintain E_{ii} for each seller unchanged at the initial value.

7. And others (e.g. Bishop) have held that as a definitional matter monopolistic competition must have these properties, for otherwise the case would be indistinguishable from pure competition. The latter may be denied on the ground that monopolistic competition with approximately horizontal sales curves is not the equivalent of pure competition if selling costs and product determination are incorporated into the model.

group case of all novelty is considered below. Here two things may be simply noted. There is no good evident reason, logical or empirical, for believing that Chamberlin's postulates to support the slope of dd' in monopolistic competition must be valid ones.[8] And a generalized approach to his basic market classification via the route of cross-elasticities of demand, possibly backed by some propositions concerning the underlying consumer indifference maps, at once suggests the possibility of an elaborated variety of solutions for Chamberlin's product-differentiated market categories.[9]

Although the formal definition of the categories in Chamberlin's rudimentary market classification turns out to have more than a taxonomic importance, a more substantive issue has been whether the connected theory of markets could be improved by introducing initially a finer subclassification of markets. This may be done by employing as principles of

8. First, the finite value of E_{ji} found with some minimal number of sellers sufficient to qualify as a 'large group' can clearly be at once small enough to indicate that all pairs of products are distinctly imperfect substitutes and large enough that $E_{ji}(n-1) = E_{ii}$ is extremely large for each seller. Second, though some decline of E_{ji} with increases in n may seem plausible, there is no particular reason to suppose that any such decline of E_{ji} need be great enough to keep E_{ii} from increasing with n, in the event that there was a significant departure from perfect elasticity for the sales curve before n increased. Chamberlin effectively argues as if, in the fully symmetrical case, $E_{ji} = k/(n-1)$, where k is a constant with a relatively small absolute value, as suggested in footnote 6 above. This is clearly a special and arbitrary assumption.

9. It may be noted that Bishop, fearful of the pitfalls inherent in assumptions of infinite numbers and of industry demands with own-price elasticities of zero (which we reject or neglect here), hedged in his own final market classification along the following lines:

	$-E_{ii}$	$-E_{ii}/E_{ji}$
Near-pure competition	$\to \infty$	large
Significantly differentiated competition or pure monopoly	$< \infty$	large
Near-pure oligopoly	$\to \infty$	small
Significantly differentiated oligopoly	$< \infty$	small

This end result does not fit well with his incisive exposition of classification principles in twenty preceding pages of his major article (1952). Heiser (1955) effectively criticizes Bishop's final retreat from a fully interpreted Triffin criterion.

classification added attributes of market structure other than numbers of sellers and degree of product differentiation, and also by recognizing with respect to some attributes more than a dichotomous distinction such as that between 'many' and 'few' sellers. If the theory is to be improved in this way, the addition of principles of classification and of market categories must be quite limited, because the primary function of an *a priori* theory – to produce generalizations – would not be fulfilled if a classification including very numerous market categories were employed. None the less, some elaboration of the original Chamberlinian classification has seemed promising.

Elaboration of the Chamberlinian market classification by recognizing more than a dichotomous distinction with respect to seller concentration seems clearly indicated within the magnum category of oligopoly. In an empirically relevant theory, oligopoly broadly construed embraces not only industries populated by 'a few sellers, all large', with circular interdependence for every pair, but also any industry in which at least one pair of sellers has such circular interdependence, even though it includes other smaller sellers having circular interdependence neither *inter se* nor with their large rivals. Furthermore, fewness of sellers is both a broad and a loose concept, so that oligopoly defined in general terms embraces both industries with very high seller concentration in which the strength of recognized interdependence might be expected to be dominant, and industries with only moderate seller concentration in which such interdependence, though present, is relatively weak. The writer has thus previously suggested a slightly elaborated market classification that not only distinguishes pure and heterogeneous oligopolies but also subclassifies each of these types according to degree of seller concentration and presence or absence of a competitive fringe of small sellers (see Bain, 1952, pp. 268–70). The theoretical rationale of this subclassification of oligopoly, and its potential as a basis for a more adequate theory, are discussed below in the consideration of the theory of oligopoly.

I have also suggested that the Chamberlinian market classification may be fruitfully elaborated by introducing a third principle of classification – the condition of entry to an industry.

It is notable that Chamberlin generally assumed both free entry (except for exact imitation of differentiated products) and the neglect by established sellers of the threat of entry, even for the market category of oligopoly, thus incidentally arriving at some implausible equilibrium solutions. Repair of this theory through elaboration of assumptions requires initially sub-classifying oligopolies and single-firm monopolies according to the heights of barriers to the entry of additional sellers (Bain, 1954). The exploitation of the implications of the added assumptions, involving an additional theorem, is also discussed in the subsequent section on the theory of oligopoly. Let us turn first, however, to issues concerning the extent of monopoly power under monopolistic competition.

Market power under monopolistic competition

Chamberlin assumed as a central market model a large group of small sellers purveying differentiated products (relatively close but not perfect substitutes to buyers) and then intuitively concluded that the *ceteris paribus* demand curves of individual sellers would be negatively sloping with a price elasticity that, though relatively high, would not approach infinity. He also assumed that these *dd'* demand curves would slope smoothly, no kinks occurring at the going or any other output, and that their price elasticities would not increase as the number of sellers increased. Given these assumptions plus those of U-shaped cost curves, of his version of free entry and of 'symmetry' of position as among all sellers, he derived his famous long-run group equilibrium for the 'large-group case' as an alternative to purely competitive long-run equilibrium. His novel conclusions under these assumptions were that a long-run equilibrium would be reached with no excess profits, with all sellers operating slightly below optimal scale, and with every seller continuing to exercise a modest degree of monopoly power. He put his major emphasis on this model and these conclusions, and in consequence his theory at first came to be identified mainly with them.

In retrospect this is unfortunate, for his reformulated theory of oligopoly, on which he spent much less time, had greater empirical relevance and more revolutionary implications for price theory, whereas his theory of large-number monopolistic competition was undermined by implicit assumptions concerning consumer preference patterns even more than by his special symmetry assumptions, and was open to attack from numerous directions.

As seen above, a significantly sloping dd' for the individual seller cannot be unequivocally deduced from the assumption of a large number of symmetrical sellers of products that are close but imperfect substitutes (have finite price cross-elasticities). If the number of sellers is absolutely large (let us say a hundred or more), it is additionally required that all price cross-elasticities be very small. Then, in one sense at least, the various products are individually quite poor substitutes for each other, pair by pair, and, moreover, the cross-elasticities must become smaller as the number of sellers increases. These were implicit assumptions in *Monopolistic Competition*, made explicit by Chamberlin only after others brought them to light. If we reject them, the general structural definition of monopolistic competition is consistent with *ceteris paribus* sales curves that are price elastic enough that the difference from infinite price elasticity is negligible. Then in monopolistic competition individual sellers would not necessarily have monopoly power, and the long-run group equilibrium would appear – *until product variation and selling costs are brought into play* – potentially to resemble very closely that of pure competition. When nonprice competition through product variation and sales promotion are recognized and incorporated into the theory, however, predicted market performance in monopolistic competition remains potentially distinctive even if individual sellers are essentially devoid of conventional monopoly power.

The preceding, moreover, suggests only one of the bases for revising Chamberlin's formulation of the individual seller's demand curve in monopolistic competition. In a notable article Nicols (1947) went behind the sorts of cross-elasticities of demand that Chamberlin had implicitly assumed for the large-group case, to uncover what had also been implicitly assumed concerning the maze of individual buyer preferences among the numerous differentiated products assumed to be offered. His most important expressed suggestion was that in order for individual sellers to have *ceteris paribus* sales curves that were both negatively and smoothly sloping (devoid of kinks) over any relevant interval, they would have to be supplying 'scale-of-preference' buyers each of whom ranked all available products in some particular way (from most to least preferred), and that in addition different buyers or subgroups thereof would need to assign a reasonably full variety of different preference rankings to the various products.

One revealing corollary of the existence of a mixed lot of scale-of-preference buyers may be illustrated as follows. Suppose 101 sellers form a group, each with a differentiated product and each with 500 buyers when the sellers are charging equal prices. The scale-of-preference conditions would require that if any seller A raised his price by say 1 per cent (equivalent to all other sellers lowering their prices by approximately 1 per cent) he would have 100 buyers who whould shift to other sellers, with one of these 100 shifting to each of the other sellers, because each shifting buyer had a different 'next-best' product on his preference scale, and these 100 were the most easily detached of his 500. Then seller A's cross-elasticity of demand with respect to every other seller for his price increase would be 0·2, and his own elasticity of demand for his price increase would be −20. Conversely, if seller A cut his price by 1 per cent, each of his 100 competitors would have one most-easily detached buyer who put A's product 'next-best' in his list, so that by cutting his price A would gain one buyer from each of his 100 competitors, and would have the same cross-elasticity of demand (0·2) with respect to every other seller, and the same own-price elasticity of demand (−20) for his price decrease as for his price increase. Thus A's *dd'* curve would have a continuous slope at the ruling output, as Chamberlin had it. As further successive price increases or decreases by any one seller were considered, comparably scale-of-preference properties of buyers' interproduct preference patterns would be required to secure the continuity of slope of any sellers' demand curve.

As Nicols suggested, this implicit assumption concerning a complex combination of scale-of-preference buyers is on *a priori* grounds, and apparently in terms of empirical relevance, a special assumption that we would not in general expect to be fulfilled. If it is not, alternative buyer-preference patterns could lead to individual sellers' demand curves being 'obtusely kinked', or more elastic beyond going output than short of it. To take an extreme case, suppose in the preceding example that all of the buyers from any one seller preferred his product to all those of all competing sellers, though some preferred it more strongly than others and could thus be detached only by larger price difference; but that all such buyers were indifferent as to their choice among the other 100 products, viewing them effectively as perfect substitutes. Each buyer would be a one-product man with weaker or stronger loyalty, and all other competing products would be indifferent choices *inter se* to him. Then, assuming symmetry, if a 1 per cent decrease by any one seller A would attract one 'most detachable' buyer from each of 100 competitors, he would encounter a cross-elasticity with each competitor again of 0·2 and an own-elasticity of demand of −20, *for his price decrease*. But if A raised his price by 1 per cent (equivalent to all his competitors lowering their prices by about one per cent) he would lose only his one 'most detachable' buyer to some competitor, and his own-elasticity of demand *for his price increase* would be only −0·2. (His 'average' cross-elasticity of demand with the other 100 sellers would be 0·002.) Then his *ceteris paribus* demand curve would clearly have an obtuse kink at his going output. Moreover, if somewhat higher values of cross-elasticity of demand are assumed (e.g., 2·0 instead of 0·2 for A's price decrease, and an 'average' of 0·02 for his price increase) his own demand curve would approach perfect elasticity for his output increases (−200 in this example), whereas it would be substantially less elastic for his output decreases (−2 in this case). Here Nicols obtained a very elastic seller's *dd'* by familiar reasoning concerning cross-elasticities and numbers, but obtained it only for output increases (price decreases) as he abandoned the scale-of-preference assumptions in Chamberlin's model.

Nicol's suggestions were significant for several reasons. First, he revealed clearly that Chamberlin really failed to explore formally the implications of his theory on the level of the theory of consumer choice, and thus neglected to forge an analytical system incorporating product differentiation that led logically forward from the theory of consumer behavior through the theory of the firm and to his theory of the market in monopolistic competition. In making this revelation, Nicols suggested the importance of 'completing' the Chamberlinian theory by building it from an adequate foundation theory of consumer behavior in the context of differentiated products. (Nicols himself merely scouted this territory.) Second, he properly identified the Chamberlinian solution for the large-group case as a distinctly special one and suggested the existence of a variety of equally plausible alternative solutions that might be profitably explored. Third, in introducing the notion that with some sorts of buyer-preference patterns (such as that featuring buyers each of whom views one product as superior and all others as indifferent choices) sellers in monopolistic competition may face *ceteris paribus* demand curves that are obtusely kinked at going output and very elastic beyond it, he suggested a model for monopolistic competition in which dynamically unstable prices within some equilibrium range may readily be deduced (as elementary experimentation will show), thus generating an interesting new hypothesis concerning long-run equilibrium tendencies in monopolistic competition.[10]

A full reconsideration of Chamberlin's model of and solution for the large-group case suggests: (a) that the model and the solution are special rather than general, mainly because they rest on special implicit assumptions concerning consumer behavior, his symmetry assumptions representing a lesser, if superficially more obvious, departure from generality; (b) that in the general case the existence of significant degrees of monopoly power should not characterize such monopolistic competition; and (c) that its distinctive features emerge when selling costs and product variation are incorporated into the model. Manipulation of these decision variables clearly opens the probability (if the symmetry assumption is abandoned or

10. Nicols's own special case of a monopolistic competition in which a significant fraction of buyers are totally unattached (view all products as perfect substitutes) and in which, therefore, each seller faces a perfectly elastic demand curve in the relevant range of output (any kinks being displaced to occur at smaller than going outputs), indeed gives purely competitive results, but the case is as uninteresting as it is special.

collapses) of equilibria with systematic price, product and selling-cost differences among sellers even though none has perceptible monopoly power. It is possible, however, that buyer-preference patterns may be such in some instances that the seller possesses monopoly power for price increases but not for price decreases, in which case a price 'yo-yo' effect is suggested.

The theory of oligopoly

The Chamberlinian contribution that was individually most important in implementing and giving vitality to his classification of markets was his discovery and formulation of a sophisticated theory of oligopoly. Cournot and others had played about with the model of duopoly as a theoretical curiosity, under assumptions that were internally inconsistent with the definition of the model. Chamberlin recognized oligopoly as a significant broad category of markets, introduced alternative assumptions that were implicit in the definition of the model and drew the main outlines of a theory of oligopoly resting on these assumptions.

His most important assumption, of course was, that of 'mutual dependence recognized' (or 'circular interdependence' as others have called it) among the sellers in an oligopolistic industry. Chamberlin was quick to see that, given such interdependence plus a sort of comprehensive symmetry in rival sellers' situations and a complete absence of time lags in every seller's response to the price or output changes of the others, the member firms of an oligopoly should move inevitably to a joint monopoly price. (Specific conditions necessary to validate this conclusion include, in addition to instantaneous responses, identical market shares that cannot be influenced by price cuts or otherwise, and identical cost functions – all generally implied or expressed by Chamberlin.) He completed the blocking out of an elementary theory by suggesting that nonfulfillment of one or more of the necessary conditions for a joint monopoly solution for oligopoly could lead to any of a range of price outcomes between the joint monopoly and competitive limits – in either pure or heterogeneous oligopoly.

It must be recognized that Chamberlin did not develop a

complete and fully articulated theory of oligopoly (in part because he held himself forever bound by symmetry assumptions). Only about twenty of the 176 text pages of the first edition of *Monopolistic Competition* were devoted to his own theory of oligopoly, and many of them were discursive. But he revealed the need for a complete theory of oligopoly, demonstrated the crucial importance in such theory of his own concept of circular interdependence and suggested the critical structural characteristics of oligopolies (other than fewness of sellers) that would have to be formally recognized in a more complete theory. At the same time, he left a great deal of work to be done by other theorists.

Reactions in subsequent years to Chamberlin's innovation have been varied. There was some initial tendency to consign the theory of oligopoly to an early limbo on the grounds that in the *general* case all that was to be found was a maze of interdependent conjectures about rivals' reactions and an indeterminate equilibrium solution. Others chose to develop a theory for oligopoly only under special institutional assumptions such as that a cartel or a viable and well-observed price or market-sharing agreement existed, and to neglect the rest. This pursuit was not entirely fruitless, for the exploration of the theory of oligopoly with express agreements revealed some fundamental tendencies within oligopolies that a more generalized theory would have to recognize and account for.[11] Much later, various attempts were made to arrive at a general theory of oligopoly through the application of the theory of games. To date these have not proved very successful (the *n*-person nonzero-sum game with coalitions admitted seems to be the appropriate general model) but they have shown us how to reach a Cournot duopoly solution the hard way.

Others have attempted positive elaborations of a general theory of oligopoly along the lines that Chamberlin's work suggested, by exploring the internal logic of the oligopolistic situation and, without reliance on special institutional assumptions, tracing the implications of an added range of empirical generalizations that may be incorporated into the theory as assumptions. Perhaps the most significant general work in

11. This quality is particularly apparent in Patinkin (1947).

this tradition is William Fellner's *Competition among the Few* (1949), which incorporates a brilliant and lucid general statement of the logic of oligopoly in its first chapter and then proceeds to develop a theory of qualified or limited joint-profit maximization. Fellner's general theorem is that within any oligopoly there are likely to be conditions and motives present that oppose or mitigate the intrinsic drive toward joint-profit maximization and engender a market performance that, although not competitive, falls short of or deviates from monopolistic performance. Although he properly notes as relevant conditions such things as incompleteness of coordination in the nonprice dimensions of seller decisions and safety-margin considerations in the presence of uncertainty, he strikes at the heart of the problem when he notes that only qualified joint-profit maximization and quasi-agreements are generally possible because of the unwillingness of the individual oligopolist to yield up his sovereignty at all fully for the sake of joint-profit maximization, except in exceptional circumstances.

Fellner specifically emphasizes this reluctance as a pervasive deterrent to the emergence of perfect cartels (in which firms would pool their resources and earnings and agree on interfirm compensations) whenever cost functions are nonhorizontal or differ among firms or when product differentiation is present. But the thesis is readily generalized and extended (a) to identify comparable deterrents within oligopolies that forestall agreements to charge an approximately monopolistic price, and (b) to explain difficulties that make several sorts of imperfect collusion (e.g., collusion at a submonopoly level of price, imperfectly observed collusion, collusion on price *cum* rivalry for market shares) predictable possibilities or probabilities. Fellner recognizes this in a general way, but does not pursue the point very far.

A generalization of Fellner's thesis might take the following form: if an oligopoly is defined as being composed of several independently owned and controlled firms, its members intrinsically have two or three conflicting motives. One is the motive for joint profit maximization (most probably long-run maximization), because all would like to divide the largest profit pie. Such joint maximization is exactly obtainable via a perfect cartel or, if that is barred by law, attainable to a reasonable approximation through price and kindred agreements that may be reached tacitly by nothing more than 'implicit bargaining', for example, as offers to agree are made and accepted or rejected through press releases. Another motive, however, is present because of the fundamental antagonism of interests of separately owned entities: each oligopolist would also like to increase his share of joint profits at the expense of his rivals and is willing to do so even if his action reduces joint profits, provided that the absolute amount of his separate long-run profit is increased. This motive does not vanish simply because there is also a mutual interest in maximum joint profits, and because it does not, the movement by oligopolists toward joint-profit maximization (even of the approximate sort attainable without perfect cartels) is not a foregone conclusion. A motive corollary to the general antagonism of interest among rival oligopolists is that of each to protect his sovereignty; this deters him from exposing himself to loss through agreements or treaties comprehensive enough that his rivals can hurt him without hurting themselves by failing to observe or abrogating the treaties or agreements. This consideration places a definite constraint on the probable scope and content of tacit or express agreements and, even on the degree to which they represent attempts to approach joint monopoly pricing or selling-cost or product policies.

All of the preceding being recognized, pricing and related policies and market performance within oligopolies depend on the relative operational strength of joint-profit maximizing and antagonistic motives in particular situations. This relative strength of motives in turn depends on the specific characteristics of the oligopolistic market – characteristics that effectively determine the probability of success of antagonistic pricing and related policies in enhancing the profit positions of individual sellers. If these structural characteristics are such as to render antagonistic policies unprofitable to sellers who undertake them, generally or with respect to certain decision variables (price, product, selling cost), then collusive action for joint-profit maximization generally, or with respect to given variables, is predictable. If these characteristics tend to render antagonistic actions profitable to some or all of the rival sellers, independent profit-maximizing motives come into at least limited play. Then it is predictable that collusive monopoly outcomes will be whittled away in some degree by independent actions (clandestine price cutting, product competition, etc.); that agreements will initially not aim so high as joint-profit maximization because they would then be too vulnerable to defections; or that agreement with respect to one variable (e.g., price) may be accompanied by limited antagonistic policies with respect to another (e.g., product).

The structural characteristics of oligopolies that seem to be most important in determining the relative importance of joint-profit-maximizing policies and antagonistic policies include, in addition to the state of market information and other considerations affecting the promptness with which rivals can respond to each others' actions: (a) the degree of seller concentration, or more generally the number and size distribution of sellers in the market; and (b) the effective differentiability of the product, which establishes the scope for independent product adjustments or variations that are not readily or rapidly matched by rivals.

The importance of the degree and pattern of seller concentration is obvious as we distinguish oligopolies with only a very few large sellers from those with a somewhat greater number of large sellers, their number being small enough that circular interdependence is still readily inferred. In addition we may distinguish subcategories of each of the preceding classes according to whether or not the oligopolistic industry also includes an appreciable competitive fringe of small sellers who do not have circular interdependence with the large ones. In highly concentrated oligopolies, circular interdependence tends to be so strong (the effect of each seller's price or related adjustments on each of the others so great) that antagonistic actions tend to be rapidly and fully 'punished' and thus discouraged; joint-profit-maximizing actions are then likely to be dominant, leading toward monopolistic market performance.

In moderately concentrated or more dilute oligopolies, the self-policing mechanism of circular interdependence, though present, is weaker, encouraging limited antagonistic actions, profitable to those who undertake them, as a pull against joint-profit-maximizing action. (Limited antagonistic action may be expressed through independent clandestine price concessions to individual buyers, leading toward 'chaotic' price discrimination, through independent forays in product variation and increases in sales-promotion budgets, etc.) Price, product or selling-cost policies may then not be held at the joint-profit-maximizing level both because tacit agreements are selectively violated and because the terms of the agreements themselves are adjusted to mitigate destructive violations. A profit-maximizing principle that is a hybrid of joint-profit-maximization and independent-profit-maximization may in effect be the working principle. The probability of this happening is enhanced if the oligopolistic industry is in fact made up of an oligopolistic core and an appreciable competitive fringe of small firms, for reasons so obvious as not to require discussion. The preceding suggests that an elaborated theory of oligopoly should rest on a structural subclassification of the general oligopoly category to recognize three or four degrees and patterns of seller concentration, and that, at least as probability judgements, different market conduct and performance may be predicted for each subcategory.

Further subclassification is suggested according to the effective differentiability of the product the industry sells. With products having high effective differentiability, limited antagonistic action in the area of product policy and related sales promotion are tentatively predictable even with high seller concentration and even with joint-profit-maximizing collusion on prices; a less restricted antagonistic action is indicated for oligopolies that are moderately concentrated and that have significant competitive fringes of small sellers.

The preceding theory, like Fellner's, is not a 'complete' theory of oligopoly according to criteria ordinarily applied, principally because it does not tie its assumptions to its conclusions by a complete process of deductive reasoning that would lead unequivocally to unique predictions of market performance for each of several subcategories of oligopoly. It does provide a framework for a complete theory, the development of which (if possible) would require the introduction of some added concepts and assumptions, among them the values of both price and quantity cross-elasticities, and the 'pivot man' or 'policeman' seller whose policies limit the scope of the antagonistic policies of others. Such a generalized theory may emerge if sufficient time and ability are devoted to the problem. Meanwhile, this quasi-theory is of some value as a source of refutable hypotheses to be tested through empirical studies.

One relatively recent elaboration of the theory of oligopoly (and of monopoly) has involved the introduction of (a) the concept of the condition of entry (or height of barriers to entry) to oligopolistic industries as an added significant dimension of their market structures; (b) the theorem that established firms will tend to recognize threats of entry and deter it by 'limit pricing' below the monopoly level if that is more profitable to them in the long run than charging higher prices and inducing entry; and (c) further theorizing concerning the conditions under which they will and will not follow limit-pricing policies.[12] This theory has not yet had its fullest obviously attainable formal development. In its present rudimentary form it proposes a new range of hypotheses concerning the pricing and related policies and the market performance of oligopolists and suggests the validity for theoretical purposes of further subclassifying oligopolies according to the height of the barriers to entry to them. A notable aspect of this theory is that it finds a new role for product differentiation – namely, as one of the main types of barrier to entry – which might be held to be as important as the role Chamberlin assigned to it. Its full development depends on the application of Chamberlin's novel construct. As far as the genesis of the theory goes, the writer must give further credit to Chamberlin, whose implausible 'high-tangency' solution for heterogeneous oligopoly (where all established sellers were supposedly oblivious to threats of entry and to the long-run effects of entry on their profits) fostered a desire to arrive at a more plausible solution.

The consideration of theories involving barriers to entry and limit pricing has suggested incidentally the desirability of extending the theory of long-run equilibria in oligopolistic industries to comprehend the determination of market structures,

12. See Bain (1954, 1956). One aspect of this theory was independently developed, on somewhat special assumptions, by Sylos-Labini (1956).

especially in the dimension of degree and pattern of seller concentration. Such an extension should comprehend among other things the systematic classification of certain models of oligopolistic behavior, such as price warfare to weaken or eliminate rivals, as representing disequilibrium situations and reflecting dynamic processes of market adjustment. Some tentative work has been done on this front, which remains open for exploration.

Equilibria involving product determination and selling costs

If Chamberlin's theory of oligopoly was most important in developing the implications of his market classification, second in importance would be his elaboration of price theory by introducing product and selling cost as variables that the firm manipulates along with price, quantity of output and production cost. Through this elaboration he clearly suggested the possibility and presumptive importance of a multidimensional theory of the firm and of industry equilibrium with greatly enhanced empirical relevance. He also implied the need for developing an elaborated set of criteria of market performance, to include socially optimal product quality and variety and a socially optimal size of selling costs (in addition to 'efficiency' criteria referring to marginal cost-price relations, scale of firm and excess capacity), against which theoretically predicted performance in the dimensions of product and selling cost could be measured.

The major reasons that Chamberlin's innovation in this area has failed to have a vital impact on subsequent theoretical literature seem to be that Chamberlin himself did not develop any normative system to match his predictions concerning market performance in the dimensions of product and selling cost, that these predictions of his were almost devoid of normative content, and that theorists later have conspicuously failed to remedy his omissions by developing a coordinate set of norms. Distinctly secondary reasons for this lack of strong impact would include the facts that, being restricted to formal analysis via two-dimensional geometry, Chamberlin was unable to develop fully the interactions of five variables and larger numbers of intervariable relationships in arriving at equilibria for the firm or industry, and that most of his predictions in this area were so general in character as scarcely to be susceptible to empirical refutation. These latter deficiencies have become readily remediable with advances in related branches of theory and in mathematical economic theory generally.

Chamberlin's own failure to develop or attempt to develop the sort of norms described is consistent with his general disinclination to delve into the theory of consumer behavior, even though the need for the development of some aspects of this theory was clearly implied by his theories of markets and of the firm. This is a disinclination already identified as being responsible for the fact that major parts of his theory rested partly on a foundation of unexplored implicit assumptions and thus ran to special solutions. But he contributed a great deal as it was, and it is puzzling that others have not pursued the theoretical inquiries that he neglected by working over the area of consumer preference theory to provide norms at least for 'ideal product'.

Norms for selling costs are elusive creatures, because of the direct action of selling costs on consumer preference patterns. However, the road toward developing the concept of buyers' price–quality–quantity preference functions,[13] defining optimal coadjustment of these variables and deducing the extent to which market performance within each of several market structures tends to diverge from such an optimum is fairly well marked and appears to be passable. The best explanations available for a general failure to push along this road are that it is rough and can be navigated only with quite advanced technical equipment, that many economic theorists have been temporarily beset by a disenchantment with normative economics and that those with the most adequate technical equipment are more interested in other problems or perhaps never heard of this one. Yet a careful study of Chamberlin's theory of group adjustment including product variation clearly

13. These preferences might be reflected, for example, in maps of indifference curves relating price to quality, quantity being given, or quantity to quality, price being given – or in more complex four-variable functional relationships linking price, quality, quantity and the level of satisfaction.

suggests propensities toward product qualities that are 'excessive' from the standpoint of buyer welfare, under any of a number of constellations of buyer price-quality preferences, and an analysis of this suggestion at the level of rigorous formal theory would clearly be important.

Chamberlin's own analysis of decision making by the firm and of equilibrium for the group when price, quantity, production cost, selling cost and product are all variable is well known. He developed partial solutions for various trios of variables, each including production cost and quantity – taking as the third variable successively price, product and selling cost – and avoided most of the more obvious pitfalls of this procedure through literary interpolations that qualified his partial solutions by considering the coordinate influence of the adjustment of another variable. Then he poured together the partial solutions into a general solution that says nothing more than that the firm will seek a *maximum maximorum* position in which all partial marginal-equality conditions are simultaneously fulfilled, and that the group will do likewise after exit or entry. Insufficient emphasis was perhaps placed on the fact that two of the partial marginal-equality conditions could be fulfilled at points and with intervariable relationships inconsistent with a *maximum maximorum*, and the interplay of all the variables could not be adequately analysed with the equipment at hand. A conspicuous omission from relevant empirical generalizations entered as assumptions in Chamberlin's theory was one concerning the relation of the demand for a seller's output (represented by price, quantity being given, or by quantity, price being given) to increase in product quality. A related omission was the failure to distinguish markets in which all buyers have identical price–quality or quantity–quality indifference maps from those in which buyers differ systematically in this regard – and thereafter to explore the relevance of this distinction.

Chamberlin's theoretical models involving selling cost and product were thus not productive of many formal hypotheses that were meaningful in the sense that they were conceivably susceptible of empirical refutation. If there is product differentiation, selling costs will be incurred and be covered by price.

With respect to the outcome of group product adjustment, 'the most that can be said is that it [the exact point of equilibrium] will be characterized by (a) the equation of cost and price and (b) the impossibility of a "product" adjustment by anyone which would increase his profits' (Chamberlin, 1933, p. 97 of 8th edn). The equilibrium product under monopolistic competition is inevitably 'inferior' because of sellers' monopoly power, but this really turns out to mean only that product quality is slightly lower than if we had monopolistic competition without such monopoly power, so that the term 'inferior' is devoid of normative connotations. About the most that is made of selling costs is Chamberlin's deduction (to abbreviate a prolonged argument) that the competitive use of selling costs will virtually enlarge the markets of individual sellers by concentrating a given industry demand in the hands of fewer sellers (and perhaps by enlarging industry demand), that this virtual increase will not be fully offset by consequent price increases, and that firms undertaking selling costs will thus operate at larger scales than otherwise. This is a conclusion that if generally supportable is of much interest mainly in the context of the inefficiently small scales or excess capacity that Chamberlin's rather special solutions for monopolistic competition and oligopoly predict.

The foregoing might be construed as expressing a dim view of Chamberlin's contribution so far as it introduced selling costs and product variation into the theories of the firm and of markets. It is really dim, however, only with respect to Chamberlin's formal exploitation of the constructs he introduced and to the inadequate underpinning of his argument in the area of the theory of consumer choice. A consistent positive view is that he opened up a fruitful territory for theorizing that should by now have been explored far more thoroughly than it has, because of both its policy implications and its general theoretical interest. His formal models, together with his literary commentary on them, are a rich source of informal and implied hypotheses concerning market performance in the dimensions of product and selling cost that clearly invite formal development, just as the need for feeding much more normative content into his models is implied.

However, the payoff from his crucial constructs and derived rudimentary models in this area has been slow in coming – much slower than that from his innovation of the theory of oligopoly. Properly neglected are miscellaneous regurgitations and reformulations of Chamberlin's three-variable partial solutions (mostly emphasizing selling costs as the more quantifiable of the added variables), because by and large they added nothing to and sometimes subtracted from what we already had. Abbott (1955) made a valiant effort to develop the theory of product determination. Although he contributed significantly to the theory of the 'horizontal' equilibrium of products (degree of differentiation) (Abbott, 1955, pp. 143–52), in dealing with 'vertical' product equilibrium (level of quality of all products in a group) he succeeded mainly in demonstrating unmistakably that on an inflexible price-is-given assumption it is possible to reach nonsense conclusions concerning both the level of product quality a market will reach and the positions of firms *vis-à-vis* exploitation of scale economies – albeit displaying considerable technical ingenuity *en route* (pp. 152–70). In subsequent argument he unfortunately failed to eradicate this blight or to arrive at an improved general solution for product determination where price is also variable.

At present, the blueprint for the development of the product and selling-cost phases of Chamberlin's theory calls for many additional building blocks; without these blocks the full potential impact of his pioneering work in the area of multivariate analysis on the theories of the firm and of the industry remains largely unrealized. Correspondingly, its major impact has so far been registered on the conceptual structure of empirical work in the field of industrial organization.

Conclusion

A concluding synopsis of the foregoing may be omitted in favor of some general remarks about Chamberlin's broad contribution to microeconomic theory and subsequent contributions that his work has inspired or should inspire.

Chamberlin's *Monopolistic Competition* had its wellsprings in the brilliance, originality, breadth of view and rigor of intellect of its author. His most important contribution to price theory was one of broad conceptualization and of organization or reorganization of ideas. In this function he stands pre-eminent as an original architect of a new system of price theory. He has been perhaps less outstanding, though indubitably competent, as a 'construction man' who followed his own blueprints, in that he has built only pilot models on selected assumptions (being a bit unwary about implied assumptions), but he certainly has built enough to point the way to the fulfillment of his master architectural plan. He has been perhaps least outstanding as a self-critic. In thirty years of active work following the initial publication of *Monopolistic Competition*, he did not really revise it although it remained his major interest and went through eight editions. He has tended to resist rather than accept and benefit from numerous criticisms and suggestions, and has been curiously reluctant to go on with the main construction job he began on completing the manuscript first published in 1933.

Examination of his main contributions would suggest that he contributed most importantly to the theory of markets by introducing the construct of a market classification based on distinctions among market structures and on a brilliant identification of those dimensions of market structure that provided the most significant principles of classification. Of substantially equivalent importance were his contributions to the theories of the firm and of markets, through his innovation of 'mutual dependence recognized' for firms in oligopoly and through his introduction of a multivariate theory of the firm's market policy and of market equilibrium. He contributed very little, however, to the theory of consumer choice, even though his theories of the firm and of markets cried out for such a contribution. Partly in consequence, the notable deficiency of these theories was their comparative lack of normative content.

Thus Chamberlin passed on to theorists both an enormous opportunity and an exciting challenge to implement his broad architectural plans and to explore the *terra nolum cognita* he had viewed from a distance. What has been the quality of the response to this opportunity and challenge, within the general confines of *a priori* microeconomic theory, and where have there been conspicuous failures to respond?

First, his taxonomy of market structures has been systematized and regularized on a formal level, and also deliberately elaborated as logic and observation have dictated, with resultant improvement, albeit at the cost of questioning certain of his primary deductions concerning the sufficient conditions for the existence of monopoly power. Tentative advances along this line, however, have been marred generally by a failure to refer back at all sufficiently to the theory of consumer choice.

Second, much less has been done in developing his model of large-numbers monopolistic competition. Retrospective evaluation of his original work has suggested that this Chamberlinian model was a much less important novelty than his theory of oligopoly, at any rate except so far as it incorporated selling cost and product as decision variables. That the seller in such monopolistic competition should be viewed as possessing significant monopoly power remains seriously in doubt – a doubt that arises only in very diminished degree with respect to the oligopolist. Moreover, oligopolistic markets seem empirically more important than those that combine atomism with product differentiation. Given this doubt, theoretical progress has nonetheless been made toward recognizing that large-numbers monopolistic competition may generate a variety of special and distinctive types of market performance, of which the original Chamberlinian type was only one.

Third, exploitation or development of Chamberlin's germinal theory of the firm and industry in situations where selling costs and products as well as price and output are variable has been quite limited. This seems explicable in part by a passing shift of economists' interests to other matters (or to types of national economies in which allocation of resources among different sorts and qualities of consumer goods is hardly the central problem), and in part by their failures to recognize (here Chamberlin did not explicitly draw a road map) the need for a correlative probing of the theory of consumer choice – and to probe it.

Finally, perhaps the most fruitful effort devoted to exploiting the potential of Chamberlinian theory has centered on the theory of oligopoly, and not improperly so if empirical relevance is introduced as a criterion. Some successes have been scored in

Joe S. Bain 285

this area, resulting from endeavors that would probably not have been launched lacking a *Monopolistic Competition*. That this should be the main area of successful efforts to advance Chamberlinian theory matches well with the fact that Chamberlin wrote mostly of the theory of markets, and implies some things about the habits and limitations of most economic theorists. Yet in spite of comparative success in exploiting the potential of Chamberlin's ideas in this area, both generally and with regard to the analysis of conditions of entry, we still have something resembling fuller architectural plans much more than completed theories.

From this we might infer a dismal fate for sophisticated price theory, but of necessity only if fads and fancies continue to tempt theorists always to abandon the half-explored claim in order to join a new gold rush. A resurgence of interest in the actual allocation problems of an affluent enterprise economy, as distinct from its growth problems, may engender the development of a much more adequate neo-Chamberlinian microeconomic theory than we now have.

References

ABBOTT, L. (1955), *Quality and Competition*, Columbia University Press.
BAIN, J. S. (1952), *Price Theory*, Holt, Rinehart & Winston.
BAIN, J. S. (1954), 'Conditions of entry and the emergence of monopoly', in E. H. Chamberlin (ed.), *Monopoly and Competition and their Regulation*, Macmillan, pp. 215–41.
BAIN, J. S. (1956), *Barriers to New Competition*, Harvard University Press.
BAIN, J. S. (1964), '*The Theory of Monopolistic Competition* after thirty years: the impact on industrial organization', *Amer. econ. Rev., Pap. Proc.*, vol. 54, pp. 28–32.
BISHOP, R. L. (1952), 'Elasticities, cross-elasticities and market relationships', *Amer. econ. Rev.*, vol. 42, pp. 781–803.
BISHOP, R. L. (1953), 'Reply', *Amer. econ. Rev.*, vol. 43, pp. 916–24.
BISHOP, R. L. (1955), 'Reply', *Amer. econ. Rev.*, vol. 45, pp. 382–6.
CHAMBERLIN, E. H. (1933), *The Theory of Monopolistic Competition: A Re-Orientation of the Theory of Value*, Harvard University Press, 8th edn, 1962.
CHAMBERLIN, E. H. (1953), 'Elasticities, cross-elasticities and market relationships: comment', *Amer. econ. Rev.*, vol. 43, pp. 910–16.
FELLNER, W. (1949), *Competition among the Few*, Knopf.
FELLNER, W. (1953), 'Elasticities, cross-elasticities and market relationships: comment', *Amer. econ. Rev.*, vol. 43, pp. 898–910.

FRIEDMAN, M. (1961), 'More on Archibald versus Chicago', *Rev. econ. Stud.*, vol. 30, pp. 65–7.

HEISER, R. (1955), 'Elasticities, cross-elasticities and market relationships: comment', *Amer. econ. Rev.*, vol. 45, pp. 373–82.

KALDOR, N. (1935), 'Market imperfection and excess capacity', *Economica*, new series, vol. 2, pp. 33–50.

KOOPMANS, T. C. (1957), *Three Essays on the State of Economic Science*, McGraw-Hill.

MACHLUP, F. (1937), 'Monopoly and competition: a classification', *Amer. econ. Rev.*, vol. 27, pp. 445–51.

NICOLS, A. (1947), 'The rehabilitation of pure competition', *Quart. J. Econ.*, vol. 62, pp. 31–63.

PATINKIN, D. (1947), 'Multi-plant firms: cartels and imperfect conditions', *Quart. J. Econ.*, vol. 61, pp. 173–205.

SYLOS-LABINI, P. (1956), *Oligopoly and Technical Progress*, trans. E. Henderson, Harvard University Press, 1962.

TRIFFIN, R. (1940), *Monopolistic Competition and General Equilibrium Theory*, Harvard University Press.

12 William J. Baumol

Models of Economic Competition

William J. Baumol, 'Models of economic competition', in P. Langhoff (ed.), *Models, Measurement and Marketing*, Prentice-Hall, 1965, pp. 143–68.

Probably the first thoroughly sophisticated piece of mathematical economic analysis, the work of a Frenchman, Augustin Cournot (published in 1838), was a *competitive model*. Indeed, even today, that model continues to be illuminating. It will be described later in this chapter, not as an historical curiosum, but as an important piece of up-to-date economic analysis. Thus, it can be seen that interest in the analysis and description of the competitive process began very early and continues to be a major and common concern of the economic theorist, the operations researcher and the businessman. In recent decades, one of the most imaginative breakthroughs in mathematical economics, the theory of games, can be placed in this area. Another fundamental development, mathematical programming, is of considerable relevance. Both of these will be discussed in this chapter.

The vital importance of this subject to the businessman hardly requires emphasis. The planning of his strategies, as well as his countermoves to the decisions of his rivals, is clearly critical to the success and survival of his operation. Yet, despite the importance of this area and despite the spectacular intellectual contributions that have been made toward its analysis, much of our understanding is in a state that is far from satisfactory, especially from the point of view of direct practical application. In making this statement, I wish carefully to avoid selling competitive theory short. Management has already learned a great deal from it and the solution of many of management's problems can be rendered far more tractable with its assistance. However, it is important to avoid claiming too much, and the reader must be warned that there are too many important questions the theory cannot even pretend to answer.

Objectives of the firm

To understand how firms behave (or how they should be expected to behave), it is first necessary to determine what the company is trying to achieve. This determination is not so trivial as it may at first appear. It can have an important bearing on the conduct of the firm. Yet, it is often extremely difficult to answer in any particular situation.

Difficulties in determining company objectives

In many cases, companies have issued public relations statements purporting to describe their goals. However, these assertions, which proclaim that the firm lives exclusively to support progress, motherhood and the American way of life, are hardly to be taken seriously. In practice, management is simply too busy dealing with its day-to-day operating problems to have time for a calm introspective look at its long-run aspirations. Indeed, it is by no means clear that management is well equipped to make such a study, even if it did have the time to do so. Who of us is in a position to undertake a convincing statement of our own motivations in any particular act or decision? Moreover, as will presently be indicated, the analysis of objectives may involve subtle problems of consistency that are not obvious to the nonspecialist. A final and very important obstacle to the investigation of motivations arises out of the complexity of the modern corporation. A corporation is rarely a monolithic decision-making organism. Decision power and responsibility are divided and dispersed, partly because of the nature of the organizational structure, partly because it is simply impossible for top management to undertake the myriad of minor decisions that must be made in a firm. This being the case, there can perhaps be no single set of objectives which characterize the aims of the company as a whole. Rather, company targets must somehow be considered the result of the diverse objectives pursued by the many decision makers who effectively operate it.

Some alternative goals

What are the goals of the typical company? Standard economic analysis unambiguously tells us that the company usually has one single target – it seeks to make as much money (total net profit) as it possibly can. Recently, this assertion has been questioned from two different points of view. First, it has been suggested that profits are not the only interest of management and, indeed, other goals may frequently have higher priority. Second, it has been argued that management may not try to *maximize* anything – that a more modest goal may be all it hopes to achieve. This latter argument will be discussed in the next section. For the moment, let us only list some of the other aims that may be pursued by management.

There is reason to believe, for example, that many businessmen are very highly concerned with the rate of growth of the firm – the rate of growth of its sales (the total value of all items sold by the company) or of its assets, or even the rate of growth (more than the current level) of its profits. They are also apt to assign great weight to the company's sales volume *per se* and to its market share.

Here we must be careful not to confuse means and ends. Sales are not important *only* to those whose target is maximal dollar volume. The profit maximizer must also watch his sales because low and declining volume is apt to be a poor way to bring in profits. To him, however, sales are only an instrument for turning out profits, whereas to a sales maximizer (or to a sales-growth maximizer) the reverse is apt to be the case – profits will be a means for financing selling activities and expansion. Therefore, although there is likely to be some similarity of behavior in the two types of firms, *it will be far from identical.* The sales maximizing firm will, even in the long run, usually sell more and earn less money than does the profit maximizing company.

Only one objective to a company

This brings up another significant point – management can only serve one master at a time. Though it is apt to be frustrating, it must be recognized that it is generally impossible to maximize more than one achievement. We cannot at the same time maximize profits, rate of growth of sales, minimize costs and minimize risk, etc. For example, the growth maximizer must be prepared to undertake special risks and to subject his company to higher costs than if he were content to let it drift or remain static. Once the company's central objective is determined, its efficient pursuit requires the subordination of all other aims.

Thus, management is placed in an unenviable position. Faced with a variety of attractive objectives, it must be reluctant to reject all but one. Compromise is, indeed, possible. We may choose to maximize neither profits alone nor sales alone, but some weighted average index number of the two. However, it is essential to avoid trying to pursue all goals at the same time and, by attempting to run off in all directions at once, working towards none of them efficiently. This is a lesson that is neither always obvious in practice, nor is it always heeded in the heat of day-to-day decision making.

Some other alternatives

Several other alternative objectives may be mentioned before concluding this section. A conservative management may give primary emphasis to the firm's survival and may seek to minimize risk. A self-centered management may seek to maximize its own direct remuneration or the value of the stock options that often constitute so important a portion of its compensation. Maximization of the returns to stockholders may sometimes be the company's primary goal. Finally, despite some natural skepticism, it must be recognized that some sort of public service goals are often apt to characterize the aims of top management.

Thus, goals are likely to vary from company to company, and any company is likely to vary its objectives with the passage of time. In analysing the competitive behavior of any particular firm at any particular date, it is essential to understand which goal, or combination goals, it holds, because the strategies that are most appropriate for a company with one set of objectives are most unlikely to be optimal for a firm with other goals.

The logic of the pursuit of objectives
The meaning of explicit maximization

In the preceding section, the words *maximum* and *minimum* occurred with considerable frequency. These may be taken as synonymous with the most efficient pursuit of whatever objectives the company may have chosen for itself. Now, it is as apt to appear at first glance that any management in its right mind maximizes, and in some trivial sense it probably does. That is, only a pathological management will consciously and deliberately make a decision that (in the long run) reduces the firm's level of achievement. A profit-maximizing management may, with its eyes open, subject the company to a temporary loss, but only if it believes that this will pay off and with dividends in the long run.

Maximization, or at least explicit maximization, means more than this. It implies that management has examined all (or at least a representative subset) of the full range of possibilities and has decided, after due deliberation, on the method that best furthers its objectives. This is something that is rarely encountered in practice. What business firm, which has decided to operate sixty regional sales offices, has first carefully examined the consequences of *each* of the available alternatives (fifty-nine offices, fifty-eight offices, sixty-one offices, etc.)? How often is a decision to spend 2 million dollars on new product development buttressed by explicit evidence that *no* other expenditure level is likely to serve the company better?

Difficulties in explicit maximizing calculations

This sort of optimality analysis is usually not undertaken for a variety of reasons. To some extent, hidebound tradition, lack of managerial time, outright laziness or poor thinking may play its role. But more important are the very real obstacles to such an analysis. Often, the requisite data are simply not available, or they may be very imperfect and expensive to obtain. The calculation of the effects of alternative research and development budget levels is an extreme case of this lack of analysis, involving large elements of guesswork and speculation. However, even in deciding the consequences of changes in a relatively measurable item, alternative inventory levels, accurate data are not easily come by.

A second difficulty in making a full optimality analysis is the sheer magnitude of the task of going through the entire range of comparisons. In choosing what number (from say one to one hundred) of sales offices to operate, there are one hundred alternatives to be studied and compared. However, if we adjoin to this decision the problem of deciding on the location of the offices, the matter gets entirely out of hand for a straight-forward comparison process. The number of possible combinations involved in choosing, for example, twenty-five sales headquarters from among the one hundred largest American cities is absolutely astronomical. Indeed, it can be shown to be a number that leaves billions and even trillions far behind. Back-of-the-envelope calculations break down completely in the face of such a massive comparison and decision problem.

The differential calculus

In these circumstances, it becomes essential to devise more effective techniques for scanning and comparing the vast array of possibilities and coming up with the selection of the alternative that maximizes the firm's level of achievement (at least under whatever simplifying assumptions are needed to make the problem tractable). A variety of informal devices have been employed for this purpose. Most noteworthy for us are the two systematic techniques that do the job: differential calculus and mathematical programming. The differential calculus is a branch of mathematics invented by Newton and Leibnitz not many decades after the Pilgrim fathers dropped anchor in Massachusetts Bay. The basic idea of the method can be explained very simply. Suppose we have found, by statistical methods, a mathematical relationship between the level of profits, P, and advertising expenditure, A. For purely illustrative purposes, assume the equation were

$$P = 10 + 0 \cdot 8A - 0 \cdot 02A^2.$$

This equation implicitly describes what would happen in each of the very large number of alternative advertising budget decisions. For example, it shows that if ten (million) dollars were budgeted for this purpose, profits would be

$$P = 10 + 0 \cdot 8(10) - 0 \cdot 02(100) = \$16 \text{ (million)}.$$

Similarly, the effects of any other budget level can be computed with the aid of our equation. However, which of these many possibilities *maximizes* profits? The differential calculus enables us to compute the marginal or incremental profitability of advertising – it tells us how much any additional expenditure on advertising will add to company profits. This is illustrated in Figure 1, which is a graph of our advertising profit equation.

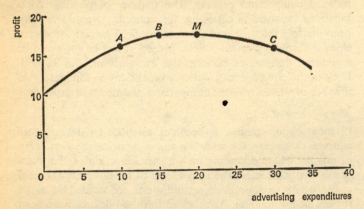

Figure 1

This shows, for example, that an increase in our advertising expenditure from 10 to 15 million dollars will raise company profits from 16 to 17·5 million (points *A* and *B* on the graph) – that is, approximately an increase of 1·5 million dollars in net profits for 5 million in added advertising budget – a $300,000 incremental profit per million dollar change in advertising outlay.

The differential calculus gives us a formula for this incremental profit, which in this case can be shown to be

incremental profit = $0.8 - 0.04A$.

Looking at our graph, we note that at the left of the profit maximizing point, *M*, the curve goes uphill as we move to the right; that is, increasing advertising *adds* to profit. Therefore, incremental profit is positive and we see that at any of those points, such as *A*, we have not carried our advertising far enough. On the other hand, at any point to the right of *M*, we have over-advertised – our incremental advertising payoff is *negative* because the increase in advertising outlay is not matched fully by the increase in its gross profit return. Near *M*, the optimal point (where the curve is neither going uphill nor downhill), the incremental payoff is approximately zero. That is, we will have used up every opportunity to increase profit by advertising and, thus, further advertising outlay yields a zero incremental profit return.

This reasoning can now be used to determine the optimal advertising level with the aid of our (second) *incremental* profit equation. We are looking for the point where incremental profits are *zero*, for we have seen that the optimal point has this characteristic. Hence, we want a value of A, such that

incremental profit $= 0.8 - 0.04A = 0$,

i.e. for which

$0.8 = 0.04A$ or $A = 20$.

The graph confirms that this is the optimal solution.

This, then, is the essence of the first of the two standard optimization techniques – the differential calculus. Among all the many possibilities, we find the optimal one by calculating the incremental profit (or incremental sales if we are sales maximizers, etc.) and then computing the values of the decision variables that make this incremental yield equal to zero; that is, those values of the variables that leave zero unused opportunity to add anything to company profits.

Mathematical programming

Many economic maximization problems have one complicating feature that precludes the use of calculus. They involve limited resources or confining product specifications which state in effect, 'It is permissible to maximize, but only after you have taken care of certain requirements and provided you stay within your budgeted resources.' Clearly, such requirements, which the mathematician calls *constraints*, make things harder for the firm and usually mean that the company cannot do as well in pursuing its objectives. Limited plant capacity can reduce sales and profits. Demanding product specifications may be expected to raise costs and possibly cut into profits.

Where the firm is subjected to such constraints, such as a ceiling on the available amounts of resources and a floor on standards of performance, information about an absolute maximum that ignores these limitations can be of very little use to management. A calculus computation that tells the firm its profits will be maximized if the company produces 8000 units of its product per day is not very helpful if funds and plant capacity constraints prevent it from manufacturing more than 6500 units. Thus, one requires a special procedure that determines the best thing the company can do *within the limitations imposed by its constraints.*

Mathematical programming is the name given to the body of techniques that has been developed to deal with constrained maximum problems. Though the problem had been formulated earlier in Hungary and the Soviet Union, as well as in the United States, it was not until the late 1940s that George Dantzig invented a practical method of solution. Though several alternative methods now exist, variants of Dantzig's original technique, the simplex method, continue to constitute the most effective known procedure. Recent developments, many of which are also due to Dantzig, now permit the relatively rapid solution on electronic computers of problems of really astonishing magnitude – problems involving literally many thousands of different variables and constraints.

There is no point in giving a detailed description of the nature of the simplex method. Very briefly, it can be characterized as a systematic trial and error approach. For example, in selecting the advertising media that maximize the special audience that the advertiser reaches for his given budget, the first step is to select some arbitrary set of media that might, by some stretch of the imagination, conceivably do the job. From this original set, one determines which of the media makes the smallest net audience contribution and replaces it by budgeting the released funds for some other medium that is calculated to make the largest possible incremental contribution of any medium not included in the original trial set. In this way, media are tried and replaced in such a manner that the audience obtained always grows until one finally runs out of audience increasing opportunities. Then, the (constrained) maximal solution will have been found. We will have determined the very largest audience that the advertiser can obtain out of the fixed amounts of money he has allocated for the purpose (his constraint).

Of course, such a brief and intuitive description must make the procedure sound simpler than it really is. But the fact of the matter is that, like so many revolutionary ideas, at least the basics of linear programming are quite simple once you understand them.

The satisficer

We have strayed from our basic subject – economic models of what firms do when they compete. The last two sections have described methods for calculating maximizing strategies – for determining what decisions best achieve whatever goals happen to have been adopted by management.

As stated earlier, some writers have recently begun to question whether firms maximize anything at all. In particular, Herbert Simon has argued that the businessman, knowing his own limitations and the limited accuracy of the data and calculation procedures available to him, adopts a more modest goal. He wishes to obtain conditions that are thoroughly viable, but which offer no assurance of producing for him the best of all possible worlds. Thus, the failure to scan all of the relevant possibilities before reaching a decision, far from constituting an imperfection in the businessman's procedures, is a logical consequence of the nature of his aspirations. Simon has used the term *satisficing* to designate this sort of managerial behavior.

Rules of thumb: optimally imperfect decisions

This or perhaps a very closely related view asserts that one can overdo perfectionism in the decision-making process. Better information and finer calculations can be highly expensive and, although they make possible better and more profitable decisions, there comes a point where the gain is no longer worth the cost; that is, where more carefully calculated and better informed decisions will add less to company returns than the additional expenses that these refinements incur. Therefore, it is clear that there is a limit to the effort management should expend on a decision. When this point is reached, though the decision will remain imperfect, it can be asserted that the decision process is optimal in a deeper sense, that is, considering both the effects of the decision and the costs of the decision process, the company will have done as well as is humanly possible. We can say that such a decision is optimally imperfect, and that further calculations and care in the decision process would have been an act of irrational perfectionism. Viewed this way, the behavior of the satisficer becomes the very essence of rationality.

The widespread use of rules of thumb in business decision making may be considered a manifestation of the imperfectability of the decision process. A rule of thumb is the ideal tool for low cost approximative decision making. A well-designed rule that has been built and tested by long experience may yield very satisfactory results. It can substantially reduce the costs of pricing, inventory control and many other decision processes, produce a high degree of consistency in company policies, and make it easier for upper managerial echelons to evaluate and keep track of actions taken on the basis of delegated authority.

Of course, a poorly designed rule of thumb can be very costly. It is not very difficult to show convincingly that many of the rules of thumb currently used in business decisions lead to highly undesirable results. Indeed, the bulk of the successes of the operations researchers have occurred when they have encountered cases of managerial reliance on such inefficient rules. But it must be emphasized that, in these cases, the operations analysts have not, in effect, sought to eliminate rules of thumb completely. Rather, their procedure has been to replace the current rules with others that (although a little more complex and sophisticated) give far more acceptable results.

Types of competitive situation

The economist has been concerned with a wide variety of competitive situations, many of which have been given what must be to the layman weird and unattractive names. Monopsony, oligopoly and bilateral monopoly[1] are among the terms familiar to the specialist. Although several of these forms of

1. For those who are curious, a *monopsonist* is the single purchaser of some product or service (just as a monopolist may be defined as a single seller of a commodity). *Oligopoly* refers to an industry consisting of a relatively small number of large firms. *Bilateral monopoly* is the monopolist selling to a monopsonist.

competitive situation are likely to be of little direct interest to firms large enough to undertake an organized marketing program, it is desirable that several of the most frequently discussed cases be described in order that the point of view of the economist be clearly displayed.

Pure competition

The model that has played a central role in much of the economic literature is that of *pure competition*. Curiously, this limiting and somewhat artificial case, which to the economist represents the ultimate in competitiveness, is, in the eyes of the businessman, apt to be totally devoid of competitive activity.

To meet the requirements of pure competition a situation must satisfy three main conditions:

1. Each firm in the industry must be so small as to constitute an insignificant portion of the market. Thus, any increase or decrease in the amount of product that it offers for sale will make no noticeable difference to the over-all supply–demand situation. Therefore, the firm is shorn of all power to influence price by modifying the quantities it supplies and price is determined impersonally and automatically on the market.

2. To complete the elimination of all power in the hands of the businessman, it is required that his product be totally undistinguishable from that of other companies in the industry. Thus, the consumer has no motivation to shop around or to prefer any one seller to any other.

3. Finally, firms must always be free to open up for business in the industry and to produce identical products on the same terms as other producers who are already operating. Similarly, companies who find it desirable to close up shop must be free to do so without hindrance. This requirement serves to preclude continuing and excessive profits (or losses), because high profits will quickly attract new firms who will flood the market with their product to an extent sufficient to drive prices down and eliminate 'abnormal' profits.

It is noteworthy that in this peculiar situation there is no room for any normal marketing activity. There are no salesmen, no advertisers and no designers of distinctive packages, because any seller can dispose of as much of his output as he wishes at the going market price. This case is not as far removed from reality as may at first appear. The stock market and some of the grain markets are frequently cited as examples. An ordinary investor who wishes to sell some of his holdings of a particular security, say common stock of a large automobile firm, can sell either five shares or fifty shares at the current price, which he cannot influence. His customers do not care whether they buy from him or from anyone else; indeed, they rarely if ever know from which seller they have made their purchase. No such seller ever has any motivation to advertise or package his wares attractively.

Clearly, this is not *active* competition. Each seller is, in effect, so downtrodden, so shorn of power, that he does nothing about his rivals. Rather, he must passively accept the verdict of the great impersonal mechanism, the market, which settles most matters for buyers and sellers alike.

Why, then, is the economist so interested in this very special sort of circumstance? Partly because the analysis of this situation turns out to be particularly easy. One does not have to take account of the messy consequences of a sequence of strategies and counterstrategies, and so the model becomes extremely tractable. Many of the most complex and advanced of the economist's analytic structures are based on the case of pure competition.

There is still another reason why the economist has been so preoccupied with the pure competition case. It transpires that, granted a number of somewhat questionable assumptions, pure competition *automatically* produces prices, output quantities and an allocation of society's resources among firms and industries that is, in a sense, optimal from the point of view of society as a whole. More explicitly, pure competition guarantees that the productive processes of the economy will be carried on in a way that gives each individual every advantage he can conceivably obtain without its being taken out of the hide of others. In this sense, pure competition is said to guarantee that the productive process is efficient.

To illustrate how this works, we must first show that productive efficiency requires that, if the incremental product of any input (say one kilowatt hour of electricity) is 10 dollars when it is used by company A, an additional hour of electricity must also give 10 dollars worth of product to company B, company C and any other firm. For suppose instead that it offered only 8 dollars worth of product to company B, then it would increase society's total production to take some electric power away from B and transfer it to A where it can do more good.

How does pure competition automatically guarantee this result – that a given input will yield the same incremental return in all companies? Suppose input price is fixed at any level, say at k dollars, as it is under pure competition; that is, no company can do anything to influence this price. Then it will pay company A to buy so much of this input that (because of diminishing returns) its incremental product is equal to k dollars. For so long as k dollars of electricity brings in more than k dollars in returns, it will pay the company to keep contracting for more and more electricity. However, if the incremental return in company A equals the k dollar kilowatt hour price, and the same is true in company B, these incremental returns in the two companies must be equal to the same number, k, and hence equal to one another. By contrast, if the two companies could have hoped to influence the input price by holding off on their purchases, all bets are off and the argument breaks down.

The argument is remarkably clever and indeed valid in its limited context. Unfortunately, it is usually somewhat and often totally inapplicable in the real world. Indeed, it turns out that in an economy in which the bulk of production is *not* carried out under pure competition, the presence of one or more purely competitive industries can yield highly undesirable results. Because the individual producer in such an industry never comes face to face with a real marketing problem, the industry as a whole will tend to overproduce relative to the rest of the economy. To this phenomenon we may perhaps ascribe a very significant role in the nation's farm problem.

Therefore, it is likely to be ill-advised and inappropriate to hold pure competition up as a model for the structure and conduct of industry in practice. Unfortunately, this precaution is not always carefully observed.

Monopolistic competition

In the 1930s there was a burst of analytic activity devoted to investigation of a wide variety of competitive models other than that of pure competition. Much of this analysis has come to be referred to as *monopolistic competition* and is thereby associated with the work of E. H. Chamberlin. Broadly defined, monopolistic competition has been used to denote the entire spectrum of competitive situations. More frequently, the term refers to a very special situation – one that is only of limited interest to marketing management. This definition encompasses cases that differ from pure competition only in terms of the distinctiveness of the wares handled by different sellers. Firms remain tiny, but customers see, or think they see, a difference between the offerings of one company and another. On this definition, the monopolistic competitor is the local retailer who handles one particular make of automobile or offers some particular brand of trading stamps that are not available at his competitors.

A number of interesting results can be deduced from this model, but since it still does not get down to the main matter, active competition as it is interpreted by the businessman, there is no point in dwelling further on this construct.

Oligopoly – the larger firms case

The last of the model types to be described in this section will constitute the subject of the remainder of the chapter. This is the theory of *oligopoly*, which deals with the case of a number of firms of significant size and influence. It is here that we encounter the sort of competitive situation that constitutes our main interest. Unfortunately, it is here also that economists have been least successful in obtaining results that can be applied directly by management. Reasons for this lack of success will emerge presently.

It is interesting that the term oligopoly seems to have evoked a considerable degree of distaste in the business community, which no doubt feels that the word sounds uncomfortably similar to *monopoly*. The surprising thing is not that business-men resent being called oligopolists, but that they seem to have been less offended by the terms *monopolistic competition*. At any rate, to avoid the use of persuasive terminology, I shall, instead of oligopoly, employ the designation *the larger firms case*.

Models of competition among larger firms

It is convenient to deal with four main subcases in the analysis of the larger firm situation. These subcases can be called the independent decisions case, the accommodating decisions case, the systematic reactions case and the (game theoretic) strategic counterplanning case. The last two of these situations involve the greatest analytic complexity and each of them will be discussed at some length.

The independent decisions case

This case refers to decisions that are made by the company in a way that totally ignores the presence of competitors. It may be surprising that this possibility is even considered in a discussion of models of competition, particularly in the large firm case where the dependence of each company on the behavior and actions of others must be perfectly obvious to management.

However, here we are faced with an important application of the principle of optimally imperfect decision making. In many of its routine and relatively minor decisions, management simply cannot be bothered to take into systematic account the probable reactions of others. Indeed, it is often unnecessary to do so because, for the same sort of reason, a firm's competitors will frequently not even take note of its day-to-day decisions. As a result, the company can proceed to maximize, satisfice or calculate in whichever way it prefers, as though it were in total isolation. It is rather curious that, although economists are reluctant to admit such a possibility in their theoretical writings they have characteristically proceeded on just such a basis when they have worked as *advisors to business* on operations research problems. The most successful work of the operations re-searcher, inventory analysis, product line selection and trans-portation routing, has most frequently been applied to the larger firms because only they can afford to finance such research. Yet, in these analyses, there is almost never any allusion to a competitor and his behavior. For example, better transportation routing may improve customer service and lower costs, and in so doing it may court competitive counter-moves. However, there is no place for this consideration in the standard (and highly useful) linear programming transport-ation routing model.

It must be emphasized that, in this sort of independent routing decision making situation, calculus and programming maximization techniques have proved to be most helpful. By deciding to ignore complex interaction patterns, the remaining relevant features of the situation become sufficiently tractable for systematic data gathering and analysis to become effective.

The accommodating interaction case

A second relatively uncomplicated large-firm case is that of accommodating interaction. Here, management procedes, not with the view that competition can be ignored, but rather with confidence that rivals will react in a way that keeps the situation livable for all concerned. For example, this procedure is what one often encounters in pricing. Any one of a group of firms may find that if (after a sufficient interval of price stability) it raises the price of one of its products, competitors will increase their price correspondingly, often within a matter of hours. It requires no collusion to accomplish this result. The price change initiator need merely take care to publicize his action sufficiently and he can be fairly confident that he will not be left in isolation.

There are many reasons why this would be the case. Success-ful businessmen have typically operated long enough to observe that there is much to be gained by acting for the industry's common benefit rather than by striking out on one's own in disregard of any chaos that may result. However, this is not enough to assure accommodating reaction patterns. We all know of industries where a cut-throat competitive approach, typified by the discount house, has paid off handsomely to the 'trouble makers'.

Another, more fundamental reason why accommodating reactions may occur is the presence of considerable similarity in the products of the various competing firms. One company's steel of a given specification is not likely to be significantly better than that produced by a rival. Producers of such homogeneous items soon learn that they cannot charge a price any higher than that offered by anyone else in the industry. Moreover, company B knows when its price is lower than A's that it must either quickly raise its price to meet A's or that A will almost immediately be forced to lower its own. Faced with these two alternatives, it takes little imagination to forsee the course that B is likely to take.

Sometimes such accommodating interactions are institutionalized into a price leadership pattern. All other firms in the industry learn to imitate the pricing decisions made by company X. Once this is accomplished, it becomes extremely difficult for any one company to violate the arrangement on its own. This has been formalized in a well-known model first constructed by Paul Sweezy – the so-called *kinked demand curve case*.

In Figure 2, 10 dollars is taken to be the price that has currently been set by the price leader. Line DD' represents the demand curve for company A's product if each other firm in the industry were to match his every price move, whereas the steeper line, dd', indicates what would happen to the demand if everyone else steadfastly ignored A's price changes. Thus, note that a rise in A's price to 15 dollars would only reduce his sales to $5\frac{1}{2}$ million units if everyone else went up to a 15 dollar price (point S on line DD'). But if nobody copied A's price rise, his sales would fall all the way to 4 million (point s on dd').

Company A, not being a price leader, is likely to reason that if it raised its price above 10 dollars, it would be left high and dry. Others would not follow its example and the relevant segment of its demand curve would be Ed'. But on the downward side, things would be different. Competitors could not afford to remain aloof when he, A, cuts his price and thus threatens to steal their customers away. He would promptly become a (temporary) price leader. Thus, for cuts in price below 10 dollars, A's price changes would be followed and so curve DE becomes relevant. In short, instead of either straight line demand curve, A would be confronted in his pricing decisions by segments of both curves that together constitute the bent (kinked) demand curve *DEd'* (heavy line). In this situation, it is apt to be equally unattractive to A either to raise or lower his price from that set by the leader. This model, then, may

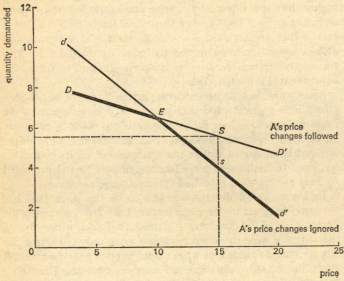

Figure 2

help to explain why price leadership arrangements, when once arrived at, appear often to prove so durable.

The Cournot systematic reaction function case

We turn next to the prototype model of explicit competitive interaction – the *Cournot reaction model*. Here, for the first time in this chapter, we find competitors taking explicit cognizance of one another's decisions and reacting accordingly. Indeed, the essence of the matter is that each firm develops dependable reaction patterns that are readily amenable to the work of the economic analyst.

Consider a graph that plots information on the prices of two competing firms (Figure 3), company A and company F, both of which are food retailers. Thus, any point in the diagram represents a *pair* of prices, one for each company. For example, point *B* represents a 90 cent company F price per pound for sirloin steak and a price of 1 dollar by company A. Suppose then that on this figure we plot a set of such points (the dots) representing statistics of F's steak prices and the corresponding

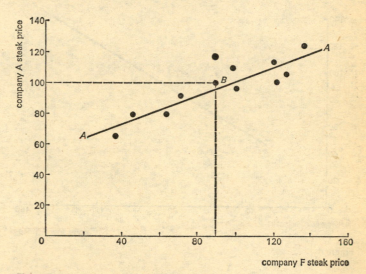

Figure 3

company A prices for a later week (say one week later). For example, point *B* may represent F's price for the week of 12 January and the A's price for the week of 19 January. This point then presumably represents A's *reaction* to F's preceding price.

Next, we fit a straight line or curve marked *AA* in the figure to these dots. This is A's *reaction curve*. In fact, it predicts A's response to every potential F price within the range of statistically observed experience.

In dealing with competitive interactions, it is essential to recognize that this sort of reaction is likely to be a two-way affair; that is, F is just as apt to react to A's decisions of the previous week as the reverse. This means that F is also likely to have a reaction curve *FF* (in Figure 4) that relates, this time, to current company F prices with past company A prices.

It should be noted that even though we are now seeking to explain company F pricing on the basis of past company A

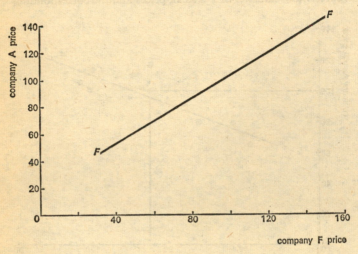

Figure 4

prices, we still measure the former on the horizontal axis and the latter on the vertical axis as we did in Figure 3. This measurement is a matter of achieving greater comparability between the two diagrams that is necessary for reasons that will become clear presently.

Reaction curves and dynamic response patterns

Reaction curves are important because they lead to analysable dynamic interaction patterns. To see this, we superimpose the company F reaction curve (Figure 4) and the company A reaction curve (Figure 3) on to one diagram (Figure 5). Suppose, now, that we happen to have at some particular date, a company F price 1.20 dollars per pound (see point F_0 in Figure 5). The time sequence of events that follows can now be forecast from the reaction curve pattern. For on the following week, if it acts in accord with its reaction curve, AA, we can predict that company A will respond by charging a price of 1.10 dollars (points C and A_1). But then, the week after that, company F will move to point D on its reaction curve and charge a price of about 1.05 dollars (point F_1), and so on. We see that in this

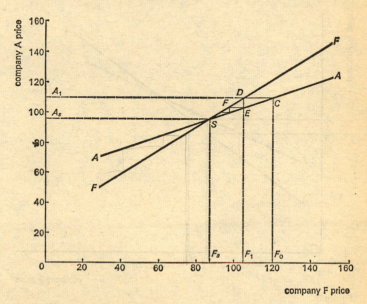

Figure 5

illustrative example a price cutting pattern has developed, but it can also be shown that after a while these prices will settle down. For the movements have been proceeding along the staircase shaped pattern C, D, E, F, etc., which goes from reaction curve to reaction curve. Eventually it will approach point S, the intersection of the two reaction curves. These prices will settle at about 88 cents for company F (point F_s) and 96 cents for company A (point A_s).[2]

2. Some reaction curve patterns, incidentally, can involve disastrous price wars. This would have happened if the positions of the AA and the FF curves had been reversed in the previous diagram, as is shown in Figure 6. Here if

This suggests that if all firms' pricing practices do accord roughly with the reaction curve analysis, we should expect to find patterns such as the following. After a period of a settled price for some item, someone finds a reason to change it, e.g., a special deal with the supplier or a new advertising gimmick.

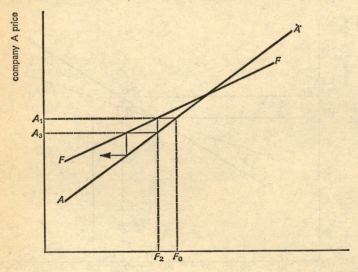

Figure 6

Then there will be a series of price changes for several weeks on the part of all the firms involved and, finally, the price will settle down again.[3]

It can be seen that reaction curves can provide a powerful tool of analysis and prediction. The preceding discussion is

company F price starts out at F_0, company A price goes to A_1, company F responds by cutting F_2, and so on – the prices will keep falling without limit until someone gives up the battle.

3. Note that if both firms react according to their reaction curves, a period of price stability can be followed by price cutting only if a reaction curve has shifted temporarily.

illustrative of the sort of calculation that can be done with its help. It indicates why the Cournot reaction curve remains so prominent in the literature that seeks to analyse the competitive behavior of larger firms.

The game-theoretic case: equilibrium solutions

A company's most reasonable course of action *vis-à-vis* its competitors depends very heavily on the assumptions it is willing to make on how the competitors are going to behave. In the game-theoretic approach to which we now turn, the firm is taken to adopt a fairly extreme assumption of this sort. In effect, it prepares for the worst. It girds itself to compete against a management, which like itself, is a skilled student and practitioner of the theory of games.

The most developed portion of game theory involves the *zero-sum two-persons game*. It is called a two-person game because it involves only two rivals. It is called zero- (or constant) sum because it deals with a situation in which one participant's gains and the other's losses cancel out precisely. Most situations are not characterized by such complete and direct rivalry. For example, an increase in a company's advertising may well add to the industry's over-all business and not just to its own. The best economic illustration of a zero-sum case that has so far been devised is a battle for market share where, if one competitor increases his market share by 5 per cent, his rival must lose out correspondingly.

The basic tool in this simple case is the payoff table. Such a table lists a number of strategic alternatives open to each of the two competitors and then indicates (in the manner of a mileage chart in a road map) what gains company A can expect to reap from each combination of moves by the two participants.

Table 1

Company A's alternatives	Company B's alternatives	
	Filter tip	Unfiltered
King size	*20*	60
Regular	*10*	80

For example, Table 1 suggests that companies A and B are tobacco firms, each of which proposes to put out a brand of cigarettes. Company A is debating between a cigarette of ordinary length and one that is king sized, whereas B hovers between choosing a filtered and an unfiltered product. Each company knows what alternatives are being considered by the other, but must make its own decision before the other's is revealed.

The table indicates, for example, that if A produces a king-sized cigarette and B selects a filter tip, A will end up controlling 20 per cent of the market. Note that it would be redundant to indicate explicitly in the table B's market share, because of the constant sum character of the situation. If A obtains 20 per cent of the market, we know at once that B's share is the remaining 80 per cent.

Company A's best decision (strategy choice) is not completely clear on the face of the situation. A king size may get him either a 60 or a 20 per cent share, whereas the ordinary size may net him either 80 or only 10 per cent. Each course has its risks and its bright prospects. Company A's management might, for example, supposing that there is a fifty/fifty chance of B adopting either of its strategy possibilities, evaluate the king-size strategy at 50 per cent of 20, plus 50 per cent of 60 equals 40, whereas the other alternative would then be considered worth 50 per cent of 10 plus 50 per cent of 80 equals 45. On this view, an ordinary length cigarette would be A's best bet.

But in this case, a more reasonable position for A to take might be the following. Company B is a well-run company and makes rational decisions. If I put out a king-sized product, they will cut my market share down to 20 per cent. If I select my other alternative, I will probably end up with only 10 per cent. Thus, I should pay attention only to the worst (minimum) payoff to each strategy (the italic figures in the table) and be content with the maximum of these minima; that is, 20 per cent. I should, therefore, decide on kings. It is easy to see why such a decision rule is called a maximin strategy. Similarly, in this case, company B would do well to employ a minimax strategy, which considers the best A could do in response to each of its strategy alternatives and picks the strategy that minimizes these maximum returns to A. Thus, if B produces a filter tip, at best, A can get 20 per cent whereas if B's cigarette has no filter, A can get as much as 80 per cent. The minimum of these maximum payoffs is, of course, 20 per cent. Thus, A's maximin strategy is kings and its maximin payoff is 20 per cent. Similarly, B's minimax strategy is filters and its minimax payoff will also be 20 per cent. Hence, if both firms reach decisions along these lines, each will, in this case, obtain the payoff it expected. Where such a coincidence occurs, the actual payoff is called an *equilibrium point*.

We should note another important characteristic of this situation. If B chooses filters, A can do no better than to choose kings (for regulars will then only give it a payoff of 10 per cent) and vice versa. A's *best* response to B's minimax strategy is its own maximin strategy. Similarly, B's best countermove to A's maximin strategy is B's minimax strategy.

But not all payoff tables have equilibrium points. This is illustrated in Table 2.

Table 2

A's strategies	B's strategies	
	Filter tip	Unfiltered
Kings	20	60
Regulars	80	10

A's maximin strategy is still K (kings) and its maximin payoff remains 20 per cent. But B's minimax strategy and payoff are U (unfiltered) and 60 per cent respectively. Here, A will use strategy K, B will choose strategy U, and A will be pleasantly surprised to obtain a 60 per cent market share payoff. The maximin and minimax payoffs no longer coincide.

Moreover, if B decides in advance that A will use its maximin strategy K, B will no longer think it wise to put out unfiltered cigarettes. Instead, it will switch to a nonminimax strategy – filters. In the absence of an equilibrium point, the decision makers are apt to be in a particularly ambiguous situation. It need no longer be true that one player's minimax strategy is the most profitable response to its rival's maximin strategy, and vice versa.

Mixed strategies

For a nonequilibrium case such as that shown in Table 2, von Neumann and Morgenstern, the fathers of game theory, came up with an extremely ingenious and suggestive approach. Clearly, it is very much to A's disadvantage to have its plan guessed by B. One way in which the management of A can avoid having its decisions anticipated is to keep the information even from itself. This it can accomplish by avoiding the making of the choice between kings and regulars, by delegating the decision to a random device, such as the toss of a coin! At first glance, this may appear to be a foolish way to do business, but when we examine the effects on the payoff table we will see a remarkable change.

Table 3

	B's strategies	
A's strategies	F	U
K	*20*	60
R	80	*10*
50/50 odds (50 per cent of K + 50 per cent of R)	50	*35*

In Table 3, the first two rows are identical with those of payoff Table 2. But a new final row has been added to indicate what happens when company A employs what is called a *mixed strategy*; that is, when a toss of coin is used to determine its plans. In this case, there will be a fifty/fifty chance that A will end up producing either kings or regulars. Suppose, that company B produces filters. A will then have a fifty/fifty chance of a payoff of 20 and a fifty/fifty chance of a payoff of 80. Hence, if B produces filtered cigarettes, A can expect (on an average toss of the coin) a yield equal to 50 per cent of 20 plus 50 per cent of 80 equals 50; that is, the actuarial value of the payoff to the mixed strategy will be 50 per cent. This payoff is the meaning of the first entry in the last row of Table 3. Similarly, the second entry, 35, is the expected payoff in the event B puts out an unfiltered cigarette. This figure is calculated in exactly the same way. It is 50 per cent of 60 plus 50 per cent of 10, where 60 and 10 are now A's payoffs for kings and regulars, respectively.[4]

Having seen how our extended table is constructed, let us examine its properties. As before, the minimum (worst) payoffs of kings and regulars are 20 and 10 per cent, respectively (the italic figures). However, the worst payoff to the *mixed* strategy is 35 per cent – an amount higher than either of the other worst payoffs! Thus, among the three possibilities so far considered, the artificial mixed strategy becomes the maximin strategy!

Actually, this piece of sleight of hand has a simple explanation in terms of what goes on by implication in this process. As was stated when we began the discussion of this game-theoretic approach, in this situation, A assumes B's management to be diabolically clever. No matter whether A chooses to produce kings or regulars, it fears that B will outguess it and take the appropriate countermeasures. If it produces kings, management feels that company B will be able to anticipate this and will produce filters as its countermove. Thus, for all practical purposes, the higher payoff to kings (a 60 per cent market share) is disregarded as a practical possibility. Similarly, the 80 per cent potential payoff to the production of regulars is also implicitly considered to be largely irrelevant. However, once a mixed strategy is employed, there is no way in which B's management can outguess A. The 60 and 80 per cent market share payoffs are restored to the status of real possibilities and it becomes legitimate to average these figures in with the lower 20 and 10 per cent payoffs in order to produce the expected return calculations for the mixed strategy that are shown in the last row of our payoff table. Thus, the higher minimum figure in that row reflects the fact that a mixed strategy makes it possible to outfox ones competitor.

Once this advantage is recognized, another option follows

4. Actually these calculations are strictly legitimate only if the entries in the payoff table are the *utilities* of the alternative payoffs, rather than the payoffs themselves. But for present purposes, this point can be ignored as a technicality. By the 'utility' of a payoff to a player we mean a quasi-psychological measure of his subjective evaluation of that payoff. Special techniques have been invented for the purpose by von Neumann and Morgenstern.

naturally. So far, we have considered choosing between kings and regulars by means of a 'fair' coin, which gave each possibility a fifty/fifty chance. But why not use a loaded coin, one that gives kings a three/five chance and regulars a two/five chance? The result is shown in the last row of Table 4 (where the first three rows are identical with payoff Table 3). We see that the change in odds has increased the maximin payoff even further. From its 35 per cent value in the fifty/fifty case, it has now gone up to 40 per cent!

Table 4

	B's strategies	
A's strategies	F	U
K	*20*	60
R	80	*10*
50/50 odds	50	*35*
3/5 to 2/5 odds (3/5 of K +		
2/5 of R)	*44*	*40*

This suggests that the management of company A will find it expedient to experiment with different ways of loading the coin. It can easily be verified that there is an optimal way of loading the coin, depending on the entries in the payoff matrix. The optimal loading is defined as the pair of odds that gives the greatest maximin payoff for the mixed strategy and it turns out that its computation is an ordinary linear programming problem.

The reader will perhaps be interested to know that in the present problem, the optimal mixed strategy for company A involves seven/eleven odds in favor of king-sized as against a four/eleven probability for regulars. He may also wish to consider why these odds offer him the same expected payoff no matter whether B produces filtered or unfiltered cigarettes; he may be sure this result is no coincidence – it is a normal characteristic of the optimal (mixed) strategy.

Of course, two can play at optimal mixed strategizing. Company B can also get a loaded coin to choose his course of action, and can load the coin in a way that best takes care of his interests. There we have the standard solution of the two-person zero-sum game. Moreover, almost miraculously, it transpires that this solution is *always* an equilibrium solution; that is, A's maximin payoff must always coincide with B's minimax payoff if they both employ their optimal mixed strategies.

Certainly the ingenuity and path-breaking nature of this approach to the analysis of competitive behavior is not to be denied.

Testing and application of the models
Empirical testing of the models

There is a fairly long and honorable tradition of industry studies in which a specific industry is investigated somewhat informally – historically, by interviews, statistically, and by whatever means are at hand. An important feature of these studies has usually been an attempt to categorize the structure of the industry in terms of the types of competition classification that were discussed. Many very able people have produced such studies and they have told us a great deal about the workings of competition in practice. However, these investigations have been oriented rather more toward problems of anti-trust policy than to assistance in business decision making or to direct testing of the theoretical models. Only in the past few years has much work been undertaken to test the models directly by confrontation with the facts and, naturally, results so far can hardly be expected to be conclusive.

Major contributions promise to emerge from some of the many business games that are currently so popular. Business games, in which a group of people, usually assisted by a computer, operate under simulated and speeded up business conditions, are usually employed primarily as a training device. But Martin Shubik, David Stern, Jeremy Stone and others are using this technique as a serious research method. Employing carefully structured experiments, they test specific hypotheses about competitive behavior, many of the hypotheses being drawn directly from the competitive models.

Interesting results about management training and its relation to accommodating behavior, about degree of approximation to maximizing decisions and about the relevance of several types of models, are beginning to emerge. For example, one study showed that in a game in which competing players are unable to communicate and collude, professional managers deliberately avoided doing things that were seriously detrimental to their opponents much more frequently than another test group (of mathematicians). The result of this 'live-and-let-live' approach was a much higher score for the managerial group as a whole.

Statistical tests of some of the models are also being undertaken. The author has completed the first stage of a statistical study on the Cournot reaction curve model. The advertised food prices of the major Philadelphia supermarket chains seemed an ideal subject. These are published at fixed intervals (once a week, before the weekend). They are the prices that must represent the essence of the chain's competitive posture since it is only these prices that attract the customer into the store. These data are readily available for a very long period of time. So far, results seem to be consistent with the hypothesis that these companies do react with sufficient consistency to permit the employment of reaction functions as a description of their behavior. However, the conclusions are still very tentative and much work needs to be done before they can be offered with any degree of confidence.

Application of the models to business

As was indicated at the beginning of this chapter, it is easy to overstate the direct applicability of some of these competitive models to current business problems. It must not be denied that all of them offer some degree of illumination by supplying helpful points of view and check lists of variables that are likely to be overlooked by a harried management.

However, concrete decision suggestions – approximations to optimal prices, inventory levels, investment criteria, etc. – have largely come from those models in which competition plays no explicit role. That is, of the four types of interaction pattern discussed in the section on competition among large firms, only the first – the case of competitive decisions in which reactions of competitors can be ignored – has so far yielded very systematic and concrete results for the businessman. Here, in some cases, the results have been spectacular, and there is every reason to believe that this sort of applied economics is only in a vigorous infancy. As the use of computers becomes more widespread, as experience in application feeds back ideas to the model builder and as the corps of specialists trained in this sort of inventive application grows, more and more can be expected of that work.

In addition, because of the ingenuity of the workmanship and the very great ability of the investigators who specialize in the theory of games and, more generally, on the analysis of competition among large firms, one can hope that, in the future, this area will add even more than useful insights and depth of general understanding.

13 Kalman J. Cohen and Richard M. Cyert

Computer Models in Dynamic Economics[1]

Kalman J. Cohen and Richard M. Cyert, 'Computer models in dynamic economics', *Quarterly Journal of Economics*, vol. 75, 1961, pp. 112–27.

The development of the electronic digital computer has been an extremely significant technological innovation for science, probably ranking on a par with the inventions of the telescope and the microscope. As the first such computer, the E N I A C, was completed less than fifteen years ago, our experience with electronic computers is still too limited for anyone to predict the ultimate significance which these machines will have in both the natural and the social sciences. However, our knowledge has increased so rapidly from the years immediately after the Second World War, when computers were viewed only as larger and faster desk calculators, that it seems worthwhile to examine some of the implications which electronic digital computers have for research methodology in the social sciences.

It is undeniable that electronic computers, when used as routine calculating devices for performing statistical analyses and clerical data processing operations, can be extremely useful in social science research. The purpose of this article is not to consider the importance of such 'routine' uses of computers in the social sciences but rather to explore the possibilities of using computers to simulate the behavior of complex social systems. The specific illustrations used are all drawn from the field of economics, but the concepts seem equally relevant to other fields of social science. We shall use the term 'computer model'

1. This paper is based on research supported by grants made by the Graduate School of Industrial Administration, Carnegie Institute of Technology from the School's Research Funds and from funds provided by the Ford Foundation for the study of organizational behavior. The authors owe a considerable debt to their colleague, James G. March, for criticisms of an early draft and for many fruitful discussions of the contents of the article.

to refer to a formal model designed for digital computer simulation. In this article, we propose to examine the characteristics of computer models and to survey some of the economic computer models that have been formulated. In addition, we shall attempt to evaluate the future achievements which might reasonably be expected from further work with computer models.

Theory construction (model building)

The professional in any science works within a framework of definitions and concepts that becomes second nature to him. As a result, basic methodological points are frequently taken for granted. In appraising a methodological innovation, however, it is useful to re-examine such points. The explanation and evaluation of computer models can be simplified by examining the nature of theory construction (model building) itself.

A theory consists of three elements – definitions, assumptions and conclusions. The following is a simple and familiar example of a theory (Stigler, 1946, pp. 4–6):

Assumptions: (a) Firms attempt to maximize profits. (b) The marginal revenue curves intersect the marginal cost curves from above. (c) The marginal curves are continuous.

Conclusion: A firm will produce that output corresponding to the point of intersection of its marginal revenue and marginal cost curves.

It is obvious that this theory depends also on a set of subject matter (extra-logical) definitions – profits, marginal cost and marginal revenue.

There are a number of relevant points that can be noted from this example. The conclusion is a logical implication of the assumptions. The language in which the conclusion is derived from the assumptions is a matter of the theoretician's choice. In general, there are three languages that have been commonly used by economists for drawing a conclusion from a set of assumptions – ordinary prose, pictorial geometry and formal mathematics. In the particular theory under discussion, it is obvious that the conclusion can be derived using any of the three languages. It would also, of course, be possible to state the assumptions and the conclusions in any of the three languages. Generally it is most convenient to state assumptions and conclusions in prose alone or a combination of prose and mathematics. The question of which language to use is answered quite nicely in the following quotation:

If mathematics is no more than a form of logical reasoning, the question may be asked: why use mathematics, which few understand, instead of logic which is intelligible to all? It is only a matter of efficiency, as when a contractor decides to use mechanical earth-moving equipment rather than picks and shovels. It is often simpler to use pick and shovel, and always conceivable that they will do any job; but equally the steam shovel is often the economic proposition. Mathematics is the steam shovel of logical argument; it may or may not be profitable to use it (Allen, 1957, p. xvi).

Another point to note is that the conclusion is true only in the sense of logically following from the assumptions. The theory must be tested empirically before it can be said that the theory 'proves' anything about the world. As has been said a number of times, it is not possible to 'prove' by an *a priori* argument that a particular proposition is true of the real world. With most economic theories, unfortunately, testing is difficult, as it is with any nonlaboratory science.[2] One important reason for this difficulty in economics is that for the most part we are dealing with static theories, whereas the world in which we must test the theory is dynamic. As a result, it is usually difficult to find satisfactory data for testing purposes. Therefore economists frequently use artifacts of one kind or another to establish a 'subjective' probability of the validity of a theory. One frequently used artifact is the determination of whether or not the assumptions correspond with the facts. This procedure has provoked a sharp attack by one economist which has resulted in an interesting controversy.[3] We do not intend to be side-tracked by this controversy, other than to comment on the fact that the practice is the result of difficulties in testing directly the

2. For a lucid and penetrating analysis of the problems of testing economic propositions see Grunberg (1957).
3. See Friedman (1953, pp. 3–43). Grunberg (1957, p. 343, fn. 26), Koopmans (1957, pp. 137–42) and Rotwein (1959).

conclusions of most theories. We mention the issue because, as will be argued below, we feel that computer models can reduce the difficulties of developing models that can be directly tested, although some new statistical problems may arise.

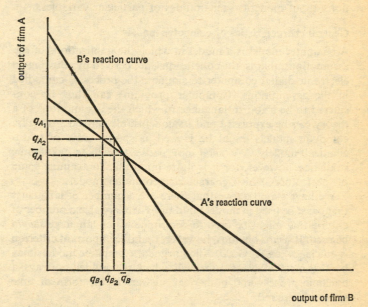

Figure 1

An additional point should be recognized about the nature of most economic theories which is relevant to the problem of testing. The point has been effectively made by Professor Samuelson (1947, p. 21):

The general method [of economic theory] involved may be very simply stated. *In cases where the equilibrium values of our variables can be regarded as the solutions of an extremum (maximum or minimum) problem, it is often possible, regardless of the number of variables involved, to determine unambiguously the qualitative behavior of our solution values in respect to changes of parameters.*

This means that the testing procedure consists in making

numerical measurements to determine whether or not the direction of change of certain parameters is the predicted direction. In general, economic theory seems more successful in yielding propositions about directions of change than propositions about numerical magnitudes of particular variables.

General characteristics of computer models

A computer model is a model in which the implications of the assumptions, that is, the conclusions, are derived by allowing an electronic digital computer to simulate the processes embodied in the assumptions. Computer programs can thus be considered to be a fourth language in which the assumptions of a theory can be expressed and its conclusions derived. Actually, computer models might be viewed as special cases of mathematical models. We shall not pause to debate taxonomic subtleties, however, for it is more important to examine some of the features which characterize computer models.

We have stated above that there are a number of languages that *could* be used in model building. There are also a number of criteria that might be used to determine which language *should* be used. It seems obvious, however, that one important criterion is efficiency, as R. G. D. Allen argued. Computer models may be the most efficient approach when the model portrays a dynamic process and numerical answers in the form of time series are desired.

The notion of a dynamic process can perhaps be made clear by reference to the simple Cournot duopoly model (see Cournot, 1897, ch. 7). In Figure 1 the reaction curves for rivals A and B are given. Each reaction curve shows the optimum output for one firm as a function of the output of its rival. In accordance with the model, the curves are drawn on the assumption that the conjectural variation terms $(q_A/\partial q_B)$ and $(\partial q_B/\partial q_A)$, are equal to zero. The dynamic process of the model can be started at any point. Assume that A is producing q_{A1}; then B will produce q_{B1}. In answer to this, A will produce q_{A2}. B will then produce q_{B2}, etc. If this simple model were analysed as a computer model, the computer would generate the time series of outputs for each firm. After the model had been run for a large number of periods, it would be clear that the outputs were tending toward the equilibrium values where A is producing $\bar{q}_A$ and B is producing $\bar{q}_B$.

In a model as simple as the Cournot model, we are generally not interested in tracing through the process by which equilibrium is reached, but only in deriving the equilibrium values. These values are easy to find by simple mathematical analysis. However, the addition of a few assumptions about the behavior of the two firms can complicate the model sufficiently so that a computer simulation will be the most efficient method for determining the implications of the model. The volume of conclusions derived from a model is within the control of the model builder. However, in complicated computer models there are, generally, a large number of potential implications generated, many of these being time series of particular numerical values.

The fact that conclusions drawn from computer models may consist of a series of numerical values has in itself a number of interesting consequences. Numerical solutions should be contrasted with the analytic solutions usually derived from mathematical models. In terms of our earlier discussion on theory construction, we could say that the conclusions sought from a mathematical model are usually in the form of relations among the variables and parameters (including, frequently, derivatives or differences of the variables or parameters), while in computer models the conclusions obtained typically are in the form of time series of specific numerical values. This suggests that computer models are less general than mathematical models. The reason for this is that the amounts of input for computer models are greater than for the usual mathematical models. The increased input places greater restrictions on the relationships among the variables and parameters and, therefore, produces a less general but more specific model. One advantage to economists of computer models is that their conclusions are presented in immediately testable form.

It should be emphasized that the above characterization does not imply that computer models are necessarily less general or mathematical models necessarily less specific. Our considerations are related primarily to questions of convenience and efficiency. It is possible to use a computer model, for example, to gain insight into the effects of rates of change of particular parameters on the results of the model. This end is accomplished by varying the parameters of the model from one simulation run to another, and comparing the output time paths which are generated. If the model can be solved analytically, however, such a result could be more easily achieved by mathematical analysis.

Comparison of computer models with operations research simulations and econometric models

In order better to understand the nature of computer models and the problems of using them, it is desirable to examine the use of simulation in the burgeoning field of operations research.[4] Additional clarification can be gained by comparing computer and econometric models.

There are two basically different approaches which can be followed in using computer simulation to study a complex system. The actual approach taken, of course, depends on the questions to be answered and the kind of information known at the time of the investigation. The approach generally taken in operations research or management science might be entitled 'synthesis'. This approach aims at understanding the operating characteristics of a total system when the behavior of the component units is known with a high degree of accuracy. The basic questions answered by this approach relate to the behavior of the over-all system. In principle, the entire system response is known once the characteristics of the structural relations are specified. If the system is complex, however, it may be difficult or impossible to determine the system behavior by current mathematical techniques. In this situation, simulation by an electronic computer can be utilized to determine the time paths traced by the system.

In social science, generally, the situation is quite the reverse.

4. A broad survey of the scope of operations research simulations can be found in Malcolm (1958). The number of operations research simulation studies which have been discussed in professional meetings or journals is too numerous to permit us to undertake here any further discussion of them (e.g. at the Sixteenth National Meeting of the Operations Research Society of America in Pasadena, California, November 1959, there were approximately twenty papers presented dealing with computer simulation).

The behavior of the total system can be observed. The problem is to derive a set of component relations which will lead to a total system exhibiting the observed characteristics of behavior. The usual procedure is to construct a model which specifies the behavior of the components, and then to analyse the model to determine whether or not the behavior of the model corresponds with the observed behavior of the total system. When this model is sufficiently complex, either because of the nature of the underlying functions or the number of variables contained in it or both, computer simulation may be the most convenient technique for manipulating the model. It is logical to call this approach to simulation 'analysis'. The actual output of the model is a set of time paths for the endogenous variables being studied by the model.

Traditional econometric models are essentially one-period-change models. Any lagged values of the endogenous variables are, in effect, treated as exogenous variables. They are assumed to be predetermined by outside forces rather than by earlier applications of the mechanisms specified in the model. Hence the output of econometric models is the determination of the values of the endogenous variables for a given time period. To determine these values for the next period, new values would have to be assigned to the lagged endogenous variables. For this reason, most econometric models should be regarded as determining the changes which take place in the world from one period to another. They should be contrasted with process or evolutionary models which attempt to exhibit the unfolding of dynamic processes over time.

The mechanisms of a computer process model, together with the observed time paths of the exogenous variables, are treated as a closed dynamic system. In such a model, the values of the lagged endogenous variables are the values previously generated by the system. Computer models may thus be forced to operate with errors in the values of the endogenous variables made in previous periods, there being no correction at the end of each period to assure correct initial conditions for the next period as in econometric models.

The contrasts between econometric and computer models have not been offered as invidious comparisons. It is clear that economics has benefited, and will continue in the future to benefit, from work in econometrics. Rather, our analysis is aimed at showing the nature and peculiar attributes of an important new research technique for social science.

Methodological problems of computer models

As with any new research technique, there are methodological difficulties connected with the efficient utilization of computer simulation. There are three basic classes of problems which arise in using computer models. These problems are the specification of functional forms, the estimation of parameters and the validation of the models.

The problem of specifying functional forms is literally an example of the 'embarrassment of riches'. Most mathematical models have been formulated in terms of linear equations in order to facilitate the attainment of analytic solutions. Since this restriction is unnecessary for computer models, the way is opened for nonlinear functions having a wide variety of forms. The solution to this problem will probably come from two sources. First, as our empirical information (the collection of which will be stimulated and guided by attempts to formulate computer models) increases, some clues as to the proper forms to use to explain and predict behavior will be available. Second, technical statistical criteria will be developed to select efficiently the proper forms of the equations, presumably on the basis of predictive power.

The problems of parameter estimation have, of course, been much discussed in statistical and econometric literature. A major advance has been the proof that unbiased and efficient estimates can be obtained only by acknowledging the simultaneity of the equations of a model (see, e.g., Klein, 1953, ch. 3). If this result carries over to computer process models, obtaining maximum likelihood estimates of all the parameters in such models will be a forbidding task.

A more feasible approach to the parameter estimation problem may be to restrict attention to the joint determination of only the current endogenous variables within a single period and to consider that the values of the lagged endogenous variables are subject to errors. The parameter estimation problem must then be considered within the framework of an 'errors in the variables' model rather than an 'errors in the equations' model. A few econometricians have investigated this kind of estimation problem, and their results may prove applicable to computer models.[5]

The likelihood of a process model incorrectly describing the world is high, because it makes some strong assertions about the nature of the world. There are various degrees by which any model can fail to describe the world, however, so it is meaningful to say that some models are more adequate descriptions of reality than others. Some criteria must be devised to indicate when the time paths generated by a process model agree sufficiently with the observed time paths so that the agreement cannot be attributed to mere coincidence. Tests must be devised for the 'goodness of fit' of process models with the real world. The problem of model validation becomes even more difficult if available data about the 'actual' behavior of the world is itself subject to error.

Although the formal details have not yet been adequately developed, there appear to be at least three possible ways in which the validation problem for process models can be approached.[6] First, distribution-free statistical methods can be used to test whether the actual and the generated time series display similar timing and amplitude characteristics. Second, simple regressions of the generated series as functions of the actual series can be computed, and then we can test whether the resulting regression equations have intercepts which are not significantly different from zero and slopes which are not significantly different from unity. Third, we could perform a factor analysis on the set of generated time paths and a second factor analysis on the set of observed time paths, and we can test whether the two groups of factor loadings are significantly different from each other.

5. Recent surveys of the state of econometric methodology regarding errors in the variables models can be found in Madansky (1959) and Sargan (1958).

6. These have all been suggested by Professor Jack Johnston, of the University of Manchester, in private conversations with the authors.

Kalman J. Cohen and Richard M. Cyert 329

Review of the literature

Although the notion of utilizing the computer as a tool in model building is still relatively new, there are several ongoing research projects and several segments of research in economics that have been completed which have followed this approach. A review of some of this work will give some specific indications of the versatility of computer models; our review is intended to be illustrative, rather than exhaustive, of the applications of computer models in economics which have been reported in the literature.

Simulation of households

A large-scale simulation which has as its ultimate goal the simulation of the total economy of the United States has been underway for several years under the direction of Professor Orcutt (Orcutt, Greenberger and Rivlin, 1958). Currently the project is concentrating on the analysis of households. The ultimate goal is to develop a general model consisting of the ten flow-of-funds sectors used in national income accounting.

The first step in Orcutt's approach is to develop a stratified sample of households classified along the dimensions of some twenty-three variables. These variables, such as race, age, sex, education, income, debt, stocks of assets, etc., are the inputs of the decision units in the model. The outputs of the household model include relevant data for forecasting population, purchases of durables, nondurables, services, and housing, net change in debt and net change in assets for the household sector.

The individual decision units of the model must be endowed with values of the various input variables in accordance with the actual system being simulated. The unit is viewed as having alternative types of behavior available. With each alternative there is associated a probability, empirically determined. Random numbers are generated to select specific actions for each unit in a manner consistent with the assigned probabilities. In this way outputs are determined for each unit. The outputs are then used to modify the inputs for the next series of decisions.

The above description is, of course, only the skeleton of the model. Orcutt discusses many other problems connected with the model such as parameter estimation, discrepancies between generated series and the actual, etc. Orcutt sees his model as providing an instrument for

consolidating past, present and future research efforts of many individuals in varied areas of economics and sociology into one effective and meaningful model; an instrument for combining survey and theoretical results obtained on the micro-level into an all-embracing system useful for prediction, control, experimentation and analysis on the aggregate level (Orcutt, Greenberger and Rivlin, 1958, p. 36).

Firm models

In another early work, Hoggatt (1957) has developed a simulation of a perfectly competitive industry. His objective was to study the stability of a model in which entry and exit conditions, as well as the formation of price expectations, are specified. The model consists of the following:

1. A market demand function dependent on two parameters.

2. A long-run average cost curve dependent on two parameters.

3. A total cost curve for each firm dependent on the same parameters as 2.

The assumption is made that entering firms will expect the then current price to prevail in the future, and they, therefore, select that plant size which will maximize profits given the current price. The usual neoclassical decision rules for determining output of the firms prevail. The model is ready to operate when the four parameters in 1 and 2, the initial number of firms and the size of plant for each firm are specified. Hoggatt begins by choosing values which give an equilibrium position for the industry. He assumes all firms to be of equal size. The output of the model is the price in the market and the production and profits for each firm. (There are also a number of other outputs which are used for analysing the system.) The demand curve is then shifted to the right by changing one of the parameters and the results studied. One interesting conclusion the model brings forth is the 'possibility that the market variables (price and industry supply) may be nearly stationary even though there is considerable entry and exit activity on the part of firms in the industry' (Hoggatt, 1957, p. 62). The model is particularly interesting as an example of the type of complex questions that can be asked of an old model with the technique of simulation.

Industrial dynamics

Another use of computer models has been made by J. W. Forrester (1958). He utilizes time lags within a system to demonstrate the types of fluctuations that can develop within a company as a result of a shock to the system, for example, an increase in demand. The model utilized consists of five component parts. These are factory, factory warehouse, distributors, retailers and customers. The customers' order rate is as an exogenous variable. There are given time lags through the whole system in terms of the delivery of goods from retailer to customer, distributor to retailer, etc., back to the factory lead time for production. There are also a series of time lags in the information system. The lags are in the timing of orders for goods, transmitted from component to component. The last aspect of the model is a description of the policy followed in placing orders at each level and the rules for maintaining inventory.

Once the parameters (time lags and policies) are fixed, the system is set in motion and can be analysed for any given customer order rate. The model is nonlinear and would be difficult to analyse by any method other than computer simulation.

Forrester also analyses a further model in which advertising is introduced with a similar set of time lags. It is clear that a number of additional variables can be introduced, and their effects on fluctuations in production, employment and investment analysed for the firm. Forrester's main aim is to utilize such analysis for the improvement of business management.

Industry analysis

Perhaps the most detailed published attempt at using computer models in economics is the study of the shoe, leather and hide industries by K. J. Cohen (1960a). This work was designed to explore the usefulness of computers in economic analysis. The models in the study are based on the empirical research of Mrs Ruth P. Mack (1956). Several different models are constructed in Cohen's study, but only the outline of the general approach will be discussed here.

The industry can be divided vertically into five segments – consumers, shoe retailers, shoe manufacturers, cattlehide leather tanners and hide dealers. The major variables on which attention is focused are the selling prices of each sector (other than consumers), the purchases of each sector (other than hide dealers), and the production of retailers, manufacturers and tanners. The models are an attempt to explain the monthly values of each of these variables from 1930 to 1940. The major exogenous variables used are disposable personal income, the Bureau of Labor Statistics consumers' price index, and hide stocks in the hands of hide dealers. As can be seen from the above descriptions, the models are formulated in terms of two major classes of variables, prices and physical flows.

The dollar expenditure on shoes by consumers is determined by disposable personal income and a seasonal factor, both exogenous variables. The physical volume of retailers' sales is simply the consumers' expenditures divided by the retail price of shoes. The retailers' receipts of shoes are determined basically by demand considerations accompanied by some price speculation on inventories: retailers always try to have available for sale at least enough shoes to meet their anticipated demand; the extent to which they try to push their inventory levels beyond this point depends upon their changing evaluations of future market prospects. The manufacturers plan their shoe production in response to retailers' orders for shoes, spreading these orders evenly over the available lead time to obtain some smoothing of production. The leather purchases by manufacturers are designed at least to provide for their current production requirements, but the manufacturers frequently build up their leather inventories beyond current needs in response to price speculation motives. The production of finished leather by tanners depends upon the relation between their leather shipments and their leather stocks but, because

Kalman J. Cohen and Richard M. Cyert 333

tanners attempt to smooth production rates, finished leather production is also tied to the previous month's production and hide wettings. Tanners' hide wettings depend upon the turnover rate of tanners' finished leather stocks, but again efforts are made to prevent rapid changes from occurring in the rate of production. Tanners' purchases of hides are determined by a reduced form relation which reflects both their current needs (the higher the rate of wettings, the more hides the tanners will order) and their view of the supply situation (the lower the price of hides last month, the more hides tanners will buy).

The retail price of shoes is determined in the models by a rigid markup on factory shoe prices. In setting the factory shoe price, manufacturers consider both the strength of consumer demand and the costs of production, as reflected in recent leather prices. Current leather price depends upon lagged leather price and current and lagged hide prices. Current hide price is determined in the models by a reduced form relation which reflects interactions between supply and demand considerations. The supply aspects are summarized in the final reduced form equation in terms of the ratio of leather and hide stocks in the hands of buyers to the leather and hide stocks in the hands of sellers; the higher this ratio, the lower the relative size of sellers' inventories, and the higher the price the sellers require to induce them to sell hides. The demand side is reflected in the reduced form equation by actual uses of hides by tanners, i.e. by hide wettings and finished leather production, and by factory shoe price, which serves as a proxy for underlying forces causing shifts in the demand schedule for hides.

There are several important interactions between prices and physical flows in the models. The physical volume of retail shoe sales is directly affected by retail shoe price. Retailers' purchases of shoes, manufacturers' purchases of leather and tanners' purchases of hides are affected, largely through price speculation on inventories, by prices which are endogenously determined. The most important converse effect in the models is the dependence of hide price upon the purchases of leather by manufacturers and the finished leather production, hide wettings and hide purchases by tanners.

Both one-period-change and process models were formulated.

Mathematically, the forms of the models are nonlinear systems of lagged simultaneous difference equations. Simulation techniques were used to trace the time paths generated by the models for all endogenous variables. These generated series were then compared with the observed values of these variables between 1930 and 1940. While these comparisons do not result in complete agreement between the hypothetical and the actual time series for the endogenous variables, they do indicate that the models may incorporate some of the mechanisms which in fact determined behavior in the shoe, leather and hide industries.

Oligopoly theory

In recent years there has been an increased emphasis on studying the decision-making processes of firms. One of the difficulties has been to find a convenient language in which a model encompassing the complex of relevant variables could be constructed. An attempt at using computer models to describe firms in a duopoly market which goes into the internal decision-making mechanisms of the firms has been described by Cyert, Feigenbaum and March (1959). It is a homogeneous duopoly, and the major decision that each firm makes is an output decision. No discrepancy between production and sales is assumed, and thus no inventory problem exists in the model. The duopoly is composed of an ex-monopolist and a firm developed by former members of the established firm.

The decision-making process postulated by the theory begins with a forecasting phase. In this phase, competitor's reaction, the market demand curve and the firm's average unit cost curve are estimated. Concurrently, a profit goal is established (goal specification phase). An evaluation phase follows, in which an effort is made to find the best alternative, given the forecasts. If this best alternative is inconsistent with the profit goal, a re-examination phase ensues, in which an effort is made to revise cost and demand estimates. If re-examination fails to yield a new best alternative consistent with the profit goal, the immediate profit goal is abandoned in favor of 'doing the best possible under the circumstances'.

Specific values were assigned to the parameters and a demand curve which varied over time was assumed. The model was allowed to run for forty-five periods. To demonstrate that the model as a whole has some reasonable empirical basis, comparisons were made with the can industry, an industry having some of the structural characteristics of the model. Specifically, the ratio of the two duopolists' profits and market shares generated by the model and the corresponding actual ratios for American Can Company and Continental Can Company were compared for forty-five periods. The predictions were viewed by the authors as satisfactorily approximating the observed data.

Future of computer models

We have examined the nature of computer models, the associated methodological problems and some of the current literature utilizing computer models. It is now appropriate to evaluate the role of computer models in social science research. We clearly maintain that computer models are an important new tool for the social sciences. Computer models should be viewed as a supplement to available procedures rather than as a replacement for all existing techniques.

The basic advantage of computer models is that they provide a language within which complex dynamic models can be constructed. In addition, and because of the richness of the language, such models can incorporate the relevant empirical variables. This does not imply that economists should no longer be interested in general models, but it does mean that economists are no longer forced to deal *only* with general models.

Computer models provide a bridge between empirical and theoretical work. The requirements of a computer model can provide a theoretical framework for an empirical investigation and, in return, the empirical information is utilized in developing a flow diagram for the model. Through this process of working back and forth, it is possible to know when enough empirical information has been gathered and whether it is of the proper quality. Once the model is simulated, a more rigorous test of the validity of the model can be made, as indicated earlier, by comparing the time series generated by the model against the actual observed behavior of the system.

Because computer models have such a large capacity for

utilizing empirical data, a burden may be placed on the actual collection of empirical information. We know of no obviously optimal procedure for gathering information that exists inside firms or inside consumers' heads. Nevertheless, this is the kind of information which economists desire and which computer models can readily handle.

Once the reduction of a system to its individual decision-making units has been accomplished, there is great hope for a solution of the aggregation problem. Thus, through computer models, we see the possibility of developing working models of the economy that will have a solid empirical basis.[7]

References

ALLEN, R. G. D. (1957), *Mathematical Economics*, Macmillan.

COHEN, K. J. (1960a), *Computer Models of the Shoe, Leather, Hide Sequence*, Prentice-Hall.

COHEN, K. J. (1960b), 'Simulation of the firm', *Amer. econ. Rev., Pap. Proc.*, vol. 50, pp. 534–40.

COURNOT, A. (1897), *Researches into the Mathematical Principles of the Theory of Wealth*, Macmillan.

CYERT, R. M., FEIGENBAUM, E. A., and MARCH, J. G. (1959), 'Models in a behavioral theory of the firm', *Behav. Sci.*, vol. 4, pp. 81–95.

FORRESTER, J. W. (1958), 'Industrial dynamics – a major breakthrough for decision makers', *Harv. bus. Rev.*, vol. 36, pp. 37–66.

FRIEDMAN, M. (1953), *Essays in Positive Economics*, University of Chicago Press.

GRUNBERG, E. (1957), 'Notes on the verifiability of economic laws', *Phil. Sci.*, vol. 24, pp. 337–68.

HOGGATT, A. C. (1957), *Simulation of the Firm*, IBM Research Paper RC–16.

KLEIN, L. R. (1953), *A Textbook of Econometrics*, Row, Peterson.

KOOPMANS, T. C. (1957), *The State of Economic Science*, McGraw-Hill.

MACK, R. P. (1956), *Consumption and Business Fluctuation: A Case Study of the Shoe, Leather, Hide Sequence*, National Bureau of Economic Research.

MADANSKY, A. (1959), 'The fitting of straight lines when both variables are subject to error', *J. Amer. Stat. Assn*, vol. 54, pp. 173–205.

MALCOLM, D. G. (ed.), (1958), *Report of the Systems Simulation Symposium*, American Institute of Industrial Engineers.

ORCUTT, G. H., GREENBERGER, M., and RIVLIN, A. M. (1958), *Decision-Unit Models and Simulation of the United States Economy*, Harvard University.

7. A more detailed discussion of the problems of and of the potential for combining individual micro-level models into an aggregate level computer model is contained in Cohen (1960b).

Kalman J. Cohen and Richard M. Cyert 337

ROTWEIN, E. (1959), 'On "the methodology of positive economics"', *Quart. J. Econ.*, vol. 73, pp. 554–75.

SAMUELSON, P. A. (1947), *Foundations of Economic Analysis*, Harvard University Press.

SARGAN, J. D. (1958), 'The estimation of economic relationships using instrumental variables', *Econometrics*, vol. 26, pp. 393–415.

STIGLER, G. J. (1946), *The Theory of Price*, Macmillan.

Part Six **General Equilibrium**

Thomas Huxley once explained that Britannia ruled the waves because of British old maids. Old maids kept cats which killed mice which ate bumble-bee combs and larvae: bumble-bees therefore flourished, and with the bees so did red clover which could only be effectively pollinated by the long tongues of bumble-bees: red clover is a staple food of British cattle, and so plenty of clover meant plenty of beef: and British tars lived on bully beef. This classic cats-and-clover story illustrates how plants and animals remote in nature are bound together in a complex web of relationships. In somewhat similar fashion, price theory explains how scattered means and ends are brought together by the push and pull of costs and demands.

General equilibrium theory might be attributed to Victorian fathers who asserted that you can have too much of a good thing. This principle – in the guise of diminishing rates of substitution, diminishing marginal products, and so on – provides the basic premise of price theory, as John S. Chipman and Francis M. Bator explain in their discussions of the convexity principle. W. Leontief depended on a different principle, that it is all a matter of proportion, to invent an operational general equilibrium theory.

14 John S. Chipman

The Nature and Meaning of Equilibrium in Economic Theory[1]

John S. Chipman, 'The nature and meaning of equilibrium in economic theory', in D. Martindale (ed.), *Functionalism in the Social Sciences: The Strengths and Limits of Functionalism in Anthropology, Economics, Political Science and Sociology: A Symposium*, American Academy of Political and Social Science, 1965, pp. 35–64.

Two pillars form the foundation of economic activity. One is the law of convexity of preferences, which states that people desire to consume a variety – or average – of products rather than limit their consumption to any one commodity alone. The other is the law of economies of production, according to which it is possible for people, by cooperating together and by combining their labor with natural resources and capital, to produce more of any one commodity than could be produced by any persons or resources alone. Thus some form of cooperation, by production and exchange, is preferable to none; yet a third principle is required, forming an arch, to explain how the fruits of cooperation are to be distributed among the participants.

Three approaches to this central economic problem warrant consideration: those of Walras, Edgeworth and Keynes. Of these, Edgeworth's two laws of contract supply the unifying principle: (a) if the number of participants is very large, the price system will often, but still not necessarily, lead to a determinate equilibrium and (b) if the number of participants is small, or if coalitions are formed, there results a basic indeterminacy leading to the possibility of deadlock. There may well be a principle at work, by which individuals pursue their interests subject to certain self-imposed restraints, in such a way that an equilibrium or order is achieved; but such a principle, if it exists, is not yet fully understood.

Equilibrium – meaning a balance of opposing forces – is a concept as fundamental in economics as it is in physics. The

1. This work was supported by grants from the National Science Foundation and the Social Science Research Council.

reason it is so fundamental is that the concept is much more complex than might at first be supposed.

In its most narrow meaning, equilibrium is a state of affairs in which things are at rest. It is obvious, however, that things which never change would not warrant much study. The real content of the equilibrium concept is to be found not so much in the state itself as in the laws of change which it implies; that is, in the tendencies to move towards it, away from it, or around it. I say 'it' guardedly; it would be more accurate to say 'them', for we cannot rule out in advance the possibility of multiple equilibria. That is not all: we cannot be sure that equilibrium always exists; thus it happens, paradoxically, that in some cases the importance of the concept derives precisely from the purely negative statement that no equilibrium is possible.

Fruitful analysis of equilibrium therefore requires analysis of stability conditions.[2] The word 'stability' has a variety of senses. Sometimes, as in the phrase 'stable price level', it signifies a state of relative constancy, that is, a state in which prices remain within certain prescribed limits. In this sense it is a kind of approximate equilibrium; it finds a close counterpart in what is known in mathematical literature as 'Lyapunov stability'. More usually, in technical economic discussions, it signifies asymptotic stability, a tendency to move towards equilibrium when the latter has been subjected to small disturbances; there is also 'global stability' which signifies a tendency to return to a particular point of equilibrium even after large disturbances. All these concepts are related, but distinct. For the most part it should be clear, from the context of what follows, which concept is intended; in technical discussions it will usually be asymptotic stability.

The above remarks are of a formal nature. Our interest in this essay is on the substantive issue of the extent to which the equilibrium concept applies to the study of the balance of economic conflict. To this we now turn.

2. For good expositions of recent research on stability, see Negishi (1962) and Newman (1961). The multitude of ways in which the equilibrium concept is used and abused in economic theory is one of the chief topics of the lively and highly recommended book by Machlup (1963, esp. pp. 43–72).

The economic order

Like most things that are familiar, the economic organization of private enterprise tends to be taken for granted. Yet many who have contemplated its workings have been struck with wonder: how is it that such a complex organization ever came about, and how can we explain that it works at all? Such an attitude has been well expressed by Frank H. Knight:

One of the most conspicuous features of organization through exchange and free enterprise, and one most often commented upon, is the absence of conscious design or control. It is a social order, and one of unfathomable complexity, yet constructed and operated without social planning or direction, through selfish individual thought and motivation alone. No one ever worked out a plan for such a system, or willed its existence; there is no plan of it anywhere, either on paper or in anybody's mind, and no one directs its operations. Yet in a fairly tolerable way, 'it works', and grows and changes.[3]

The basic idea expressed here is that of a natural working out of economic forces, a general equilibrium that results from the interaction of individuals each of whom strives for his own advantage. In the famous words of Adam Smith (1776, p. 400), each individual 'intends only his own gain, and he is in this . . . led by an invisible hand to promote an end which was no part of his intention'. This notion of a natural harmony and order goes back at least to the *laissez-faire* doctrines of François Quesnay and his Physiocrats, and can be traced back still farther to the medieval concepts of natural law (cf. Schumpeter, 1954, pp. 94–9, 110–13, 228–34).

How accurate a picture of the economic organization is this in fact? By a 'fairly tolerable' order we might mean one which stays close to some optimum which we would have to specify, according to an independent criterion. Or we might merely

3. Knight (1951, p. 31). This passage contains a qualifying footnote to the penultimate sentence stating that 'we do have a large and increasing amount of deliberate planning and control in modern society, but this means precisely the substitution of "political" for "economic" methods of organization'. See also ibid. (p. 28).

mean that a 'fairly tolerable social order' is an equilibrium which is stable in Lyapunov's sense, where the range of permissible variation is, again, to be independently specified. Since any society we can observe has some degree of conscious social control – if only laws to enforce contracts, and a judiciary and police force to implement and enforce these laws – it is clearly necessary to distinguish carefully what we mean by 'social planning and direction'. Thus as soon as we examine Knight's description more closely we recognize that it raises more questions than it answers; in fact it raises practically all the interesting questions.

The basis for exchange

It is an old scientific principle to start with the simplest cases; this has the advantage of bringing out sharply some of the basic problems involved and, furthermore, the principle is justified on the grounds that unless we can gain insight from simple cases, we cannot hope to get very far with more complicated ones.

Let us start with the simplest imaginable case, typified by Smith's well-known example: 'If among a nation of hunters, for example, it usually costs twice the labour to kill a beaver as it does to kill a deer, one beaver should naturally exchange for or be worth two deer.'[4] In such a society there would be no basis for cooperation, and none for what I think is the typically economic problem of 'voluntary conflict'. There would be a basis for appropriation, but not for exchange. Voluntary exchange would be possible, but unnecessary; each hunter would need only to distribute his time so as to obtain for himself the most preferred combination of beavers and deer. It is true that differences in strengths, productiveness or cunning could lead to appropriation by some of the product of others. But at least, even if the principle accepted was not 'to each according to his need' but 'to each according to his work', there would be an obvious way in which this principle could be understood; whereas, in more complex cases there is, as a rule,

4. Smith (1776, p. 41). This passage is usually taken as providing the original statement of the labor theory of value. However, Smith was careful to stress its exceptional nature.

no unambiguous way in which one could evaluate a person's 'work'.[5]

The peculiarly economic problem arises only when there is a basis for exchange. Such a basis would exist, for instance, if beaver and deer populated different territories, and if different groups of hunters could establish property rights in the respective territories. Sometimes this provides a natural basis for exchange, and of course this is the basis of much international trade; this is why Iceland imports bananas and exports fish. Except for such obvious geographical factors, however, the explanation of exchange on the basis of specialization in the appropriation of supplies is not a very convincing one, since it begs the question of why the appropriation by different people of different sources of supply should have been so uneven in the first place. Thus we do not get very close to a convincing explanation of exchange until we examine more deeply the nature of production.

Functionalism

In production we find the principal source of economic organization and cooperation. But here we find two very different types of explanation in the literature. The first concept is a very old one, which derives from the Platonic conception that 'all things are produced more plentifully and easily and of a better quality when one man does one thing which is natural to him and does it at the right time, and leaves other things'. In its crudest form this theory holds that inequality and diversity form the basis for a harmony of interests; 'every man has his station'. A modern exponent of this kind of viewpoint is von Hayek, who states that

only because men are in fact unequal can we treat them equally. If all men were completely equal in their gifts and inclinations, we should have to treat them differently in order to achieve any sort of social organization. Fortunately, they are not equal; and it is only owing to

5. This is the problem of imputation which was posed by von Wieser (1888). An unambiguous 'imputation' to factors on the basis of their marginal productivity depends at the very least on the existence of a unique solution of competitive equilibrium – which cannot be counted on – but it also presupposes the adoption of a competitive system. The problem is an ethical one in the last analysis.

this that the differentiation of functions need not be determined by the arbitrary decision of some organizing will but that, after creating formal equality of the rules applying in the same manner to all, we can leave each individual to find his own level (von Hayek, 1949, pp. 15–16).

Apart from the difficulty of choosing who should be the 'we' who decide how men are to be treated, this functionalistic view, if taken literally, presents an extremely optimistic picture of the predetermined harmony between individual aptitudes and economic necessity. Are we really to believe that exactly the right proportion of people will be born shoemakers and born weavers in order to contribute to the functioning of Plato's Republic?[6]

The belief that a social or economic order requires for its proper functioning a variety or inequality of aptitudes has been sometimes heard expressed in the question: 'If all men were equal, who would collect my garbage?' In a private-enterprise economy, the answer to this is quite apparent. If all men are equal and garbage-collecting is considered disagreeable, few people will wish to enter the occupation; consequently garbage collectors in a free-enterprise economy will earn higher than average incomes. This will encourage people to become garbage collectors, and at the same time make it profitable to produce mechanical garbage disposal devices and incinerators, thus preventing the wage differential from becoming excessive.

It is of course true that *in fact* there is a great variety in human talents and innate abilities, but there is no *a priori* reason why the given distribution of talents should correspond in any way to the requirements of consumption. And clearly we can just as well conceive of the diversity of talents as being too great as of its being too small. Even if there are born doctors and born lawyers, there are also born ditherers, and the system of incentives will have to be such as to induce them to 'find their level' among the various professions; and if there are too many born lawyers, some of them will have to be induced

6. Certainly Plato himself did not entertain such a simple view, since he showed in many passages a recognition of the role of education and training.

to become doctors.[7] Thus it is important to recognize the part played by devices such as the price mechanism in compensating people for undertaking disagreeable tasks, and this is the key to the understanding of any voluntary method of achieving social balance. Nevertheless, this does not imply that such compensating devices are sufficient in themselves for the attainment of equilibrium; they are doubtless necessary, but by no means the complete answer.

Economies

We have seen that one basis for exchange is to be found in differences in abilities; geographical differences formed another. But the most important has still not been mentioned, and it is that which Marshall (1890, p. 266 of 1961 edn) described by the term 'economies'. Although Marshall gave the concept a name, again we can find it clearly described in Adam Smith who, in the first chapter of *The Wealth of Nations*, described the process of pin making – a forerunner of the assembly line. No one would claim that one man was born with an innate talent for straightening the wire, and another with an inborn talent for cutting it – or that the man who sharpens the ends is very unequal to the man who fastens the heads. The important point is simply that by division of labor, more pins can be produced than would be produced by each worker separately producing an entire pin. Likewise the use of machinery duplicates and intensifies this process, and the combination of factors of production – land, labor and capital – permits the production

7. As Private Willis sings in *Iolanthe*:
Now nature always does contrive
  That every boy and every gal
    That's born into the world alive
  Is either a little Liberal
    Or else a little Conservative!
Ramsay Muir (1930) feared that the born ditherers would be easily swayed by the political parties. Whereas Hotelling (1929) feared that the political parties would be easily swayed by the ditherers. I do not, incidentally, find it possible to accept the analysis of Downs (1957). Downs believes (ibid., p. 143) that the stability of the democratic process depends on the distribution of voters on the political scale being unimodal, whereas in fact it depends on the assumption that extreme left and extreme right do not meet.

of greater quantities of commodities than could be produced by any one of them singly.

There would of course be no object to this kind of specialization unless the product could be exchanged. Presumably some forms of social organization provide direct benefits to the participants. But typically it would be pointless for workers to combine to produce pins or anything else unless they could be exchanged for products of other enterprises, since no one can subsist on pins alone; even if man can live by bread alone, he will prefer a balanced diet. In this last observation we have expression of a fundamental law of economics, that of the *convexity* of preferences. This law – first clearly perceived by Edgeworth (1881, p. 130) – states that if an individual is indifferent as between two bundles of commodities, then he will prefer any average of these two bundles to either one of them. Thus, if a certain diet of meat alone is considered no better or worse than a certain diet of vegetables alone, any weighted average – say one-third of the meat and two-thirds of the vegetables – will be preferred to either just the meat or just the vegetables. It is amazing how many economic laws stand or fall with this principle; we shall see several examples. There does not seem to be anything corresponding to this law in other social sciences.

Exchange equilibrium

A solid basis for exchange having been established, it is a useful conceptual device to imagine an economy in which different individuals have various quantities of goods at their disposal – say various quantities per period of time. To keep the argument simple, assume that no one can tolerate subsisting on one commodity alone, and that everyone comes to market with a certain amount of just one good. *Ergo*, any redistribution leaving everyone with a positive amount of each good, will make each person better off. From the previous reasoning we are entitled to assume that economies of production make it possible to produce more of each commodity than the sum total that could have been produced by each person – or factor – separately; thus cooperation has been proved advantageous.

Does this argument prove that there is, therefore, a harmony of interests, and that an equilibrium will be reached which is satisfactory to everyone? Not at all, for although advantage can be gained through cooperation, there is plenty of room for conflict over how this advantage should be divided. Let us examine how this problem has been tackled in the economic literature.

Bilateral monopoly

Menger (1871, ch. 4, esp. pp. 181–6 of 1950 edn) was one of the earliest to try to handle this problem in a fairly rigorous way, basing himself on the principle of diminishing marginal utility. He considered the case of two frontiersmen, one with a stock of horses and another with a stock of cows. He assumed that utility could be measured and added and that, say, the utility to person A of one horse was fifty units, the utility of an extra horse, forty more units, the extra utility of a third horse, thirty units, and so forth – similarly for cows. Thus if A traded his fifth horse for B's fifth cow, they would each lose ten units of utility and gain fifty, and in this way, by trading one horse for one cow, and another horse for another cow, and so forth, both traders would finally arrive at an equilibrium, beyond which it would not be of advantage for either one of them to go.

The trouble with Menger's argument was that it assumed that one horse would always exchange for one cow. In other words, Menger implicitly assumed that the terms of exchange were given in advance, but this is precisely what has to be determined. There is no reason why a sharp-witted horse-trader might not induce the cowboy to exchange two cows for one horse. Thus Menger unwittingly introduced a principle of equity, a principle which Edgeworth was later to make explicit.

In the treatment of perfectly divisible commodities Menger's analysis was more successful (Menger, 1871, ch. 5, esp. pp. 194–7). He correctly perceived that the outcome was basically indeterminate, depending on the bargaining powers of the participants. He rather spoiled this result by concluding, by means of a vague and shaky argument, that the equilibrium price would be established half-way between the limiting price ratios between which trade could be established.

Menger was certainly not the first to discover the indeterminacy of bilateral monopoly. It had been discussed in detail by Mill (1848, pp. 545–6 of 1895 edn) and was the subject of a debate between Thornton (1869, pp. 43–87) and Mill (1869). However, there was still some ambiguity about its nature until it was clarified later by Edgeworth. The nature of this ambiguity is best perceived after consideration of the theory of competitive equilibrium developed by Gossen (1854), Jevons (1871) and Walras (1874).

Competitive equilibrium

The defining characteristic of perfect competition was specified by Mill by the axiom, 'that there cannot be for the same article, of the same quality, two prices in the same market' (Mill, 1848, p. 542 of 1895 edn). Jevons later gave this principle a name: the Law of Indifference.[8] This principle made it possible to define demand and supply functions: at each collection of prices, one could determine the quantity of each commodity demanded or supplied by each trader; aggregating all the amounts people wish to hold of each commodity, at each different set of prices, and subtracting from this the total initial stock of each commodity, we obtain the aggregate excess demand for each good, expressed as a function of all the prices.

If there are n commodities, there are n of these aggregate excess demand functions. We may define 'equilibrium' to mean a solution to the equations obtained by setting all these excess demands equal to zero, that is, a set of prices for which aggregate demand is equal to aggregate supply.

The question now arises as to the 'determinateness' of this system – a satisfactory definition of 'determinateness' must still be found. There is first the question of equilibrium; can we be sure that there is a set of n prices satisfying the n equations? The affirmative assertion is called the Law of Supply and Demand, or, according to some interpretations, Say's Law.

We cannot go into all the details here, but I shall briefly sketch the main problems. First of all, the equations are not

8. Jevons (1871, p. 91 of 1957 edn) 'In the same open market, at any moment, there cannot be two prices for the same kind of article.' The words 'at any moment' actually muddled the issue, as we shall see.

independent; this proposition is known as Walras's Law,[9] which states that, whatever the market prices may be, the amount people wish to spend is equal to the amount they desire to earn. The law is usually – and wrongly – stated to mean that people spend all their incomes;[10] but people can *actually* spend all their incomes only in a state of equilibrium – this is how we define equilibrium. The amount an individual desires to earn (at given prices) is the amount of his product he desires to supply, multiplied by its price; and the amount he desires to spend is the total of quantities he desires to purchase, multiplied by their prices. If this desired net expenditure is zero, then given the excess demand for any $n-1$ commodities, the excess demand for the remaining nth commodity is determined. Therefore only $n-1$ of the aggregate excess demand equations are independent.

With $n-1$ independent equations, we might hope to solve for $n-1$ of the prices, given one of the remaining ones; but as

9. So called by Lange (1942).

If we write $x_{ij} = f_{ij}(p_1, p_2, ..., p_n)$ for the excess demand by the jth person for the ith commodity, expressed as a function of all n prices, then it is assumed that

$$\sum_{i=1}^{n} p_i x_{ij} = \sum_{i=1}^{n} p_i f_{ij}(p_1, p_2, ..., p_n) = 0 \qquad \text{B}$$

for each jth individual, whatever the prices p_i may be. Defining aggregate excess demand as $x_i = \sum_{j=1}^{m} x_{ij}$, where there are m individuals, we then automatically obtain

$$\sum_{i=1}^{n} p_i x_i = \sum_{i=1}^{n} p_i f_i(p_1, p_2, ..., p_n) = 0 \qquad \text{W}$$

which is Walras's Law. The substance of Walras's Law, however, is expressed by the budget identity (B); the rest is just arithmetic.

10. Everything in this discussion is with reference to a stationary economy, with no saving or investment. Therefore this statement should not be interpreted to mean that there is no saving – which it incidentally implies, but this is not the point. In a growing economy, 'spending' here could be taken as including purchase of bonds (saving), but it still might not be true that an unemployed worker, say, who *wishes* – but is unable – to supply his labor at the going wage, therefore *intends* to spend – on commodities *and* bonds – what he would *like* to earn. But this is exactly what Walras's Law states he *will* wish to do.

Wald (1951) emphasized, equality between the number of equations and the number of unknowns is neither necessary nor sufficient for the existence of a solution. In fact, there can be several solutions, or there can be none. The possibility of multiple equilibrium was well recognized by Walras (1874, pp. 109–11 of 1954 edn) and Marshall (1879, pp. 11–12, figs. 4 and 8 of 1949 edn). The possibility of there being no solution at all was suggested by Walras,[11] but only in recent years has it been seriously considered as a possibility, especially – in a broader context – by followers of Keynes (see Klein, 1956, p. 86).

The nonexistence of equilibrium

A very interesting example of nonexistence of a solution has been given by Arrow (1951, p. 528; see also Hurwicz, 1960, p. 42); its essentials can be described as follows. Suppose Farmer Jones has some vegetables which he has grown and wishes to market. Assume that if the price of vegetables is high enough in relation to meat, he will sell some of them and buy meat with the proceeds, but below a certain price he will just consume his own vegetables; finally, if vegetables are free, he will want to consume an indefinitely large quantity of them. On the other hand, suppose Farmer Brown has a small and insufficient supply of meat, but a bumper crop of vegetables, more than he could possibly want for himself. Then as long as vegetables have a positive price, he will wish to trade off his surplus vegetables so as to get himself more meat – which is impossible, since Jones has no meat to supply. Then vegetables will have to become a free good – but this is impossible too, since under those circumstances Jones will want more vegetables than he and Brown can jointly supply.

This can be taken as an example of the failure of Say's Law of Markets, which states that supply creates its own demand.[12]

11. Walras (1874, p. 108). I believe his example is not a legitimate one, however, since it seems to assume that both traders start out with more of everything than they want, so that there is really no economic problem.

12. Say (1821, p. 134 of 1964 edn): 'A product is no sooner created than it, from that instant, offers a market for other products to the full extent of its own value.' This statement has often been held up to ridicule on the grounds that the value might have to be zero. But Arrow's example shows that it can happen that not even a zero value will clear the market. Later on

A phenomenon rather similar to this has been observed by writers in the field of economic development (see Nurkse, 1962, ch. 1; Rosenstein-Rodan, 1943). Suppose a shoe manufacturer is contemplating setting up a shoe factory in Ruritania, and calculates that the minimum unit costs are less than the going price. He may find that he cannot market the shoes since he must produce a minimum output to achieve the calculated minimum unit cost, and in order to sell that output the price may have to go below the cost. Thus, within the context of perfect competition – where prices are assumed given and beyond any single producer's influence or control – no competitive equilibrium exists.[13]

The possibility of nonexistence of equilibrium seems puzzling at first, since it has the appearance of logical contradiction. There must be something wrong with the theory, it might be claimed; it cannot apply to reality. But this interpretation would not be correct; it assumes that reality is in equilibrium. We must distinguish between the idea that 'nothing changes' and the idea that 'nothing happens'. Obviously, something always happens! What is wrong is that the above analysis does not tell us what *would* happen; the theory is therefore incomplete.

Say has stated (p. 135): 'The glut of a particular commodity arises from its having outrun the total demand for it in one of two ways: either because it has been produced in excessive abundance, or because the production of other commodities has fallen short.' This actually corroborates the above example. Actually, it seems generally agreed now that the only authoritative and logically impeccable statement of the law is not to be found in Say's writings at all, but rather in Mill (1844, esp. p. 73 of 1948 edn). I do not find it possible to go along with Lange's definition (1942, p. 52), which appears to say that the competitive solution is one of neutral equilibrium – satisfied for all, or at least infinitely many, prices. See the valuable discussion by Becker and Baumol (1952); also Schumpeter (1954, pp. 615–24).

13. In economics treatises this problem is usually hidden by the practice of drawing diagrams with continuous curves; see, for instance, the book which I regard as gospel on these matters – Boulding (1941, p. 438). This no doubt derives from Marshall's motto: *Natura non facit saltum*, a motto which is appropriate only in a world in which there are a great many – in fact, infinitely many – small firms. Thus, the above example is one in which *natura facit saltum*. What might transpire in fact? Possibly a succession of firms entering the industry and going bankrupt – a business cycle, in other words.

For a theory to be complete it must be stated in dynamic terms. In Arrow's example described above, we must naturally ask: but what will actually happen? Possibly the price of vegetables will oscillate indefinitely, or in the long run production will be adjusted and the conditions of the problem will change. But before we can say this we must specify some laws of adjustment.

Instability and multiple equilibrium

The laws of adjustment specified by Walras were described as trials or 'tâtonnements'. Curiously enough, he described the process in words, but did not include it in his mathematics; it remained for Samuelson (1948, chs. 9–11) to do so. The principle is very simple: when the demand for a commodity exceeds the supply, its price will rise, and when the demand falls short of the supply, its price will fall. This is an old principle, described by Mill (1848, pp. 549–52 of 1895 edn) and Smith (1776, pp. 48–56) and which undoubtedly can be traced back farther still. The question as to whose behavior is represented by this process is a relevant one, to which we shall have to return.

There are two variants of this tâtonnement process that have been analysed in the literature. In Walras's original formulation, one of the prices – that of the 'numéraire' – was fixed, and if there was excess demand for a particular commodity, its price would rise relative to the numéraire;[14] this has been called the 'normalized process' (Arrow and Hurwicz, 1958). On the other hand, the 'non-normalized process' (Arrow, Block and Hurwicz, 1959) treats all commodities symmetrically; I shall confine the discussion to the latter kind of process for the time being.

The specification of a dynamic process of adjustment is what

14. Walras (1874, p. 170 of 1954 edn). A natural question to ask is what happens if there is excess demand for – or excess supply of – the numéraire? The answer is that nothing happens to the price of the numéraire – by assumption – but by Walras's Law, if there was excess supply of the numéraire there would be excess demand for other commodities. Thus if labor is the numéraire, unemployment would imply excess demand for commodities, whose prices would therefore rise. Apart from the difficulties in accepting Walras's Law in this case, there is the added possibility pointed out by Gale that if some of the commodities are inferior, some individual prices will fall, and global instability may result; cf. Gale (1963).

solves the problem of the determinacy of absolute prices.[15] In the static case, we could only solve – at best – for $n-1$ prices in terms of the remaining price; but given any initial set of prices, the Walrasian *tâtonnement* process, combined with Walras's Law, ensures that prices cannot all rise or fall proportionately.[16]

Let us see how this *tâtonnement* process works. I shall take an example which brings out the essential factors, although on the face of it it seems to be very artificial and remote from reality; this is the price that always must be paid for translating mathematics into words.[17] Suppose there are a great many bakers, each of whom has the same number of infinitely divisible loaves of bread; and an equal number of churners each of whom has a comparable amount of infinitely divisible butter. Suppose the bakers like to have approximately two slices of

15. See Patinkin (1948a, 1949a). In the first of these papers Patinkin tried to solve the problem within a static framework, but the attempt was bound to be futile. In the second, he introduced dynamic adjustment equations, but failed to realize that the differential equations themselves provided the solution to the problem. See the following footnote.

16. See Scarf (1960). For simplicity, let the rate of change of the ith price be actually equal to the excess demand for the ith commodity – the analysis does not depend on this simplification; then we can write

$$\frac{dp_i}{dt} = f_i(p_1, p_2, \ldots, p_n); \qquad i = 1, 2, \ldots, n \tag{T}$$

where $x_i = f_i(p_1, p_2, \ldots, p_n)$ as in (W) of footnote 9. Substituting these n *tâtonnement* equations in equation (W) (Walras's Law), we obtain

$$\sum_{i=1}^{n} p_i \frac{dp_i}{dt} = 0$$

which is a simple differential equation whose solution is just

$$\sum_{i=1}^{n} p_i^2 = \text{constant}.$$

That is, the prices have to stay on the $(n-1)$-dimensional surface of a hypersphere; this was pointed out by Scarf (1960, p. 162).

17. See Gale (1963, pp. 85–7). I follow here a variant of Gale's second example which, in turn, is essentially the same as the examples of multiple equilibrium of Walras and Marshall cited on page 352 and which are very familiar to all international trade theorists. Gale gives this old problem an interesting new twist, however.

bread for each pat of butter, and the churners prefer to have approximately two pats of butter for each slice of bread.[18] Finally let there be initially an equilibrium trade, in which each person keeps two-thirds of his own product and sells the other third.

Now we shall see that this is an unstable equilibrium; that is, the same kind of equilibrium as that of an egg standing on end. Suppose the price of bread is slightly increased. Then the bakers will expect to get[19] more for their bread, so they will have money left over which they will wish to spend on butter; but since bread and butter are complements, if they get more butter they will also want to keep more bread, and sell less than before. Thus the bakers will increase their demand for butter and lower their supply of bread. Similarly, the churners will be penalized by the rise in the price of bread; they will have to buy less, so they will consume less of their own butter and hence supply more.

Now as the bakers are favored by the rise in the price of bread – this is the income effect rightly stressed by Hicks (1939, pp. 67–71) – and the churners disfavored and since the bakers have a relative preference for their own product, it follows that there will be an increase in the excess demand for bread and a fall in the net demand – a rise in the net supply – for butter. Therefore, the price of bread will rise farther still and the price of butter will fall. This process will go on until a point is reached where the churners regard the two commodities as substitutes, which might well be the case in practice: if a churner is poor enough, and if bread is dear enough, he may increase the proportion of butter in his diet and rely on it as a good; it is also possible – but not necessary to the argument – that as a baker gets richer and butter gets cheaper, he may pamper himself by increasing his relative consumption of butter. In this way the price of butter may be prevented from falling too far, and a

18. By 'approximately' I wish to convey the idea that these proportions are not completely rigid, but will be modified if relative price differences are sufficiently great.

19. They cannot *actually* get more; they can only *expect* to get more, since this new price cannot be an equilibrium price. This is the kind of snarl which forced Walras to limit himself to hypothetical transactions.

stable equilibrium will be reached, but it is certainly conceivable that butter might never become a substitute for bread, in which case its price might fall to zero, leaving the churners destitute.

There is an interesting lesson to be learned from the example just considered: a competitive solution is not necessarily the 'fair' solution. If, in the example, the price of bread had initially been reduced rather than raised, the system would instead have converged to an equilibrium that favored the churners. Thus both 'unfair' solutions are possible competitive equilibria, but the 'fair' one is an unstable equilibrium, and therefore could not be achieved within the framework of the competitive system. The assumptions are perhaps not entirely typical, but certainly not absurd; in international trade, for instance, the existence of transport costs can have the effect of inducing inhabitants of different countries to prefer the consumption of their own products.

When more commodities are taken into account, the situation becomes even more complicated. Scarf[20] has furnished an example of global instability when there are three commodities; there is in his example just one equilibrium state and it is asymptotically unstable – it happens to be stable in Lyapunov's sense, which means that prices would fluctuate within a certain range.

So let us come to our original question: is there 'determinate equilibrium' within the competitive system? The answer depends, of course, on what we mean by the terms. If equilibrium is globally unstable but stable in Lyapunov's sense then it might still be called 'determinate' provided the range of fluctuation is sufficiently small. Even if equilibrium is globally stable convergence to equilibrium may be intolerably slow. In our example of the bakers and churners, equilibrium is stable for small disturbances, but a sufficiently violent disturbance could set the system moving to the other stable equilibrium; whether this movement is large or small, in practice, or whether the disturbances will be sufficiently great is, of course, an empirical question. There are some important sufficient conditions, such

20. Scarf (1960, pp. 161–3). Another has been given by Gale (1963, pp. 81–5) where, however, one of the prices is assumed to be rigid – according to the normalized process.

as the condition that all commodities be 'gross substitutes' – a rise in any price leads to a rise in the excess demand for all other commodities – in which it is known that global stability prevails.[21] It is generally doubted now that this condition can always be expected to hold. Returning to the question: is competitive equilibrium determinate? The answer must be: it all depends.

Edgeworth's Law of Contract

We must return to a more fundamental question. It is not enough to describe how the system of perfect competition works; we must explain how it would ever arise.

Consider a situation of bilateral monopoly in which Alfred has a certain quantity a of apples and Benjamin has a quantity b of berries – it will be convenient to assume that both commodities are infinitely divisible. Is it possible that there could be a state of stable competitive equilibrium between Alfred and Benjamin?

In a purely formal way, the answer is yes. For each person we can define a demand function: in principle, Alfred could, for each price of berries per apple, determine how much of his apples he would be willing to trade in return for berries, all at that price; similarly for Benjamin. But the situation is artificial; it assumes that the traders are ignorant of each other's situation. As soon as Alfred learns that Benjamin is anxious to sell his berries, he will hold out for a better price; Benjamin must pretend not to be eager to sell his berries, and Alfred must pretend to disdain them. All this is very familiar to anyone who has visited an oriental bazaar.

As Edgeworth suggested (1881, p. 109), Jevons's Law of Indifference is rather meaningless in this case. If there is to be just one bargain, and if there is just the one market, then the Law of Indifference is trivially satisfied, but pointless. The relevant feature of perfect competition is to be found in what Lange (1938, p. 86) called the 'parametric function of prices'; even though a trader, by withholding a commodity, can raise

21. This was established by Marshall – who called it the 'normal' case – for the case of two commodities and two countries (1879, pp. 11 and 21 of 1949 edn).

its price – or can generally affect prices by his actions – he is assumed to act *as if* the market price was given and beyond his control.

This led Lange to characterize the competitive system in the following interesting way:

The system of free competition is a rather peculiar one. Its mechanism is one of *fooling* entrepreneurs. It requires the pursuit of maximum profit in order to function, but it destroys profits when they are actually pursued by a larger number of people. However, this game of blindman's buff with the pursuit of maximum profit is possible only as the size of the business unit is small and the number of entrepreneurs is consequently large (Lange, 1938, p. 117).

It has long been recognized in a rather vague way that perfect competition requires a large number of competitors. For in this case, any one participant can have only a small effect on any price; so it does not seem outrageous to assume that he believes he cannot have any effect on the price. Still, in strict logic this is a little troublesome; how large is 'large'? And if the number of competitors is 'quite large' will the resulting situation be 'quite close' to the perfectly competitive one? Or might it be radically different? And more important still, why should the price system arise at all?

The core of an economy

It was one of Edgeworth's finest accomplishments to find an answer to this problem. For a variety of reasons the significance of his results seems to have gone largely unnoticed until quite recently, when attention was drawn to it by Shubik (1959), who showed that it could be reformulated as a problem in game theory. This led to a significant contribution by Scarf (1962), followed by an elegant and important paper by Debreu and Scarf (1963), which rigorously generalizes Edgeworth's result.

The principle supplied by Edgeworth was that of *recontracting* (1881, pp. 18–19). A contract among any number of traders is a conditional allocation of the products among the participants; a recontract is a reallocation among some subset of participants, and is assumed to take place – without others' consent – whenever all members of such a subset can improve their position thereby. If a contract cannot be amended in this way by recontract, it is considered to be a 'final settlement'. The collection of final settlements is called the 'core' – generalizing Edgeworth's concept of the 'contract curve'.

Edgeworth's First Law of Contract states that as the number of participants approaches infinity, the core shrinks to the set of competitive equilibria; this was stated in the form: 'Where the numbers on both sides are indefinitely large, and there are no *combinations*, and competition is in other respects *perfect*, contract is determinate' (Edgeworth, 1881, pp. 146–7; also p. 20). Today we would have to qualify this, as we saw some examples of indeterminacy even in perfect competition: (a) it can happen that no competitive equilibrium exists, (b) it can happen that there exists a competitive equilibrium which is globally unstable, or (c) there may be multiple equilibria, leading to the possibility of violent swings from one equilibrium to another.[22]

Edgeworth's Second Law of Contract states simply: 'Where competition is imperfect, contract is indeterminate' (Edgeworth, 1881, p. 147). This is the situation of deadlock; both parties have an interest in arriving at some settlement rather than none, but some principle of arbitration has to be adopted if any settlement is to be made.

I shall now briefly sketch the proof of Edgeworth's First Law, following the treatment of Debreu and Scarf as well as the original treatment by Edgeworth.

The parity theorem

Let there be a certain number n of apple growers, all with identical preferences, and each with a apples; and an equal

22. Kaldor (1934). Kaldor defines equilibrium to be 'determinate' if, starting from a given position, the equilibrium reached is independent of the process of adjustment. Another possible definition would be independence of the initial position, the range of the initial position being specified in advance; from this point of view the indeterminateness of 'neutral equilibrium' is a limiting case of multiple equilibrium. The statement in the text thus needs to be qualified by the *caveat* that some process other than the Walrasian *tâtonnement* process could lead to stability where the latter leads to instability. As Edgeworth himself pointed out in his review of Walras's *Elements*, 'Professor Walras's laboured lessons indicate *a* way, not *the* way, of descent to equilibrium' (see Edgeworth, 1889). Edgeworth's own method does lead to stability when equilibrium exists; see footnote 24 below.

number n of berry growers, also with identical preferences, and each with b berries. What I shall call the *parity theorem* states that in any final settlement all the apple growers must finish with equal quantities of apples and of berries, and all the berry growers must finish with equal quantities of apples and of berries. Since there are n traders of each kind it follows that the entire settlement can be decomposed into n identical trades between couples.

The proof rests heavily on the assumption of the convexity of preferences.[23] It is basically quite simple. Suppose the settlement was not as described above. If the apple growers do not end with the same holdings of apples and berries, then one of them must be worst off, from all their points of view; call him the underdog. In the exceptional case in which apple growers might be indifferent among the various bundles which they hold, then we shall pick any one of these apple growers and call him the underdog. Similarly, if the berry growers do not all end up with identical holdings one of them will be the underdog. Now all we have to do is prove that the two underdogs – one apple grower and one berry grower – will recontract and upset the original settlement.

This is shown as follows. Consider a hypothetical new bundle of apples and berries which is simply the average of the respective holdings of apples and berries allotted to the apple growers in the present settlement; by the convexity assumption, this would be preferred by the apple underdog to his present holdings. Similarly, the average holdings allotted to the berry growers in the present settlement would be preferred by the berry underdog to his present holdings. Now add up these two average bundles, the resulting bundle is just the average holdings of apples and berries by all traders, that is, consisting of a apples and b berries. Therefore the two underdogs could obtain these average bundles just by redistributing their own initial holdings between themselves.

The argument is easily extended to the case of many commodities. It will always be to the advantage of the underdogs, one of each type, to recontract.

23. What follows is merely a translation into words of the proof of theorem 2 in Debreu and Scarf (1963, p. 241).

The limit theorem

The limit theorem is harder to prove, and I shall attempt only to sketch Edgeworth's original method of reasoning, which at least provides a good understanding of what is involved (Edgeworth, 1881, pp. 35–9).

Consider the case of two apple growers, Alfred and Arthur, and two berry growers, Benjamin and Bartholomew. Let the apple growers each have a apples to start with and the berry growers b berries. From the parity theorem, we know that the settlement can be decomposed into a settlement between Alfred and Benjamin and an identical settlement between Arthur and Bartholomew. Now we shall show that there are some contracts which these couples could arrive at if they were isolated from each other, that will necessarily be broken when they are in communication.

Suppose Alfred and Benjamin enter into a contract which is as unfavorable as possible for Alfred; that is, Alfred barely prefers to enter into it, rather than just keep his a apples. If the two couples are in communication, then from the parity theorem it follows that Arthur must have the same unfavorable contract with Bartholomew. Now we shall see that this pair of contracts is unstable and cannot be maintained.

Again we make use of the crucial convexity assumption. All we have to observe is that Alfred can easily induce Arthur to forsake Bartholomew, in the following way. If Arthur abandons Bartholomew, he is left with his a apples; Alfred, on the other hand, has x apples and y berries as a consequence of his settlement with Benjamin. Suppose he offers to split his holdings with Arthur; then he and Arthur will each hold an average bundle consisting of half of Alfred's bundle of x apples and y berries, and half of Arthur's bundle of a apples and no berries. Since we assumed that they both barely preferred the bundle (x, y) to the bundle $(a, 0)$ in the first place, it follows from the convexity assumption that they are now better off; so much better off, in fact, that they can afford to reduce their consumption of both commodities slightly, giving some extra to Benjamin so that the latter will be willing to be a part of the recontract.

The new arrangement cannot be a final settlement either,

since Benjamin and Bartholomew end up with different allocations, in violation of the parity theorem. So Bartholomew, who has been left in the lurch, will strike back in and make an offer which is still more favorable to the apple growers. The final settlement reached by this process will necessarily leave Alfred and Arthur better off.[24] And so as more and more traders are introduced, the number of possible final settlements narrows down to the competitive equilibria.

Edgeworth (1891, see pp. 318–19 of 1925 trans.) made the interesting observation[25] that, if the Bs were workers and the As employers, the workers' advantage could not be upset in the way just described, since no man can serve two masters – that is, Benjamin could not work for both Alfred and Arthur. Thus a natural argument is found for sticky wages.

The possibility of coalitions

An obvious objection that could be made to Edgeworth's process is this: if a collection of traders – say the berry growers – should learn to understand the nature of this bargaining process, they would soon realize that by forming a coalition they could maintain their monopoly advantage. In the above example Benjamin made an agreement which was temporarily beneficial to himself, but it rebounded in the end to his own disadvantage. If Benjamin and Bartholomew had made a hard and fast agreement, this never would have happened.

Against this type of argument, Hotelling (1929, pp. 48–9) has objected that in practice conditions are constantly changing, and consequently agreements need not just to be maintained but to be continually revised; and if just one trader should need cash at a particular moment, he could by his actions break up the entire coalition.

It is very hard to make generalizations, except for these two: (a) competition is unlikely to come about automatically unless

24. The dynamic process involved here was developed more fully by Edgeworth (1881; see also pp. 310–12 of *Papers Relating to Political Economy*. See also Marshall (1890, pp. 791–3, 844–5; see also pp. 791–8 of vol. 2) as well as Marshall's review of *Mathematical Psychics* (1881). The problem has since been analysed in great generality by Uzawa (1962).

25. Schematic examples such as this should, however, be taken with a grain of salt, since several important aspects of reality are left out.

there is just the right balance between ignorance and knowledge and (b) competition is unlikely to be maintained unless it is socially enforced. As Lange said, it is a game of blindman's buff, and it requires at least some deliberate social control to enforce the rules of the game. And such social control is unlikely to come about unless competition produces palatable results.

The Keynesian system

One of the most interesting kinds of equilibrium that have been discussed is that which Keynes (1936, p. 15) described as 'involuntary unemployment'. This is a state of affairs in which workers are willing to work at the prevailing wage, but are unable to find work.[26] In other words, it is a situation in which the supply of labor exceeds the demand.

Within the Walrasian framework – the nonnormalized *tâtonnement* process – an excess of supply over demand in the labor market should lead to a fall in wages; therefore it could not be compatible with 'equilibrium' in the strict sense of the term. This has led Patinkin to say: 'Thus Keynesian economics is the economics of unemployment *dis*equilibrium' (Patinkin, 1956, p. 235; see also 1949b). But this is only true if the classical mechanism is assumed to work; Keynes did not believe it did, but he confounded economists by a double argument. First, money wages would not fall; second, even if they did, real wages would not fall, so the fall in money wages would not do any good. This leaves the question of whether unemployment is 'voluntary' or 'involuntary' hanging in the air.

From what has already been said about the Walrasian *tâtonnement* process, it is obviously not in accord with the Keynesian analysis. Keynes assumed that if workers lowered their money wage, this would be followed by a proportionate fall in all other prices, and therefore the real wage rate would remain unchanged; and so long as the real wage rate remains above the real marginal productivity of labor – the extra output obtained with extra labor – unemployment will continue. Keynes (1936, p. 14) also observed that workers' relations were with individual employers, and that they had little reason to place themselves

26. Keynes's definition is actually somewhat different from this. Here I follow Haberler (1946, pp. 237–8).

at a relative disadvantage with respect to other workers by lowering their wages; this point which has not received sufficient attention, is closely related to Edgeworth's observation that wages are sticky because no man can serve two masters.

Keynes's argument, which has been developed by Lerner (1939) and Tobin (1941),[27] goes somewhat like this: first, if money wages fall, then other factor prices will fall instantaneously; second, through the forces of competition and the fall in demand, commodity prices will soon follow suit, until the original price ratios are restored. Tobin questioned the likelihood that other factor prices would fall; however, there is an obvious reason why most of them would. Capital and land are almost always owned by firms or secured by bonds, and so the situation is just *as if* these factors were leased to the firms at perfectly flexible prices. Only if workers had guaranteed annual – or decennial – wages would their situation be at all comparable.

The argument purporting to show that commodity prices would fall proportionately is much more shaky, yet nobody in this field ever seems to have questioned it. The method employed by both Lerner and Tobin is one of 'comparative statics': if all factor prices fall, then as long as their employment does not rise immediately, competition and the fall in money demand will bring down commodity prices until they reach their previous ratio to the factor prices. This ignores the possibility that factor prices, in the meantime, may have fallen farther still – as long as labor is unemployed, undoubtedly this will be the case; and it depends on the fall in prices preceding any increase in employment. Actually the *lag* of commodity prices behind factor prices is exactly what is crucial in bringing about a fall in real wages.[28]

27. The interpretation here is my own, but I do not believe it strays too far from the spirit of Keynes's approach; see Keynes (1936, chs. 2 and 19).

28. The most questionable assumption is Walras's Law. With it, money wage flexibility is unnecessary, since unemployment implies excess demand for commodities. Without it, and with flexible wages and prices – the non-normalized *tâtonnement* process – one may conjecture that equilibrium may quite likely be stable, but this type of adjustment process has not been studied, although it is similar to the Hahn process in many respects; see Negishi (1962). Walras's Law really plays the same role as the Pigou effect, discussion of which follows.

The Keynes effect and Pigou effect

Most economists, however, have accepted the argument that under competition, prices would be perfectly – or infinitely – flexible, but have offered alternative explanations as to how full employment equilibrium would be restored. First of all, Keynes's explanation – the so-called Keynes effect – was that there would be less need for cash balances after wages and all prices had fallen; hence they would be invested in bonds, whose price would rise, lowering the rate of interest, and raising investment; and although the last step in the argument is not usually mentioned, presumably the increase in investment, by raising the stock of capital, augments the marginal productivity of labor and brings about full employment without a fall in real wages being necessary.

The other explanation is in terms of the real-balance effect – which Patinkin (1948b; see also p. 271 of *Readings in Monetary Theory*) called the Pigou effect.[29] This states roughly that the motive for saving will be to a great extent dissipated when the deflation brings about a rise in the real value of cash balances; therefore, the rate of consumption expenditures will increase, and this will prevent commodity prices from falling too fast, hence real wages will fall and full employment will be restored. Presumably this argument, referring to the *rate* of consumption, is applicable only to those who were already saving part of their income.

Thus the Pigou effect restores full employment by making possible a fall in real wages, whereas the Keynes effect restores full employment by bringing about an increase in the marginal productivity of labor.[30] Viewed in this light, wage rigidity appears not so much as 'money illusion' on the part of unions as political astuteness. In the classical world, full employment is

29. The term owes its origin to Pigou (1943); in his revision, Patinkin acknowledged that the idea had older origins, and indeed was much more fully developed by Haberler (1946, pp. 491–503).

30. Two qualifications should be made here. One is that it is just as reasonable *a priori* to assume that a rise in real balances will cause a withdrawal of labor from the market as it is to assume that it will bring an increase in consumption – the first being an increase in leisure. Hence to the extent that the supply of labor is thus reduced, the fall in the real wage will

brought about by a fall in real wages; in the Keynesian world, rigid wages and unemployment cause a pressure for public expenditures, increasing the output of public goods and generally increasing the marginal productivity of labor. Unemployment, which is considered 'voluntary' within the context of a classical world – since it could be removed by a lowering of real wages – becomes 'involuntary' when considered with reference to a Keynesian world (see Haavelmo, 1950). In this respect, and in broad outlines, unemployment is seen as a form of deadlock, an aspect of Edgeworth's Second Law of Contract – the indeterminateness of equilibrium in the absence of perfect competition.

The equilibrium of expectations

The fundamental nature of economic equilibrium is that of mutual compatibility of expectations (see von Hayek, 1949, ch. 2). The special feature of the competitive price system which makes it so interesting is that if prices and certain rules of the game are considered as data by individuals and firms, then it makes sense for these individuals or firms to maximize utility or profit subject to these fixed constraints; the resulting process often – but not necessarily – is globally stable and hence determinate. But such a system only works if the supposed data are indeed treated as such, and are not themselves the object of maximization.

Long ago Pantaleoni[31] observed that in order for a 'want' to exist there had to be not only a wish but also a belief in the possibility of achievement. This is an old idea; revolutions are brought about not because people are poor but because they discover that they can alleviate their poverty. People accept inclement weather in good humor; they might no longer do so if the weather could be controlled, and thus the possibility of weather control would bring about new conflicts. If people truly accept their fate as inevitable, then the chances for a social order – equilibrium – are undeniably good. But as Mrs

---

not be so great. Second, before the operation of the Keynes effect could increase the marginal product of labor, which would take a long time, it would – like the Pigou effect – also put a cushion under the fall in prices and lead to a temporary fall in real wages.

31. Pantaleoni (1889, p. 40 of 1957 edn). The Italian word is *bisogno*.

Robinson (1951, p. 189) has remarked: 'The hidden hand will always do its work, but it may work by strangulation.'

In the classical world of perfect competition, there is not much difficulty in determining, for any individual, what is achievable and what is not. Thus it is fairly easy to define what are the wants, and equally easy to discover the constraints. An optimal social order can be conceived of as a system in which the constraints imposed on individuals are just sufficient, and no more stringent than necessary, to admit of a determinate solution to the simultaneous maximizing activities of its members. If there are too many constraints, there is a needless lack of freedom – the constraints could properly be called coercive; and if there are too few, there is necessarily a certain kind of disorder, or indeterminateness.

When this basic indeterminacy exists, it is no longer clear what are the 'wants', since it is no longer apparent what is achievable or to what extent. It is not that the principle of maximization becomes invalid; it just becomes meaningless, since nobody knows what he can maximize and nobody knows what are the constraints. Simon (1957, p. xxv) has said: 'While economic man maximizes . . . his cousin, . . . administrative man, satisfices – looks for a course of action that is satisfactory or "good enough".' But what is 'good enough'? One man's level of aspiration is another man's level of desperation; what is 'good enough' for one person may be 'too bad' for another. We should perhaps say instead: polipolistic man maximizes subject to clearly defined constraints, whereas oligopolistic man must either struggle chaotically or else negotiate over the constraints. In fact what is usually observed is a combination of the two: a slow struggle, accompanied by the mutual acceptance of certain informal constraints.

Thus price competition tends to be avoided in oligopoly by tacit mutual agreement, because it leads to chaos – indeterminacy. Other kinds of constraints come to be adopted, which lead to short-run stability, but allow for slower long-run tests of bargaining strength. The competitive price system provides one kind of system of constraints that can be expected to work when the number of participants is large. If the number of participants is small it requires a certain amount of ignorance or *naïveté* in order to work; who would increase his output and base his calculations on a given price, pretending not to know that his action would lower the price? Thus the competitive price mechanism cannot be expected to provide a stable framework under conditions of oligopoly; some other principle is needed.

In the words of Edgeworth (1881, p. 51): 'The whole creation groans and yearns, desiderating a principle of arbitration, an end of strifes.' In the pattern of traditions, customs and inhibitions, it may, perhaps, be possible to discern a mutually acceptable game, in which all participants maximize their utility subject to these informal constraints. Though such a principle may exist, we are still quite far from discovering it.

References

ARROW, K. J. (1951), 'An extension of the basic theorems of classical welfare economics', in *Proceedings, 2nd Berkeley Symposium on Mathematical Statistics and Probability*, University of California Press, pp. 507–32.

ARROW, K. J., and HURWICZ, L. (1958), 'On the stability of the competitive equilibrium, I', *Econometrica*, vol. 26, pp. 522–52.

ARROW, K. J., BLOCK, H. D., and HURWICZ, L. (1959), 'On the stability of competitive equilibrium, II', *Econometrica*, vol. 27, pp. 82–109.

BECKER, G. S., and BAUMOL, W. J. (1952), 'The classical monetary theory: the outcome of the discussion', *Economica*, new series, vol. 19, pp. 355–76.

BOULDING, K. (1941), *Economic Analysis*, Harper & Row.

DEBREU, G., and SCARF, H. (1963), 'A limit theorem on the core of an economy', *Int. econ. Rev.*, vol. 4, pp. 235–46.

DOWNS, A. (1957), 'An economic theory of political action in a democracy', *J. polit. Econ.*, vol. 65, pp, 135–50.

EDGEWORTH, F. Y. (1881), *Mathematical Psychics*, Kelley.

EDGEWORTH, F. Y. (1889), 'The mathematical theory of political economy', *Nature*, vol. 40, pp. 434–6.

EDGEWORTH, F. Y. (1891), 'On the determinateness of economic equilibrium', *Giornale degli Economisti*, series 2, vol. 2, pp. 233–45. Abridged translation in *Papers Relating to Political Economy*, vol. 2, Franklin, 1925, pp. 313–19.

GALE, D. (1963), 'A note on global instability of competitive equilibrium', *Nav. Res. Log. Quart*, vol. 10, pp. 81–7.

GOSSEN, H. H. (1854), *Entwickelung der Gesetze des menschlichen Verkehrs*, Frager, 1889.

HAAVELMO, T. (1850), 'The notion of involuntary economic decisions', *Econometrica*, vol. 18, pp. 1–8.

HABERLER, G. (1946), *Prosperity and Depression*, United Nations, New York.

HICKS, J. R. (1939), *Value and Capital*, Clarendon Press.
HOTELLING, H. (1929), 'Stability in competition', *Econ. J.*, vol. 39, pp. 41–57.
HURWICZ, L. (1960), 'Optimality and informational efficiency in resource allocation processes', in K. J. Arrow, S. Karlin and P. Suppes (eds.), *Mathematical Methods in the Social Sciences*, Stanford University Press, pp. 27–46.
JEVONS, W. S. (1871), *The Theory of Political Economy*, Kelley, 1957.
KALDOR, N. (1934), 'A classificatory note on the determinateness of equilibrium', in *Essays on Value and Distribution*, Duckworth, 1960, pp. 13–33.
KEYNES, J. M. (1936), *The General Theory of Employment, Interest and Money*, Macmillan.
KLEIN, L. R. (1956), *The Keynesian Revolution*, Macmillan.
KNIGHT, F. H. (1951), *The Economic Organization*, Kelley.
LANGE, O. (1938), 'On the economic theory of Socialism', in B. E. Lippincott (ed.), *On the Economic Theory of Socialism*, University of Minnesota Press, pp. 57–143.
LANGE, O. (1942), 'Say's Law: a restatement and criticism', in O. Lange, F. McIntyre and T. O. Yntema (eds.), *Studies in Mathematical Economics and Econometrics*, University of Chicago Press, pp. 49–68.
LERNER, A. P. (1939), 'The relation of wage policies and price policies', *Amer. econ. Rev., Pap. Proc.*, vol. 29, pp. 158–69.
MACHLUP, F. (1963), *Essays on Economics Semantics*, Prentice-Hall.
MARSHALL, A. (1879), *The Pure Theory of Foreign Trade*, London School of Economics, 1949.
MARSHALL, A. (1881), 'Review of *Mathematical Psychics*', *Academy*, vol. 19, p. 457.
MARSHALL, A. (1890), *Principles of Economics*, vol. 1, Macmillan Co., 9th variorum edn, 1961.
MENGER, C. (1871), *Principles of Economics*, Free Press, 1950.
MILL, J. S. (1844), 'On the influence of consumption on production', *Essays on Some Unsettled Questions of Political Economy*, London School of Economics, 1948, pp. 47–74.
MILL, J. S. (1848), *Principles of Political Economy*, vol. 1, Appleton-Century-Crofts, 5th edn, 1895.
MILL, J. S. (1869), 'Thornton on labour and its claims, I', *Fortnightly Rev.*, new series, vol. 5, pp. 505–18.
MUIR, R. (1930), *How Britain is Governed*, R. R. Smith.
NEGISHI, T. (1962), 'The stability of a competitive economy: a survey article', *Econometrica*, vol. 30, pp. 635–69.
NEWMAN, P. (1961), 'Approaches to stability analysis', *Economica*, vol. 28, pp. 12–29.
NURKSE, R. (1962), *Problems of Capital Formation in Underdeveloped Countries*, Blackwell.

PANTALEONI, N. (1889), *Pure Economics*, Kelley, 1957.

PATINKIN, D. (1948a), 'Relative prices, Say's Law and the demand for money', *Econometrica*, vol. 16, pp. 135–54.

PATINKIN, D. (1948b), 'Price flexibility and full employment', *Amer. econ. Rev.*, vol. 38, pp. 543–64. Reprinted with revisions in *Readings in Monetary Theory*, Blakiston, 1951, pp. 252–83.

PATINKIN, D. (1949a), 'The indeterminacy of absolute prices in classical economic theory', *Econometrica*, vol. 17, pp. 1–27.

PATINKIN, D. (1949b), 'Involuntary unemployment and the Keynesian supply function', *Econ. J.*, vol. 59, pp. 360–83.

PATINKIN, D. (1956), *Money, Interest and Prices*, Row, Peterson.

PIGOU, A. C. (1943), 'The classical stationary state', *Econ. J.*, vol. 53, pp. 343–51.

ROBINSON, J. (1951), *Collected Economic Papers*, Blackwell.

ROSENSTEIN-RODAN, P. N. (1943), 'Problems of industrialisation of Eastern and Southeastern Europe', *Econ. J.*, vol. 53, pp. 202–11.

SAMUELSON, P. A. (1948), *Foundations of Economic Analysis*, Harvard University Press.

SAY, J. B. (1821), *A Treatise on Political Economy*, Kelley, 4th edn, 1964.

SCARF, H. (1960), 'Some examples of global instability of the competitive equilibrium', *Int. econ. Rev.*, vol. 1, pp. 157–72.

SCARF, H. (1962), 'An analysis of markets with a large number of participants in *Recent Advances in Game Theory*, Princeton University Press, pp. 127–55.

SCHUMPETER, J. A. (1954), *History of Economic Analysis*, Oxford University Press.

SHUBIK, M. (1959), 'Edgeworth market games', in A. W. Tucker and R. D. Luce (eds.), *Contributions to the Theory of Games*, vol. 4, Princeton University Press, pp. 267–78.

SIMON, H. A. (1957), *Administrative Behavior*, Macmillan Co., 2nd edn.

SMITH, A. (1776), *An Inquiry into the Nature and Causes of the Wealth of Nations*, vol. 1, Dent, 1933.

THORNTON, W. T. (1869), *On Labour*, vol. 1, Macmillan.

TOBIN, J. (1941), 'A note on the money wage problem', *Quart. J. Econ.*, vol. 50, pp. 508–17.

UZAWA, H. (1962), 'On the stability of Edgeworth's barter process', *Int. econ. Rev.*, vol. 3, pp. 218–32.

VON HAYEK, F. A. (1949), *Individualism and the Social Order*, Routledge & Kegan Paul.

VON WIESER, F. (1888), *Natural Value*, Kelley.

WALD, A. (1951), 'On some systems of equations of mathematical economics', *Econometrica*, vol. 19, pp. 368–403.

WALRAS, L. (1874), *Elements of Pure Economics*, Allen & Unwin, 1954.

15 Francis M. Bator[1]

The Simple Analytics of Welfare Maximization

Francis M. Bator, 'The simple analytics of welfare maximization',
American Economic Review, vol. 47, 1957, pp. 22–59.

It appears, curiously enough, that there is nowhere in the
literature a complete and concise nonmathematical treatment
of the problem of welfare maximization in its 'new welfare
economics' aspects. It is the purpose of this exposition to fill
this gap for the simplest statical and stationary situation.

Part I consists in a rigorous diagrammatic determination
of the 'best' configuration of inputs, outputs and commodity
distribution for a two-input, two-output, two-person situation,
where furthermore all functions are of smooth curvature and
where neoclassical generalized diminishing returns obtain in all
but one dimension – returns to scale are assumed constant.
Part II identifies the 'price–wage–rent' configuration embedded
in the maximum problem which would ensure that decentralized
profit- and preference-maximizing behavior by atomistic
competitors would sustain the maximum-welfare position.
Part III explores the requirements on initial factor ownership
if market-imputed (or 'as if' market-imputed) income distribution is to be consistent with the commodity distribution
required by the maximum-welfare solution. Part IV consists in
brief comments on some technical ambiguities, e.g. the presumption that all tangencies are internal; also on a number of
feasible (and not so feasible) extensions: more inputs, outputs
and households; elasticity in input supplies; joint and intermediate products; diminishing returns to scale; external interactions. The discussion is still stationary and neoclassical in
spirit. Then, in part V, the consequences of violating some of the
neoclassical curvature assumptions are examined. Attention is

1. The author is indebted to R. S. Eckaus and R. M. Solow for suggestive
comment.

given to the meaning, in a geometric context, of the 'convexity' requirements of mathematical economics and to the significance of an important variety of nonconvexity – increasing returns to scale – for 'real' market allocation, for Lange–Lerner type 'as if' market allocation, and for the solubility of a maximum-of-welfare problem. Finally, part VI contains some brief remarks on possible dynamical extensions. A note on the seminal literature concludes the paper.[2]

I. Inputs, outputs and commodity distribution

Take, as given:

1. Two inelastically supplied, homogeneous and perfectly divisible inputs, labor services (L) and land (D). This 'Austrian' assumption does violate the full generality of the neoclassical model; elasticity in input supplies would make simple diagrammatic treatment impossible.

2. Two production functions, $A = F_A (L_A, D_A)$, $N = F_N (L_N, D_N)$, one for each of the homogeneous goods: apples (A) and nuts (N). The functions are of smooth curvature, exhibit constant returns to scale and diminishing marginal rates of substitution along any isoquant (i.e. the isoquants are 'convex' to the origin).

3. Two ordinal preference functions, $U_X = f_X (A_X, N_X)$ and $U_Y = f_Y(A_Y, N_Y)$ – sets of smooth indifference curves convex to the origin – one for X and one for Y. These reflect unambiguous and consistent preference orderings for each of the two individuals (X and Y) of all conceivable combinations of own-consumption of apples and nuts. For convenience we adopt for each function an arbitrary numerical index, U_X and U_Y, to identify the indifference curves. But the functions have no interpersonal implications whatever and for any one individual they only permit of statements to the effect that one situation is worse, indifferent or better than another. We do require consistency: if X prefers situation α to situation β and β to γ, then he must prefer α to γ; indifference curves must not cross. Also,

---

2. Anyone familiar with the modern literature will recognize my debt to the writings of Professor Samuelson. Reference is to be made, especially, to Samuelson (1947, ch. 8, 1950, 1956).

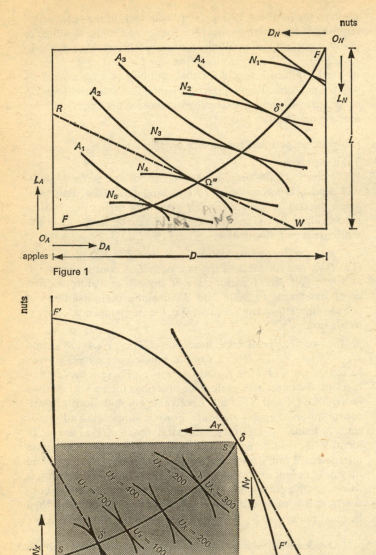

Figure 1

Figure 2

satiation-type phenomena and Veblenesque or other 'external' effects are ruled out.

4. A social welfare function, $W = W(U_X, U_Y)$, that permits a unique preference-ordering of all possible states based only on the positions of both individuals in their own preference fields. It is this function that incorporates an ethical valuation of the relative 'deservingness' of X and Y.

The problem is to determine the maximum-welfare values of labor input into apples (L_A), labor input into nuts (L_N), land input into apples (D_A), land input into nuts (D_N), of total production of apples (A) and nuts (N), and, last, of the distribution of apples and nuts between X and Y (A_X, N_X, A_Y, N_Y).

From endowments and production functions to the production-possibility curve

Construct an Edgeworth–Bowley box diagram, as in Figure 1' with horizontal and vertical dimensions just equal to the given supplies, respectively, of D and L, and plot the isoquants for apples with the south-west corner as origin and those for nuts with origin at the north-east corner. Every point in the box represents six variables, L_A, L_N, D_A, D_N, A, N. The problem of production efficiency consists in finding the locus of points where any increase in the production of apples implies a necessary reduction in the output of nuts (and vice versa). The diagram shows that locus to consist in the points of tangency between the nut and apple isoquants (FF).

From this efficiency locus we can read off the maximal obtainable combinations of apples and nuts and plot these in the output (AN) space. Given our curvature assumptions we get the smooth concave-to-the-origin Pareto-efficient production-possibility curve $F'F'$ of Figure 2.[3] This curve, a consolidation of FF in Figure 1, represents input–output configurations such that the marginal rate of substitution (MRS) of labor for land in the production of any given quantity of apples – the absolute value of the slope of the apple isoquant –

3. This presumes, also, that the intrinsic factor intensities of A and N differ. If they did not, $F'F'$ would be a straight line – a harmless special case. (See page 408.)

just equals the marginal rate of substitution of labor for land in the production of nuts.[4]

The slope (again neglecting sign) at any point on the production-possibility curve of Figure 2, in turn, reflects the marginal rate of transformation (MRT) at that point of apples into nuts. It indicates precisely how many nuts can be produced by transferring land and labor from apple to nut production (at the margin), with optimal reallocation of inputs in the production of both goods so as to maintain the MRS-equality requirement of Figure 1. It is the marginal nut-cost of an 'extra' apple – or the reciprocal of the marginal apple-cost of nuts.

From the production-possibility curve to the utility-possibility frontier

Pick any point, δ, on the production-possibility curve of Figure 2: it denotes a specific quantity of apples and nuts. Construct an Edgeworth–Bowley (trading) box with these precise dimensions by dropping from δ lines parallel to the axes as in Figure 2. Then draw in X's and Y's indifference maps, one with the south-west, the other with the north-east corner for origin. Every point in the box again fixes six variables: apples to X (A_X) and to Y (A_Y), nuts to X (N_X) and to Y (N_Y), and the 'levels' of satisfaction of X and Y as measured by the ordinal indices U_X and U_Y which characterize the position of the point with respect to the two preference fields. For example, at λ in Figure 2, $U_X = 300, U_Y = 200$. Note again, however, that this 200 is incommensurate with the 300: it does not imply that at λ X is in some sense better off than is Y (or indifferent, or worse off).

The problem of 'exchange-efficiency' consists in finding that

4. In marginal productivity terms, MRS, at any point, of labor for land in, e.g. apple production – the absolute value (drop all minus signs) of the slope of the apple isoquant (Figure 1) – is equal to

marginal physical product of land
————————————————
marginal physical product of labor

in apple production at that point. In the symbolism of the calculus

$$\left(\frac{\partial L_A}{\partial D_A}\right)_{\Delta A = 0} = \frac{\partial A/\partial D_A}{\partial A/\partial L_A}.$$

locus of feasible points within the trading box where any increase in X's satisfaction (U_X) implies a necessary reduction in the satisfaction of Y (U_Y). Feasible in what sense? In the sense that we must exhaust the fixed apple–nut totals as denoted by δ. Again, the locus turns out to consist of the points of tangency, SS, and for precisely the same analytical reasons. Only now it is the marginal subjective rate of substitution of nuts for apples in providing a fixed level of satisfaction for X – the absolute slope of X's indifference curve – that is to be equated to the nut–apple M R S of Y, to the slope, that is, of *his* indifference curve.

From this exchange-efficiency locus,[5] SS, which is associated with the single production point δ, we can now read off the maximal combinations of U_X and U_Y obtainable from δ and plot these in utility ($U_X U_Y$) space ($S'S'$, Figure 3). Each such *point* δ in output space 'maps' into a *line* in utility space – the $U_X U_Y$ mix is sensitive to how the fixed totals of apples and nuts are distributed between X and Y.[6]

There is a possible short-cut, however. Given our curvature assumptions, we can trace out the grand utility-possibility frontier – the envelope – by using an efficiency relationship to pick just one point from each trading box contract curve SS associated with every output point δ. Go back to Figure 2. The slope of the production-possibility curve at δ has already been revealed as the marginal rate of transformation, via production, of apples into nuts. The (equalized) slopes of the two sets of indifference contours along the exchange-efficiency curve SS, in turn represent the marginal rates of substitution of nuts for

5. This is Edgeworth's contract curve, or what Boulding has aptly called the 'conflict' curve – once on it, mutually advantageous trading is not possible and any move reflecting a gain to X implies a loss to Y.

6. Each *point* in utility space, in turn, maps into a line in output-space. Not just one but many possible apple–nut combinations can satisfy a specified $U_X U_Y$ requirement. It is this reciprocal point-line phenomenon that lies at the heart of Samuelson's proof of the nonexistence of community indifference curves such as would permit the derivation of demand curves for apples and nuts. The subjective 'community' M R S between A and N for given fixed A and N, e.g. at $_\delta$ in Figure 2, would surely depend on how the A and N are distributed, i.e. on which $U_X U_Y$ point on SS is chosen. Hence the slope of a 'joint' XY indifference curve at $_\delta$ is not uniquely fixed by AN.

apples for psychic indifference (the same for X as for Y). The grand criterion for efficiency is that it be impossible by any shift in production *cum* exchange to increase U_X without reducing U_Y. Careful thought will suggest that this criterion is violated unless the marginal rate of transformation between apples and nuts as outputs – the slope at δ – just equals the common marginal rate of substitution of apples and nuts, as consumption 'inputs', in providing psychic satisfaction.

If, for example, at δ one can get two apples by diverting resources and reducing nut-output by one, a point on SS where the (equalized) marginal rate of substitution of apples for nuts along indifference curves is, e.g. one to one, permits the following 'arbitrage' operation. Shift land and labor so as to produce two more apples and one less nut. Then, leaving X undisturbed take away one nut from Y and replace it by one apple. By our assumption that $MRS = 1$ both X and Y are left indifferent: U_X and U_Y remain unaltered. But we have an extra apple left over; since this permits raising U_X and/or U_Y, the initial situation was not on the $U_X U_Y$ frontier.[7]

To be on the grand utility-possibility frontier (*BB* of Figure 3), then, MRT_δ must equal the (equalized) MRS of the indifference contours along the SS associated with δ. This requirement fixes the single $U_X U_Y$ point on SS that lies on the 'envelope' utility-possibility frontier, given the output point δ. Pick that point on SS, in fact, where the joint slope of the indifference curves is exactly parallel to the slope at δ of the production-possibility curve. In Figure 2 this point is at δ', which gives the one 'efficient' $U_X U_Y$ combination associated with the *AN* mix denoted by δ. This $U_X U_Y$ combination can then be plotted as δ'' in Figure 3.[8]

Repetition of this process for each point on the production-

7. The above argument can be made perfectly rigorous in terms of the infinitesimal movements of the differential calculus.

8. Never mind, here, about multiple optima. These could occur even with our special curvature assumptions. If, for example, both sets of indifference curves show paths of equal MRS that coincide with straight lines from the origin and, further, if the two preference functions are so symmetrical as to give an SS_δ that hugs the diagonal of the trading box, then either every point an SS_δ will satisfy the $MRS = MRT$ criterion, or none will. For discussion of these related fine points see parts IV and V.

possibility curve – note that each such point requires a new trading box – will yield the grand utility-possibility frontier of Pareto-efficient input–output combinations, *BB*. Each point of

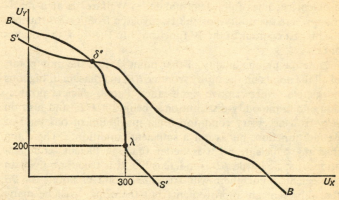

Figure 3

this frontier gives the maximum of U_X for any given feasible level of U_Y and vice versa.

From the utility-possibility frontier to the 'constrained bliss point'

But *BB*, the grand utility-possibility function, is a curve and not a point. Even after eliminating all combinations of inputs and outputs that are nonefficient in a Paretian sense, there remains a single dimensional infinity of 'efficient' combinations: one for every point on *BB*. To designate a single *best* configuration we must be given a Bergson–Samuelson social welfare function that denotes the ethic that is to 'count' or whose implications we wish to study. Such a function – could be yours, or mine, or Mossadegh's, though his is likely to be nontransitive – is intrinsically ascientific.[9] There are no considerations of *economic efficiency* that permit us to designate Crusoe's function, which calls for many apples and nuts for Crusoe and

9. Though it may provide the anthropologist or psychologist with interesting material for scientific study.

just a few for Friday, as economically superior to Friday's. Ultimate ethical valuations are involved.

Once given such a welfare function, in the form of a family of indifference contours in utility space, as in Figure 4, the problem becomes fully determinate.[10] 'Welfare' is at a maximum where the utility-possibility envelope frontier BB touches the highest contour of the W-function.[11] In Figure 4, this occurs at Ω.

Note the unique quality of that point Ω. It is the only point, of all the points on the utility frontier BB, that has unambiguous normative or prescriptive significance. Pareto-efficient production and commodity-distribution – being on $F'F'$ and also on BB – is a necessary condition for a maximum of our kind of welfare function, but is not a sufficient condition.[12] The claim that any 'efficient' point is better than 'inefficient' configurations that lie inside BB is indefensible. It is true that given an 'inefficient' point, there will exist *some* point or points on BB that represent an improvement; but there may well be many points on BB that would be worse rather than better. For example, in terms of the ethic denoted by the specific W-function of Figure 4, Ω on BB is better than any other feasible point. But the efficient point ξ is distinctly inferior to any inefficient point on or north-east of W_2. If I am X, and if my W-function, which reflects the usual dose of self-interest, is the test, 'efficient' BB points that give a high U_Y and a very low U_X are clearly less desirable than lots of inefficient points of higher U_X.[13]

10. In the absence of implicit income redistribution these curves cannot be transposed into output-space. They are not community indifference curves which would permit the derivation of demand schedules. See footnotes 6 and 13 and page 392.

11. If there are several such points, never mind. If the 'ethic' at hand is really indifferent, pick any one. If it doesn't matter, it doesn't matter.

12. Note, however, that Pareto-efficiency is not even a necessary condition for a maximum of just any conceivable W-function. The form of our type function reflects a number of ethically loaded restrictions, e.g. that individuals' preference functions are to 'count', and count positively.

13. Note, however, that no consistency requirements link my set of indifference curves with 'my' W-function. The former reflects a personal preference ordering based only on own-consumption (and, in the more general case, own services supplied). The latter denotes also values which I hold as 'citizen', and these need not be consistent with maximizing my

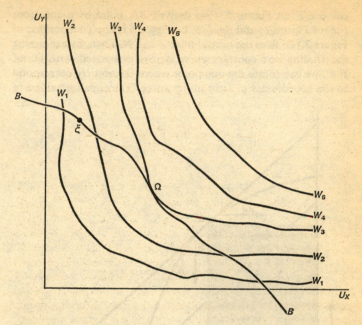

Figure 4

*From 'bliss point' to 'best' inputs, outputs and
commodity distribution*

We can now retrace our steps. To Ω on BB in Figure 4, there
corresponds just one point, Ω', on the production-possibility

---

satisfaction '*qua* consumer'. X as citizen may prefer a state of less U_X and
some U_Y to more U_X and zero U_Y. There is also an important analytical
distinction. X's preference function is conceptually 'observable': confronted
by various relative price and income configurations his consumption responses will reveal its contours. His W-function, on the other hand, is not
revealed by behavior, unless he be dictator, subjected by 'nature' to
binding constraints. In a sense only a society, considered as exhibiting
a political consensus, has a W-function subject to empirical inference
(cf. pages 392–4). The distinction – it has a Rousseauvian flavor – while
useful, is of course arbitrary. Try it for a masochist; a puritan. . . .

Francis M. Bator 381

curve $F'F'$ in Figure 5. (We derived BB, point by point, from $F'F'$ of Figure 2: and the $F'F'$ of Figure 5 is copied from that of Figure 2.) Ω' fixes the output mix: A and N. Then, by examining the trading-box contract curve $S_\Omega S_\Omega$ associated with Ω' of $F'F'$, we can locate the one point where U_X and U_Y correspond to the coordinates of Ω in utility space. The equalized slope of

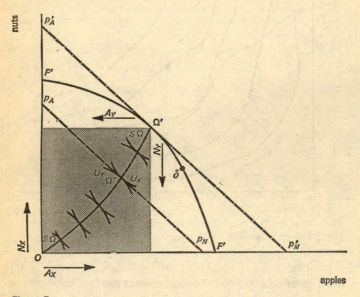

Figure 5

the indifference curves will at that point, Ω'', just equal the slope of $F'F'$ at Ω'. Ω'' fixes the apple–nut distribution implied by the maximum of W: A_X, A_Y, N_X and N_Y. Further, we cannot locate the point Ω''' on the Pareto-efficient input locus, FF of Figure 1 that corresponds to Ω' of $F'F'$. It fixes the remaining variables, the factor allocations: L_A, D_A, L_N and D_N. The maximum-welfare configuration is determinate. We have solved for the land and labor to be used in apple and nut production, for the total output of apples and nuts, and for their distribution between X and Y.

II. Prices, wages and rents

The above is antiseptically independent of institutional context, notably of competitive market institutions. It could constitute an intellectual exercise for the often invoked man from Mars, in how 'best' to make do with given resources. Yet implicit in the logic of this purely 'technocratic' formulation, embedded in the problem as it were, is a set of constants which the economist will catch himself thinking of as prices. And wisely so. Because it happens – and this 'duality' theorem is the kernel of modern welfare economics – that decentralized decisions in response to these 'prices' by, or 'as if' by, atomistic profit and satisfaction maximizers will result in just that constellation of inputs, outputs and commodity-distribution that our maximum of W requires.[14]

Can these constants – prices, wages, rents – be identified in our diagrammatic representations?[15] Only partially so. Two-dimensionality is partly at fault but, as we shall see, a final indeterminacy is implied by the usual curvature assumptions themselves.[16] The diagrams will, however, take us part way, and a little algebra will do for the rest.

The exercise consists in finding a set of four constants associated with the solution values of the maximum problem that have meaning as the price of apples (p_A), the price of nuts (p_N), the wage rate of labor (w) and the rental rate of land (r).[17]

14. Note that this statement is neutral with respect to (a) genuine profit maximizers acting in 'real' but perfectly competitive markets; (b) Lange/ Lerner-type bureaucrats ('take prices as given and maximize or Siberia'); or (c) technicians using electronic machines and trying to devise efficient computing routines.

15. To avoid institutional overtones, the theory literature usually attempts verbal disembodiment and refers to them as shadow-prices. The mathematically oriented, in turn, like to think of them as Lagrangean multipliers.

16. These very assumptions render this last indeterminacy, that of the absolute price level, wholly inconsequential.

17. Since we are still assuming that all the functions have neoclassical curvature properties, hence that, e.g. the production-possibility curve, as derived, has to be concave to the origin, we can impose the *strong* condition on the constants that they exhibit optimality characteristics for genuine, though perfect, markets. It will turn out, however, that two progressively weaker conditions are possible, which permit of some nonconvexities (e.g. increasing returns to scale), yet maintain for the constants some essentially price-like qualities. More on this in part V.

First, what can be said about w and r? Profit maximization by the individual producer implies that whatever output he may choose as most lucrative must be produced at a minimum total cost.[18] The elementary theory of the firm tells us that, for this condition to hold, the producer facing fixed input-prices – horizontal supply curves – must adjust his input mix until the marginal rate of substitution (MRS) of labor for land just equals the rent-to-wage ratio. It is easy to see the 'arbitrage' possibilities if this condition is violated. If one can substitute one unit of L for two units of D, and maintain output constant, with $w = \$10$ and $r = \$10$, it surely reduces total cost to do so and keep doing so until any further reduction in D by one unit has to be matched, if output is not to fall, by adding no less than one unit of L. In the usual diagrammatic terms, then, the producer will cling to points of tangency between the isoquants and (iso-expenditure) lines whose absolute slope equals r/w.

Reversing the train of thought, the input blend denoted by the point Ω''' in Figure 1 implies a shadow r/w ratio that just equals the MRS of labor for land in the production of both apples and nuts at that point Ω'''. $MRS_{\Omega'''}$ is given by the (equalized) slopes of the isoquants at Ω'''. The implicit r/w, therefore, must equal the slope of the line RW that is tangent to (both) the isoquants at Ω'''.[19]

The slope of RW identifies the rent: wage ratio implied by the maximal configuration. Essentially analogous reasoning will establish the equalized slope of the indifference curves through Ω'', in Figure 5, as denoting the p_A/p_N ratio implied by the solution. X, as also Y, to maximize his own satisfaction as measured by U_X, must achieve whatever level of satisfaction

18. In our flow model, unencumbered by capital, this is equivalent to producing the chosen output with minimum expenditure on inputs.

19. Again, absolute values of these slopes are implied throughout the argument. Recall from footnote 4 that the labor-for-land MRS, the absolute slope of the isoquants at Ω''' as given by RO_A/WO_A, is equal to the

$$\frac{\text{marginal physical product of land}}{\text{marginal physical product of labor}} \text{ ratio.}$$

Our shadow r/w, then, turns out to be just equal to that ratio.

his income will permit at a minimum expenditure. This requires that he choose an apple–nut mix such that the psychic marginal-rate-of-substitution between nuts and apples for indifference just equals p_A/p_N. He, and Y, will pick Ω'' only if p_A/p_N is equal to the absolute slope of the tangent (p_A/p_N) at Ω''. This slope, therefore, fixes the Ω-value of p_A/p_N.[20]

Note that this makes p_A/p_N equal to the slope also of the production-possibility curve $F'F'$ at Ω'.[21] This is as it should be. If $p_A/p_N = 10$, i.e. if one apple is 'worth' ten nuts on the market, it would be odd indeed, in our frictionlessly efficient world of perfect knowledge, if the marginal rate of transformation of nuts into apples, via production, were different from ten-to-one. Producers would not in fact produce the apple–nut combination of Ω' if p_A/p_N differed from MRT at Ω'.

We have identified the r/w and p_A/p_N implied by the maximum of W. These two constancies provide two equations to solve for the four unknown prices. Unfortunately this is as far as the two-dimensional diagrammatics will take us. None of the diagrams permit easy identification of the relationship between the input prices and the output prices. Yet such a relationship is surely implied. By the theory of the firm we know that the profit-maximizing producer facing a constant price for his product – the horizontal demand curve of the perfectly competitive firm – will expand output up to where his extra revenue for an additional unit of output, i.e. the price, just equals the marginal cost of producing that output.[22] And marginal cost, in turn, is sensitive to r and w.

It would be easy to show the implied price–wage or price–rent relationships by introducing marginal productivity notions.

20. The price-ratio relates reciprocally to the axes: $p_A/p_N = p_A\,O/p_N\,O$ in Figure 5. Along, e.g. X's indifference curve (U_X at Ω'') a rise in p_A/p_N, i.e. a steepening of $P_A\,P_N$, results in a substitution by X of nuts for apples; ditto for Y.

21. Remember, in choosing the one point on $S_\Omega S_\Omega$ that would lie on the envelope in utility space, we choose the point where the indifference curve slopes just equaled the marginal rate of transformation (see page 377).

22. Never mind here the 'total' requirement – that this price exceed unit cost – if the real-life profit-seeking producer is to produce at all. More on this in part V.

Profit maximization requires that the quantity of each input hired be increased up to the point where its marginal physical product times the price of the extra output, just equals the price of the added input. Since these marginal physical productivities are determinate curvature properties of the production functions, this rule provides a third relationship, one between an output price and an input price.

Alternatively, given our assumption that production functions show constant returns to scale, we can make use of Euler's 'product exhaustion' theorem. Its economic content is that if constant returns to scale prevails, the total as-if-market-imputed income of the factors of production just 'exhausts' the total value of the product. This means, simply, that $wL + rD = p_A A + p_N N$, and it provides a third relationship between w, r, p_A and p_N for the Ω-values of L, D, A and N.[23]

At any rate, the maximal solution implies a third price-equation, hence we can express three of the prices in terms of the fourth. But what of the fourth? This is indeterminate, given the characteristics of the model. In a frictionless world of perfect certainty, where, for example, nobody would think of holding such a thing as money, only *relative* prices matter. The three equations establish the proportions among them implied by the maximum position, and the absolute values are of no import. If the $p_A : p_N : w : r$ proportions implied by Ω are 20:15:50:75, profit and satisfaction maximizers will make the input–output–consumption decisions required for the maximum-of-W irrespective of whether the absolute levels of these prices happen to be just 20:15:50:75, or twice, or one-half, or fifty times this set of numbers. This is the implication of the fact that for the maximum problem only the various transformation and substitution *ratios* matter. In all that follows we shall simply posit that nuts are established as the unit of account, hence that

23. The condition also holds for each firm. In a competitive and constant-returns-to-scale world the profit-maximum position is one of zero profit: total revenue will just equal total cost. It should be said, however, that use of the Euler theorem to gain a relationship between input price and output price involves a measure of sleight of hand. It is only as a consequence of the relationships between price and marginal productivity (cf. the preceding paragraph) that the theorem assures equality of income with value of product.

$p_N = 1$. This then makes p_A, w and r fully determinate constants.[24]

Summarizing: we have identified diagrammatically two of the three shadow-price relationships implied by the solution to the welfare-maximum problem and have established, in a slightly more roundabout way, the existence of the third. The purpose was to demonstrate the existence, at least in our idealized neoclassical model, of a set of constants embedded in the 'technocratic' maximum-of-welfare problem, that can be viewed as competitive market prices.[25] In what sense? In the sense that decentralized decisions in response to these constants, by, or 'as if' by, atomistic profit and satisfaction maximizers will result in just that configuration of inputs, outputs and commodity-distribution that the maximum of our W requires.

III. Factor ownership and income distribution

We have said nothing, so far, of how X and Y 'pay' for their apples and nuts, or of who 'owns' and supplies the labor and the land. As was indicated above, the assumption of constant returns to scale assures that at the maximum welfare position total income will equal total value of output, and that total revenue from the sale of apples (nuts) will just equal total expenditures for inputs by the producers of apples (nuts). Also, the 'solution' implies definite 'purchase' of apples and of nuts both by X and Y. But nothing ensures that the initial 'ownership' of labor-hours and of land is such that w times the labor-hours supplied by X, wL_X, plus r times the land supplied by X, rD_X – X's income – will suffice to cover his purchases as required by Ω'', i.e. $p_A A_X + p_N N_X$; similarly for Y. There does exist some Pareto-efficient solution of inputs, outputs and distribution that satisfies the 'income = outgo' condition for both individuals for any arbitrary pattern of ownership of the 'means of production' – a solution, that is, that will place the system somewhere on the grand utility-possibility envelope frontier (BB in Figure 4). But only by the sheerest accident will that

24. For the possibility of inessential indeterminacies, however, see page 391.

25. On the existence of such a set of shadow prices in the kinky and flat-surfaced world of linear programming, see part V, below.

point on *BB* be better in terms of my *W*-function, or Thomas Jefferson's, or that of a 'political consensus', than a multi-dimensional infinity of other points *on or off BB*. As emphasized above, only one point on *BB* can have ultimate normative, prescriptive significance: Ω; and only some special ownership patterns of land and of labor-services will place a market system with an 'as imputed' distribution of income at that special point.[26]

The above is of especial interest in evaluating the optimality characteristics of market institutions in an environment of private property ownership. But the problem is not irrelevant where all nonhuman means of production are vested in the community, hence where the proceeds of non-wage income are distributed independently of marginal productivity, marginal-rate-of-substitution considerations. If labor-services are not absolutely homogeneous – if some people are brawny and dumb and others skinny and clever, not to speak of 'educated' – income distribution will be sensitive to the initial endowment of these qualities of mind and body and skill relative to the need for them. And again, only a very low probability accident would give a configuration consistent with any particular *W*-function's Ω.[27]

Even our homogeneous-labor world cannot entirely beg this issue. It is not enough to assume that producers are indifferent between an hour of X's as against an hour of Y's labor-services. It is also required that the total supply of labor-hours per accounting period be so divided between X and Y as to split

26. It is of course possible to break the link between factor ownership and 'final' income distribution by means of interpersonal transfers. Moreover, if such transfers are effected by means of costless lump-sum devices – never mind how feasible – then it is possible, in concept, to attain the Ω-implied distribution irrespective of market-imputations. But no decentralized price-market-type 'game' can reveal the pattern of taxes and transfers that would maximize a particular *W*-function. 'Central' calculation – implicit or explicit – is unavoidable.

27. If slavery were the rule and I could sell the capitalized value of my expected lifetime services, the distinction between ownership of labor and that of land would blur. Except in an 'Austrian' world, however, it would not vanish. As long as men retain a measure of control over the quality and time-shape of their own services, there will always remain an incentive problem.

total wage payments in a particular way, depending on land ownership and on the income distribution called for by Ω. This may require that X supply 75 per cent of total L; each man working $\frac{1}{2}L$ hours may well not do.[28]

But all this is diversion. For our noninstitutional purposes it is sufficient to determine the particular L_X, D_X, L_Y and D_Y that are consistent with Ω, given market-imputed, or 'as if' market-imputed, distribution. Unfortunately the diagrams used in part I again fail, but the algebra is simple. It is required that:

$$wL_X + rD_X = p_A A_X + p_N N_X,$$

and $$wL_Y + rD_Y = p_A A_Y + p_N N_Y,$$

for the already-solved-for maximal Ω-values of A_X, N_X, A_Y, N_Y, p_A, p_N, w and r. Together with $L_X + L_Y = L$ and $D_X + D_Y = D$, we appear to have four equations to solve for the four unknowns: L_X, L_Y, D_X and D_Y. It turns out, however, that one of these is not independent. The sum of the first two, that *total* incomes equal *total* value of product, is implied by Euler's theorem taken jointly with the marginal productivity conditions that give the solution for the eight variables, A_X, N_X, A_Y, ... which are here taken as known. Hence, we have only three independent equations. This is as it should be. It means only that with our curvature assumptions we can, within limits, fix one of the four endowments more or less arbitrarily and still so allocate the rest as to satisfy the household budget equations.

So much for the income-distribution aspects of the problem. These have relevance primarily for market-imputed income distribution; but such relevance does not depend on 'private' ownership of nonlabor means of production. Note, incidentally, that only with the arbitrary 'Austrian' assumption of fixed

28. All this is based on the 'Austrian' assumption that labor is supplied inelastically; further, that such inelasticity is due not to external compulsion, but rather to sharp 'corners' in the preference-fields of X and Y in relation to work–leisure choices. More than this, the W-function must not be sensitive to variations in the $L_X L_Y$ mix except as these influence income distribution.

supplies of total inputs can one first solve 'simultaneously' for inputs, outputs and commodity-distribution, and only subsequently superimpose on this solution the ownership and money-income distribution problem. If L_X, D_X, L_Y, D_Y, hence L and D were assumed sensitive to w, r, the ps and household income levels, the dimensions of the production-box of Figure 1, hence the position of the production-possibility curve of Figure 2 and 5, etc., would interdepend with the final solution values of L_X, D_X, L_Y and D_Y. We would then have to solve the full problem as a set of simultaneous equations from the raw data: production functions, tastes (this time with an axis for leisure, or many axes for many differently irksome kinds of labor), and the W-function. Three (or more) dimensional diagrams would be needed for a geometrical solution.

IV. Some extensions

We have demonstrated the solution of the maximum problem of modern welfare economics in context of the simplest statical and stationary neoclassical model. Many generalizations and elaborations suggest themselves, even if one remains strictly neoclassical and restricts oneself to a steady-state situation where none of the data change and no questions about 'how the system gets there' are permitted to intrude. To comment on just a few:

1. The problem could well be solved for many households, many goods and many factors: it has received complete and rigorous treatment in the literature. Of course the diagrammatics would not do; elementary calculus becomes essential. But the qualititative characteristics of the solution of the $m \times n \times q$ case are precisely those of the $2 \times 2 \times 2$. The same marginal rate of transformation and substitution conditions characterize the solution, only now in many directions. Nothing new or surprising happens.[29]

29. Rigorous general treatment of the $m \times n \times q$ situation does highlight a number of analytical fine points that are of interest to the pure theorist, e.g. the difficulties encountered if the number of factors exceeds the number of goods. But the qualitative economics is the same. For a full treatment from a nonnormative point of view, see Samuelson (1953–4).

2. The solution did skirt one set of difficulties that were not explicitly ruled out by assumption. We tacitly assumed that the two sets of isoquants would provide a smooth locus of 'internal' tangencies, FF, in the production box of Figure 1; similarly, that we would get such an 'internal' SS in the trading boxes of

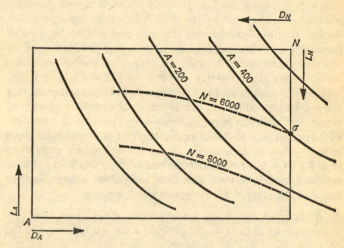

Figure 6

Figures 2 and 5. Nothing in our assumptions guarantees that this should be so. What if the locus of maximum As for given feasible Ns should occur not at points of strict tangency *inside* the box, but at what the mathematician would call corner-tangencies along the edges of the box? Figure 6 illustrates this possibility. The maximum feasible output of A, for $N = 6000$, occurs at σ, where $A = 400$; but at σ the two isoquants are not strictly tangent (they touch but have different slopes). The economic meaning of this is simple. With endowments as indicated by the dimensions of the production box in Figure 6, and with technology as denoted by the isoquants, it is not possible to reallocate inputs until the MRS of labor for land is the same in apple as in nut production. This is because apple technology (as depicted) is so land-using relative to nut production that the

$$\frac{\text{marginal productivity of land}}{\text{marginal productivity of labor}} \quad \text{ratio}$$

in apple production exceeds that in nut production even when, as at σ, *all* land is devoted to apples.

Space precludes further analysis of such corner-tangency phenomena. They reflect the possibility that the maximum-welfare solution may require that not every input be used in producing every output (e.g. no land in nut production or no brain surgeons in coal mining), and may even render one of the inputs a 'free good' (so that its total use will not add up to the total available supply). Let it suffice to assert that by formulating the maximum conditions, not in terms of *equalities* of various slopes, but rather in terms of *inequalities*; by explicit statement of the proper second-order 'rate-of-change-of-slope' conditions and by allowing inequalities in the factor-balance conditions (e.g. $L_A + L_N \geqslant L$), such phenomena of bumping into the axes can be handled; further, that only inessential indeterminacies occur in the implied shadow-price configuration.[30]

3. We stressed, above, the nonexistence of *community* indifference contours such as would provide a unique ranking, for the

30. All this can perhaps be made clearer by two examples. The essential requirement for $A\sigma$, to be at a maximum for $N = 6000$ is that the intersection at the boundary be as in Figure 6 rather than as in Figure 7. In the latter, σ' gives a minimum of A for $N = 6000$; the true maximum is at σ''. The distinction between σ in Figure 6 and σ' in Figure 7 is between the relative rates of change of the two MRSs. The price indeterminacy implied by the maximum, i.e. the fact that σ is consistent with an r/w that lies anywhere between the two isoquants, turns out to be inessential. A second example concerns the theory of the firm. It has been argued that if the marginal cost curve has vertical gaps and the price-line hits one of these gaps, then the $MC = p$ condition is indeterminate, hence that the theory is no good. As has been pointed out in the advanced literature (e.g. by Bishop, 1948) this is incorrect: what is important is that at smaller than equilibrium output MC be less than price and at higher outputs MC exceed price. It is true, but quite harmless to the theory, that such a situation does leave a range of indeterminacy in the price that will elicit *that* level of output. Such phenomena do change the mathematics of computation. Inequalities cannot in general be used to eliminate unknowns by simple substitution. On all this, see the literature of linear programming (e.g. Dorfman, 1953; Dorfman, Solow and Samuelson, 1958; Koopmans, 1951; Samuelson, 1949).

community as a whole, of various output combinations (see footnote 6). Individual marginal rates of substitution between, e.g. apples and silk shirts, equalized along a trading-box contract curve to give a 'community' MRS, are likely to be sensitive to the distribution of income[31] between gourmets and

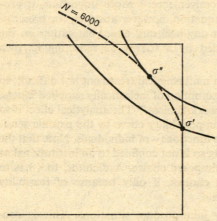

Figure 7

dandies; accordingly, community MRS at a given point in commodity space, i.e. the slope of a curve of community indifference, will vary with movements along the associated utility-possibility curve. However, once the most desirable $U_X U_Y$ combination for a given package of A and N is fixed, MRS at that AN-point becomes determinate. It follows, as recently pointed out and proved by Samuelson (1956), that if the observed community continuously redistributes 'incomes' in Utopian lump-sum fashion so as to maximize, in utility space, over the W-function implied by a political consensus, then there does exist, in output space, a determinate *social* indifference function which provides a ranking for the community as a whole of all conceivable output combinations. This function, which yields conventionally convex social indifference contours, can be treated as though a single mind were engaged in maximizing it. Moreover, in concept and if granted the

31. In terms of abstract purchasing power.

premise of continuous redistribution, its contours are subject to empirical inference from observed price-market data.

This existence theorem justifies the use of *social* indifference maps – maps 'corrected' for distribution – in handling problems of production efficiency, international trade, etc. – a substantial analytical convenience.[32] More important, it provides a conceptual foundation, however abstract, for prescription based not on just any arbitrary ethic, but rather on the particular ethic revealed by a society as reflecting its own political consensus.[33]

4. It is useful, and in a mathematical treatment not difficult, to drop the 'Austrian' assumption of inelastically supplied inputs, and introduce leisure–work choices.[34] The analytical effect is to sensitize the production-possibility curve to the psychic sensibilities – the preference functions – of individuals. Note that the empirical sense of doing so is not confined to an institutional or ethical context of nonimposed choice. A dictator, too, has to take account of such choices, if only because of feasibility limitations on coercion.

5. We assumed away joint-product situations. This is convenient for manipulation but hardly essential; the results can be generalized to cover most kinds of jointness. It turns out, in fact, that in dynamical models with capital stocks, one means for taking account of the durability of such stocks is to allow for joint products. A process requiring a hydraulic press 'produces' both stamped metal parts and a 'one-year-older' hydraulic press.

32. Note, however, that none of this eliminates the need for a *W*-function: social indifference contours are a convex function of individual taste patterns of the usual ordinal variety taken jointly with an implicit or explicit *W*-function of 'regular' content and curvature. Further, no ultimate superiority attaches to the *W*-function implied by a particular political consensus. One may disapprove of the power relationships on which such consensus rests, etc.

33. Needless to say, feasibility is not here at issue. Even on this level of abstraction, however, matters become much more difficult once account is taken of the fact that the world is not stationary.

34. If we assume only one commodity, say apples, and replace the second good by leisure (or by negative labor input); and if we let the second-good production function be a simple linear relation, our previous geometry will portray the simplest goods-leisure situation.

6. In our system the distinction between inputs (L, D) and outputs (A, N) could be taken for granted. But the distinction is clear only in a world of completely vertically integrated producers, all hiring 'primary' nonproduced inputs and producing 'final' consumable goods and services. In a Leontief-like system that allows for interproducer transactions and intermediate products, many outputs, electricity, steel, corn, beef, trucks, etc., are simultaneously inputs. It is of interest, and also feasible, to generalize the analysis to take account of, for example, coal being used not only to heat houses, but to produce steel required in the production of mining machines designed for the production of coal. Moreover, none of the essential qualitative characteristics of our maximum problem is violated by such generalization.[35]

7. What if instead of assuming that production functions show constant returns to scale, we permit diminishing returns to proportional expansion of inputs? This could be due either to inherent nonlinearities in the physics and topography of the universe, or to the existence of some unaccounted-for but significant input in limited, finite-elastic supply.[36]

35. Analytically, this is done by designating all produced goods as X_1, X_2, X_3,.... The gross production of, for example, X_1, has two kinds of uses: it is partly used up as an input in the production of X_2, X_3,..., and perhaps of X_1 (the automobile industry is a major user of automobiles). What remains is available for household consumption. The production functions have Xs on the right- as well as the left-hand side.

36. If output varies as the surface area of some solid body and 'input' as its cubic-volume, a doubling of input will less than double output – this is an example of the first kind. A typical example of the second is the instance where the production function for fishing does not include an axis for the 'amount' of lake, hence where beyond a certain point doubling of man-hours, boats, etc. less than doubles the output. There is a slightly futile literature on whether the first kind could or could not exist without some element of the second. If *every* input is really doubled, so say the proponents of one view, output *must* double. The very vehemence of the assertion suggests the truth, to wit, that it is conceptually impossible to disprove it by reference to empirical evidence. Luckily, the distinction is not only arbitrary – it depends on what one puts on the axes of the production-function diagram and what is built into the curvature of the production surface; it is also quite unimportant. One can think of the phenomenon as one will – nothing will change.

Diminishing returns to scale, as distinct from increasing returns, does not give rise to serious trouble, either for the analytical solubility of the system, or for the market-significance of the intrinsic price–wage–rent constants. It does introduce some ambiguities, however. For one thing, the 'value' of output will exceed the total of market-imputed income. This makes intuitive sense in terms of the 'unaccounted-scarce-factor' explanation of decreasing returns; the residual unimputed value of output reflects the income 'due' the 'hidden' factor. If that factor were treated explicitly and given an axis in the production-function diagram, returns would no longer diminish – since, on this view, the relative inexpansibility of that input gave rise to decreasing returns to scale to begin with – and the difficulty would vanish.[37]

In a market context, this suggests the explicit introduction of firms as distinct from industries. In our constant-returns-to-scale world the number of apple- or nut-producing firms could be assumed indeterminate. Every firm could be assumed able to produce any output up to A_Ω (or N_Ω) at constant unit cost. In fact, if we had a convenient way of handling incipient monopoly behavior, such as by positing frictionless entry of new firms, we could simply think of one giant firm as producing all the required apples (nuts). Such a firm would be compelled, nevertheless, to behave as though it were an 'atomistic' competitor, i.e. prevented from exploiting the tilt in the demand curve, by incipient competitors ready instantaneously to jump into the fray at the slightest sign of profit.

It is, however, natural, at least in a context of market institutions, to think of decreasing returns to scale, as associated with the qualitatively and quantitatively scarce entrepreneurial entity that defines the firm but is not explicitly treated as an input. Then, as apple production expands, relatively less efficient entrepreneurs are pulled into production – the total cost curve of the 'last' producer and the associated shadow price of apples become progressively higher – and the intramarginal firms make 'profits' due directly to the scarcity value of the entrepreneurial

37. The fact that the 'hidden scarce factor' view is heuristically useful does not, however, strengthen its pretension to status as a hypothesis about reality.

qualities of their 'entrepreneurs'. The number of firms, their inputs and outputs, are determinate. The last firm just breaks even at the solution-value of the shadow-price.[38]

At any rate, no serious damage is done to the statical system by decreasing returns to scale. When it is a matter of actually computing a maximum problem the loss of linearity is painful, but the trouble is in the mathematics.[39]

8. There is one kind of complication that does vitiate the results. We have assumed throughout that there exists no *direct* interaction among producers, among households, and between producers and households – that there are no (nonpecuniary) external economies or diseconomies of production and consumption. The assumption is reflected in four characteristics of the production functions and the preference functions:

(a) The output of apples was assumed uniquely determined by the quantities of land and labor applied to apple production – A was assumed insensitive to the inputs and outputs of the nut industry; similarly for nuts. This voids the possibility that the apple production function might shift as a consequence of movements along the nut production function, i.e. that for given D_A and L_A, A may vary with N, L_N and D_N. The stock example of such a 'technological external economy' (or diseconomy) is the beekeeper whose honey output will increase, other things equal, if the neighboring apple producer expands *his* output (hence his apple blossom 'supply').[40] The very

38. More precisely, the 'next' firm in line could not break even. This takes care of discontinuity.

39. It should perhaps be repeated, however, that there remains considerable ambiguity about how the imbalance between income and outlay in decreasing-returns-to-scale situations is best treated in a general equilibrium setup.

40. The other type of externality treated in the neoclassical literature, the type Jacob Viner labeled 'pecuniary', does not in itself affect the results. It consists in sensitivity of input prices to industry output, though not to the output of single firms. External pecuniary economies (as distinct from diseconomies) do, however, signal the existence of either *technological* external economies of the sort discussed here, or of internal economies among supplier firms. These last reflect increasing returns to scale along production functions – a most troublesome state discussed at length in part V.

pastoral quality of the example suggests that in a statical context such direct interaction among producers – interaction that is not reflected by prices – is probably rare. To the extent that it does exist, it reflects some 'hidden' inputs or outputs (e.g. apple blossoms), the benefits or costs of which are not (easily) appropriated by market institutions.

It should be emphasized that the assertion that such phenomena are empirically unimportant is defensible only if we rule out nonreversible dynamical phenomena. Once we introduce changes in knowledge, for example, or investment in changing the quality of the labor force via training, 'external' effects become very important indeed.[41] But on our stratospheric level of abstraction such considerations are out of order.

(b) The 'happiness' of X, as measured by U_X, was assumed uniquely determined by his own consumption of apples and nuts. He was permitted no sensitivity to his neighbor's (Y's) consumption, and vice versa. This rules out not only Veblenesque 'keeping up with . . .' effects, but such phenomena as Y tossing in sleepless fury due to X's 'consumption' of midnight television shows; or X's temperance sensibilities being outraged by Y's quiet and solitary consumption of Scotch. Nobody with experience of a 'neighborhood' will argue that such things are illusory, but it is not very fruitful to take account of them in a formal maximizing setup.[42]

(c) X and Y were assumed insensitive, also, to the input–output configuration of producers, except as this affected consumption choices. Insensitivity to the allocation of their own working time is subsumed in the 'Austrian' assumption, but more is

41. The full 'benefits' of most changes in 'knowledge', of most 'ideas', are not easily captured by the originator, even with strong patent and copyright protection. If, then, the energy and resources devoted to 'creating new knowledge' are sensitive to private cost–benefit calculation, some potential for social gain may well be lost because such calculation will not correctly account for cost and benefit to society at large. All this is complicated by the peculiarity of 'knowledge' as a scarce resource: unlike most other scarcities, just because there is more for you there is not necessarily less for me. As for training of labor: the social benefit accrues over the lifetime services of the trainee; the private benefit to the producer accrues until the man quits to go to work for a competitor.

42. For an important exception, however, see footnote 43.

required. Y's wife must not be driven frantic by factory soot, nor X irritated by an 'efficiently' located factory spoiling his view.

(d) There is still a fourth kind of externality: X's satisfaction may be influenced not only by his own job but by Y's as well. Many values associated with job-satisfaction – status, power and the like – are sensitive to one's *relative* position, not only as consumer, but as supplier of one's services in production. The 'Austrian' assumption whereby U_X and U_Y are functions only of consumption possibilities, voids this type of interaction also.

Could direct interaction phenomena be introduced into a formal maximizing system, and if so, at what cost? As regards the analytical solubility of some maximum-of-W problem, there is no necessary reason why not. The mathematics of proving the existence or nonexistence of a 'solution', or of a unique and stable 'solution', or the task of devising a computational routine that will track down such a solution should one exist, may become unmanageable. But the problem need not be rendered meaningless by such phenomena.

Unfortunately that is saying very little indeed, except on the level of metaphysics. Those qualities of the system that are of particular interest to the economist – (i) that the solution implies a series of 'efficiency conditions', the Pareto marginal-rate-of-substitution conditions, which are necessary for the maximum of a wide variety of W-functions, and (ii) that there exists a correspondence between the optimal values of the variables and those generated by a system of (perfect) market institutions *cum* redistribution – those qualities are apt either to blur or vanish with 'direct interaction'. Most varieties of such interaction destroy the 'duality' of the system: the constants embedded in the maximum problem, if any, lose significance as prices, wages, rents. They will not correctly account for all the 'costs' and 'benefits' to which the welfare function in hand is sensitive.[43]

43. It should not be concluded, however, that the different types of direct interaction are all equally damaging. All will spoil market performance, almost by definition; but some, at least, permit of formal maximizing treatment such as will yield efficiency conditions analogous to those of part I – conditions that properly account for full social costs and benefits. So-called 'public goods', e.g. national defense, which give rise to direct interaction

In general, then, most formal models rule out such phenomena. There is no doubt that by so doing they abstract from some important aspects of reality. But theorizing consists in just such abstraction; no theory attempts to exhaust all of reality. The question of what kinds of very real complications to introduce into a formal maximizing setup has answers only in terms of the strategy of theorizing or in terms of the requirements of particular and concrete problems. For many purposes it is useful and interesting to explore the implications of maximizing in a 'world' where no such direct interactions exist.

V. Relaxing the curvature assumptions: kinks and nonconvexities

None of the above qualifications and generalizations violate the fundamentally neoclassical character of the model. What happens if we relinquish some of the nice curvature properties of the functions?

1. We required that the production functions and the indifference curves have well-defined and continuous curvatures – no sharp corners or kinks such as cause indeterminacy in marginal rates of substitution. Such smooth curvatures permit the use of the calculus, hence are mathematically convenient for larger than $2 \times 2 \times 2$ models. They are, however, not essential to the economic content of the results. The analysis has been translated – and in part independently re-invented – for a world of flat-faced, sharp-cornered, production functions: linear programming, more formally known as activity analysis, is the resulting body of theory.[44] All the efficiency conditions have their counterparts in such a system, and the existence of implicit

since by definition their consumption is joint – more for X means not less but more for Y – are an important example. Maximizing yields MRS conditions that bear intriguing correspondence to those which characterize ordinary private-good situations. But these very MRS conditions serve to reveal the failure of duality. [Samuelson's is again the original and definitive treatment (1954, 1955).]

44. Isoquants in such a setup consist of linearly additive combinations of processes, each process being defined as requiring absolutely fixed input and output proportions. This gives isoquants that look like that in Figure 8(c).

'prices' embedded in the maximum problem is, if anything, even more striking.[45]

2. Easing of the neoclassical requirement that functions be smooth is not only painless; in the development of analytical economics it has resulted in exciting new insights. Unfortunately, however, the next step is very painful indeed. In our original assumptions we required that returns to scale for proportional expansion of inputs be constant (or at least non-increasing) and that isoquants and indifference curves be 'convex to the origin'. These requirements guarantee a condition that the mathematicians call *convexity*. The violation of this condition, as by allowing increasing returns to scale in production – due, if you wish, to the inherent physics and topography of the universe or to lumpiness and indivisibilities – makes for serious difficulties.

The essence of convexity, a concept that plays a crucial role in mathematical economics, is rather simple. Take a single isoquant such as *MM* in Figure 8 (a). It denotes the minimum

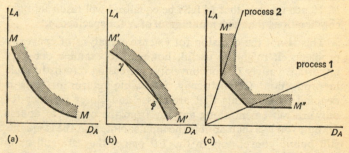

Figure 8

inputs of *L* and *D* for the production of a hundred apples, hence it is just the boundary of all technologically feasible input combinations that can produce one hundred apples. Only points on *MM* are both feasible and technologically *efficient*, but any point within the shaded region is *feasible*: nobody can prevent me from wasting *L* or *D*. On the other hand, no point

45. A little diagrammatic experimentation will show that the geometric techniques of part I remain fully adequate.

on the origin side of *MM* is feasible for an output of one hundred apples: given the laws of physics, etc., it is impossible to do better. *Mathematical convexity obtains if a straight line connecting any two feasible points does not anywhere pass outside the set of feasible points.* A little experimentation will show that such is the case in Figure 8(a). In Figure 8(b), however, where the isoquant is of 'queer' curvature – MRS of *L* for *D* increases – the line connecting, for example, the feasible points γ and ϕ does pass outside the 'feasible' shaded area. Note, incidentally, that an isoquant of the linear programming variety, as in Figure 8(c), is 'convex' – this is why the generalization of (1) above was painless.[46]

What kind of trouble does nonconvexity create? In the case of concave-to-the-origin isoquants, i.e. nonconvex isoquants, the difficulty is easy to see. Look back at Figure 1 and imagine that the old nut-isoquants are really those of apple producers, hence oriented to the south-west, and vice versa for nuts. Examination of the diagram will show that the locus of tangencies, *FF*, is now a locus of minimum combinations of *A* and *N*. Hence the rule that MRSs be equalized will result in input combinations that give a minimum of *N* for specified *A*.[47]

3. This is not the occasion for extensive analysis of convexity problems. It might be useful, however, to examine one very important variety of nonconvexity: increasing returns to scale in production. Geometrically, increasing returns to scale is denoted by isoquants that are closer and closer together for outward movement along any ray from the origin: to double output, you less than double the inputs. Note that the isoquants still bound convex sets in the *LD* plane (they are still as in Figure 8a). But in the third or output dimension of a two-input, one-output production surface, slices by vertical planes through

46. It is important not to confuse mathematical convexity with curvature that appears 'convex to the origin'. Mathematical convexity is a property of *sets* of points, and the set of feasible output points bounded by a production-possibility curve, for instance, is convex if and only if the production-possibility curve itself is *'concave* to the origin' (or a straight line). Test this by the rule which defines convexity.

47. A minimum, that is, subject to the requirement that no input be 'wasted' from an engineering point of view, i.e. that each single producer be on the production function as given by the engineer.

the origin perpendicular to *LD* will cut the production surface in such a way as to give a boundary such as *VV* in Figure 9. It is evident that *VV* bounds a nonconvex set of feasible points, so the full three-dimensional set of feasible input–output points is not convex.

The effect of such nonconvexity in input–output space can be classified with respect to its possible implications for (a) the

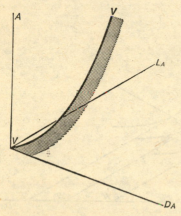

Figure 9

slopes of producers' average cost (AC) curves; (b) for the slopes of marginal cost (MC) curves; (c) for the curvature of the production-possibility curve.

Increasing returns toale and AC curves

It is a necessary consequence of increasing returns to scale that at the maximal configuration of inputs, outputs and input prices, producers' AC curves decline with increasing output. By the definition of increasing returns to scale at a given point τ of a production function, successive isoquants in the neighborhood of τ lie closer and closer together for movement 'northeast' along the ray from the origin through τ (Z in Figure 10). As Figure 10 is drawn, the ray Z happens also to correspond to an expansion path for the particular r/w ratio denoted by the family of isocost lines $R'W'$: each $R'W'$ is tangent to an isoquant along Z. Given $r/w = |$ tangent $\theta|$, a profit-maximizing apple producer will calculate his minimum total cost for various levels of output from input–output points along Z. But along Z the equal cost $R'W'$ tangents in the neighborhood of τ lie closer and closer together for increasing output, as do the isoquants.

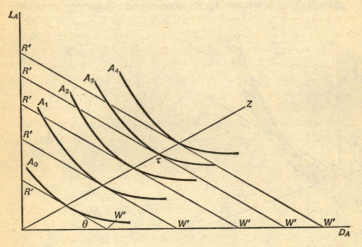

Figure 10

This implies that the increase in total cost for equal successive increments in output declines. *Ergo*, the AC curve at τ for $r/w = |$ tangent $\theta|$ must be falling.

Suppose the expansion path for $r/w = |$ tangent $\theta|$ happened not to correspond to the ray Z, but only to cross it at τ. The intersection of A_4 with Z would not then mark the minimum-cost input-mix for an output of A_4, hence the increase in minimized total cost between A_3 and A_4 would be even less than in Figure 10: the negative effect on AC would be reinforced. The point is, simply, that if for movement along a ray from the origin cost per unit of output declines, AC will decline even more should production at minimized total cost call for changes in the input-mix, i.e. departure from the ray Z.

What, then, if the maximum-of-W input–output combination

required of this particular producer is denoted by the point τ? It has just been shown that AC at τ is falling. A falling AC implies a marginal cost curve that lies *below* the average. But if τ is the Ω'''-point, the shadow-p_A will just equal MC of τ. It follows that the maximum-of-W configuration requires $p_A < AC$, i.e. perpetual losses. Losses, however, are incompatible with real life (perfect) markets; hence where increasing returns to scale prevails correspondence between market-directed and W-maximizing allocation fails. In an institutional context where producers go out of business if profits are negative, markets will not do.[48]

Increasing returns to scale has also a 'macro' consequence that is associated with $p < AC$. For constant returns to scale, we cited Euler's theorem as assuring that total factor incomes will just equal total value of output. In increasing-returns-to-scale situations, total imputed factor incomes will exceed the total value of output: $rD + wL > p_A A + p_N N$.[49]

Increasing returns to scale and MC curves

Where nonconvexity of the increasing-returns-to-scale variety results in falling AC curves, real-life (perfect) markets will fail. What of a Lange–Lerner Socialist bureaucracy, where each civil-servant plant-manager is instructed to maximize his algebraic profits in terms of centrally quoted 'shadow' prices regardless of losses? Will such a system find itself at the maximum-of-W configuration?

It may or may not. If AC is to fall, MC must lie below AC, but at the requisite Ω-output, MCs may nevertheless be rising, as for example at ϵ in Figure 11. If so, a Lange–Lerner bureaucracy making input and output decisions as atomistic 'profit-maximizing' competitors but ignoring losses will make the 'right' decisions, i.e. will 'place' the system at the maximum-of-W. Each manager equating his marginal cost to the centrally

48. Needless to say, comments on market effectiveness, throughout this paper, bear only on the analogue-computer aspects of price-market systems. This is a little like talking about sexless men, yet it is surely of interest to examine such systems viewed as mechanisms pure and simple.

49. The calculus-trained reader can test this for, say, a Cobb–Douglas type function $A = L_A^{\alpha} D_A^{\beta}$, with $(\alpha + \beta) > 1$ to give increasing returns to scale.

quoted shadow price given out by the maximum-of-W solution, will produce precisely the output required by the Ω-configuration. By the assumption of falling A Cs due to increasing returns to scale either one or both industries will show losses, but these are irrelevant to optimal allocation.[50]

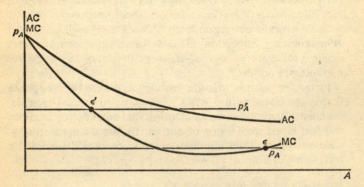

Figure 11

What if for a maximum-of-W producers are required to produce at points such as ϵ', where $p = MC$ but MC is declining?[51] The fact that ϵ' shows $AC > MC = p$, hence losses, has been dealt with above. But more is involved. By the assumption of a falling MC curve, the horizontal price line at ϵ' cuts the MC curve from below, hence profit at ϵ' is not only negative: it is at a *minimum*. A 'real-life' profit maximizer would certainly not remain there: he would be losing money by

50. There is an ambiguity of language in the above formulation. If at the maximum-of-W configuration losses prevail, the maximum profit position 'in the large' will be not at $p = MC$ but at zero output. Strictly speaking, a Lange–Lerner bureaucracy must be instructed to equate marginal cost to price or profit-maximize 'in the small' without regard to the absolute value of profit. 'Make any continuous sequence of small moves that increase algebraic profits, but do not jump to the origin.' It is precisely the ruling-out of the zero-output position, unless called for by $MC > p$ everywhere, that distinguishes Lange–Lerner systems from 'real-life' perfect markets, both viewed as 'analogue computers'.

51. This would necessarily be the case, for instance, with Cobb–Douglas type increasing-returns-to-scale functions. Such functions imply ever-falling MC curves, for whatever r/w ratio.

the minute. But neither would a Lange–Lerner bureaucrat under instruction to maximize algebraic profits. He would try to increase his output: 'extra' revenue (p_A) would exceed his MC by more and more for every additional apple produced. In this case, then, not only would real life markets break down; so would simple-minded decentralized maximizing of profits by socialist civil servants.[52]

Paradoxically enough, the correct rule for all industries whose MC is falling at the Ω-point is: 'minimize your algebraic profits'. But no such rule can save the decentralized character of the Lange–Lerner scheme. In a 'convex' world the simple injunction to maximize profits in response to centrally quoted prices, together with raising (lowering) of prices by the responsible 'ministries' according to whether supply falls short of (exceeds) demand, is all that is needed.[53] Nobody has to know *ex ante*, for example, the prices associated with the Ω-point. In fact the scheme was devised in part as a counter to the view that efficient allocation in a collectivized economy is impossible due simply to the sheer administrative burden of calculation. With increasing returns to scale however, the central authority must evidently know where MCs will be falling, where rising: it must know, before issuing any instructions at all about the solution.

Increasing returns to scale and the production-possibility curve

What is left of 'duality'? Real-life markets and unsophisticated Lange–Lerner systems have both failed. Yet it is entirely possible, even in situations where the Ω-constellation implies AC > MC with declining MC, that the maximizing procedure of part I remains inviolate, and that the constants embedded in the maximum problem retain the price-like significance. To see this we must examine the effect of increasing returns to scale on the production-possibility curve. There are two possible cases:

52. Note that a falling MC curve is simply a reflection of nonconvexity in the total cost curve.

53. Not quite all. Even in a statical context, the lump-sum income transfers called for by Ω require central calculation. And if adjustment paths are explicitly considered, complex questions about the stability of equilibrium arise (e.g. will excess demand always be corrected by raising price?)

1. It is possible for both the apples and the nut production function to exhibit increasing returns to scale, yet for the implied production possibility curve to be concave to the origin, i.e. mathematically convex (as in Figure 2). While a proportional expansion of L_A and D_A by a factor of two would more than double apple output, an increase in A at the expense of N will, in general, not take place by means of such proportional expansion of inputs. Examination of FF in Figure 1 makes this clear for the constant-returns-to-scale case. As we move from any initial point on FF toward more A and less N, the L_A/D_A and L_N/D_N proportions change.[54]

The point is that if, as in Figure 1, land is important relative to labor in producing apples, and vice versa for nuts, expansion of apple production will result in apple producers having to use more and more of the relatively nut-prone input, labor, in proportion to land. Input proportions in apple production become less 'favorable'. The opposite is true of the input proportions used in nuts as nut production declines. This phenomenon explains why with constant returns to scale in both functions the production-possibility curve shows concave-to-the-origin curvature. Only if FF in Figure 1 coincides with the diagonal: i.e. if the intrinsic 'usefulness' of L and D is the same in apple production as in nut production, will $F'F'$ for constant returns to scale be a straight line.

The above argument by proportions remains valid if we now introduce a little increasing returns to scale in both functions by 'telescoping' each isoquant successively farther towards the origin. In fact, as long as the FF curve has shape and curvature as in Figure 1, the production-possibility curve, $F'F'$ in Figures 2 and 5, will retain its convexity.

In this 'mild' case of increasing returns to scale, with a still convex production-possibility curve, the previous maximizing rules give the correct result for a maximum-of-W. Further, the constants embedded in the maximum problem retain their meaning. This is true in two senses: (a) They still reflect marginal rates of substitution and transformation. Any package

54. Only if FF should coincide with the diagonal of the box will proportions not change. The increasing returns to scale would necessarily imply an inward-bending production-possibility curve.

of L, D, A and N worth \$1 will, *at the margin*, be just convertible by production and exchange into any other package worth \$1, no more, no less: a dollar is a dollar is a dollar. . . .[55] (b) The total value of maximum-welfare 'national' output: $p_A A + p_N N$, valued at these shadow-price constants, will itself

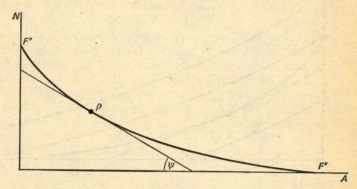

Figure 12

be at a maximum. A glance at Figure 5 makes this clear: at the price-ratio denoted by the line $p'_A p'_N$, Ω' is the point of highest output-value. As we shall see, this correspondence between the maximum welfare and 'maximum national product' solutions is an accident of convexity.

2. It is of course entirely possible that both production functions exhibit sufficiently increasing returns to scale to give, for specified totals of L and D, a production-possibility curve such as $F''F''$ in Figure 12.[56] This exhibits nonconvexity in output space. What now happens to the results?

If the curvature of $F''F''$ is not 'too sharp', the constants given out by the maximum-of-W problem retain their 'dollar is a dollar' meaning. They still reflect marginal rates of substitution in all directions. But maximum W is no longer associated with shadow-value of output. A glance at Figure 12 confirms our geometric intuition that in situations of non-convex production possibilities the bliss point coincides with a minimized

55. For the infinitesimal movements of the calculus.
56. Try two functions which are not too dissimilar in 'factor intensity'.

value-of-output. At the prices implied, as denoted by $|\tan \psi|$, the assumed Ω-point ρ is a point of minimum $p_A A + p_N N$.[57]

But with nonconvexity in output space, matters could get much more complicated. If the production-possibility curve is

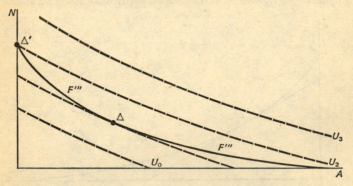

Figure 13

sharply concave outward, relative to the indifference curves, it may be that the 'minimize-profits' rule would badly mislead, even if both industries show declining MCs. Take a one-person situation such as in Figure 13. The production-possibility curve $F'''F'''$ is more inward-bending then the indifference curves (U), and the point of tangency Δ is a point of *minimum* satisfaction. Here, unlike above, you should rush away from Δ. The maximum welfare position is at Δ' – a 'corner tangency' is involved. The point is that in nonconvex situations *relative* curvatures are crucial: tangency points may as well be minima as maxima.[58]

57. For $p_A/p_N = |\text{tangent } \psi|$, $(p_A A + p_N N)$ is at its maximum at the intersection of $F''F''$ with the A-axis. Recall, incidentally that, in situations of falling MC producers were required to *minimize* profits.

58. Recall that in our discussion of part IV corner-tangencies were important in situations where no feasible internal tangencies existed. Here there exist perfectly good and feasible internal tangencies – but they are loci of minima rather than maxima. The second-order conditions, expressed as inequalities, constitute the crucial test of optimal allocation.

It is tempting, but a mistake, to think that there is a unique correspondence between the curvature of the production-possibility curve, and the

So much for nonconvexity. In its mildest form, if isoquants and indifference curves retain their normal curvature and only returns to scale 'increase', nonconvexity need not violate the qualitative characteristics of the maximum-of-W problem. The marginal-rate-of-substitution conditions may well retain their validity, and the solution still could give out a set of shadow prices, decentralized responses to which result in the maximal configuration of inputs, outputs and commodity distribution. But certain nonmarginal *total* conditions for effective real-life market functioning, e.g. that all producers have at least to break even, are necessarily violated. The shortcoming is in market institutions: the maximum-of-W solution requires such 'losses'. The important moral is that where increasing returns to scale obtains, an idealized price system is not an effective way to raise money to cover costs. It may, however, still be an effective device for the rationing of scarcities.[59]

---

relative slopes of the nut and apple MC curves. It is true that the MC_A/MC_N ratio associated with a point such as Ω' in Figure 5 must be smaller than MC_A/MC_N at any point of *more A* and *less N* on $F'F'$ (e.g. $_\delta$): the absolute slope of $F'F'$ has been shown to equal $p_A/p_N = MC_A/MC_N$, and at Ω' the slope is less steep than at $_\delta$. It is also true that along a nonconvex production-possibility curve, such as that of Figure 12, an increase in A and a decrease in N are associated with a *decline* in MC_A/MC_N. But it does not follow, e.g. in the first case of Figure 5, that at Ω' MC_A must be rising for an increase in A sufficiently to offset a possibly falling MC_N. (Remember, in moving from Ω' to $_\delta$ we move to the right along the A-axis but to the left along the N-axis.) For any departure from Ω' will, in general, involve a change in input shadow-prices, hence *shifts* in the MC curves, while the slopes of the curves at Ω' were derived from a total cost curve calculated on the basis of the given, constant, Ω-values of w and r. The point is that cost curves are partial-equilibrium creatures, evaluated at *fixed* prices, while movement along a production-possibility curve involves a general-equilibrium adjustment that will *change* input prices. Hence it is entirely possible that at say Ω', in Figure 5, both MC_N and MC_A are falling, though $F'F'$ is convex.

59. No mention has been made of the case that is perhaps most interesting from an institutional point of view: production functions that show increasing returns to scale initially, then decreasing returns as output expands further. No profit-seeking firm will produce in the first stage, where AC is falling, and A_Ω and N_Ω may only require one or a few firms producing in the second stage. If so, the institutional conditions for perfect competition, very many firms, will not exist. One or a few firms of 'efficient' scale will exhaust

VI. Dynamics

We have examined in some detail what conditions on the allocation and distribution of inputs and outputs can be derived from the maximization of a social welfare function which obeys certain restrictions (see footnote 12). We have done so, however, using a statical mode of analysis and having ignored all the 'dynamical' aspects of the problem. To charge that such statical treatment is 'unrealistic' is to miss, I think, the essential meaning and uses of theorizing. It is true, however, that such treatment buries many interesting problems – problems, moreover, some of which yield illuminating insight when subjected to rigorous analysis. Full dynamical extension is not possible here, but some indication of the directions which such extension might take is perhaps warranted:

1. The perceptive reader will have noticed that very little was said about the dimensions of A, N, L_A, D_A, L_N and D_N. The static theory of production treats outputs and inputs as instantaneous time rates, 'flows' – apples per day, labor-hours per week, etc. This ignores the elementary fact that in most production processes outputs and the associated inputs, and the various inputs themselves, are not simultaneous. Coffee plants take five years to grow, ten-year-old brandy has to age ten years, inputs in automobile manufacture have to follow a certain sequence, it takes time to build a power station and a refinery (no matter how abundantly 'labor and land' are applied). One dynamical refinement of the analysis, then, consists in 'dating' the inputs and resultant outputs of the production functions, relative to each other. In some instances only the ordinal sequence is of interest; in others absolute elapsed time, too, matters – plaster has to dry seven days before the first coat of paint is applied.

2. Another characteristic of production, on this planet at least, is that service flows are generated by stocks of physical things which yield their services only through time. Turret-lathe operations can be generated only by turret-lathes and these have

---

the market. This phenomenon lies at the heart of the monopoly–oligopoly problem.

congealed in them service flows which cannot be exhausted instantaneously but only over time. In a descriptive sense, a turret-lathe's services of today are 'joint' and indivisible from some turret-lathe's services of tomorrow. Strictly speaking, this is true of most service flows. But some things, like food, or coal for heating, or gasoline, exhaust their services much faster than, e.g. steamrollers, drill presses, buildings, etc. The stock dimension of the former can be ignored in many problems; this is not true of the latter set of things, which are usually labeled as fixed capital.[60] A second dynamical extension, then, consists in introducing stock-flow relationships into the production functions.

3. Lags and stock-flow relations are implied also by the goods-in-process phenomenon. Production takes place over space, and transport takes time, hence seed cannot be produced at the instant at which it is planted, nor cylinder heads the moment they are required on the assembly line. They have to be in existence for some finite time before they are used.

4. One of the crucial intertemporal interrelations in allocation and distribution in a world where stocks matter and where production takes time, is due to the unpleasant (or pleasant) fact that the inputs of any instant are not manna from heaven. Their supply depends on past output decisions. Next year's production possibilities will depend, in part, on the supply of machine tools; this, in turn, partly depends on the resources devoted this year to the construction of new machine tools. This is the problem of investment. From today's point of view investment concerns choice of *outputs*; but choice of what kinds and amounts of machines to build, plants to construct, etc., today, makes sense only in terms of the *input-uses* of these things tomorrow. Input endowments, L and D, become unknowns as well as data.

60. Much depends on arbitrary or special institutional assumptions about how much optimization we leave in the background for the 'engineer'. For example, machines of widely varying design could very likely yield a given kind of service. 'A lathe is not a lathe is. . . .' Further, no law of nature precludes the rather speedy using-up of a lathe – by using it, e.g. as scrap metal. In some situations it could even be economic to do so.

5. Tomorrow's input availabilities are also affected by how inputs are used today. The nature and intensity of use to which machines are subjected, the way in which soil is used, oil wells operated, the rate at which inventories are run down, etc., partly determine what will be left tomorrow. This is the problem of physical capital consumption, wear and tear, etc. – the problem of what to subtract from gross investment to get 'net' capital formation, hence the net change in input supplies.

How do these five dynamical phenomena fit into the maximum-of-welfare problem? Recall that our W-function was assumed sensitive to, and only to, X's and Y's consumption. Nothing was said, however, about the timing of such consumption. Surely not only consumption of this instant matters. In a dynamic context, meaningful welfare and preference functions have to provide a ranking not only with respect to all possible current consumption mixes but also for future time. They must provide some means for weighing apples next week against nuts and apples today. Such functions will *date* each unit of A and N, and the choice to be made will be between alternative time-paths of consumption.[61]

Given such a context, the above five dynamical phenomena are amenable to a formal maximizing treatment entirely akin to that of parts I, II and III. They are, with one qualification,[62] consistent with the convexity assumptions required for solubility and duality. The results, which are the fruit of some very recent and pathbreaking work by Samuelson and Solow (1956), define intertemporal production efficiency in terms of time-paths along which no increase in the consumption of any good of any period is possible without a decrease in some other consumption. Such paths are characterized by the superimposition,

61. Note how little weight is likely to be given to current consumption relative to future consumption if we pick short unit-periods. This year certainly matters, but what of this afternoon versus all future, or this second? Yet what of the man who knows he'll die tomorrow? Note also the intrinsic philosophical dilemmas: e.g. is John Jones today the 'same' person he was yesterday?

62. Capital is characterized not only by the fact of durability, but also by lumpiness or indivisibility 'in scale'. Such lumpiness results in nonconvexity, hence causes serious analytical troubles.

on top of the statical, one-period or instantaneous efficiency conditions, of certain intertemporal marginal rate-of-substitution requirements. But the statical efficiency requirements retain their validity: for full-fledged dynamical Pareto-efficiency it is necessary that at any moment in time the system be on its one-period efficiency frontier.[63]

Incidentally, the geometric techniques of part I are fully adequate to the task of handling a Solow–Samuelson dynamical setup for a $2 \times 2 \times 2$ world. Only now the dimensions of the production box and hence the position of the production-possibility curve will keep shifting, and the solution gives values not only for inputs, outputs and prices but also for their period-to-period changes.

There are many dynamical phenomena less prone to analysis by a formal maximizing system than the five listed above. The qualitative and quantitative supply of labor-input in the future is influenced by the current use made of the services of people.[64] There are, also, important intertemporal interdependences relating to the fact of space – space matters because it takes time and resources to span it. Moreover, we have not even mentioned the really 'difficult' phenomena of 'grand dynamics'. Production functions, preference functions and even my or your welfare function shift over time. Such shifts are compounded by what in a sense is the central problem of nonstationary dynamics: the intrinsic uncertainty that attaches to the notion of future.[65] Last, the very boundaries of economics, as of any discipline, are intrinsically arbitrary. Allocation and distribution interact in countless ways with the politics and sociology of a society ... 'everything depends on everything'. But we are way beyond simple analytics.

63. For possible exception to this, due to sensitivity of the volume of saving, hence of investment, to 'as imputed' income distribution, see Bator (1957).

64. Although labor is in many respects analytically akin to other kinds of physical capital, resources can and need to be invested to expand the stock of engineers, as to expand that of cows and machines. Machines, however, are not subject to certain costless 'learning' effects.

65. While formal welfare theory becomes very silent when uncertainty intrudes, much of economic analysis, e.g. monetary theory, trade fluctuations, would have little meaning except for the fact of uncertainty.

A historical note on the literature[66]

The foundations of modern welfare theory are well embedded in the soil of classical economics, and the structure, too, bears the imprint of the line of thought represented by Smith, Ricardo, Mill and Marshall. But in classical writing prescription and analysis are inseparably intertwined, the underlying philosophy is unabashedly utilitarian, and the central normative concern is with the efficacy of market institutions. In contrast, the development of modern welfare economics can best be understood as an attempt to sort out ethics from science, and allocative efficiency from particular modes of social organization.

The classical tradition reached its culmination in Professor Pigou's *Wealth and Welfare* (1912). Pigou, the last of the great premoderns was also, as witness the *Economics of Welfare* (1932), among the first of the moderns. But he was not the first. Vilfredo Pareto, writing during the first years of the century, has a pre-eminent claim (1909). It is his work, and Enrico Barone's after him (1935) – with their focus on the analytical implications of maximization – that constitute the foundations of the modern structure. Many writers contributed to the construction, but A. P. Lerner (1944), Abram Bergson (1938), and Paul Samuelson (1947, ch. 8) come especially to mind. Bergson, in particular, was the first to make us see the structure whole. More recently, Kenneth Arrow (1951a) has explored the logical underpinnings of the notion of a social welfare function in relation to social choice; T. C. Koopmans (1951), Gerard Debreu and others have tested more complicated systems for duality; Samuelson has developed a meaningful species of social indifference function (1956) and derived efficiency conditions for 'public goods' (1954, 1955) and Robert Solow and Samuelson have provided a dynamical extension (see Dorfman, Solow and Samuelson, 1958, esp. chs. 11, 12; also Baumol, 1952; Myint, 1948, Myrdal, 1953; Reder, 1947).

66. For a short but substantive history of the development of thought in this field, the reader is referred to Samuelson's synthesis (nonmathematical) (1947, pp. 203–19). See also Bergson (1948) and Boulding (1952). [See *American Economic Review*, vol. 47, for the complete list of references and notes – Ed.]

There is, also, an important modern literature devoted to the possible uses of the structure of analysis for policy prescription. Three separate sets of writings are more or less distinguishable. There was first, in the 'twenties and 'thirties, a prolonged controversy on markets versus government. L. von Mises (in von Hayek, 1935) and later F. A. von Hayek (1940; see also 1944) were the principal proponents of unadulterated *laissez-faire*, while H. D. Dickinson (1933), Oskar Lange (1938), Lerner (1944) and Maurice Dobb (1933) stand out on the other side. The decentralized Socialist pricing idea, originally suggested by Barone and later by F. M. Taylor, was elaborated by Lange to counter the von Mises view that efficient allocation is impossible in a collectivized economy due simply to the sheer scale of the administrative burden of calculation and control.

Second, in the late 1930s, Nicholas Kaldor (1939) and J. R. Hicks (1939, 1940) took up Lionel Robbins's (1932) challenge to economists not to mix ethics and science and suggested a series of tests for choosing some input–output configurations over others independently of value.[67] Tibor Scitovsky (1941–2a and b) pointed out an important asymmetry in the Kaldor–Hicks test and Samuelson (1950) in the end demonstrated that a 'welfare-function' denoting an ethic was needed after all. I. M. D. Little (1950) tried, but I think failed, to shake this conclusion.[68] The Pareto conditions are necessary, but never sufficient.

Third, there is a body of writing, some of it in a partial-equilibrium mode which is concerned with policy at a lower level of abstraction. Writings by Harold Hotelling (1938), Ragnar Frisch, J. E. Meade, W. A. Lewis, are devoted to the question of optimal pricing, marginal cost or otherwise, in public utility ($MC < AC$) situations. Hotelling, H. P. Wald, M. F. W. Joseph, E. R. Rolph and G. F. Break, Little, and more

67. The Hicks–Kaldor line of thought has some ties to an earlier literature by Marshall, Pigou, Fisher, etc., on 'What is income?'
68. While I find Little's alternative (see 1950, p. 105) to a welfare function ('an economic change is desirable if it does not cause a bad redistribution of income, and if the potential losers could not profitably bribe the potential gainers to oppose it') no alternative at all, his is a provocative evaluation of modern welfare theory. For an evaluation, in turn, of Little, see Arrow (1951b).

recently Lionel McKenzie, have, in turn, analysed alternative fiscal devices for covering public deficits (see Little, 1951). Last, a number of the above, notably Lerner, Kaldor, Samuelson, Scitovsky, Little, McKenzie and, most exhaustively, Meade as well as R. F. Kahn, Lloyd Metzler, J. de V. Graaf, H. G. Johnson and others have applied the apparatus to questions of gains from international trade, optimal tariffs, etc. (see Meade, 1955).

References

ARROW, K. J. (1951a), *Social Choice and Individual Values*, Wiley.

ARROW, K. J. (1951b), 'Little's critique of welfare economics', *Amer. econ. Rev.*, vol. 41, pp. 923-34.

BARONE, E. (1935), 'The ministry of production in the collectivist state', trans. in F. A. von Hayek (ed.), *Collectivist Economic Planning*, Routledge & Kegan Paul.

BATOR, F. M. (1957), 'On capital productivity, input allocation and growth', *Quart. J. Econ.*, vol. 71, pp. 86–106.

BAUMOL, W. J. (1952), *Welfare Economics and the Theory of the State*, Harvard University Press.

BERGSON, A. (1938), 'A re-formulation of certain aspects of welfare economics', *Quart. J. Econ.*, vol. 52, pp. 310–14. Reprinted in R. V. Clemence (ed.), *Readings in Economic Analysis*, vol. 1, Addison-Wesley.

BERGSON, A. (1948), 'Socialist economics', in H. S. Ellis (ed.), *A Survey of Contemporary Economics*, vol. 1, Blakiston.

BISHOP, R. L. (1948), 'Cost discontinuities, declining costs, and marginal analysis', *Amer. econ. Rev.*, vol. 38, pp. 607–17.

BOULDING, K. E. (1952), 'Welfare economics', in B. F. Haley (ed.), *A Survey of Contemporary Economics*, vol. 1, Irwin.

DICKINSON, H. D. (1933), 'Price formation in a Socialist economy', *Econ. J.*, vol. 43, pp. 237–50.

DOBB, M. (1933), 'Economic theory and the problem of the Socialist economy', *Econ. J.*, vol. 43, pp. 588–98.

DORFMAN, R. (1953), 'Mathematical or "linear" programming', *Quart. J. Econ.*, vol. 70, pp. 1–27.

DORFMAN, R., SOLOW, R. M., and SAMUELSON, P. A. (1958), *Linear Programming and Economic Analysis*, McGraw-Hill.

HICKS, J. R. (1939), 'The foundations of welfare economics', *Econ. J.*, vol. 69, pp. 696–712.

HICKS, J. R. (1940), 'The valuation of the social income', *Economica*, vol. 7, pp. 105–23.

HOTELLING, H. (1938), 'The general welfare in relation to the problems of taxation and of railway and utility rates', *Econometrica*, vol. 6, pp. 242–69.

KALDOR, N. (1939), 'Welfare propositions in economics and interpersonal comparisons of utility', *Econ. J.*, vol. 69, pp. 549–52.

KOOPMANS, T. C. (1951), *Activity Analysis of Production and Allocation*, Wiley.

LANGE, O. (1938), 'On the economic theory of Socialism', in B. E. Lippincott (ed.), *On the Economic Theory of Socialism*, University of Minnesota Press.

LERNER, A. P. (1944), *The Economics of Control*, Macmillan.

LITTLE, I. M. D. (1950), *A Critique of Welfare Economics*, Oxford University Press, Inc.

LITTLE, I. M. D. (1951), 'Direct versus indirect taxes', *Econ. J.*, vol. 61. pp. 577–84.

MEADE, J. E. (1955), *The Theory of International Economic Policy, Vol. 2: Trade and Welfare*, Oxford University Press, Inc. See also *Mathematical Supplement*.

MYINT, H. (1948), *Theories of Welfare Economics*, London School of Economics.

MYRDAL, D. (1953), *Political Element in the Development of Economic Theory*, trans. P. Streeten, Harvard University Press.

PARETO, V. (1909), *Manual d'économie publique*, Giard, Paris.

PIGOU, A. C. (1912), *Wealth and Welfare*, Macmillan.

PIGOU, A. C. (1932), *The Economics of Welfare*, Macmillan, 4th edn.

REDER, M. W. (1947), *Studies in the Theory of Welfare Economics*, AMS Press.

ROBBINS, L. (1932), *The Nature and Significance of Economic Science*, Macmillan.

SAMUELSON, P. A. (1947), *Foundations of Economic Analysis*, Cambridge University Press.

SAMUELSON, P. A. (1949), *Market Mechanisms and Maximization*, RAND Corporation.

SAMUELSON, P. A. (1950), 'Evaluation of real national income', *Oxf. econ. Pap.*, vol. 2, pp. 1–29.

SAMUELSON, P. A. (1953–4), 'Prices of factors and goods in general equilibrium', *Rev. econ. Stud.*, vol. 21, pp. 1–20.

SAMUELSON, P. A. (1954), 'The pure theory of public expenditure', *Rev. Econ. Stat.*, vol. 36, pp. 387–9.

SAMUELSON, P. A. (1955), 'Diagrammatic exposition of a theory of public expenditure', *Rev. Econ. Stat.*, vol. 37, pp. 350–56.

SAMUELSON, P. A. (1956), 'Social indifference curves', *Quart. J. Econ.*, vol. 70, pp. 1–22.

SAMUELSON, P. A., and SOLOW, R. M. (1956), 'A complete capital model involving heterogeneous capital goods', *Quart. J. Econ.*, vol. 70, pp. 884–912.

SCITOVSKY, T. (1941–2a), 'A note on welfare propositions in economics', *Rev. econ. Stud.*, vol. 9, pp. 77–8.

SCITOVSKY, T. (1941–2b), 'A reconsideration of the theory of tariffs', *Rev. econ. Stud.*, vol. 9, pp. 89–110.

VON HAYEK, F. A. (1935), *Collectivist Economic Planning*, Routledge & Kegan Paul.
VON HAYEK, F. A. (1940), 'Socialist calculation: the competitive "solution" ' *Economica*, vol. 7, pp. 125–49.
VON HAYEK, F. A. (1944), *The Road to Serfdom*, Routledge & Kegan Paul.

16 W. Leontief

Input–Output Economics

Chapter 2 in W. Leontief, *Input–Output Economics*, Oxford University Press, Inc., 1966, pp. 13–29. (First published in 1951 in *Scientific American*.)

If the great nineteenth-century physicist James Clerk Maxwell were to attend a current meeting of the American Physical Society, he might have serious difficulty in keeping track of what was going on. In the field of economics, on the other hand, his contemporary John Stuart Mill would easily pick up the thread of the most advanced arguments among his twentieth-century successors. Physics, applying the method of inductive reasoning from quantitatively observed events, has moved on to entirely new premises. The science of economics, in contrast, remains largely a deductive system resting upon a static set of premises, most of which were familiar to Mill and some of which date back to Adam Smith's *The Wealth of Nations*.

Present-day economists are not universally content with this state of affairs. Some of the greatest recent names in economics – Léon Walras, Vilfredo Pareto, Irving Fisher – are associated with the effort to develop quantitative methods for grappling with the enormous volume of empirical data that is involved in every real economic situation. Yet such methods have so far failed to find favor with the majority of professional economists. It is not only the forbidding rigor of mathematics; the truth is that such methods have seldom produced results significantly superior to those achieved by the traditional procedure. In an empirical science, after all, nothing ultimately counts but results. Most economists therefore continue to rely upon their 'professional intuition' and 'sound judgement' to establish the connection between the facts and the theory of economics.

In recent years, however, the output of economic facts and figures by various public and private agencies has increased by leaps and bounds. Most of this information is published for reference purposes, and is unrelated to any particular method of analysis. As a result we have in economics today a high concentration of theory without fact on the one hand, and a mounting accumulation of fact without theory on the other. The task of filling the 'empty boxes of economic theory' with relevant empirical content becomes every day more urgent and challenging.

This article is concerned with a new effort to combine economic facts and theory known as 'interindustry' or 'input–output' analysis. Essentially it is a method of analysis that takes advantage of the relatively stable pattern of the flow of goods and services among the elements of our economy to bring a much more detailed statistical picture of the system into the range of manipulation by economic theory. As such, the method has had to await the modern high-speed computing machine as well as the present propensity of government and private agencies to accumulate mountains of data. It is now advancing from the phase of academic investigation and experimental trial to a broadening sphere of application in grand-scale problems of national economic policy. The practical possibilities of the method are being carried forward as a cooperative venture of the Bureau of Labor Statistics, the Bureau of Mines, the Department of Commerce, the Bureau of the Budget, the Council of Economic Advisers and, with particular reference to procurement and logistics, the Air Force. Meanwhile the development of the technique of input–output analysis continues to interest academic investigators here and abroad. They are hopeful that this method of bringing the facts of economics into closer association with theory may induce some fruitful advances in both.

Economic theory seeks to explain the material aspects and operations of our society in terms of interactions among such variables as supply and demand or wages and prices. Economists have generally based their analyses on relatively simple data – such quantities as the gross national product, the interest rate, price and wage levels. But in the real world things are not so simple. Between a shift in wages and the ultimate working out of its impact upon prices there is a complex series of transactions in which actual goods and services are exchanged among real people. These intervening steps are scarcely suggested by the classical formulation of the relationship between the two variables. It is true, of course, that the individual transactions, like individual atoms and molecules, are far too numerous for observation and description in detail. But it is possible, as with physical particles, to reduce them to some kind of order by classifying and aggregating them into groups. This is the procedure employed in input–output analysis in improving the grasp of economic theory upon the facts with which it is concerned in every real situation.

The essential principles of the method may be most easily comprehended by consulting Table 1, which summarizes the transactions that characterized the US economy during 1947. The transactions are grouped into forty-two major departments of production, distribution, transportation and consumption, set up on a matrix of horizontal rows and vertical columns. The horizontal rows of figures show how the output of each sector of the economy is distributed among the others. Conversely, the vertical columns show how each sector obtains from the others its needed inputs of goods and services. Since each figure in any horizontal row is also a figure in a vertical column, the output of each sector is shown to be an input in some other. The double-entry bookkeeping of the input–output table thus reveals the fabric of our economy, woven together by the flow of trade which ultimately links each branch and industry to all others. Such a table may of course be developed in as fine or as coarse detail as the available data permit and the purpose requires. The present table summarizes a much more detailed 500-sector master table which has just been completed after two

Table 1 on pages 424–31 summarizes the transactions of the US economy in 1947, for which preliminary data were compiled by the Bureau of Labor Statistics. Each number in the body of the table represents billions of 1947 dollars. In the vertical column at left the entire economy is broken down into sectors; in the horizontal row at the top the same breakdown is repeated. When a sector is read horizontally, the numbers indicate what it ships to other sectors. When a sector is read vertically, the numbers show what it consumes from other sectors. The asterisks stand for sums less than $5 million. Totals may not check due to rounding.

Table 1 Exchange of Goods and Services in the US for 1947

Industry producing	Industry purchasing										
	1 agriculture and fisheries	2 food and kindred products	3 textile mill products	4 apparel	5 lumber and wood products	6 furniture and fixtures	7 paper and allied products	8 printing and publishing	9 chemicals	10 products of petroleum and coal	11 rubber products
1 agriculture and fisheries	10·86	15·70	2·16	0·02	0·19	*	0·01	*	1·21	*	
2 food and kindred products	2·38	5·75	0·06	0·01	*		0·03	0·03	0·79	*	
3 textile mill products	0·06	*	1·30	3·88	*	0·29	0·04		0·01		0·44
4 apparel	0·04	0·20	0·02	1·96		0·01	0·02		0·03		
5 lumber and wood products	0·15	0·10	0·01	*	1·09	0·39	0·27	*	0·04		
6 furniture and fixtures			0·08			0·01	0·01				
7 paper and allied products	*	0·52	*	0·02	*	0·02	2·60	1·08	0·33	0·01	0·02
8 printing and publishing		0·04						0·77	0·02	0·11	
9 chemicals	0·83	1·48	0·80	0·14	0·03	0·06	0·18	0·10	2·58	0·21	0·60
10 products of petroleum and coal	0·46	0·06	0·03	*	0·07	*	0·06	*	0·32	4·83	0·01
11 rubber products	0·12	0·01	0·01	0·02	0·01	0·01	0·01	*			0·04
12 leather and leather products			*	0·05	*	0·01		*	*	*	

	C1	C2	C3	C4	C5	C6	C7	C8	C9	C10	C11
13 stone, clay and glass products	0·06	0·25	*	*	0·01	0·03	0·03	0·01	0·26	0·05	0·01
14 primary metals	0·01	*	*	*	0·01	0·11	0·11	0·02	0·19	0·01	0·01
15 fabricated metal products	0·08	0·61	*	0·01	0·04	0·14	0·14	0·01	0·13	0·08	0·01
16 machinery (except electric)	0·06	0·01	0·04	0·02	0·01	0·01	0·01	0·04	*	0·01	
17 electric machinery	0·11										
18 motor vehicles	0·01	*	*	*	*	*	*	*	*	*	*
19 other transportation equipment											
20 professional and scientific equipment	*	0·01	0·26	*	*	0·01	0·01	*	0·01		*
21 miscellaneous manufacturing industries	0·06	0·20	0·04	0·02	0·02	0·01	0·01	0·03	0·03	0·56	0·04
22 coal, gas and electric power	0·44	0·57	0·06	0·14	0·05	0·12	0·22	0·07	0·19	0·27	0·04
23 railroad transportation	0·07	0·13	0·01	0·01	*	0·02	0·02	*	0·04	0·09	*
24 ocean transportation	0·55	0·38	0·03	0·14	0·04	0·12	0·12	0·03	0·10	0·47	0·01
25 other transportation	1·36	0·46	0·37	0·06	0·06	0·18	0·18	0·03	0·17	0·02	0·05
26 trade	*	0·04	0·02	0·01	0·01	0·01	0·01	0·04	0·02	0·01	0·01
27 communications	0·24	0·15	0·02	0·08	0·02	0·02	0·02	0·02	0·02	0·13	0·01
28 finance and insurance	2·39	0·09	0·03	0·02	0·02	0·03	0·03	0·06	0·03		0·01
29 real estate and rentals	0·01	0·63	0·10	0·02	0·06	0·02	0·02	0·06	0·42	0·04	0·02
30 business services	0·37	0·12	0·10	*	0·04	*	0·02	0·02	0·01	0·01	*
31 personal and repair services											
32 non-profit organizations											
33 amusements											
34 scrap and miscellaneous industries	0·20	0·02	0·02	0·01	0·01	0·25	0·25	*	0·01	0·01	0·01
35 eating and drinking places											
36 new construction and maintenance	0·20	0·12	0·04	0·02	0·01	0·04	0·04	0·01	0·04	0·03	0·01
37 undistributed	1·87	0·03	1·08	0·73	0·27	0·17	0·50	1·49	0·65	0·27	
38 inventory change (depletions)	2·66	0·40	0·12	0·19	*	0·01	0·09	0·03	0·14	0·01	*
39 foreign countries (imports from)	0·69	2·11	0·21	0·28	0·18	0·01	0·62	0·01	0·59	0·26	*
40 government	0·81	1·24	0·64	0·38	0·34	0·11	0·50	0·34	0·76	0·78	0·11
41 private capital formation (gross)	depreciation and other capital consumption allowances are included in household row										
42 households	19·17	7·05	3·34	4·24	2·72	1·12	2·20	3·14	3·75	5·04	1·08
total gross outlays	44·26	40·30	9·84	13·32	6·00	2·89	7·90	6·45	14·05	13·67	2·82

Table 1 – continued

Industry purchasing

Industry producing	12 leather and leather products	13 stone, clay and glass products	14 primary metals	15 fabricated metal products	16 machinery (except electric)	17 electrical machinery	18 motor vehicles	19 other transportation equipment	20 professional and scientific equipment	21 miscellaneous manufacturing industries	22 coal, gas and electric power
1 agriculture and fisheries	0·05	*	0·01	*							
2 food and kindred products	0·44	*	*	0·01	*	*			*	*	*
3 textile mill products	0·09	0·03		*	0·02	0·05			0·01	0·02	0·07
4 apparel	*	*				*			0·05	0·08	*
5 lumber and wood products	0·02	0·02	0·06	0·06	0·09	0·05	0·15	0·01	*		0·06
6 furniture and fixtures		0·18	*	*	0·01	0·10	0·10	0·01	*	*	*
7 paper and allied products	0·05			0·09	0·04	0·07	0·05	0·03	0·08	0·06	*
8 printing and publishing				0·01	0·01	0·01	0·03	0·02	*	0·07	*
9 chemicals	0·13	0·12	0·18	0·13	0·08	0·20	0·11	0·02	0·05	0·17	0·06
10 products of petroleum and coal	*	0·05	0·90	0·02	0·04	0·02	0·03	0·01		0·01	0·47
11 rubber products	0·05	0·01	*	0·01	0·13	0·03	0·50	0·01	*	0·04	*
12 leather and leather products	1·04			*	0·02	*	0·01	*	0·01	0·01	*

	C1	C2	C3	C4	C5	C6	C7	C8	C9	C10	C11
13 stone, clay and glass products	0·01	0·43	0·21	0·07	0·07	0·12	0·19	0·01	0·03	0·06	0·02
14 primary metals	*	0·04	6·90	2·53	2·02	1·05	1·28	0·43	0·07	0·20	0·05
15 fabricated metal products	0·02	*	0·05	0·43	1·15	0·34	0·97	0·10	0·07	0·04	*
16 machinery (except electric)		0·01	0·07	0·28	0·58	0·17	0·63	0·22	0·03	*	0·03
17 electrical machinery		0·01	*	0·24	0·03	0·86	0·62	0·12	0·03	0·02	0·02
18 motor vehicles	*	*	*	0·03		0·01	4·40	*			0·01
19 other transportation equipment		*	*				0·01	0·30			*
20 professional and scientific equipment	0·02	*	*				0·07	0·02	0·18	0·02	*
21 miscellaneous manufacturing industries	0·02	0·01	0·35	0·04	0·04	0·01	0·02	*	0·03	0·16	
22 coal, gas and electric power	0·04	0·20	0·52	0·02	0·05	0·11	0·06	0·03	0·01	0·03	1·27
23 railroad transportation	*	0·15	0·08	0·08	0·10	0·05	0·23	0·04	0·01	0·03	0·15
24 ocean transportation	0·02	0·01	0·16	0·13	0·16	0·07	*	*	*	0·01	*
25 other transportation	0·06	0·07	0·36	*	*	*	0·07	0·01	0·01	0·01	0·03
26 trade	*	0·05	0·02	0·03	0·04	0·03	0·06	0·07	0·04	0·05	0·05
27 communications	0·01	0·01	0·06	0·20	0·26	0·14	0·02	0·01	0·01	0·01	0·02
28 finance and insurance	0·05	0·05	0·06	0·02	0·03	0·02	0·02	0·02	0·01	0·02	0·05
29 real estate and rentals	0·02	0·02	0·03	0·04	0·05	0·04	0·02	0·02	0·01	0·03	0·05
30 business services	0·05	0·01	0·01	0·03	0·04	0·03	0·02	0·01	0·05	0·06	0·01
31 personal and repair services	*	0·03	0·01	0·05	0·09	0·06	0·08	*	*	*	0·02
32 non-profit organizations				0·01	0·01	*	*	*	*		
33 amusements				0·02	0·05						
34 scrap and miscellaneous industries		0·01	1·11						*		
35 eating and drinking places	0·02	0·03		0·03	0·05	0·02	0·05	0·01	0·01	0·02	0·27
36 new construction and maintenance	0·27	0·47	0·10	1·14	1·71	0·89	0·04	0·34	0·19	0·87	0·25
37 undistributed	0·03	*	0·32	*	*	*	0·41	0·01	0·05	0·16	*
38 inventory changes (depletions)	0·04		0·11	0·01	0·05		0·01	0·01	0·05	0·14	
39 foreign countries (imports from)	0·14	0·14	0·62	0·48	0·77		0·02			0·19	0·01
40 government		0·32	0·82			0·40	0·66	0·12	0·13		1·14
41 private capital formation (gross)											
42 households	1·20	2·35	5·35	4·14	6·80	3·41	3·39	1·95	0·90	2·17	5·11
total gross outlays	3·81	4·84	18·69	10·40	15·22	8·38	14·27	4·00	2·12	4·76	9·21

depreciation and other capital consumption allowances are included in household row

Table 1 – continued
Industry purchasing

Industry producing	23 railroad transportation	24 ocean transportation	25 other transportation	26 trade	27 communications	28 finance and insurance	29 real estate and rentals	30 business services	31 personal and repair services	32 non-profit organizations	33 amusements
1 agriculture and fisheries	*	*	0·01	0·07	*					0·12	*
2 food and kindred products	0·08	0·01	0·03	0·03	0·01					0·25	*
3 textile mill products	*	0·01	0·01	0·02	*				*	*	
4 apparel		*	*	0·03	*				0·03	0·02	
5 lumber and wood products		0·01	*	0·57	*		0·14	*	0·02	*	
6 furniture and fixtures	*	*	*	0·10	*		0·08	*	*		
7 paper and allied products	0·04	0·01	0·02	0·07	0·03	0·04		*	0·06	0·03	
8 printing and publishing	0·03		0·02	0·20	*	*		2·45	0·03	0·17	0·01
9 chemicals	0·27	0·09	0·45	0·06	*	0·21		0·01	0·20	0·22	*
10 products of petroleum and coal	*		0·13	*	*	*	0·78	*	0·06	0·06	*
11 rubber products			*			0·01	*		0·07	*	
12 leather and leather products						0·01			0·03	0·01	

industry	(1)	(2)	(3)	(4)	(5)	(6)	(7)	(8)	(9)	(10)	(11)
13 stone, clay and glass products	0·01	*	*	0·04	*				0·02	0·01	
14 primary metals	0·20		0·01		*					*	
15 fabricated metal products	0·03	*	0·01	0·06	*				0·03	0·01	
16 machinery (except electric)	0·06		0·01	0·01				*	0·15	*	
17 electrical machinery	0·04		0·01	0·01	0·05	0·02			0·09	*	
18 motor vehicles	*	0·08	0·13	0·02	*			0·01	1·05	*	
19 other transportation equipment	0·04		0·13								
20 professional and scientific equipment		*	*		*				*	0·18	0·05
21 miscellaneous manufacturing industries	*	*	*	0·01	*			0·01	0·05	0·05	0·05
22 coal, gas and electric power	0·44	*	0·09	0·49	0·01	0·06	3·15	0·15	0·16	0·16	
23 railroad transportation	0·41		0·06	0·08	*	0·01	0·42		0·31	0·05	
24 ocean transportation		0·22							0·03		
25 other transportation	0·19	0·04	0·25	0·31	*			0·01			
26 trade	0·03	0·01	0·42	0·20	*	*	0·13	0·15	0·01	0·02	*
27 communications	0·02	*	0·04	0·33	0·01	0·04	0·75	0·14	0·37	0·29	0·01
28 finance and insurance	0·02	0·12	0·30	1·00	0·06	0·09	0·06	0·43	0·12	0·07	0·01
29 real estate and rentals	0·02	0·01	0·15	1·96	*	1·85	0·56	0·02	0·12	0·09	0·03
30 business services	0·02	*	0·03	1·71	0·05	0·21	0·21	0·06	0·71	0·40	0·18
31 personal and repair services	0·11	0·01	0·26	1·42	0·09	0·14	0·04	0·06	0·12	0·02	0·10
32 non-profit organizations		*	*		0·02	0·11	0·03	0·07	0·56	0·08	0·02
33 amusements						0·02				0·09	
34 scrap and miscellaneous industries			0·04	0·39	0·01		0·03			0·01	0·39
35 eating and drinking places	1·12		0·01			0·11		0·02	*	0·15	0·01
36 new construction and maintenance	0·10	*	0·13	0·18	0·18	0·03	4·08	*	0·06	0·34	0·02
37 undistributed		0·04	0·03	2·59	0·01	0·71	0·36	0·31	1·13	0·91	0·22
38 inventory change (depletions)	0·04		0·08		0·03	0·10					
39 foreign countries (imports from)	0·91	0·50	0·77	3·30	0·44	1·11			0·50	0·17	*
40 government		0·26					4·00	0·21			0·32
41 private capital formation (gross)	5·70	0·90	6·20	26·42	2·15	7·93	14·06	1·08	8·20	9·41	1·50
42 households	9·95	2·29	9·86	41·66	3·17	12·81	28·86	5·10	14·30	13·39	2·94
total gross outlays											

Table 1 – continued

Industry producing	34 scrap and miscellaneous industries	35 eating and drinking places	36 new construction and maintenance	37 undistributed	38 inventory change (*additions*)	39 foreign countries (*export to*)	40 government	41 private capital formation (*gross*)	42 households	total gross output
1 agriculture and fisheries	0·02	0·87	0·09	0·17	1·01	1·28	0·57	0·02	9·92	44·26
2 food and kindred products	0·01	3·47	*	0·42	0·88	1·80	0·73	0·02	23·03	40·30
3 textile mill products	0·01	0·02	0·05	0·52	0·06	0·92	0·10		1·47	9·84
4 apparel	0·11	0·01	*	0·15	0·21	0·30	0·28	*	9·90	13·32
5 lumber and wood products			2·33	0·35	0·17	0·17	0·01	0·04	0·07	6·00
6 furniture and fixtures	0·68	0·06	0·20	0·20	0·08	0·03	0·05	0·57	1·46	2·89
7 paper and allied products	0·01	0·03	0·17	0·31	0·04	0·15	0·06		0·34	7·90
8 printing and publishing	0·03	0·04		0·68	*	0·07	0·16	0·09	1·49	6·45
9 chemicals	0·01	0·01	0·64	1·25	0·30	0·81	0·19		1·96	14·05
10 products and petroleum and coal	*		0·62	0·36	0·06	0·68	0·18	*	2·44	13·67
11 rubber products			0·06	0·47	0·09	0·17	0·02	0·01	0·71	2·82
12 leather and leather products	0·01	*	*	0·29	0·11	0·08	0·03	0·02	2·03	3·81

final demand (columns 38–42)

	C1	C2	C3	C4	C5	C6	C7	C8	C9	C10	total
13 stone, clay and glass products	*	0·06	1·74	0·36	0·10	0·21	0·02	0·01	0·34		4·84
14 primary metals	0·15	*	1·19	1·24	0·16	0·77	0·02	0·28	0·02		18·69
15 fabricated metal products	0·06	0·02	3·09	1·44	0·21	0·39	0·05	5·82	0·95		10·40
16 machinery (except electric)	0·07		0·51	2·24	0·37	1·76	0·18	1·75	1·22		15·22
17 electrical machinery	0·04	*	0·77	1·27	0·25	0·44	0·17	2·98	0·93		8·38
18 motor vehicles	0·07		0·04	0·67	0·40	1·02	0·15	1·20	3·13		14·27
19 other transportation equipment	0·01		*	0·46	0·02	0·32	1·25		0·17		4·00
20 professional and scientific equipment	0·01		0·02	0·24	0·03	0·18	0·08	0·26	0·62		2·12
21 miscellaneous manufacturing industries	0·11	0·02	0·03	0·68	0·04	0·19	0·08	0·51	1·89		4·76
22 coal, gas and electric power		0·22	0·03	0·02	0·03	0·35	0·20				9·21
23 railroad transportation	0·03	0·25	0·71	0·30	0·08	0·59	0·33	0·27	2·53		9·95
24 ocean transportation	*			*		0·16	0·31		0·10		2·29
25 other transportation	0·02					0·32	0·35	0·10	4·77		9·86
26 trade	0·09	0·10	0·57	0·17	0·04	1·00	0·05	2·34	26·82		41·66
27 communications		1·06	2·52	1·01	0·20	0·04	0·15		1·27		3·17
28 finance and insurance		0·01	0·04	0·08		0·14	0·03		6·99		12·81
29 real estate and rentals		0·07	0·40				0·22	0·80	20·29		28·86
30 business services	0·03	0·39	0·08	0·42		*	0·04		0·18		5·10
31 personal and repair services		0·06	0·13	1·17			0·08	0·27	8·35		14·30
32 non-profit organizations		0·23	0·82	0·16			5·08		8·04		13·39
33 amusements				0·01		0·13			2·40		2·94
34 scrap and miscellaneous industries			*	0·01		0·03	*				2·13
35 eating and drinking places									13·11		13·27
36 new construction and maintenance		0·07	0·01			0·02	5·20	15·70	0·15		28·49
37 undistributed		0·59	0·43								21·60
38 inventory change (depletions)	0·40			0·01							4·43
39 foreign countries (imports from)	0·07				0·34						9·52
40 government	0·07	1·41	0·47	2·19		0·83	1·31	0·22	1·32		63·69
41 private capital formation (gross)		4·20	10·73	2·27	5·28	0·85	3·46		31·55		
42 households									2·12		
total gross outlays	2·13	13·27	28·49	21·60	5·28	17·21	30·06	51·29	33·29	194·12	223·58

years of intensive work by the Interindustry Economics Division of the Bureau of Labor Statistics.

For purposes of illustration let us look at the input–output structure of a single sector – the one labeled 'primary metals' (sector 14). The vertical column states the inputs of each of the various goods and services that are required for the production of metals, and the sum of the figures in this column represents the total outlay of the economy for the year's production. Most of the entries in this column are self-explanatory. Thus it is no surprise to find a substantial figure entered against the item 'products of petroleum and coal' (sector 10). The design of the table, however, gives a special meaning to some of the sectors. The outlay for 'railroad transportation' (sector 23), for example covers only the cost of hauling raw materials to the mills; the cost of delivering primary metal products to their markets is borne by the industries purchasing them. Another outlay requiring explanation is entered in the trade sector (sector 26). The figures in this sector represent the cost of distribution, stated in terms of the trade margin. The entries against trade in the primary metals column, therefore, cover the middleman's markup on the industry's purchase; trade margins on the sale of primary metal products are charged against the consuming industries. Taxes paid by the industry are entered in the row labeled 'government' (sector 40), and all payments to individuals, including wages, salaries and dividends, are summed up in the row labeled 'households' (sector 42). How the output of the metals industry is distributed among the other sectors is shown in row 14, the figures indicate that the industry's principal customers are other industries. 'Households' and 'government' turn up as direct customers for only a minor portion of the total output, although these two sectors are of course the principal consumers of metals after they have been converted into end products by other industries.

Figure 1 The input to auto industry from other industries per $1000 of auto production was derived from the 1939 interindustry table. Comparing these figures with those for the auto industry in the 1947 table would show changes in the input structure of the industry due to changes in prices and technology

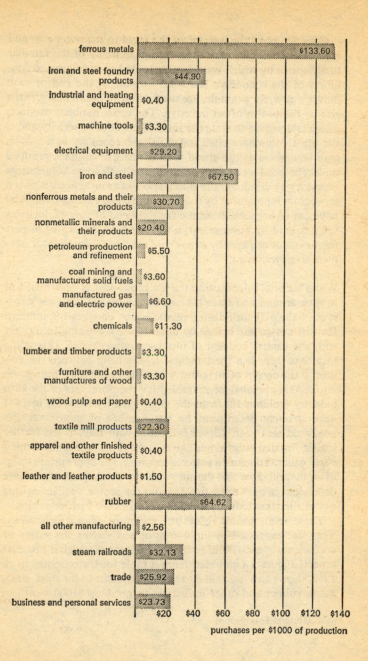

ferrous metals	$133.60
iron and steel foundry products	$44.90
industrial and heating equipment	$0.40
machine tools	$3.30
electrical equipment	$29.20
iron and steel	$67.50
nonferrous metals and their products	$30.70
nonmetallic minerals and their products	$20.40
petroleum production and refinement	$5.50
coal mining and manufactured solid fuels	$3.60
manufactured gas and electric power	$6.60
chemicals	$11.30
lumber and timber products	$3.30
furniture and other manufactures of wood	$3.30
wood pulp and paper	$0.40
textile mill products	$22.30
apparel and other finished textile products	$0.40
leather and leather products	$1.50
rubber	$64.62
all other manufacturing	$2.56
steam railroads	$32.13
trade	$25.92
business and personal services	$23.73

$20 $40 $60 $80 $100 $120 $140

purchases per $1000 of production

Coming out of the interior of the table to the outer row and columns, the reader may soon recognize many of the familiar total figures by which we are accustomed to visualize the condition of the economy. The total outputs at the end of each industry row, for example, are the figures we use to measure the size or the health of an industry. The gross national product, which is designed to state the total of productive activity and is the most commonly cited index for the economy as a whole, may be derived as the grand total of the five columns grouped under the heading of final demand, but with some adjustments necessary to eliminate the duplication of transactions between the sectors represented by these columns. For example, the total payment to households, at the far right end of row 42, includes salaries paid by government, a figure which duplicates in part the payment of taxes by households included in the total payment to government.

With this brief introduction the lay economist is now qualified to turn around and trace his way back into the table via whatever chain of interindustry relationships engages his interest. He will not go far before he finds himself working intuitively with the central concept of input–output analysis. This is the idea that there is a fundamental relationship between the volume of the output of an industry and the size of the inputs going into it. It is obvious, for example, that the purchases of the auto industry (column 18) from the glass industry (row 13) in 1947 were strongly determined by the number of motor vehicles produced that year. Closer inspection will lead to the further realization that every single figure in the chart is dependent upon every other. To take an extreme example, the appropriate series of inputs will show that the auto industry's purchases of glass are dependent in part upon the demand for motor vehicles arising out of the glass industry's purchases from the fuel industries.

These relationships reflect the structure of our technology. They are expressed in input–output analysis as the ratios or coefficients of each input to the total output of which it becomes a part. Figure 1 computed from a table for the economy as of 1939, shows how much had to be purchased from the steel, glass, paint, rubber and other industries to produce $1000 worth of automobile that year. Since such expenditures are determined by relatively inflexible customs and institutional arrangements, these ratios might be used to estimate the demand for materials induced by auto production in other years. With a table of ratios for the economy as a whole, it is possible in turn to calculate the secondary demand on the output of the industries which supply the auto industry's suppliers and so on through successive outputs and inputs until the effect of the final demand for automobiles has been traced to its last reverberation in the farthest corner of the economy. In this fashion input–output analysis should prove useful to the auto industry as a means for dealing with cost and supply problems.

The table of steel consumption ratios (Figure 2) suggests, incidentally, how the input–output matrix might be used for the contrasting purpose of market analysis. Since the ultimate markets for steel are ordinarily buried in the cycle of secondary transactions among the metal-fabricating industries, it is useful to learn from this table how many tons of steel at the mill were needed in 1939 to satisfy each thousand dollars' worth of demand for the products of industries which ultimately place steel products at the disposal of the consumer. This table shows the impressively high ratio of the demand for steel in the construction and consumer durable-goods industries which led the Bureau of Labor Statistics to declare in 1945 that a flourishing post-war economy would require even more steel than the peak of the war effort. Though some industry spokesmen took a contrary position at that time, steel production recently has been exceeding Second World War peaks, and the major steel companies are now engaged in a 16-million-ton expansion program which was started even before the outbreak of the war in Korea and the current rearmament.

The ratios shown in these two tables are largely fixed by technology. Others in the complete matrix of the economy, especially in the trade and services and households sectors, are established by custom and other institutional factors. All, of course, are subject to modification by such forces as progress in technology and changes in public taste. But whether they vary more or less rapidly over the years, these relationships are subject to dependable measurement at any given time.

Here we have our bridge between theory and facts in economics. It is a bridge in a very literal sense. Action at a distance does not happen in economics any more than it does in physics.

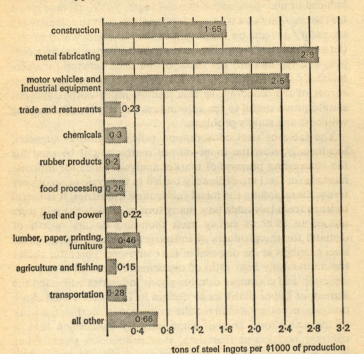

Figure 2 The output of the steel industry depends heavily on what kinds of goods are demanded in the ultimate market. This table shows the amount of steel required to meet each $1000 of the demand for other goods in 1939. The current demand for the top three items is responsible for the steel shortage

The effect of an event at any one point is transmitted to the rest of the economy step by step via the chain of transactions that links the whole system together. A table of ratios for the entire economy gives us, in as much detail as we require, a quantitatively determined picture of the internal structure of the system. This makes it possible to calculate in detail the consequences that result from the introduction into the system of changes suggested by the theoretical or practical problem at hand.

In the case of a particular industry we can easily compute the complete table of its input requirements at any given level of output, provided we know its input ratios. By the same token, with somewhat more involved computation, we can construct synthetically a complete input–output table for the entire economy. We need only a known 'bill of final demand' to convert the table of ratios into a table of magnitudes. The 1945 estimate of post-war steel requirements, for example, was incidental to a study of the complete economy based upon a bill of demand which assumed full employment in 1950. This bill of demand was inserted into the total columns of a table of ratios based on the year 1939. By arithmetical procedures the ratios were then translated into dollar figures, among which was the figure for steel, which showed a need for an absolute minimum of 98 million ingot tons. Actual production in 1950, at the limit of capacity, was 96·8 million tons.

Though its application is simple, the construction of an input–output table is a highly complex and laborious operation. The first step, and one that has little appeal to the theoretical imagination, is the gathering and ordering of an immense volume of quantitative information. Given the inevitable lag between the accumulation and collation of data for any given year, the input–output table will always be an historical document. The first input–output tables, prepared by the author and his associates at Harvard University in the early 1930s, were based upon 1919 and 1929 figures. The 1939 table was not completed until 1944. Looking to the future, a table for 1953 which is now under consideration could not be made available until 1957.[1] For practical purposes the original figures in the table must be regarded as a base, subject to refinement and correction in

1. In November 1964 the US Department of Commerce published a preliminary, and in September 1965 the final, version of the newly compiled input–output table of the US economy for the census year 1958. It contains eighty-six producing and six final demand sectors. In releasing these figures the Secretary of Commerce announced that in the future up-to-date input–output tables will be published 'as an integral part of national income and product accounts'.

accord with subsequent trends. For example, the 1945 projection of the 1950 economy on the basis of the 1939 table made suitable adjustments in the coal and oil input ratios of the transportation industries on the assumption that the trend from steam to diesel locomotives would continue throughout the period.

The basic information for the table and its continuing revision comes from the Bureau of the Census and other specialized statistical agencies. As the industrial breakdown becomes more detailed, however, engineering and technical information plays a more important part in determining the data. A perfectly good way to determine how much coke is needed to produce a ton of pig iron, in addition to dividing the output of the blast furnace industry into its input of coke, is to ask an ironmaster. In principle there is no reason why the input–output coefficients should not be entirely derived from 'below', from engineering data on process design and operating practice. Thus in certain studies of the German economy made by the Bureau of Labor Statistics following the Second World War the input structures of key industries were set up on the basis of US experience. The model of a disarmed but self-supporting Germany developed in these studies showed a steel requirement of 11 million ingot tons, toward which actual output is now moving. Completely hypothetical input structures, representing industries not now operating, have been introduced into tables of the existing US economy in studies conducted by Air Force economists.

This brings us to the problem of computation. Since the production level required of each industry is ultimately dependent upon levels in all others, it is clear that we have a problem involving simultaneous equations. Though the solution of such equations may involve no very high order of mathematics, the sheer labor of computation can be immense. The number of equations to be solved is always equal to the number of sectors into which the system is divided. Depending upon whether a specific or a general solution of the system is desired, the volume of computation will vary as the square or the cube of the number of sectors involved. A typical general solution of a forty-two-sector table for 1939 required fifty-six hours on the Harvard Mark II computer. Thanks to this investment in computation, the conversion of any stipulated bill of demand into the various industrial production levels involves nothing more than simple arithmetic. The method cannot be used, however, in the solution of problems which call for changes in the input–output ratios, since each change requires a whole new solution of the matrix. For the larger number of more interesting problems which require such changes, special solutions are the rule. However, even a special solution on a reasonably detailed 200-sector table might require some 200,000 multiplications and a greater number of additions. For this reason it is likely that the typical nongovernmental user will be limited to condensed general solutions periodically computed and published by special-purpose groups working in the field. With these the average industrial analyst will be able to enjoy many of the advantages of the large and flexible machinery required for government analyses relating to the entire economy.

A demonstration of input–output analysis applied to a typical economic problem is presented in Figure 3 which shows the price increases that would result from a general 10 per cent increase in the wage scale of industry. Here the value of the matrix distinguishing between direct and indirect effect is of the utmost importance. If wages constituted the only ultimate cost in the economy, a general 10 per cent rise in all money wages would obviously lead to an equal increase in all prices. Since wages are only one cost and since labor costs vary from industry to industry, it can be seen in the chart that a 10 per cent increase in wages would have decidedly different effects upon various parts of the economy. The construction industry shows the greatest upward price change, as it actually did in recent decades. For each industry group the chart separates the direct effect of increases in its own wage bill from the indirect effects of the wage increases in other industries from which it purchases its inputs. Giving effect to both direct and indirect increases, the average increase in the cost of living is shown in the chart to be only 3·7 per cent. The 10 per cent money-wage increase thus yields a 6·3 per cent increase in real wage rates. It should be noted, however, that the economic forces which bring increases in wages tend to bring increases in other costs as well. The advantage of the input–output analysis is that it permits the disentanglement and accurate measurement of the indirect effects. Analyses similar to this one for wages can be carried through for profits, taxes and other ultimate components of prices.

In such examples changes in the economy over periods are measured by comparing before and after pictures. Each is a static model, a cross section in time. The next step in input–output analysis is the development of dynamic models of the economy to bring the approximations of the method that much closer to the actual processes of economics. This requires accounting for stocks as well as flows of goods, for inventories of goods in process and in finished form, for capital equipment, buildings and, last but not least, for dwellings and household stocks of durable consumer goods. The dynamic input–output analysis requires more advanced mathematical methods; instead of ordinary linear equations it leads to systems of linear differential equations.

Among the questions the dynamic system should make it possible to answer, one could mention the determination of the changing pattern of outputs and inventories or investments and capacities which would attend a given pattern of growth in final demand projected over a five- or ten-year period. Within such broad projections, for example, we would be able to estimate approximately not only how much aluminium should be produced, but how much additional aluminium-producing capacity would be required, and the rate at which such capacity should be installed. The computational task becomes more formidable, but it does not seem to exceed the capacity of the latest electronic computers. Here, as in the case of the static system, the most laborious problem is the assembly of the necessary factual information. However, a complete set of stock or capital ratios, paralleling the flow ratios of all of the productive sectors of the US economy for the year 1939, has now been completed.

This table of capital ratios shows that in addition to the flow of raw pig-iron, scrap, coal, labor, and so on, the steel works and rolling mills industry – when operating to full capacity – required $1800 of fixed investment for each $1000 worth of output. This would include $336 worth of tools, $331 worth of iron and steel foundry production and so on down to $26 worth

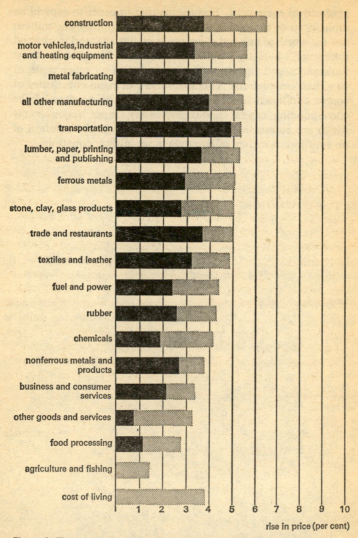

Figure 3 The price increases that would be caused by a 10 per cent increase in wages were computed from the 1939 interindustry table. The increases include the direct effect of the rise in each industry's own wage bill (black bars) and the indirect effect of price increases on purchases from others (grey bars)

of electrical equipment. This means that in order to expand its capacity so as to be able to increase its output by one million dollars' worth of finished products annually, the steel works and rolling mills industry would have to install $336,000 worth of tools and spend corresponding amounts on all other types of new fixed installations. This investment demand constitutes of course additional input requirements for the product of the corresponding capital goods industries, input requirements which are automatically taken into account in the solution of an appropriate system of dynamic input–output equations.

Part Seven In Field and Salon

'The Theory of Economics does not furnish a body of settled conclusions immediately applicable to policy. It is a method rather than a doctrine, an apparatus of the mind, a technique of thinking, which helps its possessor to draw correct conclusions.'

Lord Keynes, *Introduction to Cambridge Economic Handbooks*, Cambridge University Press, 1922.

17 Walter C. Neale

The Peculiar Economics of Professional Sport[1]

Walter C. Neale, 'The peculiar economics of professional sports', *Quarterly Journal of Economics*, vol. 78, 1964, pp. 1–14.

Professional sport promoters and owners of professional teams have long claimed a special position in respect to the monopoly laws and the constitutional prohibition against slave labor, and recently they have been deservedly successful in appeals to Congress. This paper presents the results of serious thought about the problem, serious thought engaged in *after* choosing sides on the issue. I submit that the 'firm' in professional sports is indeed in a peculiar position *vis-à-vis* our accepted way of looking at the firm in a competitive market. The basic proposition can be called the Louis–Schmeling paradox.

Louis–Schmeling paradox

If we ignore for the moment the legal reasons in the United States for avoiding a monopoly position, it is clear that the ideal market position of a firm is that of monopoly, whether to maximize profits or to maximize the comfort of life. If we consider the monopoly laws, the ideal position is as close to monopoly as the antitrust division will permit without prosecution. In brief, a firm is better off the smaller or less important the competition, and it will try to attain a situation in which it is the sole supplier.

But now consider the position of the heavy-weight champion of the world. He wants to earn more money, to maximize his profits. What does he need in order to do so? Obviously, a contender, and the stronger the contender the larger the profits from fighting him. And, since doubt about the

1. For the original stimulus to this paper I am indebted to Mr Charles Conerly of Mara University and to Coach Ole Pro of Falstaff University.

competition is what arouses interest, the demonstration effect will increase the incomes of lesser fighters (lower on the rating scale or lighter on the weighing scales). Pure monopoly is disaster: Joe Louis would have had no one to fight and, therefore, no income.

The boxing champion is the striking case, but the problem is equally great for any professional team. Suppose the Yankees used their wealth to buy up not only all the good players but also all of the teams in the American League: no games, no gate receipts, no Yankees. When, for a brief period in the late fifties, the Yankees lost the championship and opened the possibility of a non-Yankee World Series they found themselves – anomalously – facing sporting disgrace and bigger crowds.[2] If the Yankees, then, do not wish to monopolize their own league, why don't they buy out the National League? The answer is, of course, all those World Series receipts. 'Oh Lord, make us good, but not that good', must be their prayer.

Now we must face the question of whether it is possible that there is a business which, contrary to all we have learned about the business world, finds monopoly unprofitable. The answer, economists will be pleased to learn, is no – that a business monopoly is profitable in the sporting business as well as in the business of life. The first peculiarity of the economics of professional sports is that receipts depend upon competition among the sportors or the teams, not upon business competition among the firms running the contenders, for the greater the economic collusion and the more the sporting competition the greater the profits. The paradox appears because the firm in law, as organized in the sporting world, is not the firm of economic analysis; and the item sold by the sporting firm is not the product of these firms, or not entirely. We have, in fact, the phenomenon of the inverted joint product or the product joint.

2. When the San Diego Chargers of the American Football League ran roughshod over their competitors in the fall of 1961 the fans began to stay away.

The inverted joint product of the product joint[3]

We have long been used to the idea of a firm producing several products from an indivisible process. The sporting firms produce an indivisible product from the separate processes of two or more firms (in law). But the product itself is a peculiar mixture: it comes divisible into parts, each of which can be and is sold separately, but it is also a joint and multiple yet indivisible product.

To be specific, professional baseball teams produce a complex product; or in common parlance several interrelated streams of utility. There is first the saleable unit of the seat in the ball park during the game, the service sold by each firm (Yankees, Senators, and intermediates) and generally regarded as the business of and the utility produced by the sporting firm. Then there is that strange sale of the utility of TV viewing where we the people enjoy the utility while nonsporting businesses pay the bill for us.[4] However, there are two other streams of utilities. There is the pennant race enjoyed by all and paid for by none. This we call the league standing effect.

League standing effect

Of itself there is excitement in the daily changes in the standings or the daily changes in possibilities of changes in standings. The closer the standings, and within any range of standings the more frequently the standings change, the larger will be the gate receipts. Thus the free provision of the *race utility* has a favorable feedback effect upon gate receipts, and we may treat this effect as a kind of advertising. Note that this advertising is also free and that it too illustrates the Louis–Schmeling paradox in that the more successful in sporting competition the firm is, the less effective is the advertising feedback of race utility. The

3. Since a joint product refers to two products technologically resulting from a single process, we need another term for a single product resulting from discrete technological processes, and following the profession's tradition of jumbling words (value of marginal product, marginal value product) we here invert the words to symbolize single product of two processes.

4. Which raises an interesting question about whose marginal rates of substitution on what indifference map.

'league standing effect' is not limited to the consumer utility stream and the advertising feedback because it is also a marketable commodity, but not for the producers. This quirk we may call the fourth estate benefit.

Fourth estate benefit

Newspapers report the play, the outcomes, and the resulting 'league standings' of games, and these reports are a major cause of sales and therefore of direct and advertising revenues to newspapers (and of course to sports magazines): in fact, a case of economies external to the industry. Two separate sets of activities are needed to produce the game write-up – the game and the reporter–newspaper–printer–distributor complex. The former could occur without the latter, but the latter cannot occur without the former, yet the latter is the financial beneficiary of this product joint from two different economic spheres (although we must allow for the advertising feedback to gate receipts from press stories).

So far as the argument has carried us we may conclude that the product of professional sporting activity is not merely (a) the match, but also (b) the 'league standings' (or championship), the progress towards a championship or changes in the standings, topics of conversation and press reports. Furthermore, (c) a business firm – Joe Louis or the New York Yankees – cannot produce any of these streams of utilities alone. It must have the cooperation of a second business firm even to produce the game; to produce the other utilities it must have the cooperation of several business firms.[5]

The conclusion, then, is that the business firm as understood in law (and therefore in common discussion) – Louis or the Yankees – is not the firm as understood in economic theory. Rather, the firm is the league, or all professional heavyweights. Once this point is realized, the theoretical conclusion is clear: each professional sport is a natural monopoly. The several joint products which are products joint of legally separate

5. It might be argued that any firm buying inputs from another firm requires the cooperation of the second firm, but this is stretching the meaning. The cooperating firms in sports are not willing buyers and sellers from and to each other but together (and with the press) sell to third parties.

business firms are really the complex joint products of one firm, and this firm is necessarily an all-embracing firm or natural monopoly.

A natural monopoly as commonly understood is an industry in which a single firm can satisfy the market in the declining portion of its long-run average total cost curve. If defined as one in which a single firm can satisfy demand at a lower long-run average total cost than can be achieved if two or more supply the industry's product, it would be possible to have a natural monopoly where long-run costs are constant, if their level varies with the number of firms, or where average costs are rising if the minimum and rising portions are so low that any division of the market between two firms results in higher costs for both on the declining portion of the cost curve because of diseconomies external to the firm although internal to the industry.

In law a firm is regarded as a person, persons or organization having the right to own property and to contract. In economics a firm may be defined as a 'decision-making unit whose major objective is profit' (however Harry Wismer may define the term), but this definition assumes that the 'decision-making' and the 'profit-taking' units are identical, whereas in professional sports, while the legal firm takes the profits, the league makes the decisions. Professor Robert Dorfman suggests parallels to the league in trade associations, the Eastern Railway Conference, the combination of various firms for construction jobs, and the joint ventures of Gimbel's and Macy's in the United Parcel Service and the bridge connecting the stores, holding that in none of these cases have the business firms merged. But each of these organizations is a firm by the definition, 'a decision-making unit whose major objective is profit'. The railways make decisions jointly about through-routing and rates, to maximize their profits, and so small a cooperative effort as common billing by a trade association is a joint decision made to reduce costs (i.e. increase profits). In short, although legally separate, in substance the associations and conferences act as would the management of a trust or holding company in so far as they reach joint decisions on marketing and pricing and, therefore, can be regarded as merged.

If department stores were to withdraw from all businesses

except the joint ownership of a delivery firm, or if railway companies were to restrict their activities to the joint management of a terminus, one would think of them as merged for any questions of economic substance. Operations such as the cooperative selling to each other and to other buyers by plumbers, carpenters, and builders in the construction industry do parallel sporting firms in that both are multifirm plants.

Multifirm plants

Familiarity with the concept of a multiplant firm should not blind us to an occasional reversal of form created largely by the peculiarities of our law of property. The 'plant' of the construction trades is the building site. At a minimum one might say that the 'plant' of the sporting firms is the playing field, but without the league the playing field is incapable of producing the championship product, so the concept of 'plant' must be enlarged to encompass the league. Furthermore, the parallel between the building industry and the sporting firms is not complete, for the sporting firms sell an indivisible product (once divided it is no product at all) to the consumer and *contribute exactly the same inputs*. The parallel should be with two or more plumbing companies joining together to sell their services as a single source of supply. Where there is joint decision making because it is cheaper to do so, the resulting arrangement may be more easily seen as a monopoly if a (partial) cartel may be considered, as I would, a firm.

As for Gimbel's and Macy's, my mother-in-law assures me that 'everyone knows they are in each other's pockets'.[6]

An objection may be raised that one can have several leagues, and that these leagues are, or should be, competing firms. As one surveys the history and present state of the sporting trades one must admit the possibility, but one must also recognize that as a matter of observation there appears to be a strong tendency toward a single league, and this for one good reason: only a single league can produce that most useful of all products joint, the World Champion. Analytically we must regard the National League and the American League as one, for they come together

6. Mrs Paul B. Sheldon, New York City, oral communication, 23 March 1963.

each autumn to produce the World Series. Despite the differences in form, the substance of this World Series product is identical with the single league championship in the National Football League arrived at by business collusion in cooperative sporting competition between an 'eastern division' and a 'western division' team. Hereafter we should therefore refer to the two major leagues in baseball as 'divisions' within the larger league-firm.

At the present time the trade of professional football is divided in two in the United States, with a competitor in Canada. There is no meeting on the field of play between the National and the American Football Leagues. The result is an absence of sporting competition, but very strong interfirm competition between the old and new leagues. Do we, therefore, have oligopoly? Yes, in the short run, in the same way that some American railroads have tried to compete; but in the long run, no, because this is inherently a temporary state of affairs. We witnessed a similar situation just after the Second World War when the All-America Conference challenged the National Professional Football League. The result in that instance was the demise of the Conference with the older League absorbing some of the teams of the bankrupt Conference. Logically we may distinguish four cases or four possible histories of interleague business competition:

1. The Major League Baseball solution: the joining of economically competing oligopolistic firms into sportingly competitive natural monopolies.

2. The professional football solution of the forties: bankruptcy for one or the other of the economically competing firms.

3. The survival of two or more leagues because they are not economically competitive. This case occurs when the leagues are operating in different geographical areas or are inherently noncompetitive in both the sporting and economic sense, as in the case of boxers of different weights, or, a few years ago, baseball players of different colors.

4. The survival of two or more leagues which are economically competitive and which could be sportingly competitive.

The first two cases have been historically the common ones. The third case is actually rarer than one might expect. Of course, when it is patently ridiculous to compete in sport – to match a heavyweight with a flyweight – two leagues or championships coexist, but where sporting competition is prevented by geographical difference the tendency is to enlarge the area of sporting competition until in fact there is only one league. Thus we find that Australian, West Indian, Indian, Pakistani and English cricket, separated about as much as is possible (or was possible before Gagarin) merge in that great international cartel, the Test Matches. Again, soccer (mistakenly called football by literally minded foreigners), which is formally organized in teams merged in national leagues, has become a cartel of international matches. Since cartelization is necessary not only to maximization of profits but also, even especially, to maximization of output, the geographical division of the market is an inherently unstable situation usually replaced by a naturally monopolistic firm whose market region is everywhere that the sport is played.[7]

Whether or not two leagues can survive within the market area – our fourth logically possible case – depends on the facts of the matter, or, put more realistically, on the relative shapes and positions of the demand and cost functions. From the sports pages it is difficult to glean solid data to which to fit functions, but one does form the impression from the history of sports that such survival is unlikely. In effect, the argument here depends upon the acceptance of premises for which direct evidence is thin on the grounds that the conclusion reached from the premises is consistent with observation.

7. The apparent exceptions of United States and Japanese baseball and of the sportingly independent United States and Canadian football leagues partly reflect difficulties of amalgamation across national boundaries, but more important, both Japanese and Americans agree that the Japanese teams could not win an international World Series and it is thus unnecessary to prove by formal competition that the American winner is the champion. But even here when exhibition games begin to show the American superiority at its own sport is questionable, one should expect cartelization into an international league. Perhaps, too, the pressure for Canadian–United States competition is low because it is not widely believed that the Canadians might win.

The long-run cost curve of seats-at-games for the league-firm is probably flat or almost flat. As one expands the firm the quality of the product is affected by two contrary tendencies.

Diminishing quality returns

The first is diminishing quality returns because the quality of raw materials declines as less efficient inputs are drawn into the sport. One may treat this as producing an inferior product for which there is another, lower demand function for lower quality 'game seats' (which means a reduction in revenue per game seat).[8] Alternatively one may regard the diminishing quality returns as an increase in the cost of producing the same quality of game seat. In either case there is a limit to the size of the most efficient (least minimum average cost per constant quality game seat) league-firm, given by the cost function. The limit on size applies no matter how few or many leagues there are, so that one large league can provide any quantity of product as cheaply as two or more smaller firms. Thus there is no efficiency argument against monopoly, and there is a likelihood that the first league in the sport – like the first utility in a city – will become a monopoly. But any upward shifts in costs (or downward shift of quality and therefore the substitution of a new demand curve) are counteracted by the input-enthusiasm effect.

Input-enthusiasm effect

Whereas one finds that human abilities in various directions are randomly distributed in any population, one also finds that skill abilities in sports are concentrated regionally. How else can we explain the disproportionate number of first-class tennis players and cricket batsmen from Australia, or runners from Australia, England and Scandinavia, or of passing quarterbacks from Texas, other than by reference to the public attention and private concentration put into the development of these particular skills? And this input into the inputs is a result of the enthusiasm for the sport in the area, which in turn is both a consequence and a cause of the scale of operations of the sport

8. However, we know by introspection that the reduction will be small since the appeal of the seat depends mostly on the uncertainty of the outcome and on the weather.

in the area. In other words, the larger the scale of operations, the higher the quality of inputs and of products, or the lower the cost of a constant quality game seat.

When one shifts one's focus from the use of resources or the quality of product to the money costs it is reasonable to suppose that less perfect inputs (producing lower quality games) will earn a lower return, so that the cost per quality unit will not change as much as the quality changes. Both the 'enthusiasm effect' and the lower salaries of lower quality sportsmen will flatten any rising tendency in money costs consequent upon diminishing returns. Enthusiasm simultaneously increases (a) the demand for game admissions and therefore the derived demand for skilled players and hence their salaries, so that the monetary cost of each unit of the larger supply of higher quality players rises; and increases (b) the supply of skilled players. The net effect of the increase in demand on gate receipts and on derived demand will merely tend to shift the curves north-eastwards without a 'squeeze' on profits, while the underlying 'enthusiasm effect' will lower the supply schedule of inputs. Larger scale, therefore, does not necessarily increase costs more than revenue.

All this, of course, is in conformity with our economic expectations, but the supply mechanism is not market pricing. The supply of skilled inputs is developed in the sphere of amateur activity – specifically in the schools – so that the equilibrating mechanism works not through price response but through enthusiastic response and the human desire to conform to standards of group approval.

The net effect of diminishing returns, of the tendency toward constant money costs in quality units of input and of the 'enthusiasm effect' may be constant costs, increasing costs or decreasing costs. In the absence of information, I guess that the long-run supply curve of the league-firm is roughly constant for output units of games by pairs of teams.

One usually expects a constant cost industry to be competitive, *ceteris paribus*; but *cetera non sunt paria*. Even if professional sports are constant cost industries the 'World Champion utility' can only be created by cartelization. Furthermore, there is interdependence between demand and supply. The total size of the industry (in game-seats) is determined by the intersection of demand with supply, and if the long-run supply curve is horizontal, one might say that it is strategically determined by demand. But demand itself is in large part a reaction to the sporting importance of the events, the sporting importance depends upon the 'fourth estate effect' and the 'public conversation effect', and since these effects in turn depend upon the scale and universality of the championship at stake, the function will move up to the right for a more conclusive championship and down to the left if the leagues decided to avoid meeting in a play-off. Thus demand and supply tend to intersect at the point of a single, monopoly championship wherever that intersection may be (the You Don't Say Law).

On the supply side the long-run cost curve is horizontal, but the height of the curve above zero depends on the costs to the business or league-firms. These costs consist mostly of two elements: (a) fixed costs of interest or rent on the stadium capital and the cost of equipment and transportation for the firm, and (b) quasi-rents for the players. The price of any player is partly a function of his willingness to play, for the athlete need not enter the players' market since he has alternative opportunities, but once his minimum supply price is met the team firm is paying for an unreproducible talent, or a quasi-rent. If there are two firms bidding for his talents the quasi-rent will probably be higher than if there is only one bidder who is engaged with the player in bilateral bargaining. Since league firms typically prohibit multiple bidding by their team component firms counterbidding arises only when there are two independent leagues.[9] The existence of economically but not sportingly competing leagues thus raises the money costs to both leagues and so endangers profits. While in logic there is no

9. A variety of liberties and restraints characterize the quasi-rent bargaining process in professional sports. In American football the 'player draft' eliminates within-league counterbidding; in baseball the teams must bid against each other to contract with a new player but once the contract is signed the other teams cannot make counteroffers during the following years. Similar arrangements exist in other team sports, but in the sports of individual competition, e.g. boxing, the player and the business firm merge so that the quasi-rent payment to the competitor merges with his windfall profits and his income is undifferentiated.

reason why both leagues cannot continue to enjoy profits, or at least no losses, they are unlikely to do so. The salary of a player has much in common with ground rents, but the analogy must be understood to apply by lot, and is not complete. As in the result only one store actually uses one lot, so only one league employs one player. But whereas several stores can compete in a shopping area when they sell the same products because non-rental costs of and demand for the products of each store are the same, two or more leagues probably will not enjoy identical nonrental costs and demand. Transport to and from Kansas City from other points will not be the same as to and from Houston, while the urge to go to a ball game will differ from city to city (or from the Bronx to Brooklyn). Only in the unlikely event that both leagues field teams in exactly the same cities (and with exactly the same appeal to historic loyalties) will there be a no-profit-no-loss Chamberlinian equilibrium. One, there-fore, expects competitive bidding eventually to raise quasi-rents for one league or the other above the spread between its other costs and its receipts, at which point the fourth solution becomes the second.[10]

Competition exists not between teams or leagues but between sports. Paying fans and newspaper readers prefer one or another sport – I suspect largely because Dad preferred it – but shifts in taste do occur and the leagues, or even the component teams

10. Professor Benjamin Higgins pointed out that some other trades require competition to succeed. One is law, a single firm needing others to fight in court; another is fashion, the interest arising from the differences between two designers. There are perhaps more for there is no reason to believe that a 'peculiar economics' is confined to professional sports alone. However, the two examples, while requiring competition for profits, are not cases on all fours with professional sports. Fashion requires separate, econ-omically as well as esthetically, competing units and so does not tend to coalesce into a monopoly. Furthermore, the supply of fashionable goods is the product of many factories and stores all over the world, not of the designers themselves. They are more like leading architects than leading coaches. The practice of law also does not tend toward monopolization of the business firms; and unlike both sports and fashion its practice cannot be called inconsequential. The need for competition within the courts stems not from the economics of business, as it does in professional sports, but rather from the adversary structure of our system of justice. Whereas sports require sporting competition and business monopoly, fashion and law require both interfirm business as well as esthetic and legal competition.

acting independently, can encourage such shifts. Between the wars the New York (football) Giants built a loyal following by selling tickets extremely cheaply to children. Colorful people, youth leaders, immoral people, all can be used to attract attention to a sport. Ice hockey undoubtedly has increased its popularity over what it would otherwise have been by the public notice of brawls during games.

Definite divisions of the sports market seem to be characteristic. First there are the national divisions, marking off American baseball from Commonwealth cricket, American football from international soccer. Second, there are the seasonal divisions, leaving baseball dominant in the spring and summer, football in the autumn, and basketball in the winter. Third, there are divisions among social classes: cricket is upper class and soccer working class in England; baseball was the sport of the small town in America while professional football grew up in the industrial cities. Although these divisions may not be immutable they are certainly hard to change. Professional football has crept back into the late baseball season and forward into the basketball–hockey season, but efforts to establish an American soccer league in monopolistic competition with baseball (during June, July and August) have met with little favor.

Within the general framework of a whole-sport monopoly there are some additional peculiarities. We are familiar with the cobweb theorem, which depends upon next period's supply responding to this period's demand. But in professional sports we have the Roger Maris cobweb.

Roger Maris cobweb

The demand for Roger Maris's services for next year depends upon his performance this year. The cobweb has been inverted with demand reacting after a delay to supply; and the 1962 quasi-rent depended upon how ruthlessly Maris pursued the home-run mantle in 1961. Note that to introduce the concept of expectations does not alter the point, for the famous hog cycle – in which the sex urge of pigs responds to slaughtering prices in Chicago – is also one of expectations. Here one might note that an explosive cobweb is unlikely since the supply curve of talent in the quasi-rent range must be vertical and the height above the minimum price which Mr Maris will accept and the depth below the maximum which the Yankees will offer Mr Maris depends upon bargaining technique. Below the minimum which Mr Maris will take we have a horizontal supply curve and Mr Maris leaves the market.

Whether marginal analysis of input pricing will work at all is doubtful. Whereas one can speak of the marginal steel worker without naming him it seems a little foolish to speak of the marginal quarterback of the Steelers. Marginalism seems to break upon the Bobby Layne rigidity.

Bobby Layne rigidity

There are possibilities of substitution of an indirect sort. Clearly one cannot field more than eleven laborers in a football game, 'nor can one use two poor quarterbacks instead of one good one'; but one can use a better line to give a weaker passer more time or a faster fullback to make up for the absence of two first-class halfbacks. Such considerations obviously weigh with teams in their drafting and trading operations since Baltimore let Mr Lipscombe go and the Giants put more effort into finding defensive personnel than into finding new offensive backs. But here one fails to see just how the Colts and the Giants compute the marginal returns of tackles, of pass receivers, and so forth. In baseball batting averages and earned-run ratings provide a better guide to marginal productivity computations; but in both sports the value of the marginal product is only indirectly and roughly related to these sporting measures since it is the effect upon the gate receipts which counts and gate receipts have no stable functional relationship with the sporting measures. In boxing the idea breaks down completely since the entire labor input is one and always tries to be its best. Thus the ultimate of the Bobby Layne rigidity is the Archie Moore indivisibility.

Archie Moore indivisibility

Having discussed the demand and cost structure of the professional sports industry certain parallels with other industries will be apparent. The firm of economic theory is the league, and the league is a natural monopoly with demand and cost and profit adjustments always tending toward unification of all league-firms into a single *firma-firmorum*.

The plant of economic theory is the game, which requires three factors of production: namely, land, labor and labor. In different sports each of the factors has a critical minimum beyond which additions to output fall off rapidly; but the law of variable proportions is here invariable since two of the factors can be used simultaneously only in specified quantities and in some sports all three are subject to this limitation and the additional inputs logically come under the classification 'repair and renewal'. At this point one can also see the importance of institutionalism for the limits on the employment of labor trace back to ancient and irrational traditions of sportsmanlike behaviour, and to break them by, say, fielding a fifth back armed with a switch blade would be impermissible to members of the tribal society despite the fact that any United Nations expert could point out the obvious technical advantages. To my knowledge only the Canadians have adopted the fifth back, and there is no evidence in published reports that even the Canadians have equipped this man properly. On the other hand, economic sophistication of a high order is shown by the larger end zone and the elimination of the fourth down in a country with large unused areas of land and a small population.

We often think that if plant costs are constant (but here remember that the team or business firm does not constitute a plant) there can be no advantages of scale except as monopsonistic power is exerted; but we have already established those internal and external economies of scale called 'league standing' and 'fourth estate effect'. Thus we justify horizontal integration in a natural monopoly.

Vertical integration takes different forms in different sports. We would have to stretch meanings to visualize vertical integration in boxing, but we are all familiar with the phenomenon in baseball. Here one familiar with the problems of underdeveloped countries and the earlier stages of industrialization will recognize the characteristic need to recruit and commit the labor force. It is also the arena of free contract negotiation; and is finally analogous to the tomato farms held by Heinz.

In American football there is still another organization often referred to as the university. The idea is to develop commitment before recruitment largely on the grounds that it is cheaper – or rather, on the grounds that the social costs of selection and training are shifted onto the community of academics, alumni and taxpayers. But here we can go no further since this information is as well hidden as are the accounts of peasants.[11]

Variety of organization is found in the organization of recruitment more than in any other facet of the economy of professional sports. One can mention, in addition to the two forms already discussed, the feudal organization of village and county cricket, the climatic-linguistic character of ice-hockey recruitment, and less recently the religious qualifications for animal wrestling in the Roman arena. Here alone I feel economists should support the remaining elements of freedom, conflict and competition in the business organization of professional sports.

Otherwise it is clear that professional sports are a natural monopoly, marked by definite peculiarities both in the structure and in the functioning of their markets. Consequently professional leagues have every economic ground to appeal to legislatures, to courts and to the public on the ground that

We fall if you divide us;
We stand if Johnny Unitas.

11. The university farm team also appears to be the last stronghold of the third kind of integration problem. Most economists oppose integration of business firms either horizontally or vertically, but somehow manage at the same time to favor racial integration. This paradox is explained by the economic inefficiency of racial segregation, and the uneconomic character is perhaps sufficiently illustrated by an old lament of the South-west which my daddy used to sing:

There was a blackguard from the South
For our sisters he was born too uncouth;
   He couldn't play Royal's
   Or even Frank Broyles',
  So Syracuse hired the youth.

18 G. J. Stigler

The Intellectual and the Market Place[1]

Chapter 12 in G. J. Stigler, *The Intellectual and the Market Place*,
Free Press, 1963, pp. 85–99.

The intellectual has never felt kindly toward the market place:
to him it has always been a place of vulgar men and of base
motives. Whether this intellectual was an ancient Greek philo-
sopher, who viewed economic life as an unpleasant necessity
which should never be allowed to become obtrusive or dominant, or whether this intellectual is a modern man, who focuses
his scorn on gadgets and Madison Avenue, the basic similarity
of view has been pronounced.

Now you and I are intellectuals, as this word is used. I am
one automatically because I am a professor, and buy more books
than golf clubs. You are intellectuals because you are drawn
from the most intelligent tenth of the population, most of you
will go on to graduate school, and you would rather be a United
States Senator or a Nobel Laureate than the head of the Great
Atlantic and Pacific Tea Company. The question I wish to pose
to us is not whether we should love the market place – even a
professor of economics of outrageously conservative tendencies
cannot bring himself to say that the chants of five auctioneers
rival a Mozart quintet. The questions are rather: what don't we
like about the market place, and are we sure that our attitudes
are socially useful?

Let us begin by noticing that from certain important viewpoints one would have expected the intellectuals to be very

1. The present piece was written to persuade young intellectuals that we
should re-examine the traditional hostility toward private enterprise. I
suppose I should not be surprised that it has been more successful in
reaffirming businessmen in their faith. This is not an undesirable effect, but
a lecturer denouncing cannibalism naturally must view the applause of
vegetarians as equivocal evidence of his eloquence.

kindly disposed toward that system of private enterprise which I call the market place.

First, if I may introduce a practical consideration, intellectuals by and large have elevated tastes – they like to eat, dress and live well, and especially to travel. Walter Hamilton once said that our customary salutation, 'Good Day', was a vestige of an agricultural society where people were asking for good weather, and he expected city dwellers eventually to greet each other with the phrase, 'Low Prices'. If Hamilton's theory is correct, the intellectuals will come to the salutation, 'Fair Fulbright'.

Since intellectuals are not inexpensive, until the rise of the modern enterprise system no society could afford many of them. As a wild guess, the full-time intellectuals numbered two hundred in Athens in the extraordinary age of Pericles, or about one for every 1500 of population and at most times in later history the intellectuals fell far, far short of this proportion. Today there are at least a million in the United States, taking only a fraction of those who live by pen and tongue into account, or one for each two hundred of population. At least four out of every five of us owe our pleasant lives to the great achievements of the market place. We professors are much more beholden to Henry Ford than to the foundation which bears his name and spreads his assets.

Not only have the productive achievements of the market place supported a much enlarged intellectual class, but also the leaders of the market place have personally been strong supporters of the intellectuals, and in particular those in the academic world. If one asks where, in the Western university world, the freedom of inquiry of professors has been most staunchly defended and energetically promoted, my answer is this: not in the politically controlled universities, whether in the United States or Germany – legislatures are not over-populated with tolerant men indifferent to popularity. Not in the self-perpetuating faculties, such as Oxford and Cambridge from 1700 to 1850 – even intellectuals can become convinced that they have acquired ultimate truth and that it can be preserved indefinitely by airing it before students once a year. No, inquiry has been most free in the college whose trustees are a group of top quality leaders of the market place, men who, our experience shows, are remarkably tolerant of almost everything except a mediocre and complacent faculty. Economics provides many examples: if a professor wishes to denounce aspects of big business, as I have, he will be wise to locate in a school whose trustees are big businessmen, and I have.

But debts are seldom the basis for friendship, and there is a much more powerful reason the intellectual might be sympathetic to the market place: the organizing principles of both areas are the same.

An enterprise system is a system of voluntary contract. Neither fraud nor coercion is within the ethics of the market system. Indeed there is no possibility of coercion in a pure enterprise system because the competition of rivals provides alternatives to every buyer or seller. All real economic systems contain some monopoly, and hence some coercive power for particular individuals, but the amount and the extent of such monopoly power are usually much exaggerated, and in any case monopoly is not an integral part of the logic of the system.

The intellectual world, and I speak chiefly but not exclusively of scholarship, is also a voluntary system. Its central credo is that opinions are to be formed from free discussion on the basis of full disclosure of evidence. Fraud and coercion are equally repugnant to the scholar. The freedom of thought is preserved by the open competition of scholars and ideas. Authority, the equivalent of monopoly power, is the great enemy of freedom of inquiry. Competition in scholarship is in some ways more violent than in business: the law sets limits on the disparagement of a rival's product, unless it is done in a book review in a learned journal.

Just as real markets have some fraud and monopoly, which impair the claims for the market place, so the intellectual world has its instances of coercion and deception, with the coercion exercised by *claques* and fashion. But again these deviants are outside the logic of the system.

Both areas, moreover, are democratic. The intellectual believes that every able and willing young person should get a good education whatever his race or financial background. The market believes every able and willing person should be permitted to enter an industry or occupation, whatever his race or educational background. There is food for thought in the fact that racial discrimination has diminished earlier, faster, and more quietly in the market place than in political life.

The analogies could be pursued much farther, although not without danger of alienating all professors and most businessmen. I shall therefore merely mention, in passing, that both fields pay a fair amount of attention to packaging and advertising, and both fields place an absurdly high value on originality. There are also many minor differences, such as that the intellectual has no desire to know the market place, whereas the business man wishes, or at least believes he wishes, to know the world of the intellectual. The basic fact is that the intellectual believes in the free market in ideas and, what is not quite the same thing, in words.

Yet whatever the latent sympathies of the intellectual for the market place, the hostilities are overt. The contempt for the 'profit motive' which directs economic activity is widespread, and the suspicion of the behavior to which it leads is deep-seated. The charge that American society is materialistic has been recited more often than the Declaration of Independence, and has been translated into more foreign languages.

In one basic respect I believe that the criticism by the intellectuals is misplaced, and at times even hypocritical. The American economy produces many goods that are vulgar, silly, or meretricious, as judged by standards which I share with many intellectuals. It seems only proper to cite a few examples, if only to show how selective these standards are. I shall not propose the currently most popular item, the large and powerful automobile, because I have observed that mostly intellectuals of short stature criticize our cars. But other examples are at hand. I am dissatisfied with the tastes of the nine-tenths of the population which believe that non-fictional books are to be read only by young people working for their B.A. I am dissatisfied with a population whose love for interesting music is so narrow that every symphony orchestra requires subsidies. I consider it shocking that more Americans have read *The Affluent Society* than *The Wealth of Nations*.

At the risk of appearing reasonable, I wish to qualify this

complaint by observing that the tastes of the American public are more elevated than those of any other large society in history. Most societies have been judged by their cultural aristocracies – indeed in earlier periods the vast majority of the population was not even considered to be a part of the culture of the society for this vast majority was illiterate, tradition-bound, with most people living brutishly in peasant huts. Our society's tastes are judged by those of the vast majority of the population, and this majority is generous, uncomplacent and hard-working, with unprecedentedly large numbers engaged in further self-education or eagerly patronizing the arts. Our market-supported legitimate theatre, which is surely the best in the world, is a suggestive measure of popular tastes.

These qualifications are not intended to withdraw the charge that the public's tastes should be better, and for that matter, that the intellectual's tastes should be better. It is in fact a basic function of the intellectual to define the standards of good taste more clearly and to persuade people to approach them more closely. It is proper to denounce vulgarity of taste and to denounce it more strongly the more popular it is. It is permissible to reject certain desires completely – as we do when by compulsory education laws we reject the desire for illiteracy – although there is a strong presumption against the use of force in the area of tastes.

When I say that the complaints of deficiencies in tastes are misplaced when they are directed to the market place, I mean just that. The market place responds to the tastes of consumers with the goods and services that are salable, whether the tastes are elevated or depraved. It is unfair to criticize the market place for fulfilling these desires when clearly the defects lie in the popular tastes themselves. I consider it a cowardly concession to a false extension of the idea of democracy to make *sub rosa* attacks on public tastes by denouncing the people who serve them. It is like blaming the waiters in restaurants for obesity.

To escape this response, the more sophisticated intellectuals have argued that people are told what to want by the market place – that advertising skillfully depraves and distorts popular desires. There is no doubt an element of truth in this response, but it is an element of trifling size. The advertising industry has no sovereign power to bend men's will – we are not children who blindly follow the last announcer's instructions to rush to the store for soap. Moreover, advertising itself is a completely neutral instrument, and lends itself to the dissemination of highly contradictory desires. While the automobile industry tells us not to drink while driving, the bourbon industry tells us not to drive while drinking. The symphony orchestra advertises, and gets much free publicity, in its rivalry with the dance band. Our colleges use every form of advertising, and indeed the typical university catalogue would never stop Diogenes in his search for an honest man.

So I believe the intellectuals would gain in candor and in grace if they preached directly to the public instead of using advertising as a whipping boy. I believe they would gain also in virtue if they would examine their own tastes more critically: when a good comedian and a production of Hamlet are on rival channels, I wish I could be confident that less than half the professors were laughing.

The main indictment of the intellectual, however, is that the market place operates on the principle of self-interest, and in fact through competition compels even the philanthropic businessman to become self-serving. Self-interest, often described with such neutral words as egotism, greed and dog-eat-dog, is viewed as a crass, antisocial element of man's character and an economic system that rests upon, and inculcates, this motive achieves little admiration. In fact, a dislike for profit-seeking is one of the few specific attitudes shared by the major religions.

I also find naked selfishness an unendearing trait, but I have trouble in separating it from the more admirable motives related to it. A prudent regard for one's own survival is generally applauded even if the individual does not say, 'I got out of the way of the oncoming train only to spare my Sunday school class pain.' The violent endeavors of an athlete to defeat his rivals are much admired, providing the contest is more or less fair, even though the winner is expected not to say, 'I am glad I won chiefly because I'm vain, but secondarily for the honor of Sheboygan High School.'

Even in fields somewhat removed from the athletic arena, the roles of self-interest and what for lack of a better name I shall call benevolence are perplexingly interwoven. I have spent my life among college teachers, although admittedly in the most competitive branch of research and publication. In one sense the disinterest of my colleagues is beyond doubt: I have seen silly people – public officials as well as private, by the way – try to buy opinions but I have not seen or even suspected any cases in which any important economist sold his professional convictions. It is also true that many of the best professors, and many of the worst, could earn more in other callings.

But on the other hand, the motives that drive them and me are not completely clear, either. When we strive to solve a scientific problem, is ambition for our own professional status completely overshadowed by our love of knowledge? I wonder. When we write an article to demonstrate the fallacies of someone else's work, is our hatred for error never mixed with a tiny bit of glee at the display of our own cleverness? I wonder.

To shift elsewhere, I have never encountered a political candidate who said, 'I am running for office because I, with my dear wife and future administrative assistant, can earn more in politics than elsewhere.' Nor do I expect to. But the language of public interest surely covers a good many acres of self-interest.

A major source of the view that the market place places special values on self-interest, beyond those more or less evident in all human behavior, is the belief that one man's gain is another's loss, that business, like the so-called friendly poker session, is a zero-sum game. Not so.

On the one hand, it must be recognized that the great source of market gains is the productivity of the participants. Unlike the poker game, the wealth of our society has been doubling even on a *per capita* basis every twenty-five years, and the doubling has been due to the labors and ingenuity of the men in the market place. Of course there are also incomes achieved by monopoly rather than by efficiency, by fraud rather than by output, but it would be a wholly extravagant estimate that they amount to 10 per cent of the income of the market place. There is room for improvement here, but there is vastly more room to admire the prodigious production achievements of the market place.

On the other hand, I would emphasize that most of the gains from innovation in the market place are passed on to the community at large. A new idea may yield handsome profits for a time, but the rapid rush of competition soon drives the price of the product down to a modest level. Ball-point pens were first marketed at $12.50 to those penmen eager to write under water (and, judging by my experience, only under water); they rapidly fell in price and as you know are now so cheap that you have no excuse if you do not write the Great American Novel. Sears, Roebuck and Company and Montgomery Ward made a good deal of money in the process of improving our rural marketing structure, but I am convinced that they did more for the poor farmers of America than the sum total of the federal agricultural support programs of the last twenty-eight years.

It is an interesting illustration of the great influence of the intellectual that the market place itself has become apologetic of its pursuit of profit. The captains of industry now list, in a world in which public relations are becoming as important as efficiency, among their major achievements the great number of bowling alleys or college fellowships they have given to their employees. To boast that large profits demonstrate great efficiency in producing existing products and introducing new ones is considered even by them to be too archaic a form of thought for public consumption. The patron saint of economics, Adam Smith, once wrote:

I have never known much good done by those who affected to trade for the public good. It is an affectation, indeed, not very common among merchants, and very few words need be employed in dissuading them from it.

I wonder what those very few words were.

To return to the intellectuals, their dislike for the profit motive of the market place no doubt rests in part on a failure to understand its logic and workings. It is a fact painful to record that the level of economic literacy has not risen noticeably in the twentieth century. Indeed as professional economics becomes more complicated and its practitioners use an increasingly more formidable apparatus, there seems to have been retrogression in our ability to communicate with other intellectuals. Less than a century ago a treatise on economics began with a sentence such as, 'Economics is a study of mankind in the ordinary business of life.' Today it will often begin, 'This unavoidably lengthy treatise is devoted to an examination of an economy in which the second derivatives of the utility function possess a finite number of discontinuities. To keep the problem manageable, I assume that each individual consumes only two goods, and dies after one Robertsonian week. Only elementary mathematical tools such as topology will be employed, incessantly.'

But misunderstanding is not the whole explanation: I cannot believe that any amount of economic training would wholly eliminate the instinctive dislike for a system of organizing economic life through the search for profits. It will still appear to many intellectuals that a system in which men were driven by a reasonably selfless devotion to the welfare of other men would be superior to one in which they sought their own preferment. This ethic is deeply embedded in the major religions.

I personally also believe that the good society will be populated by people who place a great value on other people's welfare. This is, however, not the only attribute of the good society, and in particular in the good society a man should be free within the widest possible limits of other men's limitations on his beliefs and actions. This great ethic of individual freedom clashes with that of benevolence, for I can seldom do positive good to another person without limiting him. I can, it is true, simply give him money, but even in this extreme case where I seem to place no bonds on him, he inevitably faces the question of what conduct on his part will lead me to give money to him again. Usually I will find it hard to be content to do so little good – giving money to improve a man's food or housing or health will seem as inefficient as giving him gasoline so he will drive more often to museums. Hence when I give money I shall also insist that it be spent on housing, or on medical care for his children, or on growing wheat in the way that I think is socially desirable, or on the collected works of Burke and de Tocqueville, or Marx and Lenin. A patron tends to be paternalistic, in a nice way, of course. I am not saying that benevolence is bad, but that like everything else it can be carried to excess.

One final question on motives – why are they so important? Am I to admire a man who injures me in an awkward and mistaken attempt to protect me, and to despise a man who to earn a good income performs for me some great and lasting service? Oddly enough, I suspect an answer is that motive makes a difference – that it is less objectionable to be injured by an incompetent benefactor than by a competent villain. But I leave with you the question: are motives as important as effects?

Several charges related to the dominance of self-interest have rounded out the intellectual's indictment of the market place. First, the system makes no provision for men whose talents and interests are not oriented to profit-seeking economic activity. Second, there are cumulative tendencies toward increasing inequality of wealth, which – if unchecked – will polarize the society into a great number of poor and a few very rich. Third, the game in the market place is unfair in that inheritance of property plays an immensely larger role in success than the efforts of the individuals themselves. I shall comment briefly on each of these assertions.

The first charge is true, the market place will not supply income to a man who will not supply something which people want. People have enormously varied desires, but not enough of them wish to hire men to engage in research on ancient languages nor, sixty years ago, did they hire men to study quantum mechanics. The market place does not provide an air force or alms for the poor. It does not even supply babies. I conclude that a society needs more than a market place.

The second charge, that there are cumulative tendencies to ever-increasing inequality of wealth, is untrue. I would indeed ignore the charge for fear of reprimand from the Society for the Prevention of Cruelty to Straw Men, were it not that this straw man is so popular. In plain historical fact, the inequality in the distribution of income has been diminishing, and the diminution has been due to market forces even more than to governmental efforts. It is also worth noting that a modern market economy has a less unequal income distribution than in either centrally directed or unindustrialized economies.

The third charge, that inheritance of property plays a dominant role in the distribution of income in the market place, is an overstatement. Inheritance of property is important, but it will give some perspective to the charge to notice that property income is only one-fifth of national income, and inherited property is less than half of all property, so less than 10 per cent of all income is governed by inheritance of property.

No useful purpose would be served by trying to appraise the proper role of inheritance of property in a few passing remarks. We should have to look carefully at the effects of inheritance on incentives; we should have to look at gifts during life, which are almost equivalent to bequests; and we should have to decide whether privately endowed colleges do enough good to offset the inevitable high-living heirs – whether we can have Carleton without having Tommy Manville.

But our greatest problem would be that inheritance extends far beyond a safe deposit box full of bonds and stocks. I have told you that you are intelligent; I now add that the chief reason you are intelligent is that your parents are intelligent. Some of you, especially the younger of you, may find this unbelievable: Mark Twain said he was astonished by how much his father had learned during the short time it took Mark to grow from eighteen to twenty-one. But inheritance of ability is important, probably more important in its effects on the distribution of income than is the inheritance of property. So a full account of the proper role of inheritance would have to extend to ability, and perhaps even to name and reputation, as the junior senator from Massachusetts might agree. The social and legal institutions governing inheritance in our society are surely open to improvement, but we are unlikely to improve them if we are guided by nothing more than naïve egalitarianism.

And now to my final point. We are great believers in the human mind, we intellectuals, and of its ability to conquer an ever larger part of the immense domain of ignorance. But we have not made much use of the mind in reaching our views on the economic organization appropriate to the good society so far as its basic cultural values go. It is clear that the kinds of traits that are fostered in man are influenced by (but of course not only by) the way economic life is organized – after all, throughout history men have spent half their waking hours in economic activity.

Important as the moral influences of the market place are, they have not been subjected to any real study. The immense proliferation of general education, of scientific progress, and of democracy are all coincidental in time and place with the emergence of the free enterprise system of organizing the market place. I believe this coincidence was not accidental: the economic progress of the past three centuries was both cause and effect of this general growth of freedom. The dominant era of the free market place was in the nineteenth century. I believe, but with less confidence, that the absence of major wars in this century – the only peaceable century in history – was related to this reign of liberty. I believe, again with less confidence, that the contemporary transformation of the British public from a violent and unruly people into a population of almost painful Victorian rectitude was related to this reign of liberty.

These beliefs may be right or wrong, but they are not matters of taste. They are hypotheses concerning the relationship between economic and social organization, and are subject to analytical development and empirical testing. It is time that we did so, high time. Our ruling attitude toward the market place has not changed since the time of Plato. Is it not possible that it is time to rethink the question?

Further Reading

Part One *The Price System*

F. H. Knight, *The Economic Organisation*, Kelley, 1951.

A. P. Lerner, *Everybody's Business*, Michigan State University Press, 1961.

R. A. Radford, 'The economic organisation of a prisoner of war camp', *Economica*, vol. 12, 1945, pp. 189–201.

J. A. Schumpeter, 'The nature and necessity of a price system', *Economic Reconstruction*, Columbia University Press, 1934, pp. 170–76.

Part Two *Two Traditions*

M. Blaug, *Economic Theory in Retrospect*, Heinemann, 1968.

M. Friedman, 'Léon Walras and his economic system', *Amer. econ. Rev.*, vol. 45, 1955, pp. 900–909.

J. R. Hicks, 'Léon Walras', *Econometrica*, vol. 2, 1934, pp. 338–48.

J. A. Schumpeter, *History of Economic Analysis*, Allen & Unwin, 1954.

G. F. Shove, 'The place of Marshall's *Principles* in the development of economic theory', *Econ. J.*, vol. 52, 1942, pp. 294–329.

Part Three *Demand*

R. F. G. Alford, 'Marshall's demand curve', *Economica*, vol. 23, 1956, pp. 23–48.

K. Arrow, *Social Choice and Individual Values*, Wiley, 1951.

W. J. Baumol, 'The cardinal utility which is ordinal', *Econ. J.*, vol. 68, 1958, pp. 665–72.

G. P. E. Clarkson, *The Theory of Consumer Demand: A Critical Appraisal*, Prentice-Hall, 1963.

M. Friedman, 'The Marshallian demand curve', *J. polit. Econ.*, vol. 57, 1949, pp. 463–95.

M. Friedman and L. J. Savage, 'The utility analysis of choices involving risk', *J. polit. Econ.*, vol. 56, 1948, pp. 279–304.

N. Georgescu-Roegen, *Analytical Economics*, Harvard University Press, 1966.

J. R. Hicks, *A Revision of Demand Theory*, Oxford University Press, 1956.

K. J. Lancaster, 'A new approach to consumer theory', *J. polit. Econ.* vol. 74, 1966, pp. 132–57.

H. Leibenstein, 'Bandwagon, snob, and Veblen effects in the theory of consumers' demand', *Quart. J. Econ.*, vol. 64, 1950, pp. 183-207.

E. J. Mishan, 'Theories of consumers' behaviour: a cynical view', *Economica*, vol. 28, 1961, pp. 1–11.

P. A. Samuelson, 'Consumption theory in terms of revealed preference', *Economica*, vol. 15, 1948, pp. 243–53.

H. Schultz, *The Theory and Measurement of Demand*, Chicago University Press, 1938.

G. J. Stigler, 'The development of utility theory', *J. polit. Econ.*, vol. 58, 1950, pp. 307–27, 373–96.

Part Four *Costs*

J. S. Bain, 'Economies of scale, concentration, and the conditions of entry into twenty manufacturing industries', *Amer. econ. Rev.*, vol. 44, 1954, pp. 15–39.

H. B. Chenery, 'Engineering production functions', *Quart. J. Econ.*, vol. 63, 1949, pp. 507–31.

R. K. Diwan, 'Alternative specifications of economies of scale', *Economica*, vol. 33, 1966, pp. 442–53.

R. Dorfman, 'Mathematical, or linear, programming: a nonmathematical exposition', *Amer. econ. Rev.*, vol. 43, 1953, pp. 797–825.

W. Z. Hirsch, 'Manufacturing progress functions,' *Rev. Econ. Stat.*, vol. 34, 1952, pp. 143–55.

J. Johnston, *Statistical Cost Analysis*, McGraw-Hill, 1960.

H. Leibenstein, 'The proportionality controversy and the theory of production', *Quart. J. Econ.*, vol. 69, 1955, pp. 619–25.

F. T. Moore, 'Economies of scale – some statistical evidence', *Quart. J. Econ.*, vol. 73, 1959, pp. 232–45.

J. Viner, 'Cost curves and supply curves', G. J. Stigler and K. Boulding (eds.), *American Economic Association Readings in Price Theory*, Irwin, 1952.

Part Five *Markets*

(a) Perfect competition

R. H. Coase, 'The problem of social cost', *J. Law Econ.*, vol. 3, 1960, pp. 1–44.

J. Robinson, 'Rising supply price', *Economica*, vol. 8, 1941, pp. 1–8.

G. J. Stigler, 'Perfect competition, historically contemplated', *J. polit. Econ.*, vol. 65, 1957, pp. 1–17.

J. N. Wolfe, 'The representative firm', *Econ. J.*, vol. 64, 1954, pp. 337–49.

(b) Monopolistic competition

G. C. Archibald, 'Chamberlin versus Chicago', *Rev. econ. Stud.*, vol. 92, 1961–2, pp. 2–28.

H. Brems, *Product Equilibrium in Monopolistic Competition*, Harvard University Press, 1951.

E. H. Chamberlin, *The Theory of Monopolistic Competition*, Harvard University Press, 7th edn, 1956.

E. H. Chamberlin, *Towards a More General Theory of Value*, Oxford University Press, Inc., 1957.

R. F. Harrod, *Economic Essays*, Macmillan, 1952.

R. E. Kuenne (ed.), *Monopolistic Competition Theory, Studies in Impact*, Wiley, 1967.

J. Robinson, *The Economics of Imperfect Competition*, Macmillan, 1933.

G. J. Stigler, *Five Lectures on Economic Problems*, Longman, 1949.

(c) Duopoly and oligopoly

J. S. Bain, *Barriers to New Competition*, Harvard University Press, 1956.

W. J. Baumol, *Business Behavior, Value and Growth*, Macmillan Co., 1959.

R. L. Bishop, 'Duopoly: collusion or warfare', *Amer. econ. Rev.*, vol. 50, 1960, pp. 933–61.

W. Fellner, *Competition Among the Few*, Knopf, 1949.

J. Hadar, 'Stability of ologopoly with product differentiation', *Rev. econ. Stud.*, vol. 33, 1966, pp. 57–60.

A. Henderson, 'The theory of duopoly', *Quart. J. Econ.*, vol. 68, 1954, pp. 565–84.

F. Modigliani, 'New developments on the oligopoly front', *J. polit. Econ.*, vol. 66, 1958, pp. 215–32.

G. W. Nutter, 'Duopoly, oligopoly and emerging competition', *South. econ. J.*, vol. 30, 1964, pp. 342–52.

K. W. Rothschild, 'Price theory and oligopoly', *Econ. J.*, vol. 57, 1947, pp. 299–320.

W. G. Shepherd, 'On sales-maximising and oligopoly behaviour', *Economica*, vol. 29, 1962, pp. 420–24.

G. J. Stigler, 'The kinky oligopoly demand curve and rigid prices', *J. polit. Econ.*, vol. 55, 1947, pp. 432–49.

J. D. Williams, *The Compleat Strategyst, Being a Primer on the Theory of Games of Strategy*, McGraw-Hill, 1954.

Part Six *General Equilibrium*

K. J. Arrow and G. Debreu, 'Existence of an equilibrium for a competitive economy', *Econometrica*, vol. 22, 1954, pp. 265–90.

R. Dorfman, P. Samuelson and R. Solow, *Linear Programming and Economic Analysis*, McGraw-Hill, 1958.

R. E. Kuenne, *The Theory of General Equilibrium*, Princeton University Press, 1963.

R. E. Kuenne, *Microeconomic Theory of the Market Mechanism*, Macmillan Co., 1968.

W. Leontief, *The Structure of the American Economy, 1919–1939*, Oxford University Press, Inc., 1951.

W. Leontief, *Input–Output Economics*, Oxford University Press, Inc., 1966.

R. G. Lipsey and K. Lancaster, 'The general theory of the second best', *Rev. econ. Stud.*, vol. 24, 1956, pp. 11–32.

E. J. Mishan, 'A survey of welfare economics, 1939–1959', *Econ. J.*, vol. 70, 1960, pp. 197–265.

P. Newman, *The Theory of Exchange*, Prentice-Hall, 1964.

E. H. Phelps-Brown, *The Framework of the Pricing System*, Chapman & Hall, 1936.

P. A. Samuelson, *Foundations of Economic Analysis*, Harvard University Press, 1948.

Acknowledgements

Permission to reproduce the Readings in this volume is acknowledged from the following sources:

1 Routledge & Kegan Paul, American Economic Association and F. A. von Hayek
2 University of Minnesota Press, and O. Lange and F. M. Taylor
3 *Quarterly Journal of Economics* and R. Frisch
4 Ernest Benn Ltd
5 American Economic Association and A. Alchian
6 Chapman & Hall Ltd
7 *Quarterly Journal of Economics*
8 Harvard University Press
9 American Economic Association and Om P. Tangri
10 Stanford University Press
11 John Wiley & Son
12 Prentice-Hall Inc.
13 *Quarterly Journal of Economics* and R. M. Cyert
14 The American Academy of Political and Social Sciences and J. S. Chipman
15 American Economic Association and F. M. Bator
16 Oxford University Press Inc.
17 *Quarterly Journal of Economics* and W. C. Neale
18 Professor G. J. Stigler
   Introduction to Part 5 McGraw-Hill Book Company

Author Index

Subject Index

Monetary Theory
Edited by R. W. Clower

Exactly what is it that distinguishes a money economy from a barter situation? And having empirically perceived the 'functions' of money in an economic organization, why do we find it difficult to order these perceptions into a logical framework? This selection of Readings presents a wide range of critical thinking about the interrelationships of 'monetary' factors, from Senior's paper on the value of money, written in 1829, to Johnson's analysis in 1967 of the role of money in a growth model. All the conventional wisdoms of this period are represented, assessed, and found wanting. The quantity theory of money, equilibrium analysis, Keynesian economics and the more recent considerations of economic growth, show disparate insights which remain far removed from an integrated theory of money.

'This is a book no economist, student of economics or even dabbler in "current affairs" should be without . . . the excerpts are full, fair and enlightening; reading lists are expertly chosen, indexes full and effective' *The Times Literary Supplement*

The Theory of the Firm

Edited by G. C. Archibald

In this book of Readings, Professor Archibald brings together papers which represent the main work being done in the field.   Key methodological as well as theoretical problems are tackled in depth.

In neo-classical general equilibrium theory, firms are completely described by their production functions. Appropriately, Part One discusses the estimation of production functions and long-run costs. In Part Two, pricing and market structure are analysed assuming profit-maximization (Stigler's classic article on oligopoly and the 'kinky demand-curve' is included here). Part Three provides an exposition of the measurement and effects of monopoly. Part Four is devoted to income distribution and relative shares. Alternatives to profit-maximization, such as Baumol's sales-maximization hypothesis, the behaviour of a Soviet firm, and maximization of a managerial utility function, are examined in Part Five. The growth and size distribution of firms are covered in Part Six. Part Seven looks at linear programming and its relation with 'conventional' economic analysis.

A Critique of Economic Theory

Edited by E. K. Hunt and Jesse G. Schwarz

This trenchant set of articles brings radical criticism of mainstream economics into coherent forms. It stringently attacks the underlying assumptions of academic economics – ideas of constraints, the premise of social harmony, consumer sovereignty, the state as an impartial arbitrator, and the acceptance of the superiority of capitalism over other systems.

Part One is devoted to the rise of the neo-classical school: the shift of attention by economists from large social issues to ones of 'efficient resource allocation' is clearly exposed. The evasion of social reality by conventional economic theory is discussed in Part Two (Veblen's critical comments on the central role of the market are included here). Part Three deals with the discovery of the anomalies associated with the neo-classical concept of capital. Both the utility and labour theories of value are put forward in Part Four as fundamentally different ways of viewing the economic processes of society. The role of the state is analysed in the last Part: a contribution from Kalecki in 1943 questions whether capitalists really want full employment, and forecasts the 'political business cycle' of post-war capitalist economics.

Cost-Benefit Analysis

Edited by Richard Layard

Should India build a new steel mill, or London an urban motorway? Should higher education expand, or water supplies by improved? These are typical questions, about which cost-benefit analysis has something to say. It is the main tool that economics provides for analysing problems of social choice. Its study is also an easy way of seeing what welfare economics is all about.

This book of Readings covers all the main problems that arise in a typical cost-benefit exercise. Part One surveys the field, while Part Two deals with the valuation of costs and benefits when they occur. Part Three discusses social discount rate and the social opportunity cost of capital. The treatment of risk and income distribution is analysed in Parts Four and Five. The last Part contains a case study on the location of the Third London Airport. The editor has written a long elementary introduction to the subject and the Readings, showing how they might help one to tackle a specific illustrative problem.

The Modern Business Enterprise

Edited by Michael Gilbert

This book of twenty Readings examines not only the economic functions of the business corporation, but also the legal limitations on its activities, its internal structure and the relationship between it and the wider society.

In his introductory essay, the editor discusses the limitations of traditional single-discipline approaches to his 'problem' and develops an interdisciplinary methodology which is better able to deal with it. Part One outlines a number of theoretical approaches, moving from particular viewpoints to wider, more interdisciplinary frameworks. Control of the enterprise, both in terms of the differing interests of internal participants (managers, shareholders and employees) and of the wider society (such as government agencies and the stockmarket) is the subject of Part Two. Parts Three and Four focus on models of the firm which clearly demonstrate the link between its economic goals and its organizational structure and control. The last Part examines the social, economic and political impact of corporate activity.